BROTHER ARTIST

A Psychological Study of Thomas Mann's Fiction

James R. McWilliams

UNIVERSITY
PRESS OF
AMERICA

Library of Congress Cataloging in Publication Data

McWilliams, James R.
    Brother artist.

    Includes bibliographical references.
    1. Mann, Thomas, 1875-1955--Criticism and interpre-
tation. I. Title.
PT2625.A44Z74734   1982   833'.912   82-20243
ISBN 0-8191-2857-0
ISBN 0-8191-2858-9 (pbk.)

FOR GUNVOR

ACKNOWLEDGMENTS

I would like to thank my colleague Edward Diller for his many perceptive insights, valuable contributions and stylistic suggestions in helping me turn my dissertation into this book. Also, an expression of gratitude to the Penrose Fund of the American Philosophical Society for its assistance in the form of a research grant and to the Development Fund of the University of Oregon for the financial support it granted me at a crucial time.

I am also indebted to the S. Fischer and Alfred A. Knopf Publishers for their kind permission to quote extensively from Thomas Mann's published works and their English translations.

AUTHOR'S NOTE

This study, an outgrowth of my Ph.D. dissertation, was completed in 1968. In 1980 I decided to revise this first, unsatisfactory version of the book, without altering in any significant way, however, its conclusions. I have not considered here the secondary literature on Thomas Mann after 1968.

All citations from Thomas Mann's writings are taken from the Gesammelte Werke in zwölf Bänden--Collected Works in Twelve Volumes--(Oldenburg: S. Fischer, 1960) and are given in English in the text of this study. The only exceptions are quotations from Gedanken im Kriege--Thoughts in War--, 1914, in Das Thomas Mann-Buch, ed. Michael Mann (Hamburg: Fischer Bücherei, 1965) and from Thomas Mann Briefe: 1889-1936 and 1937-1947--Thomas Mann Letters: 1889-1936 and 1937-1947--, ed. Erika Mann (Frankfort on the Main: S. Fischer, 1962 and 1963).

When not rendered into English by myself, all translated passages are the work of Helen T. Lowe-Porter except for those of Armin L. Robinson from The Tables of the Law in The Ten Commandments, ed. Armin L. Robinson (New York: Simon and Schuster, 1944), of Willard Trask from The Black Swan (New York: Alfred A. Knopf, 1954), and of Richard and Clara Winston from The Story of a Novel (New York: Alfred A. Knopf, 1961).

CONTENTS

I. THE PATTERN OF GUILT   1

II. BUDDENBROOKS   15

III. THOMAS MANN'S PYRRHIC VICTORS   51

IV. THE REPRESSIVE OUTLOOK: FROM TONIO
KRÖGER TO DEATH IN VENICE   93

V. THE ARISTOCRATIC BEARING   159

VI. AN INTERNAL TRIANGLE: THE MAGIC MOUNTAIN   199

VII. JOSEPH AND HIS "FATHERS"   241

VIII. SEQUELS AND INTERLUDE: THE BELOVED
RETURNS, THE TRANSPOSED HEADS, AND
THE TABLES OF THE LAW   283

IX. CAVE MUSICAM   317

X. FULL CIRCLE: THOMAS MANN'S LAST WORKS   353

CONCLUSION   381

NOTES   387

THE PATTERN OF GUILT

Implicit in the nature of literary analysis is a responsibility to suspect that something significant is always lurking behind that which seems apparent and that enlightenment may come in answering a question so obvious that for a long time no one even bothered to pose it. Just such a consideration leads us then to ask a question about the life and works of Thomas Mann that may strike one both as bold and naive: "Why does this author, Thomas Mann, write what he does?"

One possible answer, according to his daughter, Erika Mann, is that his personal life is intimately fused to his literary creations as an indistinguishable autobiography: "It seems hardly possible to separate the man from his work, particularly in a case like Thomas Mann, whose work is so intimately bound up with his personality. All his books, and even the great literary essays, are autobiographical in character. . . ."[1] And Thomas Mann himself has repeatedly acknowledged that his writing is a kind of definition, a projection, or a literary duplication of his own nature: "My image, my personal experience, my dream, my pain? I am not speaking about you, not at all, you can be assured of that, but about myself, and I mean myself. . . . I am still portraying little figures . . . and they represent no one else at all but myself."[2] In an essay of 1910, he asserted: "As if I ever had had anything to do with any other subject matter than with my own life. Who is a poet? One, whose life is symbolic."[3] Perhaps Mann's final word on this point is that "poets who basically give themselves desire that people recognize them, for it is not so much a question of the fame of their creative works as it is of the fame of their living and suffering."[4] And to Mann's own comments may be added the telling statement of one of his good friends, Arthur Eloesser: "Thomas Mann himself is his own best biographer. . . . His writing is already autobiographical, a continuous personal confession; he has never worked with anything else but that which was most personal. . . ."[5]

In view of the confessed autobiographical nature of his works it is not at all surprising that Mann's protagonists are artists or kindred souls. But, contrary to what one might expect, Mann depicts his protagonists, or, as he calls them, his "symbolic replicas," as morbid creatures who doubt all values and often life itself. They are either outright cynics or neurotic wastrels; bankrupt personalities or, if successful in their vocation, unhappy misfits, outsiders, pariahs of society, or ascetic recluses; irresponsible failures or infantile weaklings; sexual deviates or impotent mysognists. One critic has even enumerated the epithets which Mann himself applies to the artist protagonists in his various works: "adventurer, ape, impostor, swindler, charlatan, actor, criminal, and gypsy . . . boaster, dabbler, buffoon, clown, vagabond, jester, hanger-on, Lucifer, fool, prince, mountebank."[6]

Mann continued to disparage the artist as late into his career as 1939. In his essay of that year, <u>Brother Hitler</u>, he compared him to Adolf Hitler, the supposed object of his loathing and contempt; according to Mann the following description could apply to both the dictator and to the artist:

> I spoke of moral chastisement, but must
> we not recognize, whether we like it or
> not, an embodiment of artistic genius
> in the phenomenon? In a shameful way
> everything is there. . . . The lack of
> a fixed mode of living, the social and
> psychic Bohemianism, the arrogant re-
> jection of any honorable activity, . . .
> the ridiculous and lamentably vague
> notion of being called by destiny, . . .
> in addition to that the bad conscience,
> guilt feelings, the fury against the
> world, the revolutionary instinct, the
> compelling need to justify and prove one-
> self, the unconscious accumulation of
> explosive compensatory urges, the drive
> to conquer and subjugate, and the dream
> of seeing the world at the feet of the[7]
> one it once spurned. . . .

The artist, in terms of Mann's own emphasis, is therefore a suspicious and questionable figure, disreputable and evil.

Taking Mann at his word,--that the little figures he depicts are no one other than himself--we may go on to examine the pattern of behavior and the discrepancies in conduct of these characters with whom he identifies. We find, for example, that Detlev

2

Spinell of Tristan possesses a conscience that eats
away at him and that a troubled conscience also burdens
the protagonist of The Clown, Jacoby of Little Lizzie,
and Schiller of A Weary Hour. Hanno of Buddenbrooks
wishes his own death and Hans Castorp of The Magic
Mountain chooses it willfully. In Gladius Dei Hieronymus is afflicted by a conscience which undermines
his health. In the nameless dread which hounds the
hero of Disillusionment and Gustav Aschenbach of Death
in Venice we detect similar expressions of a guilty
conscience. Tonio Kröger too is "an artist with a
guilty conscience," one who feels "the Mark" on his
brow. Siegmund of the opera The Valkyrie in the tale
The Blood of the Walsungs and Detlef of The Hungry
are similarly branded. Mann's heroes suffer from a
consistent sense of guilt which is betrayed by their
pangs of conscience and their compulsive need for
atonement. The protagonist may even reveal a wish for
death in order to find release from his guilty existence.

Thomas Mann likes to use the term branded to denote the man marked by guilt. Sometimes the hero's
guilt is represented symbolically by a physical handi-
cap: the crippled frame of the hero of Little Herr
Friedemann, the heart condition of Paolo Hofmann in
The Will to Happiness, the withered arm of Klaus
Heinrich in Royal Highness, the deformed body of
Cipolla in Mario and the Magician, and the club-foot
of Anna von Tümmler in The Black Swan. In other
stories, psychic distortions or obsessions become obvious substitutes for physical deformities. Tonio's,
Detlef's, and Siegmund's mark is an hallucinatory projection of their deep-seated sense of guilt. Savonarola
in Fiorenza, Adrian Leverkühn in Doctor Faustus and
Gregorius in The Holy Sinner seek acquittal from the
indictment of their conscience through mortification
of the flesh, while the protagonists of The Way to the
Cemetery, The Fight Between Jappe and Do Escobar, and
Joseph either desire or actually provoke punishment
at the hands of persons known or unknown to them.

Guilt is a condition of life, but it dominates
Mann's heroes to the point of paralysis, leads them to
negate life, and brings out their self-destructive
tendencies. The obsessive nature of the sense of guilt
cannot be stressed too heavily here, for the Mannian
hero feels the dire compulsion to seek continual expiation. Hence, there is the perpetual note of suffering and self-flagellation with its accompanying note of

approval throughout the works of Thomas Mann. Even the
titles of some works reflect this: <u>Disorder and Early
Sorrow</u>, <u>Sufferings for Germany</u>, <u>The Starving</u>, <u>A Weary
Hour</u>, <u>Suffering and Greatness of the Masters</u>, and
<u>Suffering and Greatness of Richard Wagner</u>.

This element of suffering and guilt has not gone
unnoticed by critics.[8] One particularly solid observation reads as follows: "While they need not be conscious of it, Mann's sick artists enjoy their afflic-
tions, or, at least, they approve of them. They experience their disease as a form of self-destruction or
self-punishment, as a source of excitement, as a sin,
as guilt, or excess, and as a source of superiority."[9]
This commentator concludes: "By the twenties, Mann's
artist has subdued his bad conscience, but it has not
disappeared. Joseph's trickeries and the punishment
of pit and prison still point to the former obsessive
sense of guilt which had found its most radical expression in the author's identification with the swindler Felix Krull."[10]

There is a wide divergence of opinion as to the
true cause of the hero's guilt. Ferdinand Lion sees
in Mann's artist a "solicitor of death and, as such,
a murderer, infinitely guilty, an enemy of the State
and society."[11] Other critics have stated or implied
that the guilty conscience is to be attributed to the
hero's failing in his commitments to the bourgeois
world.[12] For these critics friction arises between the
hero's artistic calling and his conventional bourgeois
attitude. Arthur Burkhard's explanation is as follows:
'[Mann's] writings, as I interpreted them, are primarily
concerned with the problem of his own inheritance and
career, more particularly manifest in the conflict
raging in his breast between the bourgeois origins and
his artistic profession."[13] Willy Tappolet sees a
hereditary basis for the author's conflict: "For this
conflict, conditioned by birth, is the substance from
which all of Mann's books live."[14] Tappolet is supported by Martin Havenstein who also claims that Mann
brought his guilt into the world with him.[15]

These statements, however, do not really explain
the essence of the Mannian protagonist's guilt. One
becomes what one is--a teacher, a missionary, a laborer,
a criminal, or an artist--as a result of one's inner
needs and concerns. In Thomas Mann's works the artist's
calling should therefore be considered the result rather

4

than the cause of guilt! The usual assumption is that
Mann has become the guilty artist as a result of a bold
choice rather than of a necessity precipitated by a
prior condition. But a patent confusion lies in this
effort to substitute the effect for the cause.

Tonio Kröger and Gustav Aschenbach, for example,
are prime examples of repressed instincts, who fight
a desperate battle to preserve a façade of decency.
But to consider them, along with Mann's other heroes,
guilty because they do not fit neatly into the social
fabric is to underestimate totally the intensity of an
individual problem that contributes a good deal of
fascination and excitement to Mann's writings. Because Thomas Mann's heroes deliberately stand apart
from social activities and interests or even flaunt
society, one can conclude with certainty that slight
social transgressions do not offer a satisfactory explanation for the underlying suffering and tragic note
of Mann's heroes. These characters are tormented and
crippled by a wound of a deeper nature and greater
magnitude, one that makes them impotent when dealing
with life and masochistic, often to the point of suicide, when dealing with themselves. And to attribute
the genesis of guilt to an incidental misunderstanding
between the decent burgher and Mann's suspect artist
is to fail to appreciate the deep and far-reaching
problems of these singularly troubled characters who
feel the mark of Cain on their brow--a mark indicating
a crime of no less gravity than that of murder!

If this is borne in mind, it is reasonable to
assume that the unusual behavior of the Mannian artist
goes back to an earlier psychological conflict that
lies buried in the subconscious, the earliest strata
of impressions as it were. The fact that he is compelled to act out his guilt against his own interests
and despite all his powers of reason, demonstrates
that he is incapable of recognizing its true nature
and is unable to take positive steps to alleviate the
severity of his problem.

For the sake of clarity let us pause at this point
to examine what is implied in such an extreme concept
of guilt, even at the risk of sounding like a textbook:
"Guilt . . . is the painful internal tension generated
whenever the emotionally highly charged barrier erected
by the superego (conscience) is being touched or
transgressed. . . . Most authors also include here

sexual impulses, particularly those related to incestuous drives."[16] In order for the sense of guilt to
overwhelm the individual and cause him to lead a way
of life which either spells disaster or great suffering, unconscious forces must be involved. "The dy-
namically important sense of guilt remains as such
unconscious, although the concomitant anxiety becomes
conscious. . . . Guilt must not be confounded with
apprehension, which in the context of our particular
interest is the proper designation of the 'fear of
being caught'; nor is the feeling of guilt the same as
a conscious and realistic fear of impending punishment."[17] The true origin of guilt is inaccessible to
its possessor's conscious mind; it is beyond his powers
of reason to apprehend its fundamental cause; otherwise he would be able, by an effort of the will, to
ascertain its nature, define its source, and nullify
its deleterious and self-defeating consequences. In
order to alleviate his immense burden of suffering he
would naturally become his own physician. But if man
were able to heal himself so easily, there would obviously no longer be a mental health problem in the
world.

In The Economic Problem of Masochism Sigmund
Freud, indicating that masochism is an inseparable
component of the phenomenon of guilt, defines guilt
as "an unconscious need for punishment."[18] Or, in the
words of one competent observer: "Analysis of many
activities discloses that a painful experience may be
unconsciously self-induced, for many individuals find
it easier to endure a pain inflicted from without than
to withstand the pressure of unconscious fantasies,
which, if they do break into consciousness, are perceived as torments of conscience or feelings of worthlessness."[19]

Masochism may range from erotogenic pain, when it
is a requisite condition for sexual gratification, to
various expressions of self-defeat, be it self-disparagement, humiliation, feelings of utter worthlessness, or a proneness to accident. All forms of such
willful punishment represent the masochist's desire to
expiate his sins. In order to achieve his goal of
punishment the masochist often resorts to sadism which
actually may be viewed as the reverse side of masochism.
"It can often be shown that masochism is really an
extension of sadism turned round upon the subject's
own self, which thus, to begin with, takes the place
of the sexual object."[20] Both sadism and masochism

6

are habitually found to occur together in the same
individual, although one will be more developed or predominant than the other.[21]

Two other terms of vital importance which are
necessary for an understanding of the concept of guilt
are repression and omnipotence of thoughts. Repression,
the genesis of which takes place in a child's early
life, is defined as the exclusion from consciousness
of those sexual or aggressive impulses which are incapable of gratification because they are directed
toward the child's parents. Repression does not mean
the destruction of such thoughts or wishes; because of
the pleasure attached to them they persist, and it is
consequently necessary that the prohibition against
them be maintained to prevent their reaching consciousness. A state of tension is the result, a protracted
conflict between the forbidden impulses and the prohibition.[22]

Omnipotence of thoughts signifies a type of
primitive or infantile thinking where the thought itself becomes equivalent to the actual execution of the
deed. Such a thought has a reality all its own, wholly
independent of actual facts or behavior.[23] The child's
conception of love and hate is all-consuming, his love
boundless, his hate murderous. In the belief that he
can alter the external world by envisioning the death
or his own seduction of a parent, the child incurs "a
sense of guilt that would be appropriate in a mass-
murderer. . . ."[24] In terms of highly charged and
dynamic situations involving sexual impulses, then,
the child's thoughts are seen as fused to his sexual
instincts in such a way that their reality becomes
absolute to him. The fact that the transgression is
entirely imagined does not diminish its total consequences of suffering and guilt: "But the point is
that fantasies of infants when repressed exert the
same dynamic and continued effect on the adult personality as actual experience."[25]

A well-known fact is reaffirmed here: a severe
mental conflict is the inheritance of the distant past.
Misdeeds in adult life often lead to painful but conscious remorse whereas guilt is the product of a
child's mind that, in its most pervasive aspect, is
intimately connected with infantile sexuality. Guilt
is thus regressive in nature. This regressive aspect
is graphically revealed in the portrayal of several of
Mann's heroes. Though adults, they not only assume

7

and act out the role of a small child or resemble an
infant in appearance, but they also manage to effect a
narcissistic withdrawal from a vigorous and full life.
Bibi, the child hero of The Infant Prodigy, is shown
to be, for example, already completely formed in his
personality: "As an individual he has still to develop,
but as a type he is already quite complete, the artist
par excellence."[26] Such Mannian protagonists seek
continual   atonement for guilt feelings that have
their origin in infantile sexuality based on parricidal
hatred and on a desire for incestuous union with the
mother. Hero after hero in Mann's works is shown to
be in quest of either his own mother or an obvious
mother substitute, and tale after tale deals with incest either openly or in disguised form. Each story
from the author's pen is, almost without exception,
concerned with the protagonist's search for a solution
to sexual drives in terms of a classic Oedipus complex.
The hero finds himself heavily saddled with guilt, for
his early preoccupation with incest presupposed a
crime of the greatest magnitude, parricide which would
in effect remove the threatening competitor for the
affection, love, and possession of the mother. The
passionate desire of the protagonist to take the
father's place with the mother leads to the fantasied
murder of his jealously hated rival. In the protagonist's imagination, enriched by onanistic sexual
play, pain fuses with libidinal pleasure, brutality
mixes with passion, and redemption is envisioned as
self-destruction. The true significance of the child's
involvement is summed up admirably by Charles Brenner:
"It is a real love affair. For many people it is the
most intense affair of their entire lives, but it is
in any case as intense as any which the individual will
ever experience. The description that follows cannot
begin to convey what the reader must keep in mind as
he reads it: the intensity of the tempest of passions
of love and hate, of yearning and jealousy, of fury and
fear that rages within the child. This is what we are
talking about when we try to describe the Oedipus complex."[27]

        In the Oedipal love affair feelings of aggression
against the powerful father outweigh those of tenderness. The desire to possess the mother, whatever the
cost or sacrifice, is coupled with the wish to vanquish
the father, and so the defeat of the child hero's
hated rival becomes an essential part of the fantasy
that combines sexual gratification with intense hostility. Fantasies of this kind must be followed by

a prodigious need for punishment and atonement, for the transgressions are not only crimes of extreme gravity, they are crimes committed against one's own flesh and blood. Consequently the child's conception of justice, an eye for an eye, holds permanent sway in his mental structure; the result is a wracking and unbearable sense of guilt, a complete denial of feelings of a normal order, and an all-consuming fascination with death as retribution.

From this perspective, then, we can begin to see why Mann's heroes gladly accept pain or even death as atonement for some unknown transgression, or why they flee from human contact to avoid the horror or doom which is associated with unrestricted emotions. Love especially represents an unconditional investment of feeling. If, however, this life-sustaining instinct is blunted by conflict, and sadistic impulses consequently become attached to it, then Eros will not suffice in involving the person actively and energetically in life. The result is a rebellion against life itself. Feelings of aggression and hostility are confused with tenderness. A state of ambivalence results, in which pleasure is fused to pain and sexual desires with destructive impulses. Love is then transformed into humiliation, ill-treatment, and a desire to subjugate and destroy. It also produces an act of desired atonement whereby the person, confronting the robustness of life and a demand for energetic human involvement, hears a distant echo of the death-wish and for no apparent reason falls victim to anxiety, fear, impotence, and self-reproach.

For a healthy mastery over life one's feelings of Eros must be stronger than those of Thanatos, the desire for punishment or death. This is never the case in the works of Thomas Mann. Love is never felt without a mixture of hostility and Eros is never fully distinguished from impulses of death and destruction. For the Mannian hero, love is associated or confused with dying. We obtain convincing confirmation of this from Thomas Mann himself in his essay on Schopenhauer. Here he points out the relationship between the two spheres of the sexual and the intellectual (or the repressive) as the ultimate determinant in creating a philosophy of life: "What makes him [Schopenhauer] the 'pessimist' and a denier of the world, is just the contradictory and hostile, exclusive and anguishing relation of the two spheres to each other. . . ."[28]

9

As a result of his ambivalence, a hard look at reality is denied the Mannian protagonist; instead he resorts to fantasy to fulfill those aims which are shattered by an encounter with the actual world. And it is this fantasy, heightened and enriched by repression, which determines the Mannian artist's calling.

Ambivalence, the acme of which is to equate love with death, is reflected throughout the behavior of the hero; he hates and loves at the same time; the one emotion is never divorced from the other. Unlike Mann's protagonists, the normal person does not love and hate simultaneously, but successively; for him tenderness without reservations characterizes his love. At the same time the mother-sweetheart also appears to Mann's heroes to be composed of some reassuring opposing traits: sensual but frigid; cruel but seductive; exotic but artistically German; slovenly and vulgar but yet cultured and aristocratic. This self-same ambivalence is applied to the hated rival. The father, living on in the hero's conscience, elicits opposing feelings of fear and disdain or hatred and respect. And so the insensitive businessman-father appears as both impotent and virile, cowardly and menacing. The hero's total outlook is colored essentially by this ambivalence as every aspect of his world becomes peopled with mother and father figures. Ordinary persons become projections of the father-world and are shown as unattractive and malicious, the objects of the hero's scorn and contempt.

Love for the Mannian hero is never without a measure of hostility, contempt, or loathing. Stemming from the inability to love unconditionally, a preoccupation with death therefore becomes the keynote of Thomas Mann's works. Mann consequently places such great emphasis on the Love-Death music of Richard Wagner's Tristan and Isolde, for in death one becomes almost innocent again; only in death can real expiation of guilt take place.

Of all the arts, it is, interestingly, music which is most directly involved in the author's sense of guilt. Certain passages of music call forth astonishing associations of a sexual nature. Thomas Mann's daughter, Monika, is especially struck by his attitude: "Music is the only weakness Papa has. He regards it with a mixture of adoration, envy and disdain. . . . He is too fully and wholly the man of the word--of the prosaic, the intrinsic, the ascetic--so that music for

10

him is necessarily somehow linked with sin."[29]   References to music abound in nearly all of Mann's works.
In his private life too it dominated him. The conductor
Bruno Walter reveals convincingly the magnetic attraction it had for him: "Anyway, Thomas Mann and music!
Does it not dominate him more than he himself suspects?
How enlightening that at the climactic moment of the
Joseph story the poet bids music to lead the son,
believed to be dead, into his father's arms, that the
supreme pathos of an incomparable human event is dis-
solved in the lovely song of the child Serach!"[30]

        Bruno Walter reports further: "I also made them
[Thomas and Katja Mann] acquainted with Pfitzner's
Palestrina. Mann's essay on the subject sounded the
very depths of this work. I also recall my playing for
him the second act of Tristan and my amazement at his
unbelievably thorough knowledge of the work when he
subsequently pointed out that I had omitted the soft
E-flat of the trumpet at the words 'Das bietet dir
Tristan.'"[31] Monika Mann again reinforces the portrait
of Mann the musician: "And nearly always when Papa is
listening to music he arouses in me the idea that he
is more musical than most musicians taken together but
that, had he chosen it or been chosen by it, he would
have fallen into an abyss. Its inarticulateness would
have corrupted him and delivered him to the devil."[32]

        Monika Mann's insight is a revealing one. Because
music is directly associated with the artistic mother
and incestuous passion, Thomas Mann could not possibly
yield himself to it completely. Vicarious enjoyment,
dilettante-like participation or disciplined and intellectual criticism were permissible, but the potential
nirvana of music prohibited his unconditional surrender
to it. Music was for him in a sense complete chaos,
whereas in the written word he had an art in which he
could limit, restrain, or gloss over suppressed forces
with threatening associations. It is no accident, then,
that Doctor Faustus is probably the fullest expression
of Mann's inner conflict. Its hero, Adrian Leverkühn,
is not a writer, but instead a devout musician, and as
such he has been designated as Mann's guiltiest artist
figure. Furthermore, there is no doubt that this novel
cost Mann the greatest measure of creative agony.[33]

        Mann's own dignity, bearing, and caution became
the salient feature of his epic style, growing as they
did out of distrust of direct emotional expression.
Consequently, a robust and earthy attitude is lacking

throughout his works. Maximilian Schochow has commented on this reserve and restraint: "It [reserve] is manifested even in all the external ways of style. Strong 'emotions' are avoided, dramatic expressions suppressed, the climaxes are instrumented so as to echo softly. . . . Seldom does one find a love-scene, and if it cannot be avoided, then it is invested with a certain lack of sensuality, almost a fear of saying a decisive word, a parsimony of gesture, which creates an ascetic effect."[34]

Strong sensations are attenuated by degress in his prolix style until they are finally vented without danger. Afraid of giving open expression to the unconscious wishes he is reluctant to face, Mann is forced to resort to subterfuge. For example, laughter, the welcome relief of tension, becomes in his works a leitmotif of dissolution.

Mann also abhorred the Bohemian type who fails to subordinate himself to discipline and order; he distrusted anyone, for that matter, who gave free expression to his feelings. The word "Bohemian" is an epithet which never fails to convey a feeling of repugnance on his part. Full enjoyment of the artist's calling, hedonism in art, unorthodoxy of emotions, all this without the suffering pangs of atonement, is charged with too much psychic pain for him to be able to disregard completely.

Mann's method of writing reveals the opposite of the Bohemian concept of creativeness. How close to religious penance, indeed, a veritable mortification of the flesh, are the following words of Mann concerning his struggle to create:

> Every morning a step, every morning a place in the text--that is simply my way, and it is based on necessity. . . . As far as I am concerned, it means clenching my teeth and slowly setting one foot before the other; it means practicing patience, being idle half the day, lying down to sleep and waiting it out in order to see if it will perhaps go better tomorrow when my mind is rested. My way of working requires an extraordinary patience, if I am to finish anything of greater scope, keep faith with what I have once undertaken, not

12

run away, or not take hold of something
new or seductively youthful. What do I
mean by patience? Sullenness, stubborn-
ness, self-discipline, and the taming
of my will, all told a regimen which one
can conceive of only with difficulty and
under which my nerves, and you may believe
me, are strained to such a degree that I
am ready to scream.[35]

Here Thomas Mann is virtually describing a tormented soul, persecuted by his justice-seeking inner
conscience. Confirmation of this creative suffering,
this self-inflicted torture, this painful penitence,
is made readily available by his close friends and
relatives. We learn from his daughter Erika how far-
reaching was his drive to create and how it dominated
him all his life, even on his vacation: "In point of
fact, since he had been a writer, Thomas Mann had never
had any real holidays. His work was suspended only
during his lecture tours or when he was ill in bed with
a temperature, and now in Sils, as at home, it was his
work that dictated the program of the day."[36] Yet
despite all this pain and anguish he could never fully
allay the insidious doubt he had about his artistic
creations. Erika Mann reveals how he had refused to
send off his just completed manuscript of Death in
Venice to the Neue Rundschau, for which it had been
commissioned. Only his wife's arguments finally convinced him that this work, which many critics claim
to be his masterpiece, was good enough for publication.[37]

Now it is time for us to turn to the works themselves in order to determine how the concept of guilt
can throw new light upon their meaning, and how guilt
operates as the common denominator of the hero's behavior. Close attention will be given to the many ways
in which the Mannian hero manifests his guilt: his
obsessive drive to toil, his inordinate insistence
upon decent dress and proper manners; his compulsive
search for precision in his art; his drive for atonement through self-imposed suffering and isolation; his
self-doubt, submission and passivity, or even outright
masochistic pleasure; his lack of differentiation between love and hatred; his fear of women; his death-
wish and his deviational behavior. It will also be
noted that his fundamental abhorrence of life, an
extension of his self-doubts, is never totally absent
from his thoughts and that the mental complexes which

13

the Mannian artist as an adult has inherited from his
early life are never fully overcome.

Certain leitmotifs, attitudes, and types of behavior are so striking in their recurrence throughout
Mann's works that they must reflect the author's life
or view of life; for the basic organization of the
human psyche remains constant even though the details
which constitute the creative parts of each episode
may vary. The motifs can then be considered the real
autobiographical patterns of the artist's works, and
they can be used to constitute a body of information
from which one can predict the actions of Mann's
characters and throw new light on the author's attitudes regarding the often elusive content of his works.

BUDDENBROOKS

Although <u>Buddenbrooks</u> is Thomas Mann's first major work, it is frequently considered the most genuine achievement of his career. This book came at a crucial time in Mann's life, pouring out as it did the abundant content and residue of childhood experiences still burdening him. The works which preceded this one were small forays into the general sphere of the same subject matter, but in <u>Buddenbrooks</u> Mann deals with a major eruption of <u>material from</u> the subconscious that embraced in a unified sequence the basic experiences, reactions, and judgments of his childhood. The result is a singular great work in which Mann spares us no details about his family and his criticism or condemnation of it. In this work he was simultaneously at one with his material and opposed to it, trying to reveal the true nature of his feelings as a young man and at the same time trying to conceal experiences and memories that were too embarrassing for comfort. The result of being the victim, prosecutor, and judge of his own self and family is that a number of incongruities in perspective and interpretation arises to plague literary analysts and readers, problems which have not yet been satisfactorily answered.

<u>Buddenbrooks</u> records the gradual decline of a commercial family of Lübeck over four generations: from that of the great-grandfather Johann Buddenbrook to the second generation of the grandfather of the same name; then Mann deals with the third generation, the father Thomas and his siblings, and finally with the last heir, Hanno, whose early death seals the fate of the whole dynasty. Though the focus is on one family, the basic impression the novel produces is the re-creation of an entire age mirrored by the North German patrician class of the middle nineteenth century. This authentic reflection of the past contributes much to the novel's universality and is greatly responsible for its becoming a masterpiece of German and world literature. In fact, Thomas Mann received the Nobel Prize for literature in 1929 chiefly on the strength of <u>Buddenbrooks</u>, which, according to the Swedish Academy at the time, "had been generally acknowledged in the course of years as one of the classical works of contemporary literature."

The Actual Hero of <u>Buddenbrooks</u>

15

Who is really the hero of Buddenbrooks? This question will probably be objected to as obviously academic, if not downright superfluous, and of being of no true import for an evaluation of the novel. On the contrary, we insist that the answer to this question is of crucial significance for an understanding of the work. What is involved is the first real test of the Mannian conception of "Brother Artist." Most readers would assume it was Hanno if Thomas Mann had not insisted in no uncertain terms that it was the non-artistic businessman Thomas Buddenbrook! This unpredictable and barely supportable denial of the obvious--for even in a hurried perusal of the book Thomas will strike the reader as unsympathetically petty and narrow--holds the key to a problem that Mann would have preferred to have critics overlook. Mann was not inclined to write detailed analyses of his works in order to help readers interpret them; but in this case he wanted to impose his opinion that Thomas Buddenbrook was the hero of the novel. In order to prove his claim that Thomas was the protagonist, Mann states that he gave him his own dearest experience: the reading of Schopenhauer. But the text shows clearly that the experience did not take hold, that Thomas Buddenbrook was too insensitive to grasp the beauty and intent of the Schopenhauer text, and that in spite of the "elevating experience" he died in a ludicrous and degrading manner.

Additional questions regarding characters and the genesis of the novel manifest themselves in a close reading of the text. Why, for example, did Mann turn from the story of the artist (the theme of everyone of his other works) to write a history of four declining generations of one family? The subtitle implies that the author wished to describe the decline of a family, but the text of the work clearly reveals that the downfall of the family really begins here in the third generation when biological "decadence" is infused into the clan from without! And why does the decline of the Buddenbrook family occur at the same time as that of many other leading families of Lübeck? And what, precisely, is meant by decline or decay in the Mannian context?

As answers for these questions become evident, certain implications should emerge which permit us to draw conclusions about the final purpose of this far-reaching work. To this end let us begin with the most intricate of the problems--the confusion whether the businessman Thomas Buddenbrook or his son Hanno, the artist figure, is the actual protagonist of <u>Buddenbrooks</u>.

The uncertainty surrounding the hero can be surmised from Hans Eichner's remarks:

> The life of Hanno Buddenbrook is made up of the author's childhood memories, but it is not a matter here of simple autobiography with a changed outcome. Thomas Mann conferred at least as much of his own personal experiences on Senator Thomas Buddenbrook, the father of Hanno. The senator's ethic of duty, that is, his obstinate willingness to sacrifice his life for accomplishment, an attitude which Mann celebrated later in the figure of Gustav Aschenbach, already links Thomas Buddenbrook directly to his creator. Above all, Mann gave his Schopenhauer experience to Thomas Buddenbrook.[1]

From this and Mann's own confirmation it would appear that the matter has already been settled and that the question of the hero of <u>Buddenbrooks</u> is only an academic exercise. However, when we take a close look at Thomas and Hanno Buddenbrook, we will find that, despite Mann's categorical statements, only Hanno, the last of the Buddenbrooks, can be the hero and an emanation of the author. Genealogical aspects notwithstanding, <u>Buddenbrooks</u> does <u>not</u> represent an exception among Mann's works. Everywhere else in Mann's fiction the hero is an artist, an artist type, or bears the unmistakable characteristics of the artist. The protagonist of <u>Buddenbrooks</u> is no exception.

Hanno's role and behavior clearly shows that only he possesses that mental structure which is truly consistent with all of Mann's heroes. In him, the effects of guilt are most pitiless and their connection with art, specifically music, are most explicitly demonstrated. The emotional and instinctual impact music makes on Hanno identifies him with his creator, not to mention with many other Mannian protagonists.

Frank Donald Hirschbach has pointed out with real justification the sexual nature of Hanno's indulgence in music:

To Hanno Buddenbrook music is the source
and the focus of his sexual drives. Like
his mother he pours all his suppressed
sensuality into music. With the precocity
and early disillusionment which is peculiar
to many of the children in Mann's works,
he seems thoroughly familiar with the
pleasures of sex of which he has never
partaken. There are two scenes which
show Hanno at the small organ, indulging
in musical fantasies. . . . The careful
reader will discover that they are accurate
step-by-step descriptions of the sex act,
including the ensuing fatigue.[2]

One of the passages crucial to Hirschbach's interpretation reads as follows:

After dinner Hanno . . . awaited his
mother at the piano. They played the
Sonata Opus 24 of Beethoven. In the
adagio the violin sang like an angel;
but Gerda took the instrument from her
chin with a dissatisfied air, looked at
it in irritation, and said it was not in
tune. She played no more, but went up to
rest.
Hanno remained in the salon. He went
to the glass door that led out on the
small veranda and looked into the drenched
garden. But suddenly he took a step back
and jerked the cream-colored curtains
across the door, so that the room lay in
a soft yellow twilight. Then he went to
the piano. He stood for a while, and his
gaze, directed fixed and unseeing upon a
distant point, altered slowly, grew blurred
and vague and shadowy. He sat down at the
instrument and began one of his fantasies.
. . .
The resolution, the redemption, the
complete fulfillment--a chorus of jubila-
tion burst forth, and everything resolved
itself in a harmony--and the harmony, in
sweet ritardando, at once sank into another.
It was the motif, the first motif! And now
began a festival, a triumph, an unbounded
orgy of this very figure, which now displayed a wealth of dynamic color which
passed through every octave, wept and

18

shivered in tremolo, sang, rejoiced,
and sobbed in exultation, triumphantly
adorned with all the bursting, tinkling,
foaming, purling resources of orchestral
pomp. The fanatical worship of this
worthless trifle, this scrap of melody,
this brief childish harmonic invention
a bar and a half in length, had about it
something stupid and gross, and at the
same time something ascetic and religious--
something that contained the essence of
faith and renunciation. There was a
quality of the perverse in the insatia-
bility with which it was produced and
revelled in: There was a sort of cynical
despair; there was a longing for joy, a
yielding to desire, in the way the last
drop of sweetness was, as it were, ex-
tracted from the melody, till exhaustion,
disgust, and satiety supervened. Then,
at last; at last, in the weariness after
excess, a long, soft arpeggio in the minor
trickled through, mounted a tone, resolved
itself in the major, and died in mournful lingering away.

Hanno sat still a moment, his chin on
his chest, his hands in his lap. Then
he got up and closed the instrument. He
was very pale, there was no strength in
his knees, and his eyes were burning.
He went into the next room, stretched
himself on the chaise-lounge, and remained
for a long time motionless.[3]

After careful examination, it becomes obvious
that a definite modification of Hirschbach's interpretation would be closer to the truth. It is not, as
he suggests, a heterosexual union which is involved or
implied, but rather an autoerotic indulgence. That it
is a question of a child's self-gratification is confirmed by his conversation with his school friend
Kai just prior to the last scene:

Hanno was silent a moment. A flush came
upon his face, and a painful confused look.
"Yes, I'll play--I suppose--though I
ought not. I ought to practice my sonatas
and etudes and then stop. But I suppose
I'll play; I cannot help it, though it only
makes everything worse."

19

> "Worse?"
> Hanno was silent.
> "I know what you mean," said Kai
> after a bit, and then neither of the lads
> spoke again.
> They were both in a strange age. Kai
> had become very red and was glancing at
> the ground without lowering his head.
> Hanno looked pale. He was frightfully
> serious, his eyes had clouded over, and
> he kept glancing to the side. (I, 744)

What is obviously stressed here is Hanno's guilt feelings about masturbation. His words disclose that he is going to do something which he knows is forbidden, and his furtive and covert manner attest to the fear of punishment, should he be found out.

The association of sex and music for Hanno and for Thomas Mann himself should not be underestimated. Music in Mann's works is an irresistible and seductive attraction, a luxurious gratification, but at the same time the ultimate in danger because music and mother are indivisibly associated. Music is an experience of the highest erotic pleasure with a maternal partner but at the cost of paralyzing mental anguish.

It is no coincidence that immediately following the clandestine scene of sex and music mentioned above, the culmination of a day in the life of Hanno Buddenbrook, the author describes Hanno's death in the most pitiless fashion. R. Hinton Thomas makes the following pertinent observation about the end of Hanno's life: "In no other major work was Mann more directly involved emotionally in his theme, yet none can match, for example, the coldness of the apparently scientific account, of aspects of Hanno's final illness. . . ."[4]

The guilt incurred by Hanno's intemperate excess in music exacts the ultimate toll; only in death is it fully cancelled. This is also the case with the hero of Doctor Faustus. The composer Leverkühn needs to punish himself as penitential payment for a life dedicated to music, and he does so by willfully contracting the syphilis which eventually causes death.

Twice earlier in the narrative Hanno is permitted to go to the opera:

> As compensation for a particularly pain-

20

ful visit to Herr Brecht (the dentist)
he had been taken to the opera for the
first time; sitting beside his mother in
the dress circle, he had followed breath-
less a performance of Fidelio, and since
that time he had heard nothing, seen
nothing, thought of nothing but opera,
and a passion for the theater filled him
and almost kept him sleepless. With unspeakable envy he looked at people like
Uncle Christian, who was known as a regular
frequenter and might go every night if he
liked: Consul Döhlmann, the broker Gosch
--how could they endure the joy of seeing
it every night? (I, 533-534)

Freud associates a visit to the dentist or pulling
teeth with punishment by castration, and here, no less,
Hanno can enjoy without reservations the luxury and
danger of music only after being subjected first to
physical punishment in the dentist's office.

There are other aspects to Hanno's behavior which
typify him as the Mannian artist hero. The artist's
self-doubt is a part of him: "What about my music,
Kai? There is nothing to it. Shall I travel round
and give concerts? In the first place, they wouldn't
let me; and in the second place, I will never really
know enough. I can play very little. I can only
improvise a little when I am alone" (I, 743). This
doubt of his art, his calling, his strength, is a
projection of the guilty mind, for the origins of his
aesthetic fantasy are, although pleasurable in the
extreme, inextricably linked with forbidden joys.
His repeated transgressions seem to prove to him his
lack of strength; and suspecting in himself a debility
of an evil nature, he convinces himself of his own
worthlessness and that of everything connected with
his existence. What ensues, is a tacit yearning for
death, for only in death is there a promise of an
ultimate remission from sin: "I'd like to sleep and
never wake up. I'd like to die, Kai! No, I am no
good. I can't wish for anything" (I, 743). It is as
if pleasure were derived from a constant preoccupation
with the thought of death, release through the anticipation of final absolution. And in this connection
his great affinity for the sea as a symbol of finality
plays a role. Thomas Mann, who has often proclaimed
his love of the sea, states in Lübeck as an Intellectual

21

<u>Way of Life</u> (1926): "The sea is not a landscape, it is the expanse of eternity, of nothing, and of death, a metaphysical dream. . . ."[5]

Pertinent to the total characterization of a Mannian principal figure is always some identification with or resemblance to the author. Here, for example, there is little doubt that Hanno's struggle in school was written from bitter personal experience. Mann's own attitude toward music, his toy puppet theater, his delight in vacationing at Travemünde, and his tendency to daydream characterize meaningfully in terms of auto-biography the child hero of <u>Buddenbrooks</u>.

Of greater importance is that Hanno Buddenbrook, with his extreme death-wish, is one of Mann's most personal and intense creations. Not to ascribe to Hanno the hero's role is to render him unique among the tortured heroic souls throughout the author's works and to disregard Thomas Mann's inner kinship to his artist protagonists. Such a view also overlooks the tragic impact which Hanno confers upon the novel. But for full corroboration of this premise, we must turn our investigation to Thomas Buddenbrook, the al-leged protagonist of this monumental work.

The case for Thomas Buddenbrook is essentially that stated in the previously cited passage by Hans Eichner: Thomas' professed dedication to achievement in his calling and the inspiration he receives from reading Schopenhauer--an experience so meaningful in Mann's own life. But as far as the Schopenhauer experience is concerned, Eichner is subject to quali-fication. Contrary to his statement and to Mann's own words in his <u>Sketch of my Life</u> (1930) that he inserted his heartfelt personal experience into the novel in order to prepare Thomas Buddenbrook for death, the great Schopenhauer experience is meaning-less for him.[6] It produces <u>no</u> lasting effect on Thomas Buddenbrook.

Nevertheless, in his Schopenhauer essay of 1938, Mann again insists that Thomas is his hero and he re-states his purpose in making use of the philosopher's thoughts on death in <u>Buddenbrooks</u>:

> Whoever is interested in life, I said in
> <u>The Magic Mountain</u> is particularly
> interested in death. That is the trail of
> Schopenhauer, deeply imprinted, valid

throughout life. It would also have
been Schopenhauerian if I had added:
"Whoever is interested in death seeks
life in it"; and I did say it, if less
epigrammatically, as a very young writer,
when it was a matter of bringing Thomas
Buddenbrook, the hero of my early novel,
down to his death; and I granted him to
read that great chapter On Death who myself as a young writer, twenty-three or
twenty-four years old, was just fresh
from its impact. It was a great joy and
I have taken occasion in my recollections
to speak of it, and tell how I needed not
to keep an experience like this to myself;
that a beautiful opportunity at once came,
to bear witness, to return thanks; that
there was straightway a place to use it
creatively. To him, the suffering hero
of my novel of bourgeois life, which was
the task, the burden, the virtue, the home
and blessing of my young years, I gave the
dear experience, the high adventure; I
poured it into his life, just close to the
end, I wove it into the narrative and made
him find life in death, liberation from
the bonds of his wearied individuality,
freedom from a role in life which he had
regarded symbolically and presented with
courage and capacity, but which had never
satisfied his spirit or his hopes and had
been a hindrance to him in achieving something other and better.[7]

However we interpret this scene in the novel, it
certainly does <u>not</u> let Thomas Buddenbrook find life
in death, nor does it elevate him. We have only to
note the remarkably confused after-effects of the
experience on him:

"I shall live," he whispered into his
pillow. He wept, and in the next moment
knew not why. His brain stood still, the
vision was quenched. Suddenly there was
nothing more--he lay in dumb darkness.
"It will come back," he assured himself.
And before sleep inexorably wrapped him
round, he swore to himself never to let
go this previous treasure, but to read and
study, to learn its powers, and to make

inalienably his own the whole conception
of the universe out of which his vision
sprang.
    But that could not be. Even the next
day, as he woke with a faint feeling of
shame at the emotional extravaganzas of
the night, he suspected that it would be
hard to put these beautiful designs into
practice. (I, 659)

And soon thereafter he rejects the works of
Schopenhauer unequivocally:

    He never succeeded in looking again
into the precious volume--to say nothing
of buying its other parts. His days were
consumed by nervous pedantry: harassed
by a thousand details, all of them unimportant, he was too weak-willed to arrive at a reasonable and fruitful arrangement of his time. Nearly two weeks after
that memorable afternoon he gave it up--
and ordered the maid-servant to fetch the
book from the drawer in the garden table
and replace it in the bookcase.
    And thus Thomas Buddenbrook, who had
held his hands stretched imploringly up-
ward toward the high ultimate truth,
sank now weakly back to the images and
conceptions of his childhood. He strove
to call back that personal God, the Father
of all human beings, who had sent a part
of Himself upon earth to suffer and bleed
for our sins, and who, on the final day,
would come to judge the quick and the
dead; at whose feet the justified, in the
course of the eternity then beginning,
would be recompensed for the sorrows they
had borne in this vale of tears. Yes,
he strove to subscribe to the whole confused unconvincing story, which required
no intelligence, only obedient credulity;
and which, when the last anguish came,
would sustain one in a firm and childlike
faith. (I, 659-660)

    Considering these words, it is most doubtful that
this Schopenhauer scene indicates any real identification between the author and this character. Indeed,
the indication is the very opposite judging from the

24

mocking tone of the description, the ineffectiveness
of the experience, and Thomas' resulting naive wish
to reacquire the faith of his parents. Isn't Mann
actually demonstrating here that, unlike the sensitive
artist, the middle-class businessman is capable neither
of the penetrating soul-searching of the artist nor of
absorbing any lasting value from the reading of someone
like Schopenhauer?

What purpose did the author then have in presenting Thomas Buddenbrook a magnificent gift, if this
gift, ironically (in this case almost viciously),
serves to show up the mediocrity, insensitivity, and
frustrations of the recipient? The only answer can be
that while he was trying to praise and elevate the
image of Thomas Buddenbrook, the irrepressible feeling
of hostility directed against his father became the
real content of the characterization. The point is
that the inner contradiction of actions and values
in Buddenbrooks grew out of a basic ambivalence of the
author himself toward his own family. We have begun
by indicating that confusion has arisen between the
statement and evidence that Thomas and not Hanno is
the hero of the novel and that Mann gave Thomas Buddenbrook the Schopenhauer experience out of a feeling of
love and admiration.

Serious contradictions can also be seen in the
statements on Thomas Buddenbrook's ethic of dedication
and accomplishment in his business. Even when prais-
ing the high standards, the relentless energy, and
the immaculate appearance of Thomas, the ambivalence
is obvious. The author masterfully describes the unbearable tension in Thomas Buddenbrook who, afraid of
his inner destructive urges, develops external defenses
with increasing frequency and by means of obsessive
ceremonials seeks to hold tight rein over them:

> He was harassed by a thousand trifles,
> most of which had actually to do with up-
> keep of his house and his wardrobe; small
> matters which he could not keep in his
> head, over which he procrastinated out of
> disgust and upon which he spent an utterly
> disproportionate amount of time and
> thought. . . .
> Nowadays it was nine o'clock before he
> appeared to Herr Wenzel, the old barber,
> in his nightshirt, after hours of heavy
> unrefreshing sleep; and quite an hour and

a half later before he felt himself ready
and panoplied to begin the day, and could
descend to drink his tea in the first
story. His toilette was a ritual consist-
ing of a succession of countless details
which drove him half mad: from the cold
shower in the bathroom to the last brush-
ing of the last speck of dust off his
coat, and the last pressure of the tongs
on his mustache. But it would have been
impossible for him to leave his dressing
room with the consciousness of having
neglected a single one of these details
for fear he might lose thereby his sense
of immaculate integrity--which, however,
would be dissipated in the course of the
next hour and have to be renewed again.
(I, 612-613)

Thomas' frantic efforts to preserve his <u>dehors</u>
are the mark of a man struggling to hide an intolerable
burden of guilt beneath an orderly exterior. In
striving for his imaginary perfection he is caught
in a vicious circle of repetitive compulsion, for his
unconscious doubt remains untouched by such measures.
This <u>manie de perfection</u> in his dress hides the decay
within. His immaculate white shirt fronts symbolize
a remission from his sins. Along with the specially
tailored suits they signify the outward strength and
steadfastness necessary to meet the practical requirements of the day and manifest a seriousness of mood
and devotion to duty. For in his attitude towards his
work, his reason for existence, there likewise occur
the same futile attempts to hide guilt. It is no
wonder then that Thomas Buddenbrook utters with such a
ring of conviction the following words to his Bohemian
brother Christian: "I have become what I am because
I did not want to become what you are. If I have inwardly shrunk from you, it has been because I needed
to guard myself--your being, and your existence, are a
danger to me--that is the truth" (I, 580).

However, there is an important distinction to be
made between Thomas Buddenbrook and the artist hero.
Whereas the latter's obsessional drives are channeled
into the perfection of his creative art, Thomas' uncertainty is mechanical and not only uncreative, but
actually destructive. Only at first is it adequately
sublimated. Later his acts go over into useless,
time-consuming trivialities which, under pressure to

26

be repeated again and again, paralyze his ability to cope with the challenges of everyday competitive life.

The resemblance between Thomas and the Mannian hero is thus a superficial one. That there is a resemblance at all can be satisfactorily explained as follows: the burgher's single-mindedness, relentless diligence, outward respect, and emphasis on propriety, in short, the impeccable dehors of Thomas Buddenbrook and later Mannian heroes, is a visual projection of the guilty artist whose own inner state is a disorganized torment, a chaos of destructive impulses. The artist hero takes his cue from his conception of middle-class respectability and thereby attempts by means of physical ritual to check the dangers within himself. And the fact that the dangers are imminent is seen in other works in which he is not always successful in maintaining the repression of his instincts. His sense of propriety also reveals his abhorrence of the Bohemian, a theme which runs like a leitmotif throughout the early works of Mann.

Mann sets a pattern of ambivalence that is reinforced in the vast majority of his writings, an ambivalence that originated for him in the intimacy of his own family. Looking beyond the surface to the bottom of this relationship, we find that Thomas Buddenbrook is actually the antagonist of this novel and it is at his feet that the blame for the decline of the family must be placed: his choice of a marriage partner infuses decay into the family, his is also the conclusion that the business which sustained and bolstered the clan for generations should finally be liquidated, and he blunders even from beyond the grave by appointing a pompous, incompetent person to execute the terms of his will.

Autobiography goes beyond the naming of a few familiar places and describing one's personal experiences. Mann's own ambivalence reveals itself most profoundly as he tries to praise the symbolic pater familias of the Buddenbrooks and succeeds only in denigrating him.

Coming to Terms with the Father

Referring again to Thomas Mann's statement that Thomas Buddenbrook is the hero of the novel, we find it a curious experience to follow the way in which he is exposed and diminished throughout the work. The

amount of the dowry was the real motivation for his
marriage proposal to Gerda. In his relations with his
brother Christian, he is bitter and heartless, although
(except for the scene after the Frau Consul's death)
Christian, in keeping with his name, turns the other
cheek. Towards Hanno he is harsh and lacks understanding, and to his mother, in the scene concerning the
disposal of the deceased Clara's dowry, cruel and
grasping. His honesty comes into question in connection
with the Pöppenrade negotiation--his partner Marcus
washes his hands of the whole affair. For that matter,
the whole world which Thomas represents is questioned.
The implication throughout the novel is that the businessman is, as Christian jokingly states, a swindler.
There are certainly more than a few embezzlers in the
novel: Grünlich, Kesselmayer and their Hamburg col-
leagues, Bock, Goudstiker, Peterson, Maßmann and Timm,
and finally Weinschenk and Kaßbaum. (Weinschenk merely
happened to get caught in a "routine" illegal manipulation.) In any event, the man of commerce needs
to be ruthless as Thomas himself realizes:

> For the first time in his career he had
> fully and personally experienced the
> ruthless brutality of business life and
> seen how all better, gentler, and kindlier
> sentiments creep away and hide themselves
> before the one raw, naked dominating in-
> stinct of self-preservation. He had seen
> that when one suffers a misfortune in
> business, one is met by one's friends--
> and one's best friends--not with sympathy,
> not with compassion, but with suspicion,
> cold, cruel hostile suspicion. (I, 469-470)

Needless to say, Hanno despises the very thought of
such a career.

    Chapter five of part ten begins with a description
of Thomas as a rapidly aging man of almost laughable
vanity. Gerda, on the other hand, has scarcely altered
in these eighteen years; she has small, close-set,
blue-shadowed eyes that cannot be trusted. Her personality is so cool, so reserved, so repressed, so distant
that it is evident to the people of the city that the
marriage of these two opposing types is a frigid one
at best or an adulterous one at worst. Gerda's intimate
friend is René Maria von Throta, an army lieutenant
who plays music with her up in her room while Thomas,

not daring to enter, waits and listens.* And not only is Thomas the cuckold, but he is ignored and scorned by his rival as well, who refuses all official invitations from him and confines himself to the free and private company of the mistress of the house. However, Thomas is more concerned about his reputation than he is about an honest relationship to his wife. Though he knows perfectly well what is going on between von Throta and Gerda, his only decision in the matter is to attempt to keep everybody in ignorance of his mortification.

At this point Thomas Buddenbrook begins to be reduced to a small, helpless man who pathetically sits downstairs, "an aging man" listening while, "above, his wife makes music with her lover" (I, 647). Again using musical terms, the author follows at length the sexual experiences of Gerda and her paramour down to the following conclusion:

> Then, overhead in the salon, the harmonies would rise and surge like waves, with singing, lamenting, unearthly jubilation; would lift like clasped hands outstretched toward Heaven; would float in vague ecstasies; would sink and die away into sobbing, into night and silence. But they might roll and seethe, weep and exult, foam up and enfold each other, as unnaturally as they liked. (I, 646)

Thomas' sexual impotence is implied. Repeatedly described as too old now for his young wife, he is revealed as unable "to make music," i.e., he does not have the sexual capacity to "play."

Von Throta, Gerda's music partner, slips into the story and out again as a ghostly lover with no further significance unless we adduce some psychological identity between him and Hanno. Hanno's concealed-revealed proximity to the scene of their playing, his own practice sessions with his mother Gerda and his expression of guilt during and after the episodes--he lowers his eyes, he cannot complete a sentence when addressed, he

---

*Mann's own house in Lübeck was often open to the officers of the city garrison.

tries to avoid his father as though he himself were in some way connected to the guilty act--demonstrates in any case an intimate knowledge of what is going on. It is safe to say that von Throta and Hanno are doublet forms of the same identity, that the lieutenant is a wish fulfillment of the hero, representing, as he does, Hanno's infantile and omnipotent fantasy of possessing the mother. Through René von Throta, Hanno vicariously indulges in music with his mother to the exclusion of his father.

In a desperate moment Thomas tries to restore intimacy and rescue himself from his loneliness, but instead of trying to reinstate himself in a normal way with his wife, he turns imploringly to his son. When Hanno realizes after a few seconds that this father is really lonely and is seeking some measure of sympathy and understanding from him, a brief rapport is established and the statement is made that "where fear and suffering were in question, there Thomas Buddenbrook could count on the devotion of his son. On that common ground they met as one" (I, 650). But this moment provides only a false hope that any respect or mutual understanding can be developed between the two, for Thomas almost immediately thereafter (as if to show that he does have some pride and power after all) begins to press Hanno all the more sternly to prepare himself to take over the business. At the same time his health rapidly begins to deteriorate, and as he becomes most depressed, he chances on the writings of Schopenhauer.

We now know that this elevating spiritual experience, which the author claims to be the apex of Thomas' life did not take hold at all, so we must ask ourselves what results, if any, it precipitated!

First of all, Thomas strives to recall the personal, Christian God of his childhood to sustain himself. But here too doubts and cynicism overwhelm him, so "having come to such an unsatisfactory ending of his attempts to set his spiritual affairs in order, he determines at least to spare no pains over his earthly ones, and to carry out a plan which he had long entertained" (I, 661). His new determination stems, however, from the bitterness of not having been able to find spiritual peace, and it does not reveal any real fatherly concern but rather distrust of his son and a retaliatory desire to punish that which he associates with his frustrations and misery. The object of his hostility and recipient of his punishment becomes Hanno, the

only one he can reach and who in appearance and remote
behavior is so much like his mother: Hanno, who would
be capable of fully understanding and profiting from
a reading of this Schopenhauer that he himself cannot
really comprehend; Hanno, the only one small and helpless enough to become the victim of Thomas' hatred and
grief. We will remember that earlier in this episode
Thomas thinks about reproaching his wife and throwing
her admirer out of his house, but he is afraid of embarrassment in the first case and of the futility in
the second, for "one did not call her to account"
(I, 648). In this episode, too, he feels rejected,
frustrated, and as alone as he did after the failure
of the Schopenhauer experience, and here again the
aftereffect of defeat is expressed in his relationship
to Hanno.

Thomas Buddenbrook decides to make out his will--
the last verdict and judgment of a man upon his family.
This must sound ominous and threatening to the eavesdropping Hanno, who escapes upstairs to practice his
music for an hour. Later, when the lawyer in a long,
black overcoat and his father are discussing the will,
Hanno must stand in ignorance, like a Kafaesque figure,
in front of the door to see that the judges are not
disturbed. Clutching his sailor's knot with one hand,
feeling with his tongue for a doubtful tooth, and
listening to the earnest subdued voices which can be
heard from the inside, Hanno waits there in stoic
anxiety like a person whose fate is being decided on
by higher powers. The sexual symbolism here is also
obvious, as are the thoughts of death and guilt which
occupy his mind.

The plan which Thomas intends to carry out denies
Hanno his natural right of inheritance and terminates
the raison d'être of the Buddenbrook line. Thomas
makes the decision here which is the immediate cause
of the downfall of the Buddenbrook clan. Although the
finances and resources of the family business are still
strong and well-founded, Thomas stipulates that all is
to be liquidated within one year after his death; and
so, with one stroke he demolishes the sustaining
strength of the Buddenbrook family and in terms of
retribution settles accounts for his own frustrations
with his family.

Seldom in literature has a father been so debased
as Thomas Buddenbrook is in Chapter VIII of Part 10.
His brother cannot shed a tear for him. His wife's

31

reaction to his death is one of "horror and disgust, . . . with a look of anger, distraction and shrinking" (I, 681). She does not bemoan his passing in a single instance but rather criticizes him for having died in such a dirty fashion, in the gutter: "'Oh, it is insulting, it is vile, for the end to have come like that!'" (I, 681). Little Hanno, as always when his anxieties are running high, is clutching his sailor's knot, listening to the death rattle of his father, and looking at his father's filthy clothes hanging over the chair. The ludicrous and disturbing babbling and gurgling noises the father makes as he lies dying are repeated too often to be mere description any longer. They indicate the revulsion that the family has towards Thomas' death. Thomas is further debased by the humorous device of collapsed solemnity, which turns the scene into a grotesque scenario of discomfort and ridicule. Tony begins to sing a prayer, but then forgets the words, and everybody shivers with embarrassment; Hanno coughs hard and pretends his coughs are sobs. The final straw is, of course, when Hanno, copying names of people to notify of his father' death, begins to laugh so hard and uncontrollably that he has to be sent up to bed. There is even an addition al anticlimactic debasement in the rumor that goes around town that Thomas Buddenbrook had died of a bad tooth. "'But goodness,' they rejoined, 'People don't die of a bad tooth. . . . was ever the like heard!'" (I, 688). The final outburst of laughter shifts the death scene into the realm of grotesque comedy.

Yes, Thomas dies an absurd and undignified death when he succumbs, presumably, to a toothache after a harrowing visit to the dentist's. Symbolically Thomas has been emasculated, for in Freudian terms his demise is sexually conditioned as he, deprived of the potency that determines his superiority in the unequal contest with Hanno, ignominiously collapses on the muddy street His pathetic demise can be contrasted with the "honest" death of Hanno.

The images of his father persist in Hanno's unconscious as a vital reality, and so, still living in fear of his father's jealousy and still burdened with the guilt of incestuous desires, he is still subject to the specter of the menacing Thomas. Hanno's fantasies surrounding his compulsive habit of self-gratification pile on his conscience an increased burden of guilt for which the only punishment must be death, if there is to be any real justice at all. Through

the device of omnipotence of thought, the Oedipal
fantasies about removing the father to enjoy the mother
freely have become a reality for Hanno. But what he
could not anticipate was the effectiveness of the subconscious lex talionis, which demands an eye for an
eye, a tooth for a tooth. In thought Hanno imagined
his father's death, and when Thomas actually died,
Hanno became guilty of parricide and had to pay for
the crime with his own life. All his hostilities and
affection are now turned inward against the self and
expressed in Mann's carefully detailed description of
Hanno's onanism (I, 747-750). Hanno is compulsive in
his autoeroticism, a compulsion whose full implications
he cannot understand. He visualizes them in symbols
rich in images significant to him and describes the
accompanying actions in terms of musical harmonies,
"welling up uncontrolled from the keyboard, as they
shaped themselves under Hanno's laboring fingers"
(I, 749). Completely withdrawn into his own narcissistic world, he ponders his physical capacity for
erotic experience in musical symbols:

> He sat a little bent over the keys, with
> parted lips. . . . What was the meaning
> of what he played?. . . . The fanatical
> worship of this worthless trifle, this
> scrap of melody, this brief, childish
> harmonic invention only a bar and a half
> in length. . . . (I, 749-750)

That same evening, after a stand-off game of chess (a
barren intellectual exchange rather than an emotional
one) with his mother he goes to his room and until
after midnight thinks again of his harmonium, but he
"played in thought only, for he must make no noise"
(I, 751). Playing is his great source of satisfaction.
It is the production of a maze of fantasies with regard
to sexual wish fulfillment--his preoccupation, his
gratification, and his burden in life!

Let us gather together some of the introductory
threads of thought. Thomas Mann has asserted that he
gave the heroic father, Thomas Buddenbrook, his own
favorite Schopenhauer experience out of a feeling of
admiration and affection, but from what we have seen
of the way he treated the father, we must conclude that
Thomas is everything but the figure of a hero. The
only person who seems to bewail his death to any degree
is Tony, but even she goes on to criticize him bitterly.
Nevertheless, after having gone to great lengths to

33

rebuke and belittle the character of Thomas Buddenbrook, it is reasonable that the author should come back years later with a determined effort to establish him as the persevering hero of the novel. The only way to explain this ambivalence is to recognize that, in this most autobiographical of all his works, Mann's hostilities simply got away from him in an effort to settle accounts with his father. Primarily, Mann was writing in defense of his own childhood position, trying to belittle his opponent and chief critic while gaining public sympathy for himself as he suffered the inner fate of Hanno. There is no doubt that he did succeed admirably on both counts. However, the reverse pose of ambivalence has constantly remained to plague him in his work and conduct. In his praise of the bourgeoisie in later works he often echoes hollow phrases of fidelity that he is still loyal to the world of his father, that in spite of the fact he is a writer he has not become a Bohemian, that in dress and comportment (on the surface at least) he has become like his father. Externally, then, up to the very end of his career it became one of Mann's underlying desires to reinstate himself through apologia and disguise in the good graces of his introjected father whom he feared more than he respected.

That this confusion concerning Hanno as the real hero is deliberate and that Mann intentionally misleads the reader by compounding this confusion in his later writings, certainly needs no further documentation; but Henry Hatfield emphasizes the point so well in another context that he deserves to be quoted. Significantly, Hatfield entitles his chapter on Buddenbrooks "The World of the Father": "Mann tell us that his mood at the time was made up of 'indolence, a bad conscience as a bourgeois, and the secure sense of latent talents.' For the 'bad conscience' there were presumably two reasons: his rejections of any sort of middle-class career, and his choice of the decay of his own family as a subject. At times, Mann must have felt that he was committing an indiscretion if not a downright betrayal."[8]

In view of Thomas Mann's known emphasis on propriety in his private life, his imprudent depiction of his own family seems exceedingly strange.* From

---

* Thomas Mann's belief in the sanctity of his

James Cleugh we learn of the impact the novel had on
the city of Lübeck itself. It raised a storm there,
certain citizens complaining bitterly of being cruelly
caricatured. Mann was vindictively attacked and four
years after the appearance of the novel a futile legal
action was introduced against him. In 1906 Mann himself felt compelled as a protective measure to write
a defense, (Bilse and I), of his treatment of Lübeck
in Buddenbrooks, asserting therein an author's right
to make use of his own experience.[9] The impact Buddenbrooks made on Lübeck is surprising if one considers
that, as many critics have claimed, it is hardly a
novel about Lübeck, but rather about the decay of one
single family.

The Genesis of the Novel

The implications in these conjectures about Mann's
"betrayal" are not yet exhausted. The autobiographical
factor has further overtones, especially in the second
half of the novel, where Hanno makes his entrance for
the first time. Mann tells us that the creation of
Buddenbrooks, to a great extent, proceeded backwards.
We learn from Lübeck as an Intellectual Way of Life
that the novel originally dealt only with the artist
figure and his relationship to his father: "The work
grew in my hands; everything took atrociously much more

---

private life is clear from the remarks of his brother-
in-law Klaus Pringsheim: "In discussing such personal
matters as my private feelings about and personal encounters with Thomas Mann, it is indeed very hard to
choose what should be said and what had best remain
unsaid, for it is in bad taste to air family affairs
in public; and especially in the Pringsheim and Mann
families great opprobrium is attached to the public
discussion of family matters, unless it be in the
necessary explication or elaboration of what is already
in the public domain. Thus when I speak of Mann (and
this is the first and probably the last time that I
do so publicly), I am subconsciously mindful of his
and my aunt's reproachful glance or wagging finger
warning me that I must be truthful and must not say
anything that I do not really know or firmly believe."
Thomas Mann in America und sein Verhältnis zur Politik
--unpublished manuscript in the Thomas Mann Archive,
Zurich--(Lawrence, Kansas, 1962), p. 2.

space (and time) than I had dreamt. While I had actually been only interested in the story of the sensitive
latecomer Hanno and at most in that of Thomas Buddenbrook, everything that I had thought of being able to
treat only as historical background assumed a very
independent and peculiarly justifiable form. . . ."[10]
And from the following citation one gathers that the
genealogical structure of the work appears as an afterthought or expedient: "I designed it at the age of
twenty-three, or better said, I began to write it; for
the word design could give the impression that I had
planned it as it then became and had had a clear idea
of what I was undertaking with it."[11]

      This is a strong indication that Thomas Mann wrote
a good deal of the second half of the Künstlerroman
before he turned to the genealogical aspect. In any
event he did switch from the problem of the artist to
the history of his family. Such a shift from the inner
world of the artist occurs nowhere else in Mann's works
His heroes are artists and suffer the artist's curse.
One wonders what Mann had hoped to gain, especially
since the two parts, the one historical, the other
psychological, have to a great extent little in common
and, though ingeniously fused, are not without signs
of this disparate composition. By doubling the already
long novel he also risked his chances of getting it
published. That lengthy novels were at that time un-
fashionable is confirmed in his Sketch of my Life:
"Critics were out of sorts and were asking, whether
the many volumed tomes were perhaps again to become
the fashion. They compared the novel with a truck
stuck in the sand with its wheels spinning."[12] Yet,
with the expansion to two volumes, Mann makes his work
more than twice as long as his professed model, Renée
Mauperin by the Goncourt brothers. The same was true
with his Scandinavian prototypes: "In its size too,
my aim had been to write something corresponding to the
books of Kielland and Jonas Lie: two hundred pages,
no more, in fifteen chapters--I still remember how I
had set it up."[13]

      His publisher, Samuel Fischer, was extremely
dubious about accepting the novel in its present length
form, especially since the sale of Mann's first collection of short stories had gone very poorly:

            If you think it possible to cut your work
            by about half, you would then find me very
            much inclined in principle to publish your

book. A novel of 65 closely printed
gatherings is for our present day life
practically an impossibility. I don't
think many people will find the time or
have the power of concentration to digest
a novel of this size. I know that I'm
demanding a lot from you and that that
perhaps means you will have to write the
book over completely, but as a publisher
I can't take any other course of action.
Perhaps the theme is too large and extensive for your command of epic breadth;
perhaps, however, you would also discover
that a greater thematic concentration would
be to the advantage of the work.[14]

Thomas Mann's answer, reported by his daughter
Erika,--"The most beautiful letter in his whole life"
--was a direct refusal. Without a moment's hesitation
he stated that Buddenbrooks' length was essential to
the quality of the work and that it would either be
published in its entirety or not at all.[15]

Mann's refusal can in all validity be ascribed
to his uncompromising position with regard to his art.
But from his letters to his brother Heinrich, we learn
that artistic integrity was not his sole concern at
that time. After weeks of waiting for word from the
Fischer company he became deeply depressed and even
thought of abandoning his career in art: "Well, if
no one wants the book, I think I'll become a bank
official."[16] How serious this intention was--to become a member of the business world which he abhorred
and which he placed in such a bad light in his novel--
may never be known. However, Thomas Mann, who later
described himself as young and lonely and an unknown
beginner in the art of the written word, was then in
financially straitened circumstances.[17] Mann had in
fact placed his way of life as well as his career as
an artist in jeopardy by his reply to his publisher,
and when he finally received favorable news from Fischer
he was overjoyed and immensely proud: "So then, fame
and greatness in spite of the length. While I was
working on the novel, my secret and painful ambition
had continuously been directed towards fame. . . .
Sometimes my heart pounds immediately at this thought
[that Buddenbrooks is no ordinary novel]."[18]

The reason that Thomas Mann did not consider
Buddenbrooks an ordinary novel was that he had exposed

here his own family and rendered his most personal
memories immortal. Buddenbrooks has frequently been
designated as a roman à clef. Many writers have as a
matter of course pointed to the actual people standing
behind the characters. Thomas Mann's son, Golo, states
with certainty: "In his first novel, Buddenbrooks,
there is indeed practically no character at all which
is fictitious except for the Bavarian, Permaneder.
The second husband of Tony Buddenbrook, the Aunt Elisabeth whom I used to know, was not a Bavarian but a
Swabian from Eßlingen on the Neckar. Apart from this,
the only really fictitious thing about Buddenbrooks
is the name Buddenbrook itself."[19] Victor Mann, the
author's younger brother, devotes considerable space
to his first meeting with his uncle, "Christian Buddenbrook," in reality Friedrich Lebrecht Mann; and Arthur
Eloesser in his Thomas Mann biography specifies who
the real prototypes for most of the characters are
including even the maid Ida Jungmann. According to
them, Mann's own father, Thomas Johann Heinrich Mann,
became Thomas Buddenbrooks, the father of Hanno.

        Likewise it would seem only natural to expect
Gerda Buddenbrook, Thomas Buddenbrook's wife and Hanno's
mother, to be equated with Mann's mother. Although in
her case the opinion is somewhat divided, the external
evidence does point up overwhelming similarities between the two.[20] Both Gerda and Julia Mann, exotic
in origin and manners, came to Germany in order to
marry a North German businessman. Both created a
sensation on first arrival in Lübeck; both stayed a
short while at a boarding house run by a hunch-backed
woman, and both were musical to the core. In Hatfield's
opinion "Thomas Buddenbrook is closely modeled after
Mann's own father, and his exotic wife Gerda would
seem, to a lesser extent, reminiscent of Mann's mother,
Julia Da Silva-Bruhns."[21] We receive support from the
statement that Gerda is only "reminiscent of Mann's
mother" from Viktor Mann, who paints a picture of a
devoted mother, neither cold, austere, moody and infirm
like Gerda Buddenbrook nor "fiery," "passionate,"
"negligent," and "impulsively lewd" like Consuelo
Kröger, the mother in Tonio Kröger.[22] In short, we
understand (but with reservations) why Hatfield and
others feel constrained to deny the exact equation:
Julia Mann = Gerda Buddenbrook.

        It is interesting to hear Thomas Mann's answer to
such speculation. Because of critics' interpretations
he felt compelled to defend the portrayal of his mother.

> I wish the public had not been so ready
> in identifying certain figures in my
> tales with those of real life. More
> than one critic, convinced that I was
> bound by strict autobiographical consid-
> erations, has unhesitatingly cited phrases
> with which I characterized the mother of
> my hero in Tonio Kröger in such a way as
> if they were words which I had written
> about my own mother. That, however,
> things are not quite so simple is shown
> by the fact that the corresponding woman
> figure in Buddenbrooks, Hanno's mother,
> Gerda Arnoldsen, evinces no similarity
> with Tonio's mother except in her musical-
> ity and her being from a distant place.
> Which figure then is now the real image
> of my mother?[23]

Despite Mann's equivocal statement, his portrait
of Gerda Buddenbrook is compatible with the typical.
In her passionate attachment to music with its sexual
connotations, the cold and haughty, yet adulterous
Gerda is similar to the heroines throughout the works
of Thomas Mann. She, like other Mannian women, is a
perilous attraction for the hero and reflects the
ambivalence to be found in his conception of love.
Though inaccessible, these women are seductive and
provocative temptresses; though exotic and of patrician
station they are the instrument of pain or mortification
to the hero, and though sometimes slovenly and debased
they are the forbidden wife or paramour of a titled
and respected rival.

Two Halves of a Novel

When we divide the novel into distinct artistic
halves, we find that Hanno's position as a protagonist
is strengthened. Episodic in the total work, the
chapter which describes one day in Hanno's life in-
contestibly assumes singular importance for the role
of the artist-hero, whereas the significance of the
father, Thomas, fades in perspective.*

---

*The average length of the chapters in Buddenbrooks
consists of five pages; there is only one truly long
chapter, the one day in the life of Hanno, and it is
nearly twice as long as the next longest.

A comparison of the two halves of the novel reveals that the author has gained a great deal by enlarging the tale of the artist to the narrative of four generations. A series of unforgettable scenes--three weddings, the Grünlich, Schwarzkopf, and Permaneder episodes, the Revolution in the city, and the magnificent description of a feast--are all told with great vitality, and each character is full flesh and blood. The diabolical Kesselmayer, for example, lives for only a few pages, but the force of his characterization is felt long afterwards. So it is with Morten Schwarzkopf, Bendix Grünlich, and Alois Permaneder.

The first half of the novel belongs to Thomas' sister, Tony; it is her story and she makes the most of it. She has her entrance on the very first page, and at the end of the volume she is still in the limelight. Thomas and Christian are, for a time anyway, on foreign soil. It is Tony's story but at the same time it is also the story of a child. In the leitmotifs which characterize her we are reminded of her immature bearing: her quivering upper lip and the way she throws back her head and tucks in her chin. Besides the manner in which she behaves under pressure we see her juvenile pranks, quixotic emotions, and her spiteful attitude towards the religiously-minded guests. And it is not just that the other members of the household refer to her as a child on several occasions, the author himself frequently describes her as such. By these intrusions Thomas Mann tones down her importance for the total work. For although she is essentially the only surviving member of the Buddenbrook family, her function is not central to the purpose of the novel. She is rather the connecting link which helps to achieve a better fusion of the two disparate halves: the genealogical novel and the story of the artist. As a foil around whom significant conversations take place, she is the confidante of all and through her the pace of the novel achieves a certain briskness.

Tony is also one of the most irrepressible creations of Thomas Mann. Her tremendous naiveté breaks through all the inhibitions and restraints of the particular situation no matter how serious. The end result is that she is irresistible. Erich Heller has summed her up admirably: "She is comic--and one of Thomas Mann's most successful comic creations--because she has hopelessly incongruous ideas. If the

Great Flood were upon her, she would find complete relief in being angry about the inadequacy of the weather
forecast."[24]

The second volume, by comparison, which begins
significantly with the christening of Hanno, is more
thought provoking. Besides Pfühl's theories on music
and the scene dealing with a volume of Schopenhauer
there is the psychological factor. Almost every detail, even Thomas' quarrel with Christian and Hanno's
hours in school, as forcefully as they are told, are
seen through the eyes of a depth psychologist. It is
interesting in this respect to compare the animation
of the Grünlich bankruptcy scene and the Tony-Morten
idyll in volume one with, respectively the dark overtones of the Weinschenk affair and Hanno's last sojourn
at Travemünde in volume two. The trivial poetaster
Hofstede al the beginning of the novel can also be
compared to the real artist Pfühl in the second volume.

So the question of the disparity and necessity of
the two parts presents itself again: Why did Mann
bring in more information on his ancestors, and why
did he refuse to cut the length of his work even in
face of the possibility of giving up his career as a
writer? By merging Thomas with many Buddenbrooks, the
author utilizes sheer space to diffuse the intensity
of the spotlight which would otherwise shine furiously
on Thomas Buddenbrook and on his hostility towards his
son. Thus the focus on the Buddenbrook genealogy in
the first volume detracts from the significance of the
second and consequently reduces the emphasis on the
father-son conflict. Mann commits real indiscretions
in expressing his inner feelings about this conflict,
and for this reason, he was not able to cut the novel
in half. For him, the first volume alone would have
failed to convey his real intent, and the second
volume would have too readily exposed his own hostile
feelings to the harsh light of day.

In the light of these conjectures it is possible
to reach some new conclusions about Buddenbrooks. The
genealogical novel can now be interpreted as a screen
for the novel of the artist and the family history as
a mask for the embarrassingly stark description of an
immediate family situation. Behind the theme of decline lurk the profound fears and sins of the artist
himself, while the concept of decline represents in
effect partial atonement for the author's transgressions. Thus, in Buddenbrooks, as in all the other

works of Thomas Mann, the basic desideratum is not the
history of familial decadence but rather the artist's
inner problem of existence, the problem of the guilt-
ridden nihilist with a fragile hold on life.

Decline and the Critics

Without exception the critics of Buddenbrooks
have felt the need to explain away the decline of this
patrician family of Lübeck. Eichner, a key representative of one school of thought, states that "The way
in which this decline takes place is, however, not
brought about politically or sociologically, but rather
metaphysically."[25] By this Eichner and others mean
that the philosophy of Schopenhauer, reinterpreted by
Nietzsche, stands behind the concept of genealogical
decline. But whatever applied role the philosophies
of Schopenhauer and Nietzsche play in the family's
decline, the ultimate "why" in the critics' terms
still remains unsolved. One wonders if decline is
considered an inevitable process or if it is to be
understood as a slow but constant biological process.
Or is it a metaphysical one? Are four generations
really needed as a pre-condition for this atrophy?
And how does it follow that a loss of vitality and
capacity for life is an inexorable consequence from
one generation to the other or that a problematical,
doubting nature is the product of heredity?

Perhaps it is best to deal with an immediately
answerable question: Is the novel about the downfall
of a single family or of a whole age? Several critics,
perhaps taking their cue from the author, have seen in
Buddenbrooks the decline of a whole cultural era: "It
is the decline of the bourgeoisie which in the most
pregnant moment is conceived of as the decline of a
family."[26] There is some evidence to support this view,
as Wolff demonstrates:

> Decline is not identical with downfall,
> for whereas downfall can be brought about
> by chance, decline presupposes a systematic
> downgrade motion; and although Mann does
> not treat the theme in detail, so much is
> clear from the beginning: the fate of the
> Buddenbrooks is not a special case but
> rather a typical phenomenon. The Raten-
> kamps, whose house old Johann Buddenbrook
> had just acquired, were once an old and
> respected family which has now died out,

and at the end of the novel the young
aspiring Hagenström family steps into
the place which the Buddenbrooks had
previously occupied; some other families
who appear in the background, the Krögers,
Duchamps, etc., suffer the same fate. The
decline which brings an end to the Buddenbrook family is thus a regular phenomenon
in the families of the well-to-do Hanseatic
merchants of the novels. . . .[27]

Wolff could have added to the list of families on
the downgrade: Köppen, Kaßbaum, Möllendorpf and
Döhlmann, not to mention the Krögers, a branch of the
Buddenbrooks. Do these families also go through the
same metaphysical or biological process, as the Buddenbrooks do, in the course of four generations? Does
genealogy play a significant part in the fate of these
other families as well? Do they decline in the same
manner as the Buddenbrooks--through a decrease in
robustness combined with heightened artistic sensitiv-
ity? The answer is negative on all counts.

Decline is linked directly to the material fortunes of the Buddenbrook firm as well as to the physical
health of the individuals. The irretrievable sense of
loss from the sale of the old house in the Meng street
and the liquidation of the firm are concrete indications
of the fall from greatness. Yet, curiously, both the
financial ebb and the decline in health are not an
organic part of the family's history but are accidental
and induced from without. At his death Thomas Buddenbrook left behind on paper 650,000 Marks, a sum nearly
equal to the firm's capital after the death of his
father, so actually the firm is as strong as in the
time of old Johann Buddenbrook. But because of the
terms of Thomas' last will and testament, in which the
business must be liquidated within a year, the firm's
property and later Thomas' house are disposed of by
the executors Kistenmaker, Marcus, and Gosch on hurried
and unfavorable terms. The collapse of the Buddenbrook fortune is then in reality the result of an ill-
made will, executed all too literally by men whose
incompetence, as is stressed, plays a decisive role.

Likewise the utter physical exhaustion of the last
male Buddenbrook heir, Hanno, is a question of dubious
biology. Hanno is evidently decadent at birth. Yet
such a concept is scientifically questionable; it
"would seem to be an instance of the triumph of theory

over artistic judgment."[28] Of greater significance is
the fact that Hanno's inborn predicament, like his
affinity to music, is conditioned solely by his mother
who married late into the family: "Bluish shadows lie
in the deep corners on both sides of the nose, and
these give the little face, which is hardly yet a face
at all, an aged look not suited to its four weeks of
existence. But, please God, they mean nothing--for
has not his mother the same?" (I, 396).

So the deterioration of the family begins with
the arrival of the unhealthy, ultra-refined and artistic Gerda. Her entrance into the family, it can be
said, insures its downfall, and, because she as an outsider is the chief cause of decline, any inherent
genealogical weakness must be called into question.
In any case the history of the two previous generations
has no real meaning for the decline that really begins
in the third generation.

This observation receives further support from
the fact that Hanno's cousin (also of the third generation), Erica Grünlich, the daughter of Tony, is healthy
to the core--a point carefully emphasized in the novel.
Further confirmation is to be had from Wolff in his
discussion of the problem of the hyprocrisy of marriage
in Buddenbrooks. According to him it is the generat-
ing force of love that is lacking in the marriage of
Gerda and Thomas:

>The marriage is all the more objectionable,
>since even Gerda, whose father, despite
>his wealth, plays the violin like a
>gypsy, is a typical phenomenon of deca-
>dence. Possessing a genuine artistic
>nature, she is interested exclusively
>in her violin playing and is therefore
>incapable of any real devotion in her
>relationships with people, even with her
>husband. In this respect she stands in
>stark contrast to Anna, the little flower-
>girl, whom Thomas had loved in his youth,
>but had given up for Gerda, although Anna
>is fervently devoted to him. And inasmuch
>as we see her again at the end of the novel
>as the mother of numerous healthy children,
>we are forced to conclude the following:
>if Thomas had followed the voice of his
>heart, had he disregarded social prejudice
>and married Anna, he would have then be-

come a happy person and the father of
happy and healthy children as well. His
overemphasis on money and other social
values is responsible for his early collapse as well as for the extinction of his
family.[29]

The point is perhaps more accurately stated as
follows: If Thomas had married someone who was healthy
instead of the decadent Gerda, he would have had
healthy offspring. Wolff plays down the importance
of social class in his discussion of the unnatural
conditions upon which marriages among the patrician
families of Lübeck are contracted. He is of the opinion that marriage for gain plays a subordinate role in
the problem of degeneration.[30] Actually it plays no
intrinsic role at all! Two cases in point are Gotthold
Buddenbrook and Erica Grünlich, who, though they con-
tract love matches, do not infuse new vitality into
the clan. Likewise the marriage between Clara Buddenbrook and Sievert Tiburtius, which seems to have been
based on mutual affection, leads nowhere.

Most critics apparently feel that the decline of
the Buddenbrook family is the end result of its increased spiritualization or "intellectualization."
This position asserts that there is a gradual development of a more sensitive temperament and a gain in
artistic awareness that leads in turn to a loss of
vitality and self-confidence. Yet old Johann Buddenbrook was in fact on a more familiar footing with art
than his grandson Thomas, and, indeed, it is only in
the last generation with Hanno (in terms of direct
succession to the leadership of the family), that
interest is again awakened in art; so there is certainly
no evidence of gradual increase in the artistic spirit.
Although Thomas' appreciation of literature is mentioned, his daily newspaper seems to hold his interest
more, and his wife Gerda selects the books which he
reads. In fact, what is really stressed is his lack
of understanding of art, especially of music. Gerda
is extremely blunt on this point: "'Thomas, once and
for all, you will never understand anything about
music as an art, and intelligent as you are, you will
never see that it is more than an after-dinner pleasure
and a feast for the ears'" (I, 509). His antipathy
toward art is further emphasized by his zeal for commercial affairs coupled with his distrust of Christian's
interest in the theater.

There is no consistent progression in the paralysis of the life force from one generation to the next.
Thomas does not possess special knowledge or insight
nor has he become a superior intellect with heightened artistic powers. His problem, like that of his
son, is psychological. He is worn down by his neurotic
compulsions while Hanno is afflicted with an exaggerated
death-wish. In other respects, Thomas is no less able
to manage his business affairs than his father. He is
not above being ruthless in the sense of Nietzsche's
will to power and is thus quite fit for survival in
the material world. Even his reason for marrying Gerda
is based on the soundest of commercial motives: "I
respect Gerda Arnoldsen deeply, but I simply will not
delve deep down enough in myself to find out how much
the thought of the large dowry, which in such a cynical
way was whispered into my ear that first evening, contributed to my feeling" (I, 290).

If anyone displays a weakening of strength coupled
with artistic inclinations, it is Christian Buddenbrook.
But his life does not lead directly to the last male
heir of the Buddenbrook family. Moreover, we doubt
that Christian's function is to stand for a link in a
genealogical chain. Instead he is probably intended
to represent the unproductive Bohemian artist type
whom the author and many of his heroes abhor and reject
uncompromisingly. He can be readily viewed as a caricature of the artist who gives into his impulses instead of holding them in check with iron self-discipline. In contrast to Mann's true artist figures, who
impose a harsh physical regimen upon themselves and
even exult in pain and discomfort, Christian continually
complains of his ailments and possesses no stoical
strain at all. He is really not intellectual either,
and his activities, bordering most of the time on the
inane and usually dealing with the tasteless cabaret
theater, give him no spiritual insight.*

---

*Nowhere does Thomas Mann's aversion to and fear
of the Bohemian come forth more strongly than in his
outline (in A Sketch of My Life) of the suicide of his
younger sister Carla in the year 1910. Though not
much more than a perfunctory sketch, it stresses,
needlessly, her unsettled life, points up her failings,
and does not spare some of the more personal details,
somewhat sordid in character, of the events leading
to her act of self-destruction. This misfortune,
which the author called a betrayal, occasioned the

It is tenuous to claim that Consul Buddenbrook represents an intermediate step between old Johann and Thomas in the inexorable march towards the collapse of the life force. He is not the first stage in the paralysis of the will, for he is quite capable of bold and even ruthless negotiations, willing even to sacrifice his daughter's happiness for the sake of profit. Likewise his feelings for his half-brother Gotthold (in the tenth chapter of part one), where it comes to the question of yielding to the latter's demands or not, are in the final analysis, just as unrelenting as his father's feelings about Gotthold. What sets him apart from old Johann is his hypocrisy, not a weakening of the will. The elder Johann appreciates fully his son's ability, recognizing "that his son and associate was often his superior when it came to a quick decision upon the advantageous course" (I, 48).

In the first volume there is, aside from Christian's instability very little to indicate the family's approaching destiny. Only in the third generation with Thomas Buddenbrook, beginning with the second volume, does the subtitle, "Decline of a Family," take on any significance. As one critic notes, Thomas' final prostration is curiously incongruous with his vigor at the beginning: "In the case of Thomas Buddenbrook this decadence cannot be foreseen at all from the beginning. No one can suspect that this young enterprising executive will collapse in decay in a relatively few years."[31]

By the terms of his will, Thomas Buddenbrook, the punishing father, gains a measure of revenge on Hanno for being excluded from his wife's affections. The

---

only outburst of deeply-felt emotion in the entire cool and objective autobiographical outline. It must be brought to mind that A Sketch of My Life was written twenty years after the suicide, time enough, presumably, for the author to achieve distance and a sense of restraint. And when we compare Thomas Mann's account with that of his brother Viktor in There Were Five of Us, we feel the incongruity all the more. Not a word of detraction is uttered by the latter when speaking of his sister; on the contrary, the sense of great personal loss is conveyed by unalloyed feeling.

financial decline of the Buddenbrook clan is thus the end result of personal animosity between father and son, both rivals for Gerda's understanding and affection. Thomas' calculated vindictiveness confirms the paternal hostility which the child Hanno projects onto his father. Likewise, the other aspect of decline, Hanno's tainted biology, plays its role in the aims of Oedipal retributive justice that destroys both father and son. Hanno's congenital debility and his musical inclinations are derived from his mother. Remembering that Hanno's music is inseparable from incestuous fantasies, we conclude that his death through typhus is logically aligned with his transgressions. His frenzied self-indulgence at the piano, combining the highest sensuality with parricidal hate, produces a sense of guilt that finally undermines his will to live and increases his yearning for absolution of his sins, no matter what it entails. The penalty which Hanno pays for his erotic indulgences is disease of a symboli order: a biological stigma that fits the needs of justice. This function of disease as the ultimate atonement anticipates the novel <u>Doctor Faustus</u> where disease is again made to serve as the expiation.

One can only conclude that the imposed theory of decline is another mask to cover or apologize for the artist's guilt-ridden conscience. Thomas Mann, burdened with concerns that grew out of the frustrating and debilitating conflicts of his own family, put his life too obtrusively on display before a curious public The overwhelming need to be punished, arising originall from Oedipal transgressions, is sublimated into a destructive darkness--decline--which descends haphazardly on the clan. Yet, in the middle of this impending disaster, a sensitive, tender, perceptive artist figure arises in whom a sense of guilt is so strong that he looks forward to his death as a final punishment and atonement. He distinguishes himself mostly by his harassed awareness of his guilt and his unshakeable knowledge that death will soon come to him in repayment for his sins.

Hanno Buddenbrook with his extreme death-wish is one of Mann's most intense and autobiographical creations. Not to ascribe to Hanno exclusively the hero's role is to render him unique among the tortured heroic souls throughout the author's works and to disregard Thomas Mann's inner kinship for his artist protagonist. Such a view also overlooks the tragic impact which Hanno confers upon the novel. His pitiless death, which seals the fate of the family, represents the climax of the work and, with a note of awful finality, brings the novel to a close.

The imposition of a kind of mythological concept of tragic fate descending on the whole family thus became a social necessity for Thomas Mann. Its creation issued from a need to preserve the established forms and appearances of his family while he was, paradoxically, in the throes of surrendering to a passion to expose them. Under a veil of virtue and tragic fate, Mann transgressed the great family taboo against indiscretion, and by thinly disguising his own disapproval and hostilities in vague symbols and slightly altered characters, he was in a position to disclose a good deal about himself and his family.

Decline, then, like genealogy, was a variation on an afterthought which Thomas Mann imposed on the novel to detract from the embarrassing personal secrets which he brought out into public. The effect, to our way of thinking, was most successful in convincing the public that disease is enlightening, that death is redeeming and that a pathological desire for punishment is courageous.

Because Buddenbrooks represents the most direct and intense confrontation between the Mannian hero and the authoritarian father, it must remain the author's most authentic and basic work. Mann's betrayal of his family may also explain the popularity of this novel, for the reader immediately feels the genuineness of this work. In reviewing his early years and experiences and the personal relationships of his own family, Thomas Mann bared his soul; he permitted his inner feelings to come to the surface and did not overlay them with an excess of words, a valid criticism of his later novels.

THOMAS MANN'S PYRRHIC VICTORS

Critics who have dealt with Thomas Mann's first creative period--his shorter fiction from 1894 to 1903--have usually focussed on three stories: <u>Little Herr Friedemann</u>, <u>Tristan</u>, and <u>Tonio Kröger</u>, either dismissing the others simply as inferior or implying that they were of little consequence.[1] Wherever interest in the early stories has been shown, the emphasis has tended to be on the developing theme of the problematic artist[2] or on the external influence of Nietzsche and Schopenhauer.[3] Curiously, little has been written on the abundance of psychological insight in these works.[4] Yet, the particular psychological flavor of the stories clearly identifies them as an integral unit of Mann's total work.

The result of philosophical emphasis at the expense of the psychological is that critics have not fully grasped the one dominant and unifying theme consistent to these tales--the theme of masochism.[5] Each of these early tales is characterized by a self-pitying masochistic protagonist who precipitates a crisis in order to seek relief from his burdened conscience. The hero literally welcomes the relief which defeat or punishment affords him; and to secure it, he either provokes the angry retaliation of others or simply invites disaster by exposing himself to an emotionally charged situation. Hounded by the unbearable pressure of subconscious guilt, he attempts to overcome his anticipation of punishment by rushing forward to meet what he fears and gains his triumph over conscience at the expense of moral defeat or self-destruction. His is therefore a Pyrrhic victory in which aggression plays the strategic role, differing in violence, perhaps, but not in kind, from the music-typhus attack that leads to Hanno Buddenbrook's death and atonement for his guilty fantasies.

These early tales demonstrate in a remarkable way Freud's definition of guilt as an unconscious need for punishment. In them Mann has depicted masochism in all its forms. The dual nature of masochism, as promulgated by Freud, is also demonstrated in each of these tales. Sadism and masochism, the active and passive forms of the instinct for cruelty operate together here, for the hero relies on aggression as the instrument to gain the pleasure of pain. One of the fascinations inherent in these stories is the up-to-dateness of the author's psychology, for when Mann wrote them he was

wholly unfamiliar with Freud's works. Freud himself
tells us that people took notice of his works only
about the year 1906 or 1907, and only then in a restricted circle of the scientific world.[6] Since Mann
first reached print in 1894 and all of these stories
readily fit into the same mold, we can assert that
Mann's uncanny insights into abnormal behavior and his
remarkable understanding of the dynamic effects of unconscious mental phenomena were intuitively arrived at
before Freud formulated them as part of his psycho-
analytical theories. Before Freud, unconscious mental
processes had been under discussion among philosophers
as a theoretical concept but not as something actual
with laws of its own. To some extent these early tales
are Thomas Mann's most impressive creations, for they
reveal him to be a spectacularly original psychologist.
As a description of unconscious mental phenomena, Mann's
psychological portraits and sketches are sophisticated
and accurate, and not at all primitive, despite assertions to the contrary.[7]

Gladius Dei / Fiorenza / The Way to the Cemetery

Gladius Dei is perhaps the clearest example of
how far the Mannian artist figure goes to achieve his
masochistic goal. An uncomplicated story about Hieronymus, a recluse and friendless young man who becomes
involved in a short and unimportant argument with the
owner of an art shop, it strikingly demonstrates how
his words are not really designed to be taken on a
literal level but are calculated to antagonize and
infuriate. While it is true that the exploitation of
the sensual is a justification for his indignant protest, the undiplomatic manner with which he goes about
his task completely overshadows his supposed reason
for approaching the shopkeeper. Outraged by a painting in a store window which depicts the Madonna in a
sexually attractive way, Hieronymus asks the proprietor
Blüthenzweig to remove it.* Undismayed when the latter

---

*The family situation similar to that in **Buddenbrooks** is hinted at in this story. The Madonna is
the possession of the English-speaking businessman
Blüthenzweig--a name which conveys the fullness of
life: branch of blossoms. The Madonna's sultry eyes
ringed with shadows are like those of Gerda Buddenbrook, the cold wife but at the same time the fiery
musician. She is depicted in a sensual and provocative

refuses to listen to him, he then directs his arguments to Blüthenzweig's underpaid assistant clerk, one obviously in no position to reverse his employer's decision. Soon Hieronymus goes well beyond the issue in question to include in his denunciations all that smacks of the animal and instinctual in art. And at the end of his fiery and strident outburst he is only listening to his own voice, for he even goes so far as to command the shopkeeper to burn every art object in the store. His prolonged and truculent defiance of Blüthenzweig finally produces the reaction which Hieronymus most deeply desires. Intensely annoyed at the hero's delirium, the shopowner has him forcibly ejected from the store. On the surface Hieronymus is ingloriously routed. But in terms of his primary objective, punishment, he has successfully managed to turn the tables. Immediately after the chastisement has been administered, there are the following words: "And his eyes, rimmed with fire, wandered over the beautiful square like those of a man in a frenzy."[8] The feverish, almost voluptuous language with which Thomas Mann invests this scene implicitly shows the sensual pleasure which Hieronymus derives from the physical manhandling.

Mann has to some extent prepared the way for the dramatic scene in the art shop. The characterization of Hieronymus stands in deliberate contrast to the loose and carefree artistic world of Munich; his presence in the Bohemian quarter of the town is likened to a shadow passing across the sunny blue sky. From his monkish dress and existence we learn that he is a lonely individual who has completely shunned human contact and denied all expression to his drives. Walking along the street, he is an unwitting object of ridicule to two young girls bent on adventure. We also learn that he is a man suffering from an extreme mental burden: "What pangs of conscience, what scruples and self-tortures had so availed to hollow out these cheeks" (VIII, 200). From this portrait of a man who has rigidly harnessed his instinctual life we can understand why the sensual painting of the Madonna acts as a catalyst on his emotions. The severity of his repressive measures is responsible for his extreme and uncompromising position, and the questionable morality of the painting is only the external

---

pose with the naked and precocious child playing with her breasts.

and initial excuse for his arguments with the store owner.

Hieronymus' monastic appearance and solitary nature make him close in spirit to other Mannian protagonists, but in profile he precisely resembles Girolamo Savonarola, the Renaissance Florentine protagonist of Mann's only drama, Fiorenza. Though Fiorenza reached print three years later than the novella, it probably had its origins two years before. In fact, a close look at Gladius Dei reveals an almost Italian atmosphere in the description of the life in Munich.*

Savonarola is a counterpart to Hieronymus not only in his physical appearance but also in his fanatical attitudes. Perhaps the masochistic tendencies of the Mannian figure are best summed up by this protagonist. Threatened with death at the stake for his stand against the shameless artistic world of Lorenzo de' Medici, he replies: "'I love the fire.'"[9] Savonarola's willingness to die for his beliefs has led critics to view Fiorenza as a play about the conflict between morality and art.[10] This is a legitimate interpretation of the drama, but underlying the hero's excessive morality is his sexually-oriented anticipation of the highest pleasure. Like Hieronymus, he lashes out at the rampant voluptuousness he subconsciously desires and fears, and like him he insults and infuriates at the same time. His priestly office and power enable him to fulminate publicly against the sensual appetites, but they also give him an opportunity to fan the flames which will eventually consume him. Appalled at the profligate crowd around Lorenzo de' Medici which does not shrink back from any excess in its licentious pursuit of beauty, Savonarola is remorseless and venomous in his sermons. A special target of his attacks is Fiore, the mistress of Lorenzo. From her we learn that what had originally triggered his reckless fanaticism was his failure in love. Her description of his behavior before fame came his way indirectly reveals

---

*The strikingly magnificent blue sky, the people in the native costume of Alba Longa, and the references to Machiavelli and Piero Medici and to the Italian Renaissance painters and books of this period. The hero of Fiorenza, Savonarola, also bears the name Hieronymus as a young man.

the sexual basis of his hatred: fearing people, Savonarola had shut himself off from the company of others. Whenever there was a merry throng in the city, he had buried himself in his books, played mournful melodies upon his lute, and written what no one was allowed to read. Once when Fiore had been alone with him at dusk, he had drawn near, panting and raving, and begged her to yield to him. But when she repulsed him and struck at him he had torn himself away and fled to Bologna, where, donning priestly robes, he began to preach repentance in thundering tones. Lorenzo de' Medici later concludes it was this experience with Fiore which made Savonarola great.

Savonarola's prostration and humiliation before a woman is like several other scenes in the works of Thomas Mann. It graphically shows that his violent protest against the whole world of the senses is in reality directed against his scarcely bridled desires. It also helps to demonstrate that his yearning to be burned at the stake belies his expressed abhorrence of sensuality and goes beyond the bounds of his righteous zeal. Unable to appease his instincts by embracing a woman, Savonarola longs to be consumed by fire, to be destroyed by this external symbol of relentless sexual passion. His attitude is so inflexible and virulent that it leaves his opponents no choice but retaliation.

Both Hieronymus and Savonarola are <u>moral masochists</u>. Their need for punishment has developed into a system of morality, a way of looking at the world; it becomes the basis for a moral viewpoint--that is, the means by which they can justify their inward demand to be punished.

At the end of the drama there is a dramatic showdown between Savonarola, the representative of restraint and Lorenzo de' Medici, the exponent of sensuality. Yet, as the dialogue reveals, both men are artists. Lorenzo dwells in the luxury of the senses, but Savonarola, the articulate and eloquent monk on exhibition, unable to bear the guilt of his unrestricted impulses, is compelled to close the lid tightly on them. He thus calls himself an artist who is at the same time a saint.

Lorenzo de' Medici complements the artist monk. He is the other side of the coin whose reverse image is the ascetic who needs self-mortification as the <u>sine qua non</u> of life. As such, Lorenzo is very close

to the Bohemian figure. In his fear of death he reminds us of another character, the somewhat disreputable and questionable Christian Buddenbrook, who
anxiously shuddered at the biers of his mother and
brother. Both stand in sharp relief to the ascetic
type of artist who can only cleanse his conscience
by periodic acts of atonement.* Lorenzo's artistic
retinue is in general a profligate crowd, exuberant,
wanton and obviously not burdened by exacting consciences.

The chaste artist figure Savonarola, however,
points to the dictum of "frigid art" which finds its
fullest artistic expression in Tonio Kröger, where
the perilous impulses are securely contained by the
prophylaxis of restraint and the prohibition of emotions. From this conception of art we are perhaps
close to a true understanding of the failure, as is
generally acknowledged, of Fiorenza as a drama.**

---

*Because of his extreme attitude and hostility
towards art, Savonarola has not been readily accepted
by all critics as the protagonist of the drama. In
order to counteract such a misapprehension the author
categorically stated in a letter to a reviewer that
only Savonarola was the true object of his research
and psychological interest and that only this priest
was capable of arousing his enthusiasm. In this same
letter he also expresses his antipathy towards the
aesthetic group around Lorenzo de' Medici whom he
characterizes unfavorably as boasters, jokesters,
satyrs, and children by comparison to the protagonist's
honest sorrow. See On "Fiorenza" (1908), Works, XI;
561-563.

**The title of this drama contains an interesting
ambiguity, no doubt intentional considering Mann's
predilection for playing with names. Mann had originally planned to entitle his drama "The King of
Florence." Fiorenza is archaic for Firenze, the Italian name for Florence, but it also can apply to Fiore,
and, as such, emphasizes further the triangle situation
basic to the works of Thomas Mann and points up as
well the sexual basis for Savonarola's implacable
position. Both Fiore and the city are disparaged by
Savonarola as "wanton whores." The monk's prostration
before Fiore also places him in competition with Piero,
the practical man of life, for the affections of Fiore.

The doctrine of "frigid art" is by its very nature
inimical to the stage, on which the hero must act out
his guilt; it is incompatible with living, breathing
characters. Thus it is no accident that the hero appears for only fourteen pages out of 106 and that his
words, although forceful, are of a dialectical nature.
Only in the secondary characters, the Renaissance
artists, do we find persons suited for the stage and
even here they are only used as commentators to tell
us about the attributes of the main characters. Yet
Mann probably worked on this play for close to five
years, longer than on Buddenbrooks. From a letter to
his brother Heinrich Mann, dated December 17, 1900,
we become acquainted with the beginnings of the drama
which appeared in print in 1905.[11] The author's attempt to disengage himself from his inner feelings by
taking the path towards "frigid art" is probably the
cause behind the creative delay in his only dramatic
effort.

Another tale, in which the hero's unleashed hostility causes him to embark on a collision course is
The Way to the Cemetery. Its plot is simple in the
extreme: the protagonist Lobgott Piepsam flies into
such a paroxysm of fury at the sight of a cyclist
(continually referred to as Life, as if this were his
name) riding on a walking-path that he dies as a result.
There are, significantly, two thoroughfares in this
story: the much traveled road of life and the solitary
path to the cemetery, down which the bankrupt soul
Piepsam treads. Because of Piepsam's affinity for
death, James Cleugh is justified in regarding him as
the "eternal outcast, the decadent first cousin to the
artist, though he neither paints nor writes and has no
ear for music."[12] But supplementing this theme of the
decadent artist is the motif of punishment at all cost.

The hero's determination to wrest Florence from his
adversaries and become its king (with Fiore as the
queen), and the personification of this city as a woman
attest to another level of meaning in the title of the
work. Mann admits a double meaning in the title but
explains it as follows: "The ambiguity of the title
is, you know, intentional. Christ and Fra Gerolamo
are one: weakness, which has developed into genius,
attaining to mastery of life." Kantorowicz, p. 61.

Viewed in this light, we see that The Way to the Cemetery is practically a repetition of Gladius Dei. In both works the protagonist baits his opponent in order to secure a defeat, each time by an angry verbal assault which elicits physical force and attracts a crowd of people. Each is on exhibition. The difference, however, is that Lobgott Piepsam succumbs completely in his apoplectic rage. And where Hieronymus is eloquent and to some extent even cogent in his arguments, Piepsam is crude, inarticulate, and close to the preposterous. Another difference is that Hieronymus, as a priest, fortifies his existence by self-denial and ascetic restraint, whereas Piepsam undermines his controls by indulgence in alcohol. After losing his wife and children, Piepsam surrendered himself to drink.

But whatever their differences, their inner kinship is convincingly close. Both go to drastic extremes to seek surcease from their conscience and both attempt to buy off their inner reproaches by enduring humiliation. Their shame is easier to bear than their primary guilt.*

---

*In censuring all of the people within earshot, Piepsam reveals what is foremost in his mind: "There will come the day . . . when God shall weigh us all in the balance . . .the Son of Man shall come, you innocent rabble, and his justice is not of this world. He will hurl you into outer darkness . . ." The Way to the Cemetery (1900), Works, VIII, 195. The guilt-ridden Piepsam projects onto the "innocent" crowd his own prevalent fear of final judgment. And the sexual overtones in Piepsam's rage are revealed by one of the remarks he hurls at Life. "The Devil scratch them [sparkling blue eyes] out!" (VIII, 194). In psychoanalytic terms putting out the eyes is the symbolic equivalent of castration, the atonement for incest and parricide. The title of the story also contributes to the significance of the familial implications, for Piepsam, on his way to visit his family in the graveyard, ironically succumbs in a paroxysm of anger and follows his family literally to the grave. In the demise of Piepsam's family we note the overtones to Buddenbrooks, for in both this story and the novel each hero, the last male representative of his family, is suddenly and swiftly taken away by death while in a feverish state.

In his drinking Piepsam finds an additional instrument of self-debasement to cushion his tyrannical conscience by administering to himself a daily measure of
defeat and punishment. The use of stimulants excites the
demonic powers of the artist hero which if fully released would annihilate him. But what does not happen
to Piepsam in drink does occur in anger. In his encounter with Life, a trivial incident triggers a pow-
derkeg of pent-up confusion of fear and hate. He has
done what Mann condemns the most--he has lost full
control of himself and is overwhelmed by his own
passions.

Piepsam demonstrates in several ways the weaknesses and underlying feelings of an artist who, in
grappling with the natural impulses of life (represented by the cyclist), exposes himself to ridicule
for his adherence to a trivial law. Drinking achieves
a dual purpose; it helps dull the senses to alleviate
some of the inner burden of guilt and anxiety but at
the same time it stigmatizes him as a kind of pariah,
for the way is made free for demonic urges to reveal
themselves to public censure.

Piepsam's fury reveals that the murderous hatred
the Mannian protagonist harbors against life is very
close to the surface and easily capable of overwhelming the defenses of repression. It also shows us that
this hatred is more compelling and genuine to him than
his desire to be on good terms with people. The dire
anxiety explains why Thomas Mann intervenes several
times to comment in an incredulous tone on the behavior
of his hero. By these interruptions a balance is
restored and the stark situation of violent rage and
hostility assumes comic overtones. Here, as in other
works of Mann, repression serves to minimize the outbreak of intense emotion. In this way Thomas Mann
thus takes special pains to emphasize Piepsam's inability to master his darkest urges, as if he were
admonishing the artist not to lose complete control,
but to work rather for a successful symbolic sublimation or a satisfactory compromise-solution of his conflicts. This tale consequently resembles a story with
a moral in addition to a depiction of the inadequacy
of repression. Piepsam dies because he gives full vent
to his hostile emotions. His aggressive impulses are
released and the excessive hostility unleashed against
life brings on his own death.

Like Mann's other early heroes, Piepsam's reaction

to a disturbing trifle is simply too exaggerated considering the given situation. Piepsam goes to great
lengths to artificially create an enemy of the bicycle
rider, "Life." Essentially innocent in the encounter,
"Life" reacts in self-defense, no doubt completely
mystified at the hero's immeasurable choler. Lobgott
Piepsam himself does not even realize that he wishes
unconsciously for a defeat, that he is obeying an inner
ultimatum which dictates punishment; in short, that the
grievous necessity to assuage the overpowering unrest
within can be suspended only slightly by rational processes and that this unconscious compulsion must inexorably run its course. The crescendo of aggression
is reached from within and only superficially is the
external stimulus, "Life's" infraction on the pedestrian
path, significant.

Little Herr Friedemann / Revenged /

The Will to Happiness

        In the three tales just discussed, the protagon-
ists use the most direct and unsubtle approach to their
goal. The naked aggression which they employ dominates
the narrative thread to the extent that it overshadows
the sexual factor implicit in their behavior.   In
contrast, another set of stories, Little Herr Friedemann, Revenged, and The Will to Happiness, is characterized by features of overt sexuality. Here a woman ad-
ministers the punishment at the climax of each story
and the hero's manner is that of a voluptuary, scarcely
able to restrain his clamorous urges. Of the three,
Little Herr Friedemann is the most developed and the
most intensively concerned with the sexual torment of
the hero. It is an uncomplicated story of a lonely
cripple whose life of passive repression gives way to
emotional turbulence and suicide as the result of a
hopeless infatuation. In Friedemann we have a hero
who makes a virtue out of repression and who lives
almost exclusively in his fantasy. The solicitude he
lavishes on his illusions is worthy of a real artist.
He nurses carefully all his feelings and moods, the
sad as well as the unfulfilled desires. He loves them
for their own sake and knows that with fulfillment the
best would be over. When at the age of sixteen he witnesses the girl of his desire kissing another boy, he
promises himself never to be involved again emotionally. The verbs to hear and to listen, virtual leitmotifs in the story, characterize his passivity, his
retreat from any expression or investment of his in-

stincts.

But once he sets eyes on Gerda von Rinnlingen, his passive tranquillity is thoroughly shattered. Henceforth, every encounter, no matter how casual, causes him to pale and to become feverish. Finally, no longer able to prevent his emotions from taking their course, he drastically effects a confrontation with her. And when he impulsively releases his imprisoned feelings before her at a garden party, the result is a kind of redemption: "Then suddenly he started up from his seat, trembling all over; he sobbed and gave vent to a sound, a wail which yet seemed like a release, and sank slowly to the ground before her" (VIII, 104). The frantic nature of his actions, his uncontrollable surge of feeling, and the pitiful manner in which he grovels before Gerda, frustrates at the outset his supposed longing for a union with her. Gasping and trembling like Savonarola before Fiore, Friedemann cuts a grotesque and repulsive figure. His precipitate behavior, the expression of his most primitive drives, leaves no room for tenderness and affection but only leads to the rejection he so desperately wants.

Death is the logical extension of this climactic scene. Having transgressed the most sacred barriers erected by his conscience, Friedemann seeks immediate expiation and ends his life in the river. His punishment fits his crime, for the association of doom with the direct expression of his feelings was originally responsible for his stringent repression of his instincts.

Friedemann has also been interpreted as an epicurean whose strict control of his passions is inadequate when confronted with the will to life itself; his desire for Gerda is thus a desire for life.[13] But underneath this desire we detect the same drive for sexual release which dominated Hieronymus and Savonarola. Friedemann's choice of woman is consequently no accident. Instinctively he knows that she alone is fitted to play the role of the Nemesis in his masochistic fantasy. Thus, despite Martin Havenstein's contention, the characterization of Gerda as cruel, overbearing, faulty and one-sided, is not borne out by the text.[14] It can be understood as a logical extension of the protagonist's highly subjective needs. The reader knows only what goes on in Friedemann's mind and thus knows only Friedemann's projection of Gerda; he apprehends only the protagonist's wish ful-

fillment of her. Friedemann wants her to be pitiless
and heartless to him, an instrument by which he can
punish himself. That is why he is affected out of
proportion to the actual situation when he happens to
meet her fleetingly on the street and at the opera.
The impulse to love and destroy has become one in him
and his hate is sexualized: "Again he felt the same
surge of voluptuous, impotent hatred mount in him
. . ." (VIII, 91). Such behavior seems completely unmotivated unless one takes Friedemann's guilty conscience into consideration, for the excitement he
anticipates is mingled with a premonition of impending
doom: "Then this woman had come, she had to come; it
was his fate that she should, for she herself was his
fate and she alone. He had known it from the first
moment. . . .--her coming had roused in him all those
forces which from his youth up he had sought to suppress, feeling, as he did, that they spelled torture
and destruction. They had seized upon him with frightful irresistible power and flung him to the earth!"
(VIII, 99). In Friedemann's death by drowning we note
the symbolic return to a state of innocence.

Little Herr Friedemann's description suggests
Hanno Buddenbrook if one considers his small size, the
color of his eyes which are darkly shaded, his brown
hair parted on one side, his inwardly oriented existence, his loneliness and reserve at school, his musical ability, and his crippled position in life.* Though
the physical debility is biological in Hanno and in
Friedemann the result of an accident, the distinction
is very slight and the causes in both instances go back
to a woman.

---

*In other ways this work points to <u>Buddenbrooks</u>.
The names of some characters: Gerda, Hagenström,
Friederike, Henriette and Pfiffi, Colonel von Rinnling-
en; Friedemann's gray gabled house with its interior
description of the music room, the walnut tree in the
back yard, the festive and sumptuous evenings in Gerda's
palatial home, the presence of the military, Gerda's
musical inclinations, her sickly and nervous constitution, her red hair and the closely spaced eyes surrounded by blue shadows, her coldness to her husband
(they are childless after four years of marriage),
the implication, nevertheless, of her sensuality (her
plunging neckline), and finally her reception by the
city's social circles attendant with subsequent doubts
about her strange ways.

In these two kindred spirits can be seen the figure of the decadent artist, infantile and immature. Friedemann has no beard and his features have hardly changed since childhood. Likewise, in the words "Little Herr Friedemann," there is a continual refrain which emphasizes the diminutive size of the hero, symbolically the special existence of the artist, graphically the immature child.

As is the case with Hanno, Friedemann's artistic imaginings conjure up guilty sexual associations, and it is consequently at the opera with the strains of Wagner's music that they are crystallized. The violent upheaval he undergoes when he confronts Gerda at a performance of Lohengrin is equal to the climax of sexual passion. In this story, as in others, the mortification of the hero coincides again with the moment of pleasurable satisfaction.

Dunja Stegemann, the woman in the short sketch Revenged, is also an unwilling accomplice in the masochistic protagonist's subconscious designs, and like Gerda Buddenbrook is highly intellectual, cold and aloof. She is also foreign-born--a newcomer to the city--, cultured, extremely musical, and greatly interested in Wagner. Though she is described as excessively ugly, we are, as in Little Herr Friedemann, only acquainted with a highly subjective opinion of her appearance, the opinion of a hero who finds in her not only the instrument of pain in his self-sacrifice to humiliation, but also a witness to his suffering. Galled by her superior calm, the nameless protagonist of this story is overwhelmed by the urge to terminate his inner turbulence. Under the guise of intellectual honesty he tells her point-blank that she is ugly--the first step in the staging of his drama of pain and defeat. He follows up this attack by another when he brazenly asks her to have an affair with him. When she refuses, his manner becomes hostile and menacing: "I called out with the fury of a degenerate who is not used to holding back any thought, no matter how dirty: 'Why not? Why not? Why so coy?' And I made a motion as if to go into action."[15]

From his aggressive tone we can readily discern the familiar flight forward. His insolent remarks are designed from the beginning to sabotage his supposed desire for a love relationship with Dunja. All chance of a tender union is intentionally eliminated by the manner of his proposal. Actually, the hero is

sincere, but only on the level of his most basic subconscious needs: gratification through pain and humiliation. Thus he behaves like a sadist in order to
elicit the appropriate rejection. And because the
hero's approach is crude, it is crowned with success.
After Dunja rejects him and leaves, he stands awhile
in the middle of the room, and in a gesture of composure and resignation, strikes his forehead with his
hand and goes off to bed. He is ready for sleep, for
he has succeeded in satisfying his need for humiliation,
in soothing the anguish within. In contrast to those
protagonists who become physically involved in the
climactic situation and thereby reach a high state of
sensual excitement, he is a verbal masochist who gains
a feeling of relief from being rebuked.

Despite his words that his carnal desires are
unbridled and that he is unusually preoccupied with
sowing his wild oats, his reaction on learning of
Dunja's past love affair reveals the same crippled
sensuality that distinguishes many other infantile
heroes of Mann.

The protagonist of The Will to Happiness, Paolo
Hofmann, is also physically disabled. Suffering from
an incurable heart disease, he is forced to postpone
his marriage to Ada von Stein for five years until
all obstacles are overcome, only to die on his wedding
night.* Reflected in the story's title, according to
several critics, is the influence of Nietzsche as well
as a manifestation of the will to live.[16] This will
to live is revealed again in the words of the hero's
friend after the marriage has been consummated; he says
that it was the will to happiness alone which had enabled Paolo to master death for so long. But his words
and the title also reflect the very opposite, that
Paolo lived in constant anticipation of the extreme
pleasure to be derived from the end of his unbearable
suspense. As such the hero's desires are not far removed from the death-wish of Hanno Buddenbrook. That
he, as in the case of other protagonists, views the
woman as a means to a masochistic end can be seen
from his friend's description of Paolo's impatient

---

*Again it is an older man who comes between the
protagonist and the woman of his choice: the titled
father of Ada, Baron von Stein.

and restless torment as he awaits Ada's appearance before her house: "While he was standing next to me, everything about him was completely calm, even to a nervous twitching of the eyelids--a calmness that was powerfully tense. He had stretched his head a bit forward; the skin of his forehead was taut. He gave almost the impression of an animal that had convulsively made his ears come erect and was listening with the tenseness of all his muscles."[17] The excited anticipation which Ada von Stein produces in the hero is so extreme that it cannot be mistaken for love or affection. What he seeks in his marriage to her is an expedient challenge lying outside the sphere of tenderness. The protagonist's friend is to a certain extent aware of Paolo's underlying intentions. He implies that Paolo's behavior contains an element of aggression, even of brutality: "I have asked myself, whether he had acted badly, consciously badly to the person he married. But at his burial I saw her standing at the head of his casket, and I recognized on her countenance the expression which I had also seen on his: the solemn and resolute seriousness of triumph" (VIII, 61). Here we have again the theme of a woman, who presents an enticing possibility for union and gratification to the hero but causes, instead, the death or mortification of the male. Ada von Stein, like so many of Mann's heroines, is a destructive temptress. The reader is moved to ask at the end of The Will to Happiness why a wife should have an expression of triumph instead of sorrow at her husband's funeral! Implied is that Paolo's death is some sort of victory for her. However, we learn that Paolo regarded Ada as an opponent in combat as well as an object of desire: "And in this moment I again recognized on his face and in his entire attitude the expression, which I had observed on him, when I was to see the Baroness for the first time: the powerful, convulsively strained calm, which the beast of prey shows before he springs" (VIII, 55). Paolo lunges finally into marriage, a sexual union which puts an end to his exhausting strain. Instead of the supreme moment of affection it is a war to the death in which hatred supplants consideration, and respect and tenderness is confused with immolation and death.

Paolo's will to live is little more than a self-imposed asceticism arising from his subconscious need to hold his powerful, sensual desires in check. But behind his mask of stoic resignation rages a fierce, futile psychic battle that consumes the energies needed

to live fully in the real world. In a distorted fashion
Paolo makes repression the very purpose and goal of
his life. The father figure Baron von Stein embodies
the repression--he is the obstacle that forces Paolo
to renounce his desire for Ada--, and so the hero impulsively veers away like a small boy with only one
thing in mind: live on until he can possess the woman.
The control of sensual urges has become more important
than a healthy gratification of them and consequently,
it is only a question of time before repression can no
longer dictate, pressure becomes intolerable, and death,
the only force strong enough to checkrein the hero's
incessant urges, is welcomed for its own sake. Once
again the Mannian hero triumphs in death, a Pyrrhic
victory which delivers him from his merciless conscience.

Tobias Mindernickel / Fallen / Disillusionment

Tobias Mindernickel, a tale which culminates in
the murder of a dog, fits into the pattern of masochistic provocation which we have found to be predominant in Mann's heroes. Tobias Mindernickel is, however, handled somewhat differently. Although described
from a clinical standpoint, he is actually consistent
with other protagonists, for in making excessive demands
on his dog Esau, which are obviously impossible for the
animal to meet, he provokes an outburst of his hostile
impulses and insures that the result will spell disaster. The precipitate of his lethal attack, the dis-
obedience of his dog, is something so slight as to
discount completely its validity in direct cause and
effect motivation. With marked psychological insight
the author traces the development of the hero's masochistic fantasy from passive suffering at the hands of
the children on the street to the frustration which
ensues from his active attempts to satisfy his love-
needs.

To this pronounced sado-masochist, love is found
only in conjunction with pity and pain. An exaggerated
sense of tenderness is consequently necessary for him
in order to hold in check the extreme lurking cruelty
lodged within him, but it breaks through in an unpre-
meditated fashion despite his efforts.

The description of Tobias' face as pale and twisted
with grief just before his fatal encounter with Esau
also points up the anticipated sexual nature of his
sadistic impulse in the same way that Friedemann's
pallid and distorted countenance at the opera graphi-

cally depicts his destructive passion for Gerda.

The author interrupts the story to remark: "There was a story about this man; I tell it, because it is both puzzling and sinister, to an extraordinary degree."[18] And when the hero is on the point of murdering his dog, Thomas Mann again breaks in: "That which now happened was so shocking, so inconceivable, that I simply refuse to tell it in any detail" (VIII, 150). Although Mann tries to gain by this means a necessary aloofness from his flagrantly guilty creation, the ultimate portrait of Tobias Mindernickel, despite his bizarre characterization, is still trenchantly involved in Mann's scheme of the heroic. Tobias' lonely and practically monastic existence, independent of ordinary bourgeois employment, the hint of his patrician derivation--his clothing and a certain gesture betray that he was not of the common people among whom he lived--, and his attitude toward personal neatness are all typical. Like Herr Friedemann, Tobias has a tendency to daydream, sitting alone with his head supported by his hands. And his inflamed eyes, which cannot bear to look directly into the gaze of other people, remind us of the cripple after his meeting with Gerda von Rinnlingen.

Because Tobias is unable to neutralize his feelings of aggression, his love affair must end in disaster, for this is a love affair in which Tobias kills the thing he loves. This overdetermined relationship between Tobias and his dog is made necessary by his poverty of mature emotions. He purchases the dog, Esau, in hope of mollifying his loneliness a little, but from the start he handles the animal so dictatorially that one wonders if he really wanted it as a friend. One's early suspicions are borne out when he compulsively provokes a crisis in which he finally destroys his little companion. The vicious circle of guilt to repression to guilt is completed by his deed, for the outbreak of his destructive impulses reinforces his profound sense of sin. As in other tales discussed, the hero opens the floodgates and the result is death. But this time destruction is turned away from the self.

It might be interesting to speculate a bit here about Mann's interest in dogs, for the symbolic role they play in Mann's works alters perceptibly along with his maturity as a writer. In the tale discussed earlier, The Way to the Cemetery, a fox-terrier plays a devastating, aggressive part in Piepsam's ignominious end: "The terrier could no longer contain itself; it braced its forefeet and howled into Piepsam's face with its tail between its legs" (VIII, 195). The dog seems to be castigating Piepsam heartlessly at the moment of his most miserable defeat. Later in his career Thomas Mann moves from this depiction of utter humiliation and ludicrous helplessness of a human being at the mercy of a barking dog to a description of a man and his pet as a symbiotic, but no less ambivalent relationship: the collie Perceval in Royal Highness and the faithful Bashan in A Man and His Dog. Much later in The Holy Sinner, Mann again graphically describes the brutal stabbing of the dog Hanegriff.

In giving the dog such an important role in the psychological activities of his characters, Thomas Mann shows him to be an integral member of the group, in this story a kind of father-substitute. Assigned strong, dominant, or critical features, the animal is thus elevated to a paternal role.

From this perspective we see Tobias Mindernickel as a dramatic expression of Mann's ambivalence towards his father in the form of a pathetic struggle between frustrated hate and painful tenderness. How more dramatically can the dynamics of ambivalence be shown than in this story where a dog is tenderly coddled, injured, nursed and loved, then killed and mourned for?

There is no love in Tobias for his dog without a corresponding amount of hate, and so we have again an example of hostility winning out over an expressed desire for love and tenderness. The hero reestablishes his brooding self-pity and loneliness only by killing his pet, thereby making himself vulnerable to a repetition of the cycle of love and hate.

Our next story, Fallen, varies from this pattern only in one respect--that the hero of the tale again becomes the passive victim of his fate rather than, as Tobias, the instigator of it. In Fallen, Mann's earliest tale, and in Disillusionment the masochistic tendencies of the protagonists are depicted in a rudimentary form subordinated to the other events of the narratives. Common to both works is still the provocative factor with its rationale in the subconscious. Dr. Selten, the protagonist of Fallen, is, like the heroes already mentioned, the victim of a disastrous love affair which he relates in detail to other guests

at a dinner party. In his description it is revealed
how love and hate became synonymous in his mind. After
he has been betrayed in love by the actress Irma
Weltner, his ambivalence, as was the case with Friedemann, is complete: "Perhaps he had already learned
from these kisses, that from now on for him love was
to be found in hate, and sensual pleasure in savage
revenge. . . ."[19] That his love for Irma, despite its
consummation, scarcely differs from that of other
Mannian protagonists, is revealed by the fact that it
is he who first entertains the idea of unfaithfulness.
Dr. Selten's masochism takes the form of self-disparagement; he cannot refrain from revealing his conflict by
relating the humiliation of his love affair to the
guests at the party. His exhibitionistic display manifests itself as a compulsive gesture of penance. From
this recasting of his love affair he again experiences
its excitement and also obtains a measure of the desired punishment by reliving his rejection. His humiliation is enhanced by the natural reaction of dislike
he must receive from his dinner companions. He outrages his friends when he brutally states: "If a
woman falls today for love, she will fall tomorrow for
money" (VIII, 42). By this cynical remark he publicly
expresses feelings of his love-turned-into-hate, he
provokes the others, and he thus obtains the pleasure
of corroborating his denial of basic human affections.
Dr. Selten even feels that he is objective in cold-
bloodedly projecting his personal conflict onto the
whole world, irrespective of persons and situations,
and in ascribing base motives to all women, oblivious
that his conclusions are logical only in terms of his
punishing conscience; he is, of course, completely unaware of the subconscious reasons behind his disparaging attitude.

As the initial effort of Thomas Mann, Fallen is
an impressive work. Because of its youthful pessimism,
skepticism, and irony it drew high praise from a number
of critics.[20] In spite of the fact that it is Mann's
only story which deals basically with a "normal" love
affair, it still sets the tone for all of his works:
the romantic triangle situation, the love-hate duality,
the childish behavior of the protagonist, the characterization of the woman, and the link between sex and
music as that between love and death.*

---

*It is the only time the author describes the
consummation of a love affair relatively free of morbid

Despite his brutal cynicism, the disposition of the protagonist is that of an exceedingly sensitive person. He composes poems and finds the object of his love in an artistic counterpart, an actress in the Goethe-Theater. Mann takes pains to assure us that Selten is a real poet. But at the same time his behavior has an infantile cast. He sheds copious tears for little or no reason; indeed, his weeping is practically beyond control and out of keeping with his age. Like a child, he gives vent to intense emotions spanning the extremes; he sobs one minute and expresses immeasurable delight the next. He is also a mere boy in physical appearance, pretty, frail and beardless. He is called "little man" by his friend Rölling, to whom he relates everything concerning his love affair; the latter then treats him as if he were a child. He writes his "Mama" all about his happiness. In his personal relationship to Irma Weltner he acts like a little boy who seeks protection by clinging to his mother's skirt, for he continually desires to lie humbly at her feet and confess his love. Irma, like Gerda Buddenbrook, is unpredictable in her moods; she scolds him as if he were a child and he must beg meekly for forgiveness before she will permit him to lay his head on her lap and be caressed in a motherly fashion.

From this characterization of the protagonist we can readily view his love affair with Irma Weltner as a symbolic screen for the intense erotic involvement of a child for his mother, the fantasied recasting of an earlier traumatic love relationship. Dr. Selten tells a good story, a vivid and trenchant story, for he is reliving his own experience in the full sense of the word. Although more than a decade has elapsed since he received his psychic wound from Irma Weltner, he reacts as if it had happened yesterday. In his brusque and unpleasant bearing to the other guests, he appears as one who is still suffering from a recent injury. In a sense his story is recent and powerful, for the interim between then and now is bridged by fantasy, a direct expression of omnipotence of thoughts. When we conceive of this emotional experience as mask-

---

and perverse elements and whose aftermath is not capped by the protagonist's indifference. One must <u>wait sixty years</u> to find a similar scene of heterosexual passion in Mann's works. Only in <u>Felix Krull</u>, which appeared in 1954, did he dwell on the delights of sexual union between man and woman.

ing an intense relationship between mother and child, we can understand why this love affair is the protagonist's most profound experience, which thoroughly conditions the rest of his days, and why there is no real contradiction between Dr. Selten's hard cynicism and his lachrymose description of his love affair.

For the protagonist, there is only one consolation, and that is his triumph over the old, dignified, finely dressed gentleman who buys sexual favors from Irma Weltner. But this victory is minimized by the fact that this father-figure has usurped the love of Irma. The old gentleman is beside himself when his young rival (who incidentally now takes childish glee in his actions) orders him out of the house. He then scolds his persecutor like a father to a son: "'I'll go right now. But we'll see about this, you young scamp, you!'" (VIII, 37). Nevertheless, the old gentleman cuts a lamentable figure as he takes his leave.

Intermingled with the progression of the protagonist's love affair is the smell of lilac. This has been correctly interpreted as symbolic of decadence or decay. Contrasted to this evening mood is the advent of spring in all its glory. Additional manifestations of the fusion of life and death in this story are found in the protagonist's poem, in which yearning for death is distinguishable, and in the scene prior to his first sexual union with Irma Weltner when he gazes at the river--a body of water signifying for Mann the endless tranquillity of death. Spring, a rebirth, is an assertion of the life-force, and has its highest expression in Eros. But in this story Eros is symbolically linked with death. To love here is to die in part and be close to death, for this love is a guilty and forbidden one. The emotional impact Eros makes on the protagonist stands in sharp contradiction to his kinship with death.

Only the memory of Selten's passion remains at the end of the liaison with Erma Weltner. While he gazes at her picture, some strains of music are heard which conjure up the enjoyed pain of his experience. The sweet bliss of erotic consummation is fixed in the protagonist's mind by the sound of music--music which has played no integral role at all up to this point in the narrative.

The reason behind Thomas Mann's application of the frame technique or structure for this tale fits the psychological pattern which has been established. Hirschbach is close to the truth when he says:

> Fallen employs the technique of the Rahmenerzählung, the frame, a device frequently used by prose writers of the nineteenth century. Its chief characteristic is that it removes the author from the role of the narrator of the story and interposes another person between author and reader. Thomas Mann uses the frame in order to conceal from the reader the fact that he is vitally interested in what he is saying or, in other words, to avoid the danger of becoming pathetic.
> . . .
> Fifty-four years later after the publication of his first story Mann once more used the frame technique conspicuously in Doctor Faustus, this time to hide a vital concern for Germany and Adrian Leverkühn who symbolized her fate.[21]

Yes, Thomas Mann is vitally interested and concerned. Fallen is easily his most emotional work, for despite the use of frame the emotional intensity of the youthful Thomas Mann breaks through. As a consequence, he later repudiated Fallen as a work of art by not including it in any of his collections.

The nameless protagonist of the sketch Disillusionment is another cynic, whom we first encounter pacing up and down the square in Venice, smiling foolishly and talking to himself. The cause of his unrest, he explains, are the "great words" of good and evil, beautiful and lucky, which were a part of his childhood. Since his faith in these great words has not been matched by his experiences in life itself, he has become disillusioned and consequently lonely, unhappy, and eccentric. The hero has been shown by several critics to stand for Friedrich Nietzsche--both grew up in a small city in a pastor's family where the grand phrases of pulpit rhetoric were a daily occurrence.[22] Because of the biographical similarity between the hero and the philosopher, Wolff concludes that the hero's blunted hopes in great words represent Thomas Mann's explanation for Nietzsche's tragic fate: the philosopher's over-expectations from fine phrases were responsible for his collapse.[23] Yet there is an equally valid and more convincing explanation for the

point of this story. In the psychological portrait
of this outcast protagonist we see an affinity to those
already discussed. The description of him pacing up
and down reveals a man hunted from within, seeking
relief from psychic pain. Driven by his sense of
guilt, he seeks out a complete stranger to serve as
a witness to his suffering. Unexpectedly though, when
he unburdens himself to his listener, he fails to be
convincing. The reasons he gives for his unhappy state
are so transparent that they seem naive; yet within
the framework of the mental stress he is undergoing,
they are completely logical. His words really function
more as irritants than as explanations. He shows a
galling pride that the Fates have singled him out and
wronged him, and he deliberately attempts to destroy
his listener's pleasure in the beauties of Venice.
Like Dr. Selten he finds both a haven and a measure of
atonement in his aggressive cynicism. With this attitude he is better equipped to protect himself--that
is, to achieve isolation from the uncertainty of human
involvement and at the same time to obtain the reject-
tion he desires. This need for rejection stands in
the way of his understanding the reasons for his paralysis; by means of the abstraction, "great words,"
he is able to conceal his personal conflict from himself, to invent a rationalization which acts as a
buffer against the force of his subconscious guilt
feelings.

Reflected in the stranger's unhappy repudiation
of life is the author's own doubt of his ability as a
creative artist. The hero states that he has learned
to hate poets who desire to write their great words
on the walls of heaven. His perpetual doubt of himself causes him to question everything, even his artistic inclinations. Like the artist, he is, for safety's
sake, a perfectionist in his feelings and, unsure of
his instincts, refuses to trust their reliability in
any situation.

He claims to have loved a woman, but he himself
anticipates the doubt which this claim of having experienced a strong emotion will evoke in his listener:
"You may believe me that I do not speak without experience of life. Years ago I fell in love with a
girl. . . ."[24] He cannot love, because he cannot
feel; he is paralyzed inside, being unable to find
the slightest amount of enjoyment without psychic
torment.

Thoughts of death dominate the stranger's words: his narrow escape from a fire, his toying with suicide, and his reflection on the sea. Paradoxically, he, the hater of life, and the friend of death, is condemned to live.

Little Lizzie / The Wardrobe / Death / The Clown

Little Lizzie, The Wardrobe, Death, and The Clown "seem" to deviate from the masochistic pattern in that the provocative element is lacking or is of minor significance. But a closer look at them shows that they are not real exceptions.

It is true that Jacoby, the protagonist of Little Lizzie, seems more like a reluctant victim than one who subconsciously manipulates his own suffering. Yet he acquiesces when his wife Amra, with the aid of her illicit lover, Alfred Läutner, insists that he go upon the stage at a party and, dressed up in baby clothes, sing a song. We have here a matchless example of the dangerous sin which music represents. Jacoby's apparently harmless reverie in song is in reality a transgression of the greatest magnitude. The lethal power of music, the result of its unbearable association with the forbidden in the mind of the Mannian protagonist, exacts its toll. That is why he is able to recognize his wife's unfaithfulness in the midst of a special chord progression and why he collapses and succumbs on the spot. Jacoby is defenseless and on exhibition; he is being watched by the world and his sinful pleasure is being exposed to view. The sexual connotation is obvious. From the music Jacoby gains the insight that he has been betrayed by his wife. Once again Thomas Mann is especially explicit. Amra's part as the fatal muse who metes out the chastisement is clear from her words to Alfred Läutner just before the performance:

> And when she lay relaxed by the expression of her love, she pressed her lover's head passionately to her breast and whispered:
> "Write it for four hands. We will accompany him together, while he sings and dances. I, I will see to the costume myself. . . ."
> And an extraordinary shiver, a suppressed and spasmodic burst of laughter went through the limbs of both.[25]

74

By her desire to have Jacoby dress up in baby clothes, Amra emphasizes the infantilism and impotence in her husband-artist figure. Jacoby's insight that he is being cuckolded and that he is impotent, and consequently no match for his rival, flashes through his mind at that moment when he, dressed as an infant, is indulging in "musical" sex.

There is for Jacoby the Mannian punishment which fits his crime; he pays with his life for his involvement with music. Mann carefully emphasizes this point. The composer Alfred Läutner has struck upon a kind of music which is capable of profoundly affecting Jacoby. By means of a sudden phrasing of real art in the midst of a vulgar and humorous work, he manages to bring his insignificant talent to its highest pitch.

Jacoby's rival, Alfred Läutner, is a musician with some talent and a limited reputation. That he is by no means a true artist figure who undergoes penance to create and that he does not understand the concept of suffering for its own sake, Thomas Mann takes special pains to put across to the reader:

> This blond young man with a sunny smile
> belongs to the present-day type of petty
> artists who do not demand much from them-
> selves and whose first requirement is to
> be happy and good-natured, who employ their
> small talent to enhance their personal
> amiability and self-esteem, and who are
> fond of playing the role of the naive
> genius at social gatherings. They are
> consciously childlike, unmoral, unscrupu-
> lous, merry and self-satisfied, even
> healthy enough to enjoy their physical
> disorders, they are pleasant enough in
> their vanity, so long as that has not been
> wounded. But woe to these insignificant
> poseurs when a serious misfortune befalls
> them. They will not know how to be un-
> happy in a decent way; not being able to
> come to grips with their suffering, they
> will succumb. (VIII, 172-173)

Several times Mann emphasizes that Läutner is a man of small substance whose manners and sense of morality leave much to be desired. In keeping with this we note that the sympathy in the story gradually shifts to favor Jacoby the artist figure. Disgusting and disturbing in the beginning, he assumes with his death at the end a tragic character while his two tormentors sink in our estimation. The protagonist's suffering is stressed during his performance on the stage.

The familial situation is transparent in this tale. Alfred Läutner, typical of the representatives of life in the works of Thomas Mann, is a blond-haired and blue-eyed bourgeois. In this antagonist we have a direct link to the father figure, one who is the bitter rival for the affections of the mother. Amra, like so many of Mann's heroines, is sadistic and sensual at the same time, but despite her malice and mocking cruelty, Jacoby loves her with unequaled fervor, lies submissively at her feet, and weeps bitterly. This description of infantile behavior is reinforced by that of his physical appearance; he is so monstrously obese, that we are reminded of the baby fat of an infant.

Jacoby is one of Thomas Mann's most grotesque literary inventions. He is carefully described as repugnant beyond measure both in appearance and manner. When he approaches his wife's bed at night, he behaves in the most groveling and unmanly fashion. He humiliates and disparages himself. Behind this exaggerated depiction we detect the familiar refrain of the punishment fantasy. Jacoby incurs shame through self-abasement before his wife, but he thereby minimizes pain by temporarily relieving his conscience which is supercharged with guilt: ". . . this extraordinary colossus seemed perpetually to suffer from a plague of conscience" (VIII, 170). He finds relief from his inner torment by an attitude of complete submission.

Albrecht van der Qualen, the protagonist of The Wardrobe, also appears in some respects to be an exception, for we do not detect in him the impatient need to allay the violent pricks of his conscience.*
This character, whose name suggests a tormented soul, calmly seeks out a secret retreat on the edge of an un-

---

*But he has the Mannian characteristics of darkly shaded eyes, hair parted on one side; he is also of patrician station as shown by his elegance of dress, his polite manners, his travel accommodations, the menu he orders, and his penchant, like that of Thomas Buddenbrook, for Russian cigars and cigarettes.

familiar city; here he is free to embrace the wondrously beautiful nude woman who visits him. (This dream woman gains access to the protagonist's room by means of the cloth backing of the wardrobe.) Although there is a license to indulge in passion, Albrecht van der Qualen is really no different from the other early Mannian protagonists, for he is already dedicated to death. The doctors have given him but a few months to live. He anticipates his inevitable atonement and therefore makes full use of his freedom. This is why he is exempted from time and order and the obsessive practices which hold in check his guilty thoughts.* But even here there is the same fusion of love and hate which was found in the other tales. The stories related by the nude woman are all depressing and sad, sometimes even containing an element of horror: "But it ended badly; a sad ending; the two holding each other indissolubly embraced, and while their lips rest on each other, one stabs the other above the waist with a broad knife--and not without good cause."[26] The inspiration Albrecht van der Qualen receives from the muse-like creature is close in spirit to that of Tobias Mindernickel: the most violent cruelty is shown here to be inseparable from the moment of supreme tenderness.

With its insight into the relationship between the sexual act and the act of artistic creation, this story is perhaps the most noteworthy and exceptional among the shorter works of Thomas Mann. The nude who visits Albrecht van der Qualen every night and relates stories to him confirms the forbidden sexual element behind the artist's creativity. She does not resist whenever he passionately takes hold of her, but as a consequence

---

*A solitary traveller, he seeks out a secluded place, a veritable monastic cell in its unqualified bareness. He is completely alone, devoid of any contact with the outer world. His musing at the plight of the lady traveller with her suitcase reveals his utter separateness from human relations. Totally exempt from the demands of time, he has no watch; not only does he not know what month it is, but he is unaware of the season as well. When he takes stock of himself, we learn that he has no goal or occupation, that he is not beholden to any man and owes even God nothing; no one could be freer or more unconcerned than he.

she stays away for several evenings. Only by resistance to her charms is there an artistic fountain of
imagination; sexual fulfillment, however, stops the
flow of creation. In frustration and its consequence
of recurring tension, the fantasy of the artist soars.
Instinctual repression is made to serve in the form
of art. The more reality fails to fulfill one's
instinctual longings, that is, the more inadequately
life provides the desired gratifications, the more one
dreams and the more vivid and imaginative these fantasies become.*

According to Frederick J. Beharriell, The Wardrobe
is reminiscent of Arthur Schnitzler's works of the same
period which deal with the confusion of dream and
reality: "But while Schnitzler's dream episodes show
a clear anticipation of Freud's dream theory, Mann does
not. Certainly this dream, with its pronounced sexual
element, invites a Freudian interpretation. It does
not, however, show any conscious anticipation of Freud's
later 'Great Discovery.'"[27] In taking the dream-like
mood of this tale too literally, Beharriell has overlooked a more fundamental and more remarkable anticipation of the author: The Freudian concept of the
instinctual basis of art. In The Wardrobe Thomas Mann
has penetratingly demonstrated the later theory of
Freud that artistic creativity has its origins primarily
in sexuality.

The Wardrobe points ahead to Tonio Kröger with its
artistic program of "frigid art." According to this
doctrine, emotions and feelings hamper rather than
help the artist in his efforts to reach the heights
of creative expression. Feelings are common and banal
and not the domain of the real artist. Whenever Albrecht embraces the muse in a surge of passion, he
loses the inspiration necessary to create works of art.

Death, a brief sketch in diary form, deals with an
unnamed protagonist who attempts to will his own death

---

*The words Thomas Mann has placed in the mouth of
Lorenzo de' Medici (Fiorenza) give full confirmation
to the argument: "Oh world! Oh deepest pleasure!
Oh passionate dream of power, sweet, consuming! . . .
One should not possess. Yearning is gigantic strength,
but possession emasculates!" (VIII, 1040).

on a specific date. Instead,--so he believes--he causes
death to visit his little daughter on the night which
he had predicted for himself. We can readily regard
this work, as Frederick J. Beharriell does, as an example of the Freudian death-wish.[28] However, this
label leaves something unsaid unless we make a direct
connection between the hero's wish to die and his association of pleasure with the event. That he con-
ceives of death as a kind of penitential reward, in
much the same way as did Savonarola, is disclosed by
his words as he joyfully looks forward to the end of
his guilty existence: "I intend to thank death when
it comes, for now it cannot arrive too soon for me.
. . . How excited I am about this last moment, the
very last! Shouldn't it be a moment of rapture and
unspeakable sweetness? A moment of the greatest voluptuousness?"[29] These words leave no doubt about the
role of sex in his yearning for death. Both his longing for release from his state of tension, as well as
the tension itself are instinctively fixed. His drive
for pleasure is so great that he is completely helpless to resist it. Consequently his behavior manifests
itself as a compulsive urge to hasten the normal course
of events.

The protagonist looks forward with relish to a
release from his guilty existence. His attitude, a
reflection of his all-consuming self-doubt, is compulsively focussed on an arbitrary date, arbitrary except to the inner logic of guilt. By fixing on a precise point of time he attempts to arrange the conditions
and submerge the feeling of dread associated with death.
His rigid attitude towards time, the metronome of his
conscience, enables him to suspend the rush forward
and to prolong the sense of impending pleasure. As
with other protagonists who labor against the clock
until they are on the point of exhaustion, his relentless subservience to time serves as an effective re-
striction and control on his impatient urges.

He doubts life so completely that he yearns for
death. But his doubt even pervades this desire: "I
am alarmed at the thought of my death having something
bourgeois and commonplace about it" (VIII, 70). This
quotation reveals both the cause and the concern of
his death-wish. He wants to remove the source of his
suffering through death but fears that death may come
clothed as the common banality he wishes to escape.
In rejecting a bourgeois death, he hopes, heroically,
to rid himself of all traces of the introjected father,

even the father's world: the middle-class.*

Thomas Mann's comprehension of the psychology
of Death is more than an analysis of the hero's death-
wish. Mann, with real clarity and precision, has arrived at the profound insight that every suicide is a
psychically concealed homicide--the implication explicit in the denouement of the story. In longing for
the end of his guilty existence, reflecting as it does
the desire to remove the source of the psychic pain,
the hero sadistically and arbitrarily chooses a victim.
The author demonstrates how the subconscious demand to
put an end to the tyrannical repression of the instincts
can unleash forces of aggression which, if directed
outward, are destructive and lethal. Thus, we must
regard Mann's psychology as astonishingly modern;
indirectly he has anticipated a concept that has only
in recent years gained credence, and then only by
means of clinical research.

In The Clown (sometimes translated as The Dilettante) the hero relates the story of his unhappy and
ill-spent life: his troubled time at home and in
school, his aimless and irresponsible existence, and
his inability to establish worthwhile ties with other
human beings. This nameless misfit makes a virtue out
of self-reproach and self-detraction. He too complains
of an unusually severe bad conscience, and to substantiate his complaints he proclaims his utter worthlessness. But although he calls himself a clown, we have
only his word for it. What we see is his projection
of himself. His self-disparagement with the word
"clown" is a purposeful instrument of his wracking
conscience which inflicts perpetual self-doubt. When
he notices superiority, impatience, and contempt in the
countenance of an old friend, he is subjectively seeing that which fits his needs for punishment and therefore does nothing to counteract his friend's impression.

----

*This attitude towards the bourgeois anticipates
Detlev Spinell's hostility to the businessman Anton
Klöterjahn and Hans Castorp's higher view of death
compared with that of his uncle from the middle-class
flatland. He also predicts the stoic resignation of
later protagonists who gladly accept the blows of fate
and attain to a superior kind of suffering.

As is the case with Paolo Hofmann and Herr Friedemann, the clown is disproportionately moved by his
innocent first encounter with the woman in the story.
And the object of his affections, Anna Rainer, is likewise the haughty and aggressive type of woman who either
mocks him or gives him the impression of scorn. The
clown has a fixation for this kind of woman; she alone
is fitted to play the leading role in the fantasy of
humiliation which he nearly precipitates. To some extent he is even aware that she is essential to a subconscious aim and that his desire for her is based
less on affection than on a need to obtain a pleasurably tinged defeat: "Was I--if I might ask the ques-
tion--was I in love with this girl? Possibly . . .
but how--and why?"[30] Again Mann describes his central
character while at the point of committing himself
emotionally with the woman of his choice. In a state
of violent agitation he approaches Anna Rainer at the
bazaar. But this time he does not press the issue;
instead, he breaks off and rushes outside without
really arriving at a conclusion. He fails to achieve
the longed-for punishment which would mean the tempo-
rary end of his discontent. In contrast to other
Mannian protagonists who find atonement either in death
or in their feeling of relief from unbearable tension,
he continues to perpetuate his miserable, dissatisfied
state.

   The Clown, as has frequently been observed, points
to the larger framework of Mann's creations. The
gabled city (Lübeck), the protagonist's patrician
family with a merchant father and a musical, physically
unhealthy mother, the puppet theater, the protagonist's
relationship to schoolteachers and fellow pupils, the
sudden death of his father, and the liquidation of the
firm all remind the reader of Buddenbrooks or of
Thomas Mann's own life. The meticulously dressed
father with his cigarette case, whose health is undermined by business worries, his early death and liquidation of the business, anticipate Thomas Buddenbrook;
and the protagonist's position in a business office,
his unfitness for military service, his trip to Italy
and his stay in a modest boarding house find parallels
in the author himself. Likewise, the protagonist's
eventual accommodation to a settled and regular mode
of life is part of the autobiographical refrain. The
parallels here seem to be endless--the passive attitude
toward life, the fear of participating directly in
life's full course, the vulnerability to one's own
dangerous emotions, the rationalization leading to

disillusionment, self-doubt, and the indulgence in a make-believe puppet world, where, as in the case of Hanno Buddenbrook, sexual fantasy through music plays the dominant role: "Truly when after such a strenuous performance, I put my toy theatre away, all the blood in my body seemed to have risen to my head and I was blissfully exhausted as is a great artist at the triumphant close of a production to which he has given all that is in him. Up to my thirteenth or fourteenth year this was my favorite occupation" (VIII, 110).

It is no surprise that later in the narrative the ultimate realization of the emptiness of his life is brought about by his interest in Anna Rainer, especially since this interest is quickened and even fixed by an evening in the opera. It is music that reinforces the hunger within him and at the same time conjures up all the guilty associations and taboos connected with this forbidden pleasure. With music comes insight as to why he is unable to love; music is too closely involved with sexual guilt for him to permit indulgence in either. That is also why this protagonist is a dilettante in the pursuit of music. Although a passive enjoyer of all arts, he inclines toward that art whose danger and pleasure quotient is greatest. Thus, he has no choice but dilettantism, for to be a real musician would require a complete, unqualified involvement in his undertaking, an investment of self which is terrifying to him.

The guilt that causes him to withdraw from people also makes him deplore the Bohemian, who, without conscience, gives free rein to his dark thoughts and desires. He categorically states that he, as a person of education and spotless dress, has no desire at all to sit down with unkempt anarchists over a glass of absinthe.

Tristan

In Tristan, Thomas Mann has given us his most elaborate depiction of the course of masochism. Its hero, Detlev Spinell, leads a monastic life in the sanatorium Einfried. It is a self-induced incarceration, for nowhere in the story is he described as ailing or infirm. He weakly rationalizes his flight from the world by his interest in the institution's style of furniture. But this measure is not enough to counteract the deleterious effects of a conscience which continually weights him down and makes him

physically ill. He feels it necessary, as he confesses
to the woman of his choice, Gabriele Klöterjahn, to
lead a completely hygienic existence: to rise at an
incredibly early hour, take a cold bath, and go walking in the snow.*

Until Gabriele Klöterjahn's arrival at Einfried,
Spinell's monasticism and self-inflicted torture in his
daily routine represented a successful compromise
solution to his conflict. But like Friedemann and
the clown, and their fateful women, he completely surrenders his repose at his first sight of her. His
inordinate interest in Gabriele reaches a climax in the
darkened salon during the absence of the other patients.
Spinell begs and flatters her into playing the Liebestod
music from Tristan and Isolde. What emerges from her
accomplished performance on the piano, from her im-
passioned playing, is in itself erotic fulfillment. In
the lengthy description of the music, the yearning,
joy, and bliss of sexual consummation are only thinly
disguised. The sexual nature of this musical scene is
further emphasized in the title itself; ironically the
infantile Spinell is identified with the great lover
Tristan. The passage in question is as follows:

> Here two forces, two beings, strove
> towards each other, in transports of joy
> and pain; here they embraced, and became
> one in delirious yearning after eternity
> and the absolute. . . .

---

*In this tale there are obvious parallels to the
family triangle in Buddenbrooks. Gabriele Klöterjahn,
like Gerda Arnoldsen, is infirm and delicate and possesses the fatal deep shadows near her eyes. Likewise, her mother was no longer living when she married,
and her father and she played violin duos together.
Both create a kind of sensation when they make their
entrance: Gerda in Lübeck, Gabriele in Einfried. Like
Thomas Buddenbrook, Herr Klöterjahn is a wholesale
merchant on the Baltic Sea and retains a fond memory
of banquet suppers at home. While on a business trip
he visited his future wife's father and had some difficulty obtaining the latter's consent to marry Gabriele.
With his carious teeth, doe-like brown eyes and dark
hair, Detlev Spinell presents an external resemblance
to Hanno Buddenbrook.

Oh night of love, sink downwards and
enfold them, grant them the oblivion they
crave, release them from this world of
partings and betrayals. . . .
Their voices rose in mystic union,
rapt in the wordless hope of that death-
in-love, of endless oneness in the wonder-
kingdom of night. Sweet night! Eternal
night of love! And all-encompassing land
of rapture! . . . most gentle death! Release these lovers completely from the need
of waking. Oh, tumultuous storm of rhythms!
How find, how bind this bliss so far remote
from parting's torturing pangs? Ah, gentle
glow of longing, soothing and kind, ah,
yielding sweet-sublime, ah, raptured sink-
ing into the twilight of eternity! Thou
Isolde, Tristan I, yet no more Tristan,
no more Isolde. . . .
Beneath her flying fingers the music
mounted to its unbelievable climax and was
resolved in that ruthless, sudden <u>pianis-
simo</u> which is like having the ground glide
from beneath one's feet, yet like a sink-
ing too into the very depths of desire.
Followed the immeasurable plenitude of
that vast redemption and fulfillment; it
was repeated, swelled into a deafening,
unquenchable tumult of immense appeasement
that wove and welled and seemed about to
die away, only to swell again and weave
the <u>Sehnsuchtsmotiv</u> into its harmony; at
length to breathe an outward breath and
die, faint on the air, and soar away. Profound stillness.[31]

Despite his tumultuous emotions, whether Spinell
loves Gabriele is extremely dubious. When he hears
the other patients returning, his first reaction is
that of a guilty culprit afraid of being caught. Sel-
fishly he thinks only of flight and shows no further
concern for the fate of the woman he had previously
followed about slavishly. His actions are hardly consistent with true feelings of affection, especially
considering his indifference when the outbreak of passion proves to be fatal to Gabriele. Spinell's infatuation for Gabriele is in fact the ambivalent and
guilty love of a person whose expenditure of passionate
feelings exposes him to the anguish of a pitiless
conscience and as a consequence disqualifies him from

the role of the devoted lover.

Spinell has indulged in forbidden fruit. It is no wonder, then, that his subsequent behavior is determined exclusively by his need to come to terms with his overburdened conscience. By daring to be punished, he tempts fate in order to square accounts. Inasmuch as mature love with genuine feelings of tenderness is not a part of his passion, one would think that Detlev Spinell would have at least considered the affair closed, and would have had the desire to cover up the ignoble role he has played. Under ordinary circumstances this undoubtedly would have been the case, but with the Mannian artist figure, whose guilt is labyrinthine, social behavior is not strictly dependent on the external situation but rather subject to its own inner reality.

Without the slightest provocation he makes an enemy of Herr Klöterjahn by writing him an insulting letter. In its timing, tactlessness, and spite we have the elements of an infantile game. His confession of hatred for everything Herr Klöterjahn is and stands for is a clear act of aggression directed at a person completely unaware of his existence. We obtain a satisfactory explanation for his behavior only when we view Herr Klöterjahn as a father figure and Spinell in the role of his son, expressing his hostility as a masochistic provocation against the father. This supplements Spinell's conception of Gabriele as a queen of a group of virgins, emphasizing thereby the time when she was not possessed by the father, and denying the father's influence on her life.

The English-oriented Herr Klöterjahn is pictured for the most part unsympathetically. The manner in which he admonishes his wife is remembered by her as somewhat unpleasant, and he is more concerned about practical money matters than about the dangerous state of her health.

The masochistic provocation alone can explain why Spinell does not feel it necessary on that particular morning to punish himself by rising early in accordance with his usual conscientious routine. Subconsciously he expects, in fact anticipates, the coming punishment and the consequent atonement at the hands of Herr Klöterjahn. Mann even includes an explanation for the way Spinell reacts to Herr Klöterjahn's upbraiding-- as if he were falling out of character: "The fact was, he had given in to his natural man today and slept nearly up to midday, with the result that he was suffering from a bad conscience and a heavy head, was nervous and incapable of putting up a fight. And the spring air made him limp and good-for-nothing. So much we must say in extenuation of the utterly silly figure he cut in the interview which followed" (VIII, 256).

But in reality Spinell's late rising has less to do with atmospheric conditions than with his growing sense of guilt and nervous expectation of punishment. That Detlev Spinell expects retaliation from Herr Klöterjahn must be taken for granted. Yet he is surprised when the latter knocks on his door: "He rose and gave his caller a surprised and inquiring look, though at the same time he distinctly flushed" (VIII, 255). Why this discrepancy? We again consider the infantile role Spinell plays and visualize the child provoking his parent, testing to see how far he can go. His dare succeeds and nervous consternation precedes the punishment. And like Tobias Mindernickel during his fateful climax, this hero grows pale before his adversary.

Spinell makes only a feeble attempt to answer the verbal abuse he receives from Herr Klöterjahn, just enough to encourage the latter's assaults but not enough to defend himself. He accepts the chastisement like a repentant child: "'"Inevitable" was the word I used,' Herr Spinell said; but he did not insist on the point. He stood there, crestfallen, like a big, unhappy, chidden, gray-haired schoolboy" (VIII, 257). Herr Klöterjahn's words are more reminiscent of a family scene than a disagreement between two men. Klöterjahn calls Spinell a "skulking idiot," "pitiful wretch," "tomfool," "ass," "coward," "lazy lout," "malicious good-for-nothing," and one whose heart is "in the seat of his pants." The son's projection of his father's disapproval of his artistic calling is also reflected in the almost humorous anticlimax: "'You have a miserable hand, my young man. I wouldn't employ you in my office'"(VIII, 257).

After Herr Klöterjahn's tirade is over, Spinell's reaction is strange. No adjectives describe him in a state of turmoil or agitation, ordinarily a natural consequence of such an intense emotional scene. The mood is rather one of quiet relief, for he has found satisfaction through punishment of the guilt that plagued him. His appeased conscience now permits him to take a drink of cognac, take a walk into the fragrant spring air, and even to hum the Sehnsuchtsmotiv from the Liebestod.

Suddenly he stops as if in a state of shock. He sees before him Klöterjahn's son, shrieking in delight. This sight is too much for him and he flees in alarm.

Why is he shaken at the sight of Anton Klöterjahn, Jr.? Certainly the vehement Herr Klöterjahn represents health and vigor as much as his son and the latter's rebuke did not seem to affect Spinell particularly.

We recall that in his letter, Spinell also revealed his feeling of superiority toward the infant Klöterjahn:

> But your son, Gabriele Eckhof's son, is alive; he is living and flourishing. Perhaps he will continue in the way of his father, become a well-fed, commercial, tax-paying citizen; a capable, philistine pillar of society; in any case a tone-deaf, normally functioning individual, responsible, sturdy and stupid, troubled by not a doubt.
> Take this confession, sir. I hate you and your child, as I hate life itself, ridiculous, but yet triumphant life which you represent, the ever-lasting antipode and deadly enemy of beauty. (VIII, 254)

Father and son are on a par to him, except that the former commands a measure of respect. Spinell is forced to fall back on a higher and more noble aim to justify his position of weakness: "You are the stronger. I have no armor for the struggle between us. I have only the Intellect and the Word--the lofty weapon and avenging instrument of the weak" (VIII, 255).

The only apparent explanation for Spinell's inner collapse at the sight of the laughing baby is that for the first time he becomes consciously aware of the unequal nature of his contest with Herr Klöterjahn. The real impact of his own impotence comes home to him when he is dramatically confronted with proof of the father's virility, that the father is capable of producing a child. He realizes with stark clarity the shaky foundations of his position, and that his jealousy of Herr Klöterjahn has less to do with "the Intellect and the Word" than with a lack of virility. He is vulnerable to the insight that his strength is based on failure--his inability to love as the consequence of guilt.

An indication of this crippling deficiency is reflected in the Liebestod scene with Gabriele. She asks Spinell why he is not able to play although he understands music so well:

> Strangely enough, he could not hold out against this simple question. He colored, twisted his hands together, shrank into his chair.
> "The two things seldom happen together," he wrung from his lips at last. "No, I cannot play. But go on." (VIII, 246)

His inability to perform can be equated with his inability to love. His understanding is a substitute for love. Here we are reminded of Albrecht van der Qualen's dilemma: actual fulfillment is replaced by passion in his fantasy.

We have in the person of Detlev Spinell, the fashionably dressed aesthete-hero of Tristan, the portrait of an infantile artist. Indeed, the child in him is pronounced to a remarkable degree. Specifically he is a man in his early thirties, "whose round, white, slightly bloated face, however, exhibited not the slightest trace of a beard. Not that it was shaven-- that you could have told; it was soft, smooth, boyish, with at most a downy hair here and there" (VIII, 223). A fellow patient in the sanatorium Einfried labels him the "dissipated baby." In his manner of speech we are likewise reminded of the child who still has his share of phonetic problems: "His voice was mild and really agreeable; but he had a halting way of speaking that almost amounted to an impediment--as though his teeth got in the way of his tongue" (VIII, 225). Frau Klöterjahn reacts to him as if confronting a little boy: "'Ah!' said Herr Klöterjahn's wife; supported her chin on her hand and turned to him with exaggerated eagerness, as one does to a child who wants to tell a story" (VIII, 227). He shows delight spontaneously without special consideration for appearances; his gestures and bodily motions are not held in check by mature restraint. Whenever he especially enjoys an aesthetic experience he draws up his shoulders, spreads his hands and wrinkles his nose and his lips. Such an occasion can also call forth behavior we should expect from an exceedingly young person. In his agitation he is capable of blindly embracing the most distinguished person, be it man or woman.

Spinell is a "marked man" even among the sick; it is one of the patients with uncontrollable legs--signifying something disreputable--who pins the odious label, the "dissipated baby" on him. In his asceticism, childish behavior, and his acute need for punishment he is no different from Mann's previous heroes.

The hero of Tristan is infantile, selfish, and repulsive, but he is no Bohemian. He is too much concerned with living an ascetic life, exacting a toll of self-sacrifice for his art and thereby alleviating his punishing sense of guilt. To Hans M. Wolff, Mann disapproves of Spinell as an artist.[32] This is true only insofar as Mann makes the artist figure a whipping boy in general. Because of the onerous sense of sin the artist has to be dealt with unmercifully. But in this respect Spinell is no exception to the long line of Mannian artists plagued by a sense of worthlessness and suspected by the world at large. Nowhere is Spinell condemned for his fatal influence on Gabriele Klöterjahn; no ethical conclusions are attached to this interlude anywhere in the story. Only in provoking his "enemy" by writing a letter does he encounter critical opposition and that refers hardly to his aestheticism, as Wolff would maintain, but is directed toward his own person.

In the earlier tales the protagonist's rationalizations are manifestly obvious: Dr. Selten explains away his love-hate ambivalence by Irma Weltner's betrayal, the stranger in Disillusionment ascribes his guilt to "great words," and the clown claims that he was born with his problem. By contrast, Hieronymus, Savonarola and Spinell are close in spirit to the hero to come, Tonio Kröger. These protagonists justify themselves and their actions on a higher and more verbal plane; they are not only able to shift the blame by means of the most sophisticated reasons, but they are also articulate spokesmen and theoreticians on art and literature who often analyze their own particular role in this realm.

Tonio Kröger, the novella following Tristan, marks the turning point in the works of the young Thomas Mann; its leading character is the author's first mature

89

protagonist, one who is objectively in control of the
situation and who stoically endures his suffering and
inner torment. Perhaps Mann turned away from the type
of protagonist represented by Detlev Spinell because
he felt that he had exhausted the possibilities which
the theme of overt masochistic provocation had to offer
or because its naked expression was incompatible with
his growing fame as an author. In any event, from
Tonio Kröger (1903) to Felix Krull (1954) the author
rarely lets his protagonists put their feelings to the
test.* Instead, they usually effect a safe withdrawal
from the emotional ties of life: either by physical
seclusion or by the splendid isolation with which they
psychologically surround themselves. This is especially
true of Hans Castorp (The Magic Mountain) and Adrian
Leverkühn (Doctor Faustus) who shut themselves off from
the world, the one in a "hermetically sealed" sanitor-
ium, the other in his prison-like retreat on a farm.
This theme of isolation is carried out to the point of
caricature in the person of Gregorius in The Holy Sinner
who punishes himself by spending eighteen years on a
barren rock. In The Fight between Jappe and Do Escobar, Death in Venice, and the story of Joseph, Thomas
Mann places the emphasis on the protagonist's stoic
forbearance and the efforts he expends to resist the
temptations placed before him. Only in his dream or
vision does Gustav Aschenbach (Death in Venice) let

---

*There is one real exception: Mario and the
Magician. Its protagonist Cipolla is a spellbinder
and hypnotist who deliberately provokes the youth Mario
until the latter, driven into a state of shock, shoots
him to death. In this work the sexual element is
stressed: the names Torre de Venere and Cipolla, the
protagonist's crippled sexuality, and the repulsive and
monstrous kiss at the climax. The Blood of the Walsungs
does not strike us as exceptional. The passion of the
twins Siegmund and Sieglinde is muted by their characterization as incredibly spoiled decadents. Their embrace at the end is less an example of a sudden release
of feeling than it is of the extension of their decadent
natures. It should also be borne in mind that Thomas
Mann had second thoughts about the outbreak of affect
in these two works. He used the frame device in Mario
and the Magician and withdrew The Blood of the Walsungs
from publication at the last moment.

himself go. And in the <u>Joseph</u> tetralogy the author takes up an entire volume to demonstrate how the unflinching protagonist successfully withstands the amorous onslaughts of the Egyptian temptress, Mut.

These early stories are differentiated by the consequences of the protagonist's ultimate reward. Whether he lives or dies depends on the nature of his transgression. In each case where the expression of his repressed emotions is most complete, his release leads to his death. Exceptions are <u>Fallen</u>, which stood at the very beginning, and <u>Tristan</u> where the author treated his protagonist with a certain measure of irony.

The uncertainty concerning the characterization of some of these early protagonists is settled by viewing them from the standpoint of their demand to be punished, whether the punishment takes the form of self-disparagement, a sense of worthlessness, or physical chastisement from someone else.

These protagonists are, in terms of their masochism, one and the same, though they sometimes seem to be ridiculous and unheroic. Thus, when the protagonist of <u>The Clown</u> is viewed as the exemplar of the masochistic impulse, he is not a caricature as Henry Hatfield feels he might be.[33] Nor is <u>Gladius Dei</u>, as James Cleugh states, simply "a mixture of comedy and tragedy."[34] We must also question Hirschbach's view that Detlev Spinell "is not an artist but a man of artistic sensibilities who has studied the artist type well enough to act it."[35] It is equally dubious to interpret these heroes as lacking the sympathy of their creator. This is especially true in the case of Detlev Spinell. To Elizabeth M. Wilkinson, Spinell is a caricature of the poet,[36] and to Karl S. Weimar, he is a "perfect parody of the aesthete, Oscar Wilde in England and Stefan George in Germany. . . ."[37] However, when these various opinions are set off against the provocation-defeat polarity common to all the stories, they appear both dubious and glib. It is undeniable that Mann has depicted these early protagonists as outcasts, misfits, weaklings, or neurotic wastrels. But such characterization is simply part of the masochistic refrain.

Only in so far as he makes the artist figure inherently worthy of scorn does Mann repudiate or take a stand against his protagonists. The Mannian protagonists of these stories have to be dealt with unmercifully because they bear a crushing burden of guilt. Defeat is thus an end in itself and a way of life for them, for only in being vanquished can they achieve success and gain, no matter how dubious, their victory in life.

THE REPRESSIVE OUTLOOK:

FROM TONIO KRÖGER TO DEATH IN VENICE

As we begin an examination of Mann's later short stories, we do so with the premise in mind that they continue to crystallize as configurations of repressed Oedipal tendencies even though the content and the technique of narration undergo an abrupt change. In the short stories from Tonio Kröger to Death in Venice the reader can easily trace the apparatus of repression as a device for controlling one's underlying sense of guilt. Tension rises and searches out new avenues of release, for the stronger the hero's primordial urges become, the more strained his will must also become to control them, until finally, in Death in Venice the mechanism of repression fails as a bulwark against reality. After Tristan there is a necessity on Mann's part to assume a new pose in relationship to the dark forces that constitute for him the primus motor of creation, a pose that manifests itself in The Hungry and in Tonio Kröger as frigid art. But what occurs may best be described as a shift in emphasis rather than a change in basic nature or general outlook: passivity replaces overt provocation and release, nostalgia and self-pity replace anger and hostility, and stoic art replaces impulsive behavior. Thomas Mann now places certain harsh restrictions on his protagonists' behavior to reduce the chance of any impulsive involvement with life and to alter their psychic position from that of victim to viewer. The protagonist is no longer the grotesque, infantile misfit ready to burst into a fit of ill temper and passion. Self-pity and self-imposed isolation are now substituted for the ebullient behavior and uncontrollable agitation which afflicted the early protagonists. So, while continuing to create his stories out of psychic conflicts, Mann gains safety in distance, disguising himself as the observer of the action--the cool, disengaged narrator of his own works. To be sure, narrators appeared in the early short stories also, but there they were swiftly caught up in the emotional whirlpool of their own erratic natures instead of being distantly removed spectators, as they are in later works.

An additional shift in position in the later short stories, along with the safe withdrawal from the field of immediate conflict, allows the author to mirror his heroes in the light of his own career as a man of letters. Instead of permitting his protagonists to be motivated by repressed desires and impulse, he equips each of them with an analytically acute intellect and a broad knowledge of literature, cultural insight, and historical perspective. This new hero is often a recognized artist, successful in his vocation and ever aware of his estimable position above the middle-class. Commanding the respect and adulation of the crowd, he is not above accepting the social status and titles which people are prepared to shower on him.

Along with these changes, we also find a variety of stylistic devices and conceptual justifications to reflect Mann's increased degree of detachment--montage, irony, and stoicism. The stoic tendency, for example, to hold oneself in check, to ascetically and rigorously impose a willful order on one's life, is measured against the possibility of giving in to erratic influences and impulsive commitments to life. As Mann submits to the increasing psychic energy of repression in order to deal with threatening temptations, he withdraws to a safer and more remote position where the effects of a possible failure may not reach him. Irony, he discovers, gives him a comfortable distance from the forces challenging him, just as montage and stratification of narration help to remove the threatening, incestuous content of a story such as The Blood of the Walsungs into a distant, dream-like fantasy. This self-isolation, as we shall soon see in the later short stories, becomes the nucleus of Mann's own conception of art. Depersonalization and estrangement then usher in a plethora of subtle problems in the artist's relationship to society and serve as a key to Mann's aestheticism.

Mann's aesthetics arise out of the feeling of inner tension and only half belonging, of being a suffering voyeur rather than an active participant. Because of his desire to experience something without ever letting the experience control his total personality, he is the perennial outsider who is consigned to studying his own reactions to events in order to find, by means of reflection rather than involvement, satisfaction, admiration, and beauty in them. Every observation and study becomes, therefore, only another aspect of self-observation and is characterized by the tendency to experience everything distantly; and although relating events to one's self in this manner finally negates the full capacity to live and act, it does increase one's ability to speculate about life in the form of artistic creation.

The Hungry / Tonio Kröger

One need only to glance at the short story, The Hungry, to perceive how drastically continence and stoicism contrast to the impulsive outbreak of emotion in its predecessor, Tristan. Though not a major work (it is subtitled "A Study"), it fits the new ironic pose, and as a preliminary sketch for one of Mann's really great short stories, Tonio Kröger, one discerns in it the beginnings of a major shift in the author's concept and style from occasional impetuous involvement with the characters and events to a more remote position of philosophical detachment. Mann carries over many phrases and formulations from this study into Tonio Kröger, in addition to the proposition that art is a cold, emotionless antithesis to life and spontaneous feeling.

Detlef, the hero of The Hungry perceives the world as a receptacle for his own moral and masochistic needs. He prefers the secretive and protective comfort of darkness to the teeming social life which he interprets as menacing and dangerous for him. Genuine enjoyment is impossible in his world of silent martyrdom because it provokes inner conflict and suffering. Detlef knows that if he mingles with the life about him, he would only spoil the crowd's uninhibited pleasure; but incapable of honest self-recognition, he is forced to twist psychic necessity into a superior virtue. He relegates his unwillingness to participate in the activity around him to a special elevated position with regard to others: "Do I not, as my smile shows, see through your simple souls?"[1] And with these words he willfully turns the tables on those who are not crippled by guilt. By reversing the value of neurotic and normal behavior, he condemns a multitude of people and manages as well to keep himself safely distant from others and prevent them, in turn, from seeing through his defenses. What sets him fundamentally apart from the rest is his fear of exposure. He is paralyzed by the insight that he cannot love without compounding his anguish and remorse. He must, he confesses, look on, but not act; he must do penance through rigorous creativity, but not take direct part in life; he must suffer with knowledge but not actually love. The fictionalized love which he professes for life is punctuated with a question mark--"with scornful love" (VIII, 266) and "in insulting love for life" (VIII, 270). The element of hate here, ever present in his feelings, echoes the poisoned love of Savonarola: "What is mind,but the play of hatred? What is art, but creative yearning?" (VIII, 270). In his art the Mannian hero salvages not the love which is denied him in reality but only a yearning for it which stimulates aesthetic activity and creativeness. In his agony he bends every effort to elicit recognition, respect, and even reverence from a woman and from society as a whole. For reasons which represent at bottom little more than obsessive yet delicately artistic self-immolation, Detlef muses over his inner torment as a possible attraction to the woman for whom he yearns. "Would she notice his departure?" (VIII, 267), he asks of himself; would she recognize and appreciate his great sacrifice of life?

But Detlef, the distant and clinical observer of others, isolates only himself, and his questions become an empty, plaintive refrain which finally fades into an isolated state of self-commiseration and censure: "We lonely ones" (VIII, 265); "We denizens of the profound, mute with the monstrous weight of our knowledge" (VIII, 266); "We poor ghosts of life" (VIII, 265).

This position originates squarely in the apparatus of repression which prohibits Detlef from stepping out of his own established boundaries to really participate in life or love. To do so would be to court disaster, at least Detlef believes it would, because the world which he would like to enter--this sensuous, pleasurable world of extreme gaiety, intoxicating music, laughter, color, "food and drink, flowers and scents, dust and overheated human flesh" (VIII, 264)--is the alien and forbidden world of the father. Detlef stands outside the scene like a small boy, wanting to join the gaiety, but dares not enter or interrupt. And all the time he is feeling sorry for himself, he is acting out a smug, clever and ambivalent fantasy. "You are a warm, sweet and foolish life . . ." (VIII, 266) contrasts to "It makes my heart beat with desire and the lustful knowledge that I can reshape [life] as I will and by my art expose your foolish joys for the world to gape at" (VIII, 266-267). What he wants--love, sensual enjoyment, immediate satisfaction--is, at least to his way of thinking, denied him; so he rebels with defiance and hostility, covering feelings of inadequacy with a superiority that threatens to expose by a "word" the banality of life.

The protagonist's hostility and withdrawal from life is still a more acceptable situation than that of Mann's early protagonists who were ludicrously destroyed or severely castigated because of their emotions. In this new relationship Detlef, yearning from afar, incurs no risks. From his safe, passive world he can securely confess his love in the abstract and at the same time feel secure in the knowledge that he is no longer vulnerable. By controlling his overt emotional life, he risks no danger of the reprisals which an active involvement might bring.

Detlef's position remains ambivalent up to the very last where he continues to enforce the repression of his instincts with the imploring statements: "But we are brothers" (VIII, 269) and "Little children, love one another" (VIII, 270). Perhaps if the love becomes general enough, somehow it may include him; he at least tries to proclaim a bond with others by the words "brothers" and "children," but unfortunately his fate is a lonesome one, as we will see in the experiences of Detlef's soul-mate, Tonio Kröger.

In Tonio Kröger Thomas Mann wrote probably his most popular short story. Perhaps it is also the work which lay closest to his heart, for to a great extent it represents the author's Werther. Part of its appeal is undoubtedly due to its "felt" autobiographical elements and in this respect it is a direct expression of Buddenbrooks. Indeed, we learn from Mann's letter to his brother Heinrich, dated December 29, 1900, even before Buddenbrooks was in its final form, that he was working on a novella "of a bitterly melancholy character."[2] Erich Heller concludes, soundly, that this reference in conjunction with a subsequent letter of Mann can only mean Tonio Kröger.[3] Hans M. Wolff surmises that parts of the tale were originally designed to fit the Hanno story, that the two heroes are indistinguishable except that one is a musician and the other a writer, and that the elegiac tone of the dancing-lesson in the novella re-echoes the end of the epic work.[4] Hanno and Tonio are essentially one and the same except that Hanno dies a horrible death.* In a sense

---

*The similarity of the autobiographical details is also carried through: the hero's blue-shaded eyes, his troubles at the gothic vaulted school, the severe conflict with his teachers, his sojourn at the seashore,

Tonio dies too; for the sake of his art his feelings
must be deadened and emotions eliminated from his life.

Thomas Mann's programmatic theory of art reaches
its fullest expression in this short story. He defines
it here as being essentially opposed to life, in that
Tonio's heart must be dead, and his feelings frozen
before he can achieve the aesthetic ultimate. Instead
of confronting life, the hero effects an ever greater
withdrawal and goes so far as to make isolation a kind
of official program for the treatment of the problems
which the real--not the Bohemian--artist encounters.
The pendulum has swung to the very opposite extreme,
revealing graphically the extent of Tonio's ambivalence
and his inability to find genuine compromise upon a
middle ground. From this point on, the hero's hatred
against life is held in check by his inaccessibility,
his Olympian reserve and distance. Mann truly becomes
the "ironic" writer, for irony is that literary device
which drives a protective wedge between subjectivity
and objectivity and replaces identification and commitment with a coextensive remoteness.

This shift in position reflects a major alteration
in Mann's thinking, and becomes immediately evident in
his depiction of protagonists as successful artists.
Tonio and his followers now replace the complete failures or misfits of the earlier tales. This new genre
of artist is elevated to a position of honor and respect for the middle class; the hero stands above the
common herd; Hanno Buddenbrook has in one sense now
become a "Senator" and the artist-child takes the
position of authority and respect formerly occupied

---

his artistic inclinations and music-making, his passivity and dreaminess, his special affection for a school
comrade, his individual position in his adolescent
world; the patrician house and the walnut tree, the
harsh, fastidiously dressed father and his grain business, his early death and the liquidation of the firm,
his body lying in state, the special fascination it
exerts on the hero, the dead grandmother, the foreign
mother--from somewhere "far down on the map"--and her
"different" ways, her musical ability and her questionable morals. The basic difference is that in Tonio
Kröger a sharply delineated sketch replaces the broad
descriptive turbulence of Hanno's family relationship.

by the father--but not without a twist of conscience. What the previous heroes had attempted to gain by force or violence, the new artist achieves by the passive acceptance of public adulation. With the raising of the sensitive, child-like artist to such an admirable status, the artist emerges as a kind of noble patrician or aristocrat; but this new figure, rather than solving the basic contradictions, poses a number of questions couched in the language of an interior dialogue instead of that of the external, hostile confrontation. The unification of opposing values in one person does not result in a reconciliation or in integrity; it merely replaces external opposition with an inner polarity, with opposed tendencies which struggle for the domination of the person. In one situation, the victory may fall to the realm of order, control, and repression; in the next one to the pleasure-seeking forces of dissolution.

Another consequence of the shift from the open and outward hostility in the early tales is a new need on the part of the artist for self-definition. The early heroes knew in which camp they stood, but where is the security for a man who calls himself a "lost bourgeois," or, "a bourgeois who strayed off into art, a Bohemian who feels nostalgic yearnings for respectability, an artist with a bad conscience."[5] Here, and elsewhere, Tonio utters words which do not correspond with his innermost feelings. The extent to which he fails to back up his statements by deeds reveals his need to protect himself against the demands of life, by means of claims to a bourgeois origin, and to rationalize away his conflict with his art.

Tonio Kröger is little different from many of Thomas Mann's heroes who are burdened by a sense of guilt which inhibits them from total involvement in an active life. His sense of sin and doubt reach such proportions that he feels like a criminal indelibly branded by the mark on his brow--one symbolically equivalent to the sign of a murderer, the mark of Cain. As a result of his pitiless conscience, he is preoccupied by death as the promising end to his guilty existence; Tonio thus turns to art, a refuge which enables him to escape the claims of life.

For real artistic creativity, as conceived by him, the cold breath of death must still every human sensation, for "Feeling, warm, heartfelt feeling is always futile; only the irritations and icy ecstasies of the

artist's corrupted nervous system are artistic. . . .
It is all over with the artist as soon as he becomes a
man and begins to feel" (VIII, 295-296). Tonio disdains the non-serious artist who is unaware that good
works can only come into existence under the pressure
of a bad conscience. Whoever lives, he says, does not
work and in order to exist totally as a creative person
one must have died. Thus, paradoxically, his art exists
outside of life. Tonio continues: "Now for the 'Word.'
It isn't so much a matter of the 'redeeming power' as
it is of putting your emotions on ice and serving them
up chilled!" (VIII, 301).

    Mann attempts to promote a kind of art devoid of
the human and the personal. Yet, interestingly, the
credo of "frigid art," of being emotionally dead for
the sake of art discloses a breach in the hero's
thoughts insofar as it coincides in time with the hero's
statement that he loves life. Tonio's claim of loving
life lacks conviction, for one does not try to suppress
what one loves. Like Albrecht van der Qualen (The
Wardrobe) he finds in the cold creativity of art a
substitute for the threats and exigencies of life, and
in placing his energies in art rather than in life, he
avoids the perils of human involvement. In longing
for the blond and blue-eyed representatives of the
middle class, Tonio rationalizes his desire for an
active involvement while, at the same time, he compulsively maintains the repressive prohibition against the
release of these very emotions. As a consequence he
must dissemble in order to achieve the illusion of
loving life. Like all the ambivalent heroes of Mann
there is actually more hatred than love in his feelings
for life. The element of inner doubt which accompanies
Tonio's utterances is so strong that he seems hard put
to convince himself, much less his companion Lisaweta:
"I'm almost finished, Lisaweta. Please listen! I
love life--this is a confession. Take it and preserve
it. I have never made it to anyone else. People say,
people even have written and published that I hate life,
or fear or despise or abominate it. I like to hear
this; it has always flattered me, but that does not
make it true. I love life. You're smiling, Lisaweta
. . ." (VIII, 302).

    Lisaweta's smile does not seem very reassuring.
And at the very end Tonio writes to Lisaweta: "Do
not chide this love, Lisaweta; it is good and fruitful.
There is longing in it and gloomy envy; a touch of
contempt and bliss that is complete and chaste" (VIII,

338). He anticipates by "Do not chide" the disbelief
his words will evoke in Lisaweta.

Envy and contempt, despite the manner in which
they are modified, still contain overtones of resentment
and aversion, and are not calculated to convince Lisaweta or strengthen his case for an affirmation of life.
Equally revealing is Tonio's reference to the representatives of life as stupid. The very fact that Tonio
feels the need to endorse life categorically is perhaps
the best proof that he seriously doubts its value. What
had been a complete withdrawal or a fatal release in
the earliest stories and a veritable fury against Life
by Lobgott Piepsam, restated again by Hieronymus against
the representative of life Herr Blüthenzweig, is only
superficially canceled by Tonio's confession.* In
actuality the loathing is too deeply ingrained in the
artist crippled by guilt and unable to share in the
spontaneous enjoyment of living, the artist who cannot
love and therefore must hate. Also implied in his
words is the underlying motivation for his ambiguous
attitude. In "chaste bliss" we have a hint of the
sexual, the primary source of Tonio's guilt. Tonio's
ideal of chastity is also inimical to a genuine love-
relationship, which would demand physical contact and
the investment of one's deepest feelings. Crippled
sexually, and therefore unable to find satisfaction in
any aspect of life, he yearns for death: "There is
something I call being sick of knowledge, Lisaweta:
when it is enough for a person to see through a thing
in order to feel disgusted to the point of death (and
not feel the least bit forgiving) . . ." (VIII, 300).

By using the lofty word "knowledge," Tonio Kröger
lends an air of respectability to all his groping,
searching and resultant disillusionment. But in spite
of his attempts to cushion his disenchantment, he discovers instead of dignity and propriety his own miserable state. He is numbed by the insight of his guilty

---

*Tonio's confession of love for life should be
compared to Detlev Spinell's hostile and aggressive
letter to the epitome of life, Herr Klöterjahn. Within
the same year, 1903, Thomas Mann permits two distinct
heroes to unequivocally make a confession: one, Detlev, states that he hates life; the other, Tonio, that
he loves life.

existence. He realizes the painful truth, that he is unable to love, that he cannot compete without incurring remorse or increasing his inner travail: "To see things clearly, if even through a veil of tears, to recognize, notice, observe--and to have to put it all down with a smile, at the very moment when hands are clinging, and lips are meeting, and the human gaze is blinded by feeling . . ." (VIII, 300-301). His paralyzing insight is brought home to him at that specific moment when two people passionately embrace each other.*

Tonio Kröger's doubt of his virility is so great that he compares the artist to the papal castrato: "Is the artist really a male? We should ask a female. It seems to me that we artists are all of us something like those unsexed papal singers. . . . We sing like angels, but--" (VIII, 296-297). That is why the artist finds it difficult to create in the spring of the year, when, Tonio is told by his artist friend, "your blood tickles till it is indecent and you are teased by a whole host of improper sensations . . ." (VIII, 294). Spring is the time when life stirs; it represents the quickening of those urges which spell uneasiness and which threaten the necessary restrictions Tonio Kröger places on his instincts. He decries feelings, and with justice, for his are repressed so thoroughly as to become unmanageable if released. "After all, I'm not a gypsy in a green wagon" (VIII, 291). The emphatic tone is indispensable because deep down Tonio is just that and feels the need to deny it. Tonio therefore designates life, with its implication of desire and danger in one, as "seductive."

The dire nature of these repressed impulses, actually criminal in a literal sense--Oedipal desires coupled with feelings of parricide--, is surmised by Tonio in his opinion of his poet-banker friend who achieved his best creations while in prison. Tonio cannot escape the suspicion that the source and essence of his friend's art has less to do with his life in prison than with the reasons that brought him there.

---

*The hero's longing for death and his inability to love is also revealed by his fondness for the lines of Theodor Storm: "I would like to sleep, but you must dance." His awkwardness on the dance floor is further confirmation of his deficient virility.

Tonio does not dare to give way the least bit to his dark desires. He aids the repression by his impeccable dress, highly reminiscent of Thomas Buddenbrook, and by his gentlemanly bearing. That he is capable of yielding to his urges comes out in the description of his stay in Italy: "But since his heart was dead and without love, he fell into adventures of the flesh, descended into the depths of lust and searing sin, and suffered unspeakably" (VIII, 290). Indeed, his attitude toward the sexual is of a frantic and obsessive nature. The very intensity of his repression calls forth all the more readily that which he fears. He is flung to and fro forever between two crass extremes: between icy intellect and scorching passion, and he leads an exhausting life under the pressure of his conscience. Having thus compounded his guilt he once more embarks upon an ascetic course, abhorring with a vengeance the Bohemian. Nonetheless, inside Tonio feels himself to be a Bohemian; he therefore finds it necessary to hide this by wearing proper clothes and behaving outwardly like a respectable person. Another target of his repressive outlook is the demonic sensuality of the Italian Renaissance as typified by Caesar Borgia. No longer can he stomach the Italians and their ways. Everything they stand for is repugnant to him: their velvet blue sky, ardent wine, sweet sensuality, their animated and animal-like natures and the lack of conscience in their eyes. Their whole **bellezza** makes him nervous. Tonio's ascetic stand is close to Savonarola's and the similarity is further enhanced by Lisaweta's designation of the artist as a "saint."

Tonio has shown that it is necessity which inspires the dictum of "frigid art." The sense of deadness is employed by Tonio to shield himself from the horror of exposure. In this way he suffers chronically from the feeling of loneliness and of being cut off but not as violently as he would if he confronted directly the uncertainty which is life. His gaze is consequently focussed on the past, trying nostalgically to recover that period in which his heart once lived and at the same time attempting to escape from the reality of the present. The doctrine of "frigid art" takes on, therefore, a mantle of protection, a rationalization that not only frees him from the excesses of his inner drives, but also becomes, paradoxically, the impetus to pursue his artistic calling.

In keeping with his artistic theory is his

relationship to Lisaweta Iwanowna. He is above reproach in dealing with her, so much so that she chides
him for his excessive propriety as well as for his
faultless patrician dehors. And she can mention these
things because she is a woman who is safe for him, one
who will not cause him to become emotionally involved.
In some respects, she is a female counterpart to Tonio
Kröger: artistic, analytical, reserved, proper and
completely intellectual. Her function in the story is
not to live as a character but to perform dialectics,
that is, to be an intellectual foil to Tonio's pedagogical opinions on art. As a spokesman she helps to tone
down his realization that his beliefs rest on a shaky
inner foundation. When she tells him that he is a
bourgeois on the wrong path, she helps to dull his
awareness about his inner conflict, for with a bromide
such as this he may actually believe that he has
strayed off the bourgeois path in becoming an artist.
But the "bourgeoisie" is only a screen for the entirely
inner personal conflict. His condition goes deeper
and is determined in the fullest measure by sexual
guilt. He has no choice. Tonio announces his guilty
conscience, but in truth his claim to guilt is for the
wrong reason, the real one being repressed. His sense
of guilt is concealed by a defense, for his rationalization is less painful to him.

The same ambivalence is reflected in his attitude
toward art. He feels his art to be a consolation but
at the same time a curse. In effect he is a man condemned by an inner voice to suffer in servitude. Perhaps nowhere else in his works is Thomas Mann so explicit about the impact art has on the hero: "Don't talk
about 'profession,' Lisaweta Iwanowna. Literature is
not a calling, it is a curse, believe me! When does
one begin to feel the curse? Early, horribly early.
At a time when one ought by rights still to be living in peace and harmony with God and the world" (VIII,
297). And no matter how perfect the artist's clothing
or dignity, he feels, through guilty projection, perpetually on exhibition. Tonio feels that he would
hardly need to give a glance or speak a word before
everyone knew that he was not a human being, but something else: something eccentric, different, inimical.
Tonio's complex of guilt is so strong that he actually
feels like a criminal, and his suspicions about himself
are confirmed when he is nearly arrested by a policeman
in his home town. (Incidentally James Cleugh tells us
that the same experience happened to Mann himself.)[6]
Even his special care in his morning toilet and attire

does not prevent his special artist existence from being conspicuously suspect. Interestingly, Tonio is, as Erich Heller says, strangely reluctant to clear up the misunderstanding with the police.[7] He is really bargaining for punishment in order to placate his conscience; it is safe to say that he derives masochistic pleasure from the episode.

The domination Tonio's art has over him is compulsive in essence and explicable only by its origins in sexual tension. His art is nothing which he can shake off at will. To defend against the pressure of his clamorous instincts he undergoes penance through the familiar daily regimen of exacting discipline. By dint of ceaseless labor he draws off and expends the excitement within. He does not work like a man who works that he may live, but as one who is bent on doing nothing but work. Tonio is continually in need of exoneration. Consequently, he loathes the dilettante who hopes to pluck a single leaf from the laurel tree of art without suffering as he does, and he resents and envies the healthy individual who can live and at the same time succeed on the periphery of art.

In this Künstlernovelle, in which the didactic spirit prevails, the artist's self-doubt reaches its climax in expression. Nowhere else does Mann give expression to the artist's sexual impotence and feeling of worthlessness so succinctly as here, when he silently addresses a woman who reminds him of a schoolboy infatuation, Ingeborg Holm: "And even if I in my own person had written the nine symphonies and The World as Will and Idea, painted the Last Judgment, you would still have the eternal right to laugh . . ." (VIII, 334). For Tonio still would not be able to satisfy her in the manner of a normal man. His oath of undying faithfulness to Ingeborg, like his avowal of love for life, is hollow when contrasted to the abruptness with which he gets over his infatuation and settles for a renunciation of his longing: "Then he shrugged his shoulders and went his way" (VIII, 288).

As a female duplicate of the unthinking and unproblematical Hans Hansen, Ingeborg does not really attract the hero despite the pining sighs he emits in his schoolboy fashion. Tonio's resolve to be faithful to her runs the same course as did his friendship with Hans: "After all, he had forgotten Hans Hansen utterly, even though he saw him every day" (VIII, 288). The feeling of loss and loneliness which Tonio so poignantly expresses is, it must be remembered, self-imposed, its groundwork having been laid in its own resentment towards the father-world which Hans Hansen is associated with. It is no wonder that he is unable to establish a measure of real rapport with Hans Hansen, who is completely unaware of the significance of the line from Schiller's Don Carlos: "The king has wept." In citing these words to Hans, Tonio conjures up the whole father-son conflict of Schiller's play of sixteenth-century Spain, beginning with the competition for the mother (previously the son's sweetheart and later the queen) and ending with her becoming the property of King Philip, while the son is condemned to death: This reference to the classical tragedy must, of course, be lost on the blond and blue-eyed Hans, whose indifference to the hero's mental state has its counterpart in Herr Klöterjahn's mystified reaction to Detlev Spinell's vituperative and scathing letter in Tristan.

On board the boat to Denmark, Tonio meets a stranger with whom he looks out at the sea and at the stars. This stranger, with red eyes and red hair is a merchant from Hamburg; he is a business man who has "no literature in his soul"; he speaks poorly, mispronouncing his words; becomes sick in the storm and is revealed, in short, to be an embarrassingly crude creature. His banality, appearance, lack of stoicism and appreciation of the sea places him along with Klöterjahn and Thomas Buddenbrook--with the father figures. The man on the boat would like to talk to Tonio and even makes the attempt, but Tonio, the artist hero, disdains and mocks this unartistic delegate of life. To an even greater measure than that represented by Tonio's relationship with Hans, this brief encounter with the shipboard traveler reflects the hero's true feelings; that he is spurning the father's sphere of life rather than being rejected from it; the hatred has outstripped any feeling of love and the refusal to participate becomes the prerogative of the artist. Tonio's avowal of love for life is shown to be vacuous in his encounter with the stranger and, in the Mannian sense, a test for the artist to support his words with actions. But the artist refuses the test, and by rejecting the stranger's overtures, he openly rejects another invitation to participate in life, if only for a moment.

Why does Tonio Kröger go north? Is it to rediscover the springs of his existence, as Frank Donald Hirschbach says?[8] Perhaps Tonio goes north for this reason, but in another sense his trip can be attributed to an urge to revisit the scene of his original guilty experiences. Tonio is embarrassed by Lisaweta's shrewd guess that his real reason for the trip is to visit his home and not merely to spend his holidays in Denmark:

> "How are you going, Tonio, if I may ask? What route are you taking?"
> "The usual one," he said, shrugging his shoulders, and blushed perceptibly. "Yes, I shall touch my--my point of departure. . . ."(VIII, 306)

The use of inflectional endings in German is revealing. Tonio substitutes _meinen_ (my--to go with point of departure) for _meine_ (my), and in doing so catches himself just in time to avoid saying _meine Heimat_ (my home town).

A moment later Lisaweta knowingly says: "I shall expect a letter full of your experiences in--Denmark . . ." (VIII, 307). In her hesitation there is a hint that Tonio's trip north is incidental to a fervent desire to come to terms with the past.

Tonio does _not_ seek out people or demonstrate affections. He acts as if he has completely forgotten his confession of love for life, and by his aloofness and even contempt for his fellow men, he takes no steps to lessen his "middle-class guilt." There is actually an element of displeasure in his stay in the North, as if to confirm the argument of "frigid art" that his heart must be dead. Indeed, it is surprising how little Tonio enjoys himself except for his isolated vigil at the sea: his yearning for the final absolution of death. The Danish coast fits his needs the same way as the Travemünde beach did Hanno Buddenbrook's. Among Tonio's experiences in the North it is the mighty power of the sea which has the greatest effect on him: "His exultation outvied storm and wave; within himself he chanted a song to the sea, instinctual in its love. 'You wild friend of my youth. Once more we are united-- . . .'" (VIII, 321-322). Contrary to what he told Lisaweta, he does not concern himself with ordinary people, the commonplace representatives of life, but rather with the natural landscape, the magnificent sunrise, and the immense expanse of water. Only the powers of an impersonal nature succeed in stirring the deepest sources of his creative energies, despair and passion.

Tonio Kröger is always the outsider on his journey into the world of the bourgeois; he continually observes and never takes part unless people intrude on his self-imposed isolation. The verbs "listening" and "eavesdropping" keynote his passivity. In fact, his inert behavior makes us wish to question his own severity in regard to his art. Tonio does not consciously distill his exuberant feelings for his art; he coldly subdues his emotions from painful necessity rather than from conscious intention.

Within the story, Thomas Mann curiously invalidates his own thesis that feelings have no place in art. For no one who has read Tonio Kröger can fail to be moved by the emotional quality of this work. Thomas Mann has drawn a complete portrait of the intellectual artist who, lacking a capacity for direct feeling, cannot endure the sensual in art but rather finds in his calling a cleansing effect and the destruction of passions. Although the intellectual Lisaweta episode with its didactic tendencies is the heart of the story, its appeal to us is meager by comparison to the expression of felt sorrow and the nostalgia in the scene of Tonio's childhood. "Then his heart lived" (VIII, 281). The warm emotional tones which characterize Tonio Kröger as a young boy and his dream-like recollection later on of the same situations live in a real, aesthetic sense and are by no means banal and futile for artistic evaluation. In fact, it is the anguished undertone of self-pity and the sentimental yearning of the hero as well as the blurred and mysterious quality of the dream which give this novella its impact. It appeals poignantly to our own nostalgic attempts to escape into the past and to recapture the dream of youth. Tonio's ambivalence, plaintive and lyrical, touches a chord that echoes the loneliness in all of us.

The Infant Prodigy

In the little tale The Infant Prodigy we see the artist as immature and infantile. His immaturity, a regressive feature of the guilty hero of earlier stories, is, of course, within a legitimate setting here in the tale of the child prodigy and as a result does not convey a sense of the pathological. Yet the child prodigy's similarities to the morbid Hanno Buddenbrook are easily established. Music affects Bibi, the hero of the story, in much the same way as it did the protagonist of Buddenbrooks. In the following description of Bibi's performance on the stage there is an echo of Hanno's fervid and agitated response while at the piano, and a clear-cut indication of music's lethal power:

> Bibi did this all for the audience because
> he was aware that he had to entertain them
> a little. But he had his own private en-
> joyment in the thing, too, an enjoyment
> which he could never convey to anybody.
> It was that prickling delight, that secret
> shudder of bliss, which ran through him
> every time he sat at an open piano--it
> would always be with him. And here was
> the keyboard again, those seven black and
> white octaves, among which he had so often
> lost himself in abysmal and thrilling ad-
> ventures--and yet it always looked as clean
> and untouched as a newly washed blackboard.
> This was the realm of music that lay before
> him. It lay spread out like an inviting
> ocean, where he might plunge in and bliss-
> fully swim, where he might let himself be
> borne and carried away, where he might go
> under in might and storm, yet keep the
> mastery: control, ordain. . . .[9]

The sensations music arouses in Bibi add up to extreme pleasure modified, however, by pain and morti-fication: "Joy and lament, rapture and abysmal fall" (VIII, 344). In Bibi's aged appearance for his years and in his "strange mouse-like eyes with dull rings about them" (VIII, 344), we see traces of the decadent artist. His hair parted on the side is a familiar leitmotif and his strange, unpronounceable family name is in keeping with the irregular life of the artist who stands outside of society. Bibi's comments to himself on the public's taste recalls Gerda Budden-brook's pungent opinion of Thomas' musical compre-hension and appreciation; the public, Bibi finds, is attracted by the incidental aspects of music, those which are superficial and amusing. And, as in The Hungry, an artist figure comments on his lot: "We are all infant prodigies, we artists" (VIII, 348).

The story begins with a description of the prod-igy, then of his music and finally of his listeners, followed by comments on the impact his music has on them. From a few individuals in the audience the author manages to reiterate in part the didactic opinions on art in the Lisaweta scene in Tonio Kröger.

An old gentleman with a white beard thinks of the artist's talent as something holy like a gift from God. The businessman, again like Thomas Buddenbrook, looks on music as "a bit of tum-ti-ti-tum and white silk" (VIII, 345). The army officer expresses his acknowledgment of the mighty power inherent in art. The music teacher sees pedantically only the technical side of his playing and not the aesthetic element. A young girl is surprised that a child is capable of playing passion: "But what is that he is playing? It is passion itself, yet he is a child. If he kissed me it would be as though my little brother kissed me-- no kiss at all" (VIII, 345). The final spokesman, the music critic, sums up the child prodigy as follows: "As an individual he has still to develop, but as a type he is already quite complete, the artist par excellence. He has within him the artist's exaltation and utter worthlessness, his charlatanry and his sacred fire, his burning contempt and his secret raptures" (VIII, 346). He also sees through the impresario's exhibitionistic kiss as well as the tricks and the lie connected with art. In effect, the critic is an artist in his own right, in that he has the ability to unmask and to see through things. As a performer the child prodigy is a finished product; he possesses all the attributes of the grown-up Mannian artist whose partic- ipation in passion does not occur outside the realm of art; and it is valid to assume that the young girl's remarks will also apply to him as a man, when, like other Mannian artists, his virility will be in doubt.

Although Bibi has composed the first series of works on the program, he does not yet know how to do the actual writing. In this respect, he is similar to Hanno Buddenbrook who fantasied and dreamed at the piano as opposed to creating permanent works of art.

The resounding kiss the impresario bestows on Bibi singularly affects the audience, which responds with loud shouts and hysterical clapping: "That kiss ran through the room like an electric shock, it went right through the people and made the shivers run down their backs" (VIII, 346). But to the music critic this kiss is meaningless, even fraudulent: "Of course that kiss had to come--it's a good old gag. Yes, good Lord, if only one did not see through everything quite so clearly--" (VIII, 346).*

---

*A similar situation occurs in Mario and the Magician where the artist figure Cipolla electrifies

110

In this scene we are again apprised of the Oedipal situation; for it turns out that the businessman impresario, like a father to the infantile hero, takes his place alongside Bibi's exotic mother in the audience, and that his kiss demonstrates his business cleverness rather than true affection. When the concert is over, the action is removed further from the story of Bibi. The thread seems to break and the author focusses on new and particular faces in the crowd: the blond and blue-eyed types and "a girl with untidy hair and with arms swinging freely, accompanied by a gloomy-faced youth" (VIII, 348). In the youth there is a hint of the hero of <u>Gladius Dei</u> and the free swinging arms of the almost Bohemian girl signify perhaps the platonic relationship between her and her companion, that as artists they are incapable of tender love. On the street the girl gazes after the blue-eyed blond siblings: "She despised them, but she kept looking at them until they had turned the corner" (VIII, 348). Here is the same envy and yearning for the "Bürger" type as that which characterizes <u>The Hungry</u> and <u>Tonio Kröger</u>.

By shifting the spotlight away from the child prodigy to the audience--specifically to the critic, an artist figure--and then finally to still another artist figure, the girl with unkempt hair, Thomas Mann manages to put distance between himself and his hero. Our attention is thus not allowed to dwell on the hero's indulgence in music, an endeavor fraught with such terrible consequences for the Mannian hero. Elsewhere, whenever Mann's protagonists, Hanno Buddenbrook, Lawyer Jacoby and Adrian Leverkühn (<u>Doctor Faustus</u>), participate actively in music, they pay the full price, but here Bibi's role is signally neutralized by the emergence of the critic and the unkempt girl. The latter asserts that she too is a child prodigy. At the end of the story the focus is no longer on the child prodigy performing his music but rather on this nameless artist figure.

---

the spectators by the insolent and sadistic kiss he gives to the antagonist Mario.

A Gleam

In A Gleam, a military ball in the provincial
town of Hohendamm is the occasion for an embarrassing
incident which illuminates the relationships between
Baron Harry, his wife Anna, the artist Avantageur
(cadet officer) and the seductive singer Emmy. Here,
as in The Infant Prodigy, Thomas Mann diffuses the
spotlight, permitting it to shine in turn on each of
these figures.

It is clearly the figure of Baron Harry that
stands out from all others in the tale A Gleam. A
representative of life in its most commonplace, he
cuts an impressive but obtuse and fatuous figure in
Hohendamm. "Waltz-time, tinkling glasses hurly-burly
and smoke, voices and dancing steps. That was Harry's
world and his kingdom."[10] Harry is at home in that
commonplace world from which the discomfited and embarrassed Detlef, the hero of The Hungry, fled. Like
that Hamburg merchant whom Tonio Kröger met on board
ship, the blond Harry has no poetry in his soul, viewing music as light entertainment not to be taken seriously. His imperious order to the Avantageur to yield
the piano to another officer is indicative of his disdain for the artistic sphere. Harry's ruddy complexion
can, of course, stand for robustness and health, but
it can also reveal a choleric nature, symbolic of the
face of the punishing father figure. And significantly,
as we shall see, he has an English name to go with his
title of nobility.

The citizens of Hohendamm are accustomed to the
boisterous pranks of Baron Harry and his comrades. One
childish escapade is especially typical: On their way
home after a night of carousing, Baron Harry and his
fellow officers encounter a baker's apprentice with a
basket of bakery goods. Harry seizes the basket and
manages, as he whirls it around three times in a circle
and lets it fly into the river, to drop not a single
roll or loaf of bread. The outcries of the boy are
quickly silenced when Baron Harry makes ample restitu-
tion for the contents of the basket: "Then the boy
realized that these people were noblemen and he held
his tongue . . ." (VIII, 353). One does not criticize
Harry and his friends. They are no less lords and
masters of the town than the high patrician families
of Lübeck in Buddenbrooks. Yet Baron Harry plays the
role of a complete fool; as an unsympathetic portrait,

his rivals that of Thomas Buddenbrook.

Totally opposite in character to Baron Harry is the artistic and sensitive Avantageur. Though a soldier, he is awkward and out of place in the military milieu. The bourgeois author of a book of stories, he awakens the suspicions of his fellow officers. We readily see that the Avantageur is modeled after Lieutenant René von Throta in Buddenbrooks. He can make music, but he is, like Tonio Kröger, unable to dance and must sit on the sidelines with Baroness Anna--the suggestion of impotence and frigidity on their part-- while her husband flirts unabashedly with the other women. The Avantageur is drawn to Baroness Anna, for he belongs to her world of the spirit. But unfortunately she is indifferent to his presence.

Anna is treated shabbily by her husband, Baron Harry. Reflective and sensitive she stands in decided contrast to his brazen vitality. She appears to be a delicate creature and to have difficulty coping with her married life. In this respect she is a step closer to the decadent Gerda Buddenbrook, who was likewise incapable of giving herself up completely to a bourgeois existence.* Though she is described as being in love with her husband, there are moments when opposing feelings hold sway: "There would come moments when her hatred and scorn outweighed her love; in her heart she would call him a puppy and a trifler and try to punish him by not talking, by an absurd and desperate dumbness . . ." (VIII, 357). Only the memory of Harry's brief attack of tenderness during courtship sustains this love in the face of his behavior. He deceives his wife regularly and daily runs roughshod over her feelings.

The officers are giving their ball in honor of the Swallows, a group of female singers from Vienna. Despite their questionable reputation as barracks entertainers the Swallows are a huge success in the town. Emmy, without doubt the most beautiful of the troupe, is the object of Baron Harry's undivided attention. But Emmy is only interested in the Avantageur. She is attracted to him by his playing at the piano. To

---

*It is revealed that she, like Thomas Mann's own mother, grew up on her father's estate near the sea.

her he is noble, poetic and from another world; by
contrast, Baron Harry is an all too familiar and tedious
figure in her eyes.

Emmy shows physical traits of the typical Mannian
heroine. Her darkly tinged eyes are almond shaped--
exotic features of an exotic woman.* And like Gerda
Buddenbrook, her arrival (and that of her companions)
has an intoxicating effect on the city.

The disreputable Emmy is, curiously, in complete
sympathy with the Baroness Anna. In fact, there exists
an unspoken bond of friendship between them. They are
sympathetically drawn to each other, and when Baron
Harry, to the mortification of his wife, slips his
wedding ring on Emmy's finger, her reaction of shock
and resentment equals that of the offended Baroness.
"'You are coarse!' she said loudly in the hush and gave
the dumbfounded Baron Harry a great push" (VIII, 361).
She then rushes over to the humiliated Anna and offers
her apologies.

Baroness Anna and Emmy are elective affinities.
Together they form a complete portrait of the Mannian
heroine: Anna, the titled, strange, sensitive, delicate
and reserved wife, that is, cold and frigid--and Emmy,
the beautiful, sensual and, at the same time, disreputable woman from another country.** In A Gleam
Thomas Mann has divided the heroine into two persons.
In Baroness Anna and Emmy we have the two opposing and
ambivalent sides of the Mannian heroine: the voluptuous mother to the son, the frigid wife to the husband.*** The wedding ring game which Harry plays points
further to the inner kinship between these two women.

---

*The bared white arm, a familiar physical attri-
bute of past heroines, and the almond eyes will appear
again in the Kirghiz-eyed Clawdia Chauchat in The Magic
Mountain.

**In classical folklore the word Swallow is a des-
ignation for the pudenda muliebra.

***The blond Anna is attracted to the dark-haired
Emmy.

By using a montage to characterize the heroine, Thomas Mann anticipates among others The Blood of the Walsungs, Doctor Faustus and The Holy Sinner in which the two sides of each hero's nature are represented by two different people.

When viewed as a montage, the heroine becomes the object of competition for the two men, the father-figure and the outcast artist. We thus see that the triangle situation assumes the dominant role in A Gleam as it does in previous tales. We also see the reason for the characterization of Baron Harry as an object of derision, for Baron Harry's domain is the commonplace world of the father. With the "English" Baron Harry we approach the Oedipal situation in Tristan, where Herr Klöterjahn, with his English habits, is the obvious rival to the artist hero. Baron Harry appears to be less a rival to the Avantageur. But behind the confusion of the montage, there is the same hostility between the two opposing worlds. Baron Harry's interruption of the Avantageur's playing and the latter's unwilling submission reveal that there is no middle ground on which the two can meet. There is likewise no indication that the Avantageur, as well as Thomas Mann himself, wishes to effect a reconciliation with Baron Harry. The father figure is, in substance, ridiculed unmercifully in this story; Mann tendentiously stacks the cards against this character in order to reveal his utter contempt for this representative of life and his trivial, empty existence.

The tale is quite in keeping with Tonio Kröger. Both heroes passively view the mediocre qualities of life. And as in the previous story contemptuous superiority replaces a murderous hatred, for the passions of the hero have been subdued into A Gleam. The dance floor, so traumatic in Tonio's memories, becomes, here, in contrast, the scene where the domineering, but commonplace rival is finally vanquished. This time the representative of life rather than the hero feels the sting of public censure and scorn.

At the Prophet's

By virtue of a two-fold incongruence, the irony of this short sketch, At the Prophet's is perplexing enough to ask why this story (if it is a story at all) was ever written. The prophet himself is not at the prophet's house, and the narrator, a successful, well-dressed writer with a stiff hat and a well-trimmed

beard, is only a chance visitor at the reading of the
so-called prophet's proclamations. But he is present
in body only. His thoughts and interests are elsewhere. At this mysterious and unworldly gathering of
disciples and curiosity-seekers the young author spends
most of his time exchanging platitudes with a wealthy
woman; inquiring after her daughter, Sonja, of whom he
is especially fond, thinking about food, and musing,
in general, on the goodness of life. The banality of
the talk about Sonja, (the swelling on her foot that
had to be lanced, flowers, and courtship) is set off
against the prophet's ravings of doom and destruction.
We have two worlds here, one in the midst of the other,
with the former disclaiming and discounting the latter.

The garret of the prophet which the young writer
enters is described as a kind of limbo--dangerous and
foreboding, where "the air is so rarefied that the
mirages of life no longer exist. Here reign defiance
and iron consistency, the ego supreme amid despair;
here freedom, madness, and death hold sway. . . . Here
is the end: ice, chastity, null."[11] In this subaltern
world assertions of violence and death are enunciated
with a combination of pleasure and passion: "A fevered
and frightfully irritable ego here expanded itself, a
self-isolated megalomaniac flooded the world with a
hurricane of violent and threatening words. Christus
imperator maximus was his name; he enrolled troops
ready to die for the subjection of the globe; he sent
out embassies, gave inexorable ultimata, exacted poverty
and chastity, and with a sort of morbid enjoyment reiterated his roaring demand for unconditional obedience" (VIII, 368). But the prophet himself, Daniel,
the apparent protagonist, does not attend the reading
of his own proclamations, but sends in his place a
young man from Switzerland, in appearance an uncanny
mixture of weakness and brutality. Though this disciple bears a close resemblance to Hieronymus, the
artist figure of Gladius Dei, he is not to be associated with the latter. This moralistic fulminator is
treated with irony if not disdain; his thundering voice
failing at the end of his speech, he obviously does
not measure up as a suitable advocate for the subjugation of the world. In keeping with the repressive
outlook after Tonio Kröger, the sermonizing rebel cuts
a ridiculous figure and now belongs exclusively to the
non-artistic world of the father. We learn from Thomas
Mann's notebooks both before and after the appearance
of Tonio Kröger that the author was engaged in writing
The Lovers, a tale that left traces in a number of

works besides the one in question. The specific emphasis of <u>The Lovers</u> is on the comic figure of the cuckolded husband as a glorifier of brute strength and sensual power. A yea-sayer of life ("How strong and beautiful life is!"), he exaggeratedly worships the artistic and beautiful and the Nietzschean cult of the superman as it was popularized at the turn of the century. But while he enthusiastically adopts a Promethean stance, he comes forth as a pathetic and ridiculous figure in his physical weakness and impotence.*

The effect Daniel's proclamations have on the writer represents the point of the story. While listening to the oration, the novelist's attitude toward the sacred utterances ranges from polite patience to downright blasphemy. He has "a vision of a ham sandwich but manages to control himself manfully" (VIII, 369). When the rich lady arrives, his conversation with her is personal, human, and far removed from thoughts about the downfall of the world. This beautiful woman, vivacious and genuine, visits such affairs as these for her own amusement, from curiosity, or from boredom. Like the novelist, she obviously does not belong to this world and does not take the proclamations seriously. And after the session has concluded, the narrator's observations, although accurate for the most part, end with a fatuous statement: "In this Daniel all the conditions are present: the isolation, the freedom, the spiritual passion, the magnificent vision, the belief in his own power, yes, even the approximation to madness and crime. What is lacking? Perhaps the human element? A little feeling, a little yearning, a little love?" (VIII, 370).

---

*His portrait is best exemplified by the deceived husband in <u>Doctor Faustus</u>, the subsidiary figure Helmut Institoris: an elegant man with a touch of the English, he has smooth, blond hair, a blond moustache, and blue eyes of noble expression. He raves of beauty, power and mute instinct, loudly sings the praises of the Italian <u>bellezza</u>, and revels in the type of brutal and Dionysian Renaissance man represented by Cesare Borgia. Yet he is sickly and anxious and his affirmation of life rings hollowly when set off against the flush of tuberculosis on his cheeks. See Paul Scherrer and Hans Wysling, <u>Quellenkritische Studien zum Werk Thomas Manns</u> (Berne: Francke, 1967), pp. 25, 35, and 41.

This conclusion reveals more about the nature of the visiting novelist than it does about the prophet. In previous works the protagonist himself had been the victim of his suddenly unleashed passions, but now a light tone is adopted as the novelist hero, with amused detachment, discounts the voices of doom he hears, apparently confident of losing himself in life. Three times, and with biblical solemnity, he denies this world of death and the spirit: "Yes, he and life were certainly on good terms" (VIII, 370). By reiterating this point, he hopefully establishes a counterclaim in order to offset the demonic world of illness and horror.

In this story, we do not find the usual manifestation of asceticism and stoic suffering in the person of the artist himself. The apparent change in the posture of the artist can best be explained by the presence of a turning point in Mann's own personal life: his courtship of Katja Pringsheim, his wife to be. And the sound of the name Katja as compared to the name Sonja, which the young writer of the story keeps repeating affectionately, is too similar to disregard; especially, when girded with other allusions to the Pringsheim family such as the wealthy and attractive mother, the splendid home in Munich, the artistic activity there and the traditional graceful manner of life. And, as stated in the story, that is the very world of existence to which the young, sartorially impressive author, who has rejected his association with those grotesque and nearly sub-human forms, now aspires. He is more concerned with how he is dressed than with his former world of fanatic disorder, which, incidentally, he now summarily and primly rejects with the admonition mentioned before: it lacks the human element, a little feeling, and a little love.

Tender love can certainly be the remedy for the artist hero to counteract the poisonous effects of the hate which was released by rejection as in the case of Savonarola in Fiorenza, and, by extension, the stand-in for the prophet Daniel. That the hero is now on good terms with life is not unconditionally a matter of course, can be concluded from the fact that an approval of life is made three times in this extremely short work. It is as if the avowal were the consequence of an inner necessity—especially since it follows so soon after the categorical and supposedly final affirmation in Tonio Kröger. Can inner doubt be purged so easily? The question will be answered more decisively in subsequent short stories and in the novel Royal Highness.

A Weary Hour

The little sketch, A Weary Hour, takes in one small
hour in the life of Friedrich Schiller during which he
reflects on his struggles to create. Though A Weary
Hour deals with an historical figure, it is yet, as
Wolff states, a parable of the Mannian artist figure.[12]
On close examination, we find that the protagonist is
a remarkable facsimile of previous heroes. Like Tonio
Kröger, Savonarola, and others, he turns out to be a
moral masochist, in whom suffering is the raison d'être
of his existence. What was episodal, or merely a strand
of the narrative thread before, assumes here a well defined credo:

> But he did believe in it [pain]; so pro-
> foundly, so ardently, that nothing which
> came to pass with suffering could seem to
> him either useless or evil. His glance
> sought the manuscript, and his arms tight-
> ened across his chest. Talent itself--
> was that not suffering? And if the manu-
> script over there, his unhappy effort,
> made him suffer, was not that quite as it
> should be--a good sign, so to speak? His
> talents had never been of the copious,
> ebullient sort; were they to become so
> he would feel mistrustful. That only hap-
> pened with beginners and bunglers, with the
> ignorant and easily satisfied, whose life
> was not shaped and disciplined by the pos-
> session of a gift. For a gift, my friends
> down there in the audience, a gift is not
> anything simple, not anything to play with;
> it is not mere ability. At bottom it is a
> compulsion; a critical knowledge of the
> ideal, a permanent dissatisfaction, which
> rises only through suffering to the height
> of its powers.[13]

Writing signifies for him a compelling form of
pleasure but pleasure must be refined by pain, hence
the stoic regimen. The hunger for expiation is a dire
necessity for the artist plagued by a mordant conscience. The sense of guilt mercilessly forces the
artist to wrack his body and rub his nerves raw in
order to create. Effortless creation is suspect, identified as dilettantism, and, in any case, denied to
him, for pleasurable activity would only increase the
bite of conscience. Like Tonio Kröger, the writer also

distrusts any stimulant or drink which might lighten his burden of conscience by dulling its cautery with anesthetizing drugs. He is compelled to exercise his talent in only partial awareness that writing replaces life and may be exercised as an ascetic mortification of the flesh. He has no choice; and he calls it fate, for his urge to create is the direct consequence of libidinal impulses and not something which he can alter or dispense with arbitrarily.

The tone of affirmation, though hollow, which characterized, in some measure, the hero's uncomplicated striving for happiness in At the Prophet's gives way here to punishing mortification. Nothing has really changed. The hero's restrained love for his family has strengthened in some measure his hold on life but not enough to assuage his inner doubts. Addressing his sleeping wife, he says that, because of his mission in life, he must never belong to her exclusively. In fact, conscious withdrawal from real life, intellectualized objectivity, and the patently guilty manifestations of doubt reach a climax in this story. Physically exhausted and plagued by thoughts of complete bankruptcy and despair, Schiller's reflections turn to his youth when life coursed through his veins. If he were only young again! No matter how great the adversity was then, his mind had always recovered quickly and thrived; or as similarly stated by Tonio Kröger: "Then his heart lived." Also reminiscent of Tonio Kröger are the artist's words concerning the effort needed to create, the tone of a distantly isolated person, and the recurring self-commiseration. His nervous tension, his physical exhaustion, and his toying with sin, reveal Schiller to be cut from the same cloth as Gustav Aschenbach, the hero of Death in Venice. Sin and destruction seem more moral to him than modesty of ambition and a pursuit of a healthy life.

The art which is the fruit of a good conscience is to be disdained; for the guilty artist finds true morality only in pain and in a stoic fight against the enjoyable life. The repression is still in force in Schiller, whereas, soon, in Aschenbach it will crumble completely before the onslaught of his dangerous inner drives.

The Blood of the Walsungs

The story, The Blood of the Walsungs, brings us back, to a certain extent, to the pathology of Mann's earliest tales. Here the narrative culminates in the incestuous passion of the twins, Siegmund and Sieglinde, played against a background of Wagner's opera, The Valkyrie, with its hero and heroine (also twins) of the same names. Siegmund at first seems somewhat removed from the usual characterization of the Mannian hero, but on investigation we hear the notes of a melody sung before. He is boyish and effeminate, lacks friends and is reserved, and his passivity conveys the impression of infantile regression. It is true that a consistent set of leitmotifs is lacking--only his dark hair parted on the side and the wealthy patrician home with its view of the garden and the fountain are present. But in his compulsive attitude to his spotless appearance we are again on familiar ground. He must shave twice daily, and he takes more than an hour on his toilet for the opera. He is continually harassed by an extreme need for cleanliness, a need which causes him to spend a considerable part of the day on his dress; and a kind of dreamy paralysis accompanies his narcissistic efforts, although he and the rest of the family undergo a certain regimen by their severe punctuality at mealtime. Further, he and his siblings succeed in killing all social enthusiasm and natural warmth with their cold, critical intellectuality. Genuine feeling is uncomfortable for them, and they, distrustful of their own emotions, do not permit direct sincere expression. The whole family places the highest value on intellectual acuity, with the father, Herr Aarenhold, as the exception to the rule. He is a man of deeds and "Life" and consequently no match for the others when exchanges become too intellectualized. He is despised for his garrulousness, his lack of restraint and good taste, or, in short, the sentimental banality which is the essence of his life. Yet, they are all grieviously envious of this man, who, like the Hans Hansen of Tonio Kröger, is equal to the demands of life. But in calling attention to his strength of will, for example after he has stated that he has had to force the world to recognize him, the children's animosity falters: "The children laughed. At that moment they did not look down on him."[14]

The scene at the Wagner opera and the strange attraction the music has over the hero take us back to the ambivalent agitation of little Herr Friedemann. In the disturbing physical effect the music of The Valkyrie has on Siegmund we perceive again Hanno Buddenbrook's libidinal pleasure and pain at the piano:

A work of art! How did one create? Pain
gnawed and burned in Siegmund's breast,
a pulling anguish like a sweet harassment,
a yearning--where to? For what? It was
so dark, so infamously unclear! Two words
came to his mind: creation, passion. And
while his temples glowed and pounded, it
came to him as in a yearning vision that
creation was born of passion and was re-
shaped anew as passion. He saw the pale,
spent woman hanging on the breast of the
fugitive to whom she gave herself, he saw
her love and her destiny and knew that life
had to be like that in order to be creative.
He saw his own life, a life composed of
weakness and wittiness, indulgence and
denial, voluptuousness and clarity of
mind, comfort and opposition, splendid
security and playful hatred, a life which
substituted logic and words for experience, empty definitions for feeling--and
he felt the pulling anguish in his breast
like a sweet harassment--where to? For
what? For the work of art? Experience?
Passion? (VIII, 404)

That this passion, inseparable from the artist's
creative impulses, is strictly sexual, is unmistakably
demonstrated by his subsequent transfixed state and
ultimately, of course, by the culmination in the sexual
union with his sister.

Von Beckerath, Sieglinde's betrothed, is, as Thomas
Buddenbrook is to Gerda, considerably older than she.
He is a city official and a member of a good patrician
family. He is constantly preoccupied with business
and has no understanding of the world of art in which
the twins reside. "But, my God . . . business" (VIII,
382), von Beckerath complains with transparent vain-
glorious pride, and confirms with that and with similar
statements his cohabitation is that special well-popu-
lated realm of the many father figures who make their
appearance in all of Mann's work. But status, background, and age are not the only schism between von
Beckerath and his bride. Sieglinde will not permit
him to address her in the "thou" form that emphasizes
the bond rather than the division between people.
Sieglinde and her family made him wait a while before
they agreed on the engagement, and so, again, he had to
bear the same anxieties and indignities to which the

father, Thomas Buddenbrook, was subjected while waiting
for an acceptance from Gerda. Sieglinde mocks and
teases von Beckerath, as, for example, when she asks
if she and her brother may go to hear The Valkyrie once
more alone before the wedding. Von Beckerath is to be
excluded from the musical session, as Thomas Buddenbrook
was from that of Gerda and Lieutenant von Throta; and
von Beckerath, sensing the implied underlying intimacy
and aware of his own exclusion does not know how to
handle the response and is taken aback that anyone
would ask his permission in any matter; he thus answers
all too eagerly that they must go. He has no recourse
but to agree to that which he does not have the power
to prohibit or consciously comprehend. Von Beckerath,
being the type he is, can have no understanding of the
"musical" love between the twins.

Mann's growing tendency to double his characters
becomes evident again in the depiction of the father,
Aarenhold and von Beckerath. They complement each
other just as the mother figure, Sieglinde and Frau
Aarenhold do. The protagonist Siegmund also is comple-
mented by his namesake in The Valkyrie, as he, trans-
ported by Wagner's music, emulates the stage hero's
incestuous passion with his sister. Sieglinde doubles
as a mother figure through her betrothal to the businessman (father) von Beckerath, her similarity to the Mannian mother type, and her love for music, which she,
incidentally, enjoys with another man at a safe distance
from her would-be husband. In this work, the mysterious
significance of music is even less veiled, for it is
revealed beyond the symbolic level as a necessary state
of incestuous gratification. In no uncertain terms,
von Beckerath, a father substitute, becomes the cuckold
while the child-like son, Siegmund, enjoys the composite
wife-sister in sexual indulgence.

The bond between the sister and brother is a mutual
one. Sieglinde is as much attracted to her brother as
he is to her. She withdraws and cajols him in a flir-
tatious manner prior to the act so that one may readily
conclude that she is as much responsible for the seduction as he is. Throughout the story, the idea is
hammered home that the woman and the son really belong
together while the mature father figure is the intruder.
This concept is not only developed in the context but
also in the atmosphere of the story.

The twins are always holding hands, "although the
hands of both inclined to moisture" (VIII, 382), an

indication that what may otherwise be interpreted as
a platonic relationship does, in fact, evoke a physi-
ological response. The "although" implies that whereas
the handholding in itself may be permissible, the
"moistness" generated by close bodily contact should
perhaps prohibit the habit. But, of course, the drives
of these two lovers are greater than their sense of
prohibition--as we see at the end of the story.

But the taboos and transgressions are not dispelled
by the culminating act. Cryptically, Siegmund states
that von Beckerath ought to be grateful to them now,
for after all: "His existence will be a little less
trivial from now on" (VIII, 410). It is on this devastating note that the story ends, the implication of
Siegmund's statement being that von Beckerath's life
will be more significant now that Siegmund has copulated
with his fiancée. Siegmund feels that he has, as a
result of the union, contributed his inspired and genial
touch to a form that will now remain hallowed; and once
his creation, Sieglinde, is in the bourgeois world, his
own mark on her will also be there, the result of a
passionate moment that will, to some degree, beautify
the coarse mechanical nature of the blunt practical
man, von Beckerath.

The last line of the story has an additionally
veiled significance. It symbolically reflects Siegmund's complete victory over his hated rival. By re-
shaping the obtuse world of von Beckerath into something
loftier and more noble, he vanquishes the father for
all time. The life devoted to trivia, so unbearable
and odious to the artist, is by this means, transformed
into a realm less threatening and more contemptible,
the implication being that Siegmund has now removed his
opponent. Even if Siegmund were to die, his triumph
would still be secure, for he has externally effaced
that trifling but ever-present, ominous paternal existence. Through his sexual union with Sieglinde, Siegmund's complete and irrevocable bond with her is confirmed. He will remain a part of her always, even in
her future relationships with von Beckerath: "'You
are just like me,' said he, haltingly, and swallowed
to moisten his dry throat. 'Everything about you is
just like me--and so--what you have--with von Beckerath
--the experience--is for me too. That makes things
even, Sieglinde--and anyhow, after all, it is, for that
matter--it is a revenge, Sieglinde--'" (VIII, 410).
His hate, his desire to revenge himself on von Beckerath, has now become a fact.

In more than one sense, it is the scorned and inferior von Beckerath who lends the final purpose and justification to the union of the twins, for his defeat is the indispensable factor for the successful and satisfying achievement of their sinful adventure. First of all, it is certainly startling to notice that immediately preceding and following the sexual union between the twins, the subject of their conversation is von Beckerath rather than their private and mutual concern for pleasure. Certainly, passions are involved, but the verbal justification prior to the act and those following it are references to von Beckerath's immanent position in their lives and their wish to take revenge on him for his mere presence. He looms like a constant and unavoidable specter in the background, stimulating hate in Siegmund who cannot be rid of him.

The second point of elucidation revolves around the relationship between the twins, which, as previously mentioned but not examined in detail, has the complexion more of a mother-son than of a sister-brother relationship. Sieglinde looks after Siegmund constantly in his daily routine, even in his eating habits. At home after the opera, she asks him to eat something substantial and he responds with a petulant "No!" Like a mother, she tells him that he has not had enough to eat: "He shrugged his shoulders--or rather he wriggled them like a naughty child, in his dress coat" (VIII, 407). She then becomes annoyed with him, just as Gerda Buddenbrook did when she and her son Hanno played together just seconds before Hanno's last piano orgy. Siegmund goes up to his room and waits, confident that the "good night had not been final; this was not how they were used to take leave of each other at the close of the day. She was sure to come to his room" (VIII, 408). Siegmund's confidence is founded in the knowledge that Sieglinde is in the habit of coming to his room to give him a good-night kiss, like a mother who tucks her child into bed. Further, his utter passivity and infantile, narcissistic self-admiration before the mirror remind one of a childish fantasy at work. The suggestive nature of his fantasies is hinted at when Sieglinde knocks at the door: "He started, reddened, and moved as though to get up--but sank back again" (VIII, 409). When Sieglinde finally enters and sees him lying on the bearskin rug, she runs to him like a solicitous mother to inquire about his health: "Bending over with her hand on his forehead, stroking his hair she repeated: 'You are not ill?'" She playfully admonishes him like a child: "'You were cross . . . it was beastly of you to go away like that'" (VIII, 409). All in all, the confusion and interplay between erotic desire, antagonism against the rival, narcissistic concern, and childlike artistic fantasy become systematically intelligible when viewed in terms of Oedipal wish fulfillment.

In the light of these observations, it is certainly doubtful whether Hirschbach's designation of The Blood of the Walsungs as a subtle parody of the first act of Wagner's opera can be justified at all.[15] Music, especially Wagner's, is consistently a serious business for Thomas Mann and the musical taste of the twins is not in keeping with parody. After all, they had seen the opera many times and are keenly appreciative of it. Further, the descriptions of the opera itself, comparable in intensity to those passages already mentioned in Buddenbrooks and Tristan, demonstrate a deep comprehension and high approval, in fact veneration, for Wagner's art. And if we examine the unfolding of the opera we can just as readily postulate the view that the Siegmund of the opera supplements the Siegmund in the audience rather than contrasts with him. The former's existence is cursed, and like the artist hero he is a fugitive hunted by his own conscience and marked with a brand. Despite his odious life he possesses a strong yearning for human contact: "He sang of men and women, he had won friendship and love only to be rejected" (VIII, 400). And further, if we scrutinize the opera's antagonist Hunding, we discover that Mann finds him odious beyond all reason. Mann goes to great lengths to flagellate him with insulting epithets: "Blockhead," "lout," "sullen and clumsy," "paunchy and knock-kneed like a cow," "ox-eyes" (VIII, 399-401). In short, he is described as banal and vulgar, menacing and powerful, hostile and distrustful. In Hunding's pugnacious attitude, we see the artist figure's problematical confrontation with certain threatening aspect of "Life." We recognize here the same dichotomy of intellect versus life which characterizes Tonio Kröger. We also detect the same rationalizations.

To Hans M. Wolff, Siegmund's union with his sister represents a desire to break out of his passive state and to gain experience: "These are not the imaginary thoughts of an imaginary character, but rather represen Mann's own, easily comprehensible worries, for the author is beginning to have doubts about Tonio Kröger's gospel of coldness and of the denial of feelings."[16] Despite Wolff's opinion, the fact remains that the hero

126

solution, incest, contradicts his avowed aim of finding his way back to life. The <u>Drang zu den Menschen</u> of which Wagner's Siegmund sighs so poignantly is annulled by his guilty union with Sieglinde. Such is also the case with his double, the hero of the story itself. His desire to feel and participate, based on the realization of the emptiness of his life, is solved in a neurotic way. Indeed, he becomes more and more deeply involved in that which separates him from life. His incestuous act only increases the vicious circle of guilt and makes it thereby all the more difficult to bridge the gap. The acute danger for the total personality, which incest represents, signifies a virtual repudiation of his chances for establishing human relationships. Thus the artist figure's affectionate yearning for "Life" is still of a dubious nature, for it contains, as we gathered from the description of Hunding, an inordinate degree of hatred. The dichotomy of "<u>Geist</u>" versus "<u>Leben</u>," to use the author's favorite phrase, is superimposed on the artist's basic conflict as a mask, but never as a successful substitution.

Once again Mann felt a need to extricate himself from direct identification with the hero. In fact, in the year 1906, he held up publication of this work at the last moment. As a consequence, <u>The Blood of the Walsungs</u> did not find its way into print until 1921 and only then because the proofs of 1906 had been pirated and were circulating, much to the author's dismay, privately in Munich. Mann consented to his publisher's request to release this work only after he learned that the black market edition had already found a considerable audience in Munich.[17] It is also significant that in the first version of this tale the twins, Siegmund and Sieglinde, were unmistakably Jewish and the very last words of the story were "We have beganeft [put one over on] the goy [gentile]."[18] The significance of this original version becomes apparent when we read Thomas Mann's account of his visits to the Pringsheim house in Munich in order to court Katja at this time, the daughter (youngest child and twin) of the Jewish Professor Pringsheim:

> The atmosphere of the great family house,
> which recreated the circumstances of my
> childhood, fascinated me. I found its
> intimacy with the spirit of mercantile
> cultural elegance to be spiritualized

and made cosmopolitan in terms of the ostentatiously artistic and literary. Each of the five grown children (there were five, as was the case in our family--the youngest were a pair of twins) possessed a collection of beautifully bound books, not to mention the opulent art and music library of the lord of the house who was one of the earliest Wagnerians to recognize the great master and who, by dint of a kind of intelligent self-constraint, had not completely dedicated himself to music but instead to mathematics, which[19] he taught at the university of Munich.

The costly art objects, tapestry and bound book collections in the Pringsheim house in Munich, the preference for Wagner, and the Pringsheim twins are carried over into <u>The Blood of the Walsungs</u>. But while Thomas Mann, as Siegmund, was actually courting one of the twins and while the allusions to the real life situation are as direct as can be, the basic feel of this story takes us out of Munich and into the patrician world of Lübeck. Even while rendering an aspect of his courtship for artistic purposes, Thomas Mann allows the maternal image out of the past to override the actual moments of the present.

Originally Mann attempted to steer the reader's thoughts toward a Jewish household. Ultimately he depicted the main characters as ruthless, repulsive, and effete decadents, all of which, to some extent, directed one's thoughts away from the transgressions of Siegmund, thereby helping to mask the Oedipal theme. Even so, this tale, with its unleavened account of incest, represented a daring step for the young author. Both in its origin and in its theme, <u>The Blood of the Walsungs</u> points ahead to <u>Death in Venice</u>, in which the hero, Gustav Aschenbach, no longer able to contain the internal pressure, lets himself go, and succumbs to a guilty passion. <u>The Blood of the Walsungs</u> likewise demonstrates a loosening of controls, but Mann, in keeping with Tonio Kröger's gospel of frozen art, was not quite ready for such a drastic resolution, hence his refusal to go ahead with the publication of this story for fifteen years. Mann's decision mirrors the behavior of Gustav Aschenbach. The same desire to break free of repression is coupled, it will be seen, with an equally intense reluctance on the part of this same hero to let his demonic urges run wild.

Anecdote

Though no artist figure appears in the short sketch Anecdote, this work represents a nutshell-condensation of the Mannian artist's problem. The role of the father figure is played by the serious and bloodshot-eyed Ernst Becker. Formerly a state official and now the director of a bank, he fits Thomas Buddenbrook closely. Like Hanno's father--also like von Beckerath in The Blood of the Walsungs--Becker is much older than his wife. One wonders how this unimportant man came to marry the heavenly, charming, and beautiful Angela. This musically gifted woman who sings and plays the harp becomes a fantastic sensation in the local social world, having attained this position the moment she, as a foreigner, set foot in the town.

But this object of incredible adulation by the men of the town turns out to be utterly corrupt and decadent. Like Consuelo Kröger, she is unclean, sloppy and licentious, and like previous heroines, sadistic and capricious. Though the perfect social queen in the best circles, she is described by her husband as animal-like and loveless. At the end, Ernst Becker's nerves, like those of Thomas Buddenbrook, are frayed and he is on the point of collapse. As an adulteress, Angela Becker surpasses even Gerda Buddenbrook, Irma Weltner (Fallen) and Amra (Little Lizzie) in scandalous behavior, even deceiving her husband with menials and beggars who come to the door.

Angela Becker represents perfection through art. Her husband, on the other hand, stands for the non-artistic philistine who reviles, fears and distrusts the artistic.

Behind art's sacred effect and perfection lies the forbidden sexual element and behind the unpoetic person's suspicion of it, the guilt and imperfect inner personality of the artist himself. This short sketch succinctly focuses the artist figure's conflict based on his destructive view of love. Art, linked sexually in his mind, is inimical to the non-artistic father, indeed contains intense hostility against the father. When Becker stands up before his guests and unmercifully castigates his wife as lewd and degenerate to the chagrin and mortification of her blindly adoring admirers, he is saying in effect that the Mannian artist himself, in his parricidal desire to possess the mother and

129

cuckold the father, is culpable of the grossest deceptions and the most vicious crimes. Angela Becker's sins are, in short, identical to those which the artistic heroes in Thomas Mann's works have committed in omnipotent fantasy, and her husband's speech is equivalent to the voice of the artist's conscience. The accrued guilt of the artist demands repression which is expressed by self-disparagement as well as by the contempt felt for the maternal source and focus of the artist's passions and desires.

The Railway Accident

Life is mean and common contrasted to things of the spirit; and if that truth is not really apparent on the surface of things, it takes only a bit of insight to unmask life's commonness and reveal its banality. This is essentially the gist of the novella The Railway Accident. The narrator, in describing a minor railway accident which he once experienced, analyzes the reactions, mostly unfavorable, of some of the people involved, and by implication, contrasts them with his own. Fundamentally, the accident is merely a convenience to demonstrate the commonplace attributes of das Leben. There is, for example, a patrician gentleman with a dog, who is described as possessing incredibly bad manners. He is at home in life like Hunding of The Valkyrie in the previous story. His rage and odious behavior towards the conductor go beyond rudeness. The author goes out of his way to depict him in the most unflattering terms. There is not only a tone of brutality in his actions, but also in that of the author, who handles this representative of life with sarcasm this time, not irony. "'Leave me alone, you pig!' He used the expression 'pig,'--the epithet of a gentleman, of a cavalier, of a cavalry officer; it did my heart good to hear it."[20] Yet, after the accident, the same person loses his composure and pitiably calls upon a higher power for salvation, whereupon, the narrator ridicules him even further by designating him as "my hero" (VIII 425).

Similar depreciation awaits the other persons in the tale. The stationmaster loses control of himself, and the conductor, who in the beginning cuts a commanding figure of authority, is revealed after the train wreck to be a superstitious babbler. But the narrator is equally unimpressed by the train official whose supposed presence of mind prevented a far worse calamity than that which occurred. His sarcastic "praiseworthy

130

engine driver" indicates the kind of biting commentary which predominates throughout. His critical observations seem styled to ask: Who are these representatives of authority? Do they all have feet of clay? Is that all there is to life? Just what is this railway accident, this momentous and forgettable event of life? Is it not something intrinsically commonplace?

But if these actors in life seem foolish or ineffectual when confronted with reality, the narrator himself remains beyond reproach only because he does nothing, because he is passive the whole time. He looks on the hustle and bustle about him with complete detachment. Like Tonio Kröger, he tips the porter handsomely, no need to risk becoming involved in even the slightest chance of a challenging human relationship. In feelings as well as actions, one senses distance in looking at the world through his eyes. Others may display their emotions in a human context, but not he. His only concern is for the manuscript in his trunk in the baggage car; it may have been destroyed in the wreck. From the care he exercised in wrapping it, we obtain an indication of the agony and effort it cost him to write it. But even if it were destroyed, he knows that he would begin the work all over again: "Yes, with animal patience, with the tenacity of a primitive creature whose complex and curious work, whose product of ingenuity and diligence has been destroyed, I would after a moment of bewilderment and helplessness begin the whole thing anew from the beginning, and perhaps it would come easier this time" (VIII, 424).

True, the elegiac mood of Tonio Kröger is replaced here by a tone of derision, but the two works still have a great deal in common: the train trip; the hint of the world's suspicion of the artist by the conductor's lack of respect for him--the official does not bother to say good night to the hero, even though he pays respect to the churlishly crude gentleman mentioned above; the narrator's passionately voyeuristic observation of the exponents of the life from whom he obtains the necessary element for his art--"I could not look at him enough" (VIII, 418); and his totally compulsive behavior. But more significantly, there is a predominating hostility rather than a love for life here in the narrator's behavior. Indeed, the author has done his best in this little tale to stack the cards against the representatives of life. And it is of interest to note that even more than Tonio himself who

131

utters the proclamation of frigidity in art, the artist of The Railway Accident manages, by substituting ridicule for self-pity, to attain the desired aims of the former's credo--a kind of art which lacks human warmth. There are no feelings evinced by him regarding the dangers of the catastrophe while, on the other hand, the reactions of his fellow travelers become intense or even hysterical as befitting the banality of life. By maintaining distance through mockery, he manages to keep his feelings reserved for artistic use only. His true reactions would be perilous to him; so he turns the tables, makes a virtue out of necessity, and repudiates them.

Royal Highness

In the same year, 1909, Mann completed his second work of epic proportions, Royal Highness. It is a story about a lonely, introverted prince, Klaus Heinrich, who, ruling over a bankrupt duchy, happily finds a solution to his problems of love and finance when he marries the daughter of an American multi-millionaire. Wolff has noted distinct similarities between the novel Royal Highness and Buddenbrooks,[21] that go even beyond characterization: in both works the family (the Duchy in the later work) is in a state of decay at the time of the generation of the hero; there is the detailed description of the father's funeral and a reference to the musical mother; and we see in the person of Duke Albrecht, with his ill-health and inner kinship with death, the figure of Hanno Buddenbrook.

Royal Highness is a direct expression of Thomas Mann's marriage to Katja Pringsheim, as the author unequivocally states: "The first artistic fruit of my young married state, however, was the novel Royal Highness, and it bears the characteristics of that time."[22] Imma Spoelmann, the novel's heroine, is, like her counterpart in real life, a student of mathematics from a rich home. This work, as previous ones, is autobiographical in nature and by no means a political or social novel, or even a satire of the same, but rather the familiar story of the problematical artist, cursing and cursed by his existence. Mann is quite explicit about the artist theme, for he takes as his point of departure the following words of Schiller: "So is the poet to accompany the king, they both dwell on the heights of mankind"[23] and in a certain respect, Royal Highness is, as Mann himself acknowledged, an allegory. "Indeed, if a clever critic had called the book a didactic allegory, then he perhaps would not have praised my book aesthetically, but spiritually and morally speaking he would have hit upon it just the same."[24]

To a great extent this quotation offers a facile explanation for the novel's deficiency, as recognized by Mann himself, or at least for its lack of ready appeal.[25] In an allegory, we do not expect to find a dynamic expression of real life but rather an abstraction of and an intellectualized separation from life; and allegory may also be employed by an author as a safety device by which a particular self-detachment from the uncertainty of challenging human relations is effected. In this novel allegory permeates the atmosphere, the princely existence of the protagonist, Klaus Heinrich, and also the lives of other characters. The hero's loneliness, his passivity, his special affliction (the curse of the withered arm is equivalent to the mark on Tonio Kröger's brow) and his noble calling are easily seen as the persistent symbols which pertain to the artist figure, although a new one, the fairy-tale motif of the roses which emit no fragrance (pointing up the sterility of the artist's existence), is introduced to reinforce Mann's established and necessary image of the hero.

But it can be postulated as well that the other persons in the narrative are allegorical montages in that they stand for specific traits or attitudes belonging to the artist figure. As suggested, Duke Albrecht reminds us of Hanno Buddenbrook. He is sickly to the point of being incapacitated for life, and his inner longing for death sets him completely apart from the rest of society. His narcissism, his total antipathy to the demands of life, and his aversion to meeting routine duties readily recalls Hanno's repugnance while watching his father's business transactions.

In Raoul Überbein, the prince's teacher and dubious friend, the ascetic tendency also predominates. His ugliness and his renunciation of his instincts as a result of unrequited passion make him similar to Savonarola in Fiorenza; like the Florentine monk and other artist heroes he pushes himself to great accomplishments in his field. Überbein's friendship with Klaus Heinrich is less emotional than dialectical. A totally unreal character, he tells Klaus Heinrich that he became the hero's teacher because he saw in the princely existence the most perfectly expressed and best preserved form

133

of the exceptional on earth. At the end he commits
suicide--a deed which is timed to fit Klaus Heinrich's
engagement to be married and as such appears to assert
the failure of Überbein's doctrine of resignation.

Royal Highness, as Thomas Mann insists, represents
a shift in viewpoint as the result of his new marital
status, and a change from the severe austerity of Tonio
Kröger to a more human touch. Hans M. Wolff, in agreement with its author, views the novel as a criticism
of the earlier novella. To substantiate his view, Wolff
points to Raoul Überbein as a stand-in for Nietzsche--
Raoul Richter was Nietzsche's first biographer and the
name Überbein parodies that philosopher's concept of
Übermensch (Superman).

In Überbein we see an unqualified aversion to
close human contact, an actual horror of human warmth.
He has nothing but contempt for humanity and is "the
archenemy of all conviviality."* Überbein's suicide
and the repeated references to this teacher's influence
on Klaus Heinrich's thinking and feelings, are in precise alignment with Wolff's view that Mann is repudiat-
ing the rigorous program of Tonio Kröger. Further proof
is available directly from the author's words in On
"Royal Highness" which, when contrasted to Uberbein's
contempt for life, show that Klaus Heinrich's ultimate
position is presumably an affirmation of life and an
attempt to stand on good terms with humanity: "The
allusion-filled analysis of a princely existence as one
which is formal, unreal, more than real, in a word,
artistic, and the redemption of majesty by means of
love: That is the content of my novel, and full of
sympathy for every kind of 'special case' it preaches
humanity."26 Yet paradoxically, this epic work by
no means conveys a mood of renewal or rejuvenation;
indeed, compared even to Tonio Kröger's doctrine of
self-denial, it is lifeless and bereft of real emotion
If Royal Highness is, as the author claims, an example
of an ascetic breaking through to human contact, a
calamitous mistake has been committed somewhere! At

---

*Mann's later statement that Überbein is a comical
or droll figure is altogether without foundation. See
Observations of a Non-Political Man, XII, 490.

134

least in <u>Tonio Kröger</u>, there was an atmosphere of
sentiment and nostalgia; but here we feel at best only
sadness and moodiness in the hero. And in the love
scenes, we are not struck by passion nor even by a
healthy degree of emotion. Klaus Heinrich's relationship to Imma Spoelmann reminds us, in its intellectual
formality, of Tonio's friendship for Lisaweta. When
he, for example, unburdens himself to Baron Knobels-
dorff, the result is a detached and sober third person
appraisal replete with trivial details and repetitions
that effectively suppress the emotional content of the
scene. When Klaus Heinrich finally kneels before Imma
and confesses his love, one might really expect anything
but the plethora of details concerning the financial
and economical situation of the country that unexpectedly follows.

In fact, the novel is dominated by an emphasis
on minutiae that do not lead anywhere in an organic
sense. Though cleverly and artistically depicted at
times, the prolix observations on dress, customs, and
civic events, thoroughly detract from a picture of life
at its fullest. Even Thomas Mann himself admitted,
although with a measure of reluctance, that this was
certainly the case with <u>Royal Highness</u>:

> Here suddenly a book--one that by no means
> "developed" and "grew" naturally, very far
> removed from anything that smacks of dis-
> tension or rampant inflation, a thoroughly
> measured book infused with moderation and
> proportion, rational, transparent, intel-
> lectually dominated--dominated by an idea,
> an intellectual formula, which is reflected
> everywhere, is everywhere called to mind,
> which is made as lively as possible, which
> attempts to create the illusion of life by
> means of a hundred details and yet which
> never attains a basic, warm fullness of
> life.[27]

In the light of the author's development into a
writer of increasingly sophisticated prose we cannot
help but speculate on why Mann regressed to a kind of
joyless verbosity in <u>Royal Highness</u>. According to
Wolff, the short story <u>Tristan</u> already manifested a
critical stance toward the descriptive writing which
made up the style of <u>Buddenbrooks</u>.[28] But minus the
spark of creative inspiration, the style and content

of the Buddenbrooks novel take hold of the author again because Mann is again dealing with the same haunting figures and conflicts that drove him to write his first great work.

The state of decay in the Duchy, the dynasty to which Klaus Heinrich belongs, (of the lesser nobility), an old patrician family, reflect the story of Hanno which begins in medias res in the second half of Buddenbrooks. Klaus Heinrich's parents are again typical Mannian parents. The mother, Dorothea, is exotic and of foreign origin. She is beautiful but cold to the point where her beauty creates a hollow appearance. In some ways, Klaus is hopelessly attracted to her and reflects her interests, yet she doesn't love anyone; although (significantly, at concerts) she does manifest emotion and is even quite affectionate at times.

Klaus Heinrich's father, Grand Duke Johann Albrecht, often becomes fearfully menacing: "When the Grand Duke was angry with any member of his suite, he was wont to strip the culprit for the moment of all his titles and dignities and to leave him nothing but his bare name."[29] He is also like von Beckerath in appearance, small in stature and somewhat plain, even vulgar in the eyes of people with artistic sensibilities; and in other scenes also, we come closer to The Blood of the Walsungs than to Buddenbrooks. The hero's sister, Ditlinde (this alliterates with the name of Dorothea, his mother) and Klaus like to go "rummaging" around the secret places of the castle. During this whole scene, Klaus, like Siegmund in the Walsung story, is constantly holding his sister's hand, again implying an incestuous relationship. Both Klaus and Ditlinde have flushed faces and she is frequently anxious. When they hear a sudden noise, they become terrified--hardly a justifiable reaction if one does not look for improper and guilty behavior beneath surface appearances.

The cobbler Hinnerke appears like another specter out of Mann's past, with his blue eyes, a beard like the Grand Duke's, and a reddened face that reminds Klaus of his father. Hinnerke (alliterating with Heinrich) also has a son named Klaus Heinrich--certainly more of a conceptual bond than an accidental occurrence! Hinnerke may be seen in this mirrored context as the doublet father figure who must step in occasionally to warn the hero about possible transgressions.

The heroine, Imma Spoelmann, is supposed to represent Katja Pringsheim, but she seems to have more in common with Gerda Buddenbrook and Mann's own mother. Imma (a name which means "mother" in Hebrew) has a grandfather who lived in South America (Bolivia) and married a woman of Indian extraction. Imma, like Thomas Mann's own mother who was born in Brazil as Julia da Silva-Bruhns, is regarded as mysterious and exotic. As a young woman, Julia Mann arrived in Lübeck and became the talk of the town and when she made her social debut, she created quite a sensation as a "personality." Imma Spoelmann makes a similar entrance in the Duchy; her arrival is on everybody's lips and her social life enraptures the citizens.

Imma also fits too closely the past heroines to doubt her origin. She is petulant, critical, standoffish, and almost sadistic. She becomes strangely interested in the hero at times; and when Klaus Heinrich looks at Imma, he often finds her penetrating gaze directed at him. The hero remains passive in his behavior toward her. His remarks, designed for harmless conversation, are frequently twisted in cruel pleasure by her, but it is nevertheless she who first indicates some concern for the hero. And like Herr Friedemann, Siegmund, and others, Klaus subjectively sees only what he wishes to find.

Similar to previous heroines, Imma is a good horseback rider, where ability to ride stands in contrast to the ludicrous father-husband figure, Samuel Spoelmann, who rides an artificial horse in his house.*

Spoelmann appears to be more a rival to Klaus Heinrich than a prospective father-in-law. The author's basic conception of him was as a contrast figure to the artist, the antithesis of material wealth to the aristocracy of the soul: "The Hanseatic bourgeois type gives way to the modern capitalist."[30] Originally called Davis, the magnate Spoelmann is a reincarnation of the materialistic businessman of Lübeck, and as an

---

*The imperious Baron Harry, A Gleam, acquired his facial scar either as a result of a duel or a fall from a horse, the implication being that he too had difficulty playing the role of a consummate horseman.

American, an Englishman once removed, he can be directly associated with the unfeeling middle class. When Samuel Spoelmann makes his first entrance, he appears to be rather ordinary--the people even mistake him for Doctor Watercloose, an American physician, whose name ("Water Closet") is an obvious insult or jibe at the Anglo-Saxon-like father. He, like the many father figures, is diminutive in stature, nervous, and excitable. Samuel is a miniature Thomas Buddenbrook in actions as well as appearance. Having come into possession of immense wealth, he moves to the palace Delphinenort in the Duchy, after having had it refurbished. This palace, belonging to Klaus Heinrich's dynasty, becomes his home after his marriage. We recall that Thomas Buddenbrook had a new house built in Lübeck.

Klaus Heinrich, as the ceremonial prince of his country, is on perpetual exhibition. His existence is above that of the common herd which now looks up to him, although he still possesses the Achilles heel of the artist--impotency. When Imma asks Klaus Heinrich how long he has had his withered arm, she repeats almost verbatim Gerda von Rinnlingen's question to Friedemann, and the hero's anguished behavior and prostration is remarkably similar to the ordeal of this earlier protagonist: ". . . with a cry which sounded like an exclamation of redemption, he sank down before her" (II, 285).

The evidence of the underlying mother-wife identification is certainly convincing enough to draw the conclusion that the aristocratic artist figure is still possessed by the incestuous infantile wish to possess his mother, which in this novel is tantamount to the act of marrying Imma Spoelmann. The repressive forces, primarily in the shape of Raoul Überbein, warn against it, but the maternal-filial attraction has become too strong for the repressive apparatus to contain it. Thus, when Klaus Heinrich finally marries, the resistive force is destroyed--Raoul Überbein commits suicide. But Überbein is only one aspect of repression, the articulate, outspoken representative of a taboo. Its more pervasive aspect, fear, blankets the whole novel in an atmosphere of cold subjugation that smothers genuine emotion. The forbidden union may have been consummated, but the repressive apparatus does not allow the participants to enjoy the act. Guilt and fear of reprisal rob Klaus Heinrich's liaison of the expected pleasures, and a preponderance of objective insertions, depersonalized facts, and detracting trivia remove him from the satisfactions he desires.

Indirect discourse fills a remarkable portion of the narrative and a good deal of the novel is taken up in tracking down or pursuing rumors or reporting them. There is a constant reference to what the "people," "detractors," and the newspaper "Eilbote" say and report. Expressions such as "they said," "it was reported," "wags noted," "eye witnesses assured later," are extremely frequent. Often the matter in question is insignificant and dreary in the extreme, e.g., the feverish expectancy of the people as to whether Klaus Heinrich will present Imma Spoelmann with a bouquet of flowers on a particular occasion.

By the inclusion of such gossip and the people's preoccupation with it, Mann seeks to substantiate the lie that almost idyllic harmony reigns between Klaus Heinrich and his subjects: "Never was the happiness of a prince more inseparable from that of his country" (II, 322-323). This self-deceiving affirmation is a feeble attempt to reverse the self-doubt and its correlative loathing of the world. For the Pollyanna-insertions lack any real conviction with the result that what is finally stressed is the emptiness, triviality and hate of life itself. The implications of derision are unmistakable in the depiction of the people's activities, and behind the veil of words which proclaim a love for life we see the same antipathy which possessed Tonio Kröger. In fact, the scene at the "Bürgerball," paradoxically the liveliest one in the novel, strikes us by its negative presentation of the middle class. There are ugly overtones to this scene and we are not far off the mark if we interpret these as an attack on the burgher. In engaging "Life," Klaus Heinrich leaves himself open to embarrassing criticism. (He is rescued from his predicament by the ascetic Raoul Überbein.) The precarious existence of the hero is endangered by the crowd's hostility when he tries to enter into their activities. As Klaus Heinrich, like Tonio Kröger, sits watching the dancing, he is overcome by the urge to join in; and finally, although warned against it by his friend and ascetic proponent of withdrawal, he does participate, only to fall awkwardly on the floor. A hostile crowd closes in on him. Überbein saves him from injury, confirming through his actions the incapacity of an artist-figure to participate in normal social intercourse and the necessity of retreat behind the walls of one's own soul. Klaus wants to participate in life and in the sexual ritual of the

dance, but he cannot. It is here that the problem of
the artist hero's weakness and antagonism lies.

Klaus Heinrich, because of internal repressions
and external safeguards, does not act out his guilt
in this novel; consequently, he does not develop or
even live in a real sense. As a character he is present
only for the sake of appearances. Except for the "Bürgerball" scene only one secondary figure demonstrates
a modicum of vitality, and that is the Countess Löwen-
joul. Perhaps the reason for this is that she is drawn,
according to Viktor Mann, straight from life.[31] One
other character is life-sized and, ironically, that is
Perceval, the collie dog of Imma Spoelmann and the forerunner of Bashan in A Man and His Dog.* Whenever Perceval appears, the narrative is enlivened and animated.
Here is life in full swing, but the exuberance and
affectionate feeling which goes into this non-human
portrayal entails no risk in terms of the artist's
guilty conscience.

The Fight Between Jappe and Do Escobar

The Fight Between Jappe and Do Escobar is the
story of a battle between two young boys, described
as husky participants of a cockfight, with coxcombs
and bangles, circling or flying at one another. However, this fight, similar in appearance to an avian
mating dance, is seen on closer examination to mask
again an Oedipal situation which reveals its hidden
significance by the narrator's (and hero's) reaction to
this bloody encounter. In keeping with the Mannian
hero's predilection for passive voyeurism in the face

---

*The aristocratic Perceval is not only vitality
personified but is also in his own right a representative of life as he, in effect a symbolic extension of
the father figure Samuel Spoelmann, imitates Baron
Harry's (A Gleam) capricious escapade in spoiling a
merchant's bakery goods. And the reaction of the injured parties to Perceval, similar to that of the baker
apprentice to Baron Harry, quickly turns in his favor,
especially since the dog is discovered to be really
quite harmless, and his master Samuel Spoelmann offers,
as did Harry the humble baker boy, more than ample com-
pensation.

of the sexual side of the game of life, the narrator
shows himself to be stimulated to the point of frenzy
by the mere idea of the impending combat. In effect,
the terse description of his dream the night before
the scuffle demonstrates the superior intensity of his
fantasy when compared to the actual fight in its ridiculous absurdity:

> I experienced the agony of an overwrought
> passion for justice, the flaring, shatter-
> ing hatred, the attacks of raving impa-
> tience for revenge, in which they must
> have passed the night. Arrived at the last
> ditch, lost to all sense of fear, I fought
> myself blind and bloody, with an adversary
> just as inhuman, drove my fist into his
> hated jaw with all the strength of my be-
> ing, so that all his teeth were broken,
> received in exchange a brutal kick in the
> stomach and went under in a sea of blood.
> After which I woke in my bed with ice bags,
> quieted nerves, and a chorus of mild re-
> proaches from my family.[32]

The sado-masochistic tenor of this passage reaches
far beyond any normal anticipation of viewing fisticuffs between two teenagers. The next day, when the
actual combat is over and a general challenge is issued for others to fight, the hero can restrain himself
only with difficulty. He is ready to leap into the
fray, so strong does his excitement and passionate involvement with the situation become. The narrator, in
his voyeuristic pleasure of watching the encounter,
awaits the challenge to go out to him, personally,
"with shivers of delicious anticipation. . . . [I was]
plunged into a world of conflicting emotions . . ."
(VIII, 442). And, finally, "In an excess of self-
consciousness mingled with vanity, I was about to raise
my hand and offer myself for combat" (VIII, 442). In
a confusion of feeling that distorts and replaces love
and embrace with hitting and violence, hate and retaliation, the narrator is ready to participate, only to be
prevented by the referee.

The love and pleasure of destruction is rooted
deeply in the soul of the narrator, who views the impending battle as a perverse sexual encounter that expresses itself in terms of antagonism rather than
tenderness. According to the rules of this fight, at
the insistence of Knaak the referee, only striking

with the fist, no wrestling (i.e. embracing, hugging) is permitted.

In accordance with his dream, the narrator is in favor of this code of violent conduct, and so much so, that he insists along with the others that fists alone constitute the manly art of fighting. When the beaten Do Escobar, holding his bloody handkerchief up to his nose, says that wrestling is for cowards and that only Germans wrestle, he is quickly countered by a statement in defence of Teutonic pride: "But it looks as though the Germans know how to give pretty good beatings sometimes too!" (VIII, 443). And the spectators, proud and fraternal in feelings, roar with approving laughter.

The true Freudian implications of this fight are manifested when Do Escobar's pants continue to slip down and hinder his gladiatorial efforts. Both combatants are dressed in grown-up clothes. The hero, on the other hand, although reliving the excitement as if it happened yesterday, seems to be viewing the whole affair from a child's vantage point, as if it were projected from his memory of the past: "In my memory they [Jappe and Do Escobar] still seem as tall and manly as they did then, though they could not have been more than fifteen at the time" (VIII, 429). By implication, his feelings reflect the desire of a much younger person to participate in the forbidden activities of adults: "I kept putting myself in Jappe and Do Escobar's place and feeling" (VIII, 431). In the combatants themselves are juxtaposed the typical dichotomies of North and South, that is, the father-world of Lübeck and the maternal sphere "far down on the map." By his Low German name, Jappe represents the commercial North; a young middle-class man, blond, husky, coarse, a combination loafer and man-about-town, he comes forth as the crude embodiment of life.* The Spanish (Portuguese)

---

*Jappe hardly exists, if at all, as a first name in Germany; it is not listed in Adolf Bach's Deutsche Namenkunde. However, there is the verb Jappen, a low German word that means "to gasp for breath." This verb is, incidentally, normally applied to dogs and as such points back to Tobias Mindernickel and forward to A Man and His Dog, two tales in which the father image is reduced to the status of an animal.

Do Escobar, "an exotic and Bohemian foreigner who did not even come regularly to school but only attended lectures now and then" (VIII, 429-430), readily fits the lax female type so acutely desired by the Mannian hero. It must be remembered, too, that Thomas Mann's mother, Julia Mann, carried the sobriquet Dodo in her native Brazil. Do Escobar's volubility before the fight at first puts off the hero, in much the same way that Consuelo Kröger's strange ways come in for criticism by Tonio Kröger. In his characterization, there is hint of both the passion and the coldness which are features of the Mannian heroine; he is described as uncommonly wiry and savage, but at the same time, he appears haughty, even vain. And, in disdaining wrestling as a sport for Germans, for which he is hooted down by the crowd, he reveals himself to be aesthetically superior, if not coldly unwilling to "embrace" the representative of life. Although overwhelmed by the heavy German bear, Jappe, Do Escobar appears to the narrator to be the more heroic as well as the more civilized. His pants slip down and seal his fate as a gladiator: "But why had he taken off his suspenders? He would have done better to leave aesthetic considerations alone" (VIII, 440). What defeats him is a severe blow on the nose, which causes profuse bleeding. And so the fight ends as did the dream of the narrator, in a modified "sea of blood"--pointing up the secret and thrilling identification the hero possesses for the maternal sphere, despite its inherent dangers.

Authentic love-making, commensurate here with wrestling, is rejected with scorn and haughtiness by the German youths, who find it more entertaining to find substitute entertainment in playing leap frog, head-standing, and hand springs; although, they all agree, finally, that these are no real substitute for the violence of boxing.

When we view the hero as a passionately involved voyeur to a symbolically concealed act of sex, it becomes fairly easy to explain his excitement, his desire to get involved as well as his fear of doing so; because, as we recall, the dynamics of the Oedipal apparatus demand that beyond a glorious moment of pleasure, a climax of passion, and punishment by death is required. This also explains the narrator's dream which ends not in happy victory, but in violent agitation and an ocean of blood. The only way by which the gory pleasure and punishments of a symbolic love-death are avoided is by the interference of the referee, the

143

repressive and sublimating force: François Knaak.

To a great extent Knaak,--"not a member of society, yet paid by it as a guardian and instructor of its conventions" (VIII, 435)--is a replica of Raoul Über- bein in Royal Highness, an advocate of disengagement. His sexuality is doubted by the boys in this story, and although a dancing-master, he dances alone, never with women. He, like Überbein, is of poor and humble origins and uncomfortable in the presence of the common herd.

In this novella our thoughts automatically turn to the dancing teacher in Tonio Kröger who bears the same name. As a figure from this earlier story Fran- çois Knaak functions as rescuer of the hero who runs the risk of falling into the activities of life. Knaak banished Tonio Kröger from the dance after the latter mistakenly placed himself among the girls while dancing the moulinet, an occasion of danger that was repeated during the Bürgerball in Royal Highness. Now in The Fight Between Jappe and Do Escobar, a new François Knaak shunts aside the narrator on the verge of involv- ing himself in a rather precarious game.

The Fight Between Jappe and Do Escobar amounts to a recapitulation of the first two chapters of Tonio Kröger. It, too, begins with an account of the hero's relationship to two young boys. Tonio's friendship for Hans Hansen and Erwin Jimmerthal has its counter- part in the narrator's relationship to Johnny Bishop and Jürgen Brattström. Like Tonio, the narrator ap- pears as an intruder in the closer kinship linking Jürgen and Johnny. Shortly thereafter, the scene shifts to the arena,--in Tonio Kröger the brightly illuminated dance floor, in The Fight the hot, sunlit ring of com- bat. Finally, both works end with a statement of love or admiration for the blond and blue-eyed antagonist, but in both, the story thread and the hero's reactions to the object of his affection belie any real love on his part.

By way of introducing this story, Thomas Mann focusses on a somewhat strange friend of the narrator, a half-English lad by the name of Johnny Bishop. Throughout the story this character acts as the foil for the narrator's inner state, possessing aloofness, superficial callousness, and a sense of amusement rather than a passionate attraction to this conflict. He poses as an exponent of fisticuffs, wants others to adhere to the rules of the game, and to fight to a

fall--all, incidentally, for his amusement. At the
very end of the story, as if he were staging a moral,
the narrator proclaims his admiration for Johnny
Bishop and his peculiar superiority as a representative
of the English character. However, considering the
symbolic association of England with the middle-class
viewpoint in Thomas Mann's scheme, this profession of
esteem should be scrutinized, especially in view of
what has preceded it. Johnny Bishop takes no physical
part in the combat and is characterized as vulgar,
even vicious, as he looks forward with unreserved glee
to the coming battle. And there is a special incongruity in his bloodthirstiness, inasmuch as he is the
puniest physical specimen among the boys present:
"his childish arms which could never have given or
warded off a blow" (VIII, 431). He is described, like
Hans Hansen, as having blue eyes and blond hair and
wearing a sailor suit; but he is effeminate, being
thin, delicate, and often referred to as womanish in
appearance and dress: "He looked rather like a thin
little cupid as he lay there, with his pretty, soft
blond curls and his arms up over his narrow English
head that rested there on the sand" (VIII, 428). Johnny
puts the narrator to shame by his openness with regards
to sexual matters. Though older and more developed
than his companion, the hero cannot bring himself to
lie entirely naked on the secluded beach, as Johnny
does.

     Johnny Bishop's role takes us back to Thomas Mann's
proposed tale of 1902, The Lovers, in which an exponent
and worshiper of naked power of the Nietzschean superman, and of the cult of heightened senses and life was
to be portrayed as a physical weakling and cuckolded
husband. He is, further, an echo of Baron Harry in
A Gleam and of the rude gentleman with a dog in The
Railway Accident, both of whom serve as the focal center
for Mann's world of the father. Johnny is callous in
his amusements, coarse in his humor, but at the same
time elevated or aristocratic in bearing; yet, he is
the progeny of a businessman and also aligns himself
with a mercantile type. Johnny Bishop's closest friend,
Jürgen Brattström, exists to reveal those qualities
which attract and comfort Johnny. The initials of their
names are identical and the rhythm similar:

          As for Jürgen Brattström, I may say in
          passing that his father had made his own
          money, achieved public office, and built
          for himself and his family the red sand-

> stone house on the Burgfeld, next to Mrs.
> Bishop's. And that lady had quietly ac-
> cepted his son as Johnny's playmate and
> let the two go to school together. Jür-
> gen was a decent, phlegmatic, short-legged
> lad without any prominent characteristics.
> He had begun to do a little private busi-
> ness in licorice sticks. (VIII, 429)

As one identifies this lad with Johnny, one perceives a splitting-off process where the clean, aristocratic, socially attractive elements of the father are
paired off with banality and commonness of the business-
like, enterprising parent.

The blond, middle-class Jappe is, like the weak
Johnny Bishop, quite at home in life, even though he
is a nervous nail-biter like Thomas Buddenbrook. They
both belong to the crowd, as opposed to the foreign
and strange Do Escobar who stands alone at the end of
the story. By regarding Jappe and Johnny as a montage,
we can reconstruct Thomas Mann's ambivalent characterization of the father figure who is both stout and
puny, both manly and effeminate and both aristocratic
and of the people.

The fight Between Jappe and Do Escobar foreshadows
Thomas Mann's political confession, Observations of a
Non-Political Man. In this work of the First World
War, the paternal figure becomes the embodiment of the
English character, reduced to the position of a middle-
class dandy, a spokesman for the bourgeois Geist, and
an adherent of the tango and two-step world (dance =
combat) over which Jappe had emerged as king and which
is to Thomas Mann the epitome of a trivial and tedious
civilization as opposed to Germany's profound culture.
Johnny himself, who, ironically, represents the admirable and "peculiar superiority of the English character," rejoices in the fray, thus anticipating, in
Mann's caustic view, the belligerency of the Western
Powers in World War I. In Observations of a Non-
Political Man a slight shift takes place in that Mann
disavows any connection of the father-world with Germany
as he crystallizes the identification of the middle
class with her enemies and finds in the maternal figure
the essence of a profoundly aesthetic and musical
Germany.

Death in Venice

There is no doubt in our minds that Thomas Mann wrote his finest creation in Death in Venice. His most measured and mature use of language is to be found in this work which came at a time when the conscious pose he struck in Tonio Kröger had played itself out in the face of a more realistic expression of his inner turmoil. Death in Venice stands at the end point of Thomas Mann's severe and chaste attitude towards himself, representing in essence the failure of his conscious attempt to subdue and subjugate his feelings by refrigeration and repression. This is not to say that he becomes the exponent of uninhibited scenes of passion. But now he does resort to a less programmatic evaluation of his inner problem, creating a near perfect balance between an objective description and fervent longing, freeing himself from the indulgence in self-pity and, at the same time, dispensing with the excess of words which plagues all of his longer works both past and present.

The reader of Death in Venice is repeatedly struck by the signs of death which occur in this novella. At the very beginning, the hero Gustav Aschenbach finds himself before a Munich cemetery, deserted except for a mysterious stranger whose facial description reminds one of a death's head. From this omen of the grave, the first of a series of Stygian figures encountered by Aschenbach, there is a progression to an apocalyptic culmination in the cholera epidemic in Venice. The total effect is a powerful dirge, a paean of death which hinges on the slightest of plots.

These signs and symbols of death are more than external artistic embroidery; they are intimately correlated with the protagonist's inner mental state and are an indispensable factor in his drift towards the abyss. In Gustav Aschenbach's mind, death is the penalty which he must categorically pay for his frantic excesses. Up to now critics have not viewed these symbols as part of the psychological justification for Aschenbach's degradation. Vernon Venable sees them as literary symbols and only touches on their psychological function. In fact, he calls the first stranger a symbol of life.[33] Frank Hirschbach finds two distinct levels of interpretation in this work: "Death in Venice especially was written and is intended to be read on a naturalistic and symbolic level. Every incident in

the story as well as the story as a whole have both a
naturalistic and symbolic meaning. . . . When the
story, on the other hand, is read on a symbolic level,
it becomes the case study of the gradual deterioration
and abdication of the human will and of the artistic
will in the face of beauty."[34] While this last statement may possibly apply to the beautiful young Tadzio,
it scarcely fits the spectral strangers who precede
him. And to explain Aschenbach's problem as a failure
of the will is to obscure a good deal of the psychological penetration with which Mann invests this narrative.
It is also questionable that anything is really gained
by such a division into two distinct levels or that it
is necessary to distinguish between a human and artistic will. Instead of being interpreted as mutually
exclusive phenomena or as a departure from reality,
these and other devices in the story can be regarded
as an extension of perfectly natural forces operative
within the frame of the narrative. Indeed, it is
through these devices that Mann helps to direct his
hero's downfall and that he offers us striking evidence
of his exceptional understanding of psychology. Thomas
Mann's masterpiece can thus be viewed not only as a
literary tour de force but also as a remarkable psychological document.

As asserted above, Death in Venice marks the end
of the Tonio Kröger solution to the artist's problem
of living in a hostile world. This work, then, could
readily be subtitled: "The Failure of a Repression."
Gustav Aschenbach is an older Tonio Kröger by nearly a
decade, a Tonio Kröger without his youthful enthusiasm
or sweet nostalgia or the rationalizing force to buoy
himself up in the face of overtaxed nerves. Tonio
Kröger's position with regard to his basic drives is
the key to a real understanding of Aschenbach's fatal
deterioration. Like Tonio, Aschenbach has been living
in an emotional vacuum. He has put Tonio Kröger's
program to the fullest test, exhausting himself in
dedication to his calling. This fact has not gone unnoticed by critics, who have pointed out the artistic
kinship between Aschenbach and Tonio Kröger as well
as the similarities between them and their creator.[35]
However, it is vital that we pay even closer attention
to the psychological affinity between these two protagonists. Both heroes undergo practically the same
experiences in a very similar context, that of a simple
journey to a foreign land from their home in Munich.
In Tonio's case, it is a trip to the colder North by

way of the home of his puritanical father; Aschenbach, on the other hand, travels to a southern--maternal--clime, where sensuality and animal-like passions hold sway. Otherwise they act similarly. In his constant sitting and gazing, Aschenbach is, if we disregard the erotic overtones, close to the spokesman for frigid art, whose participation in the life at the sea resort where he stays is virtually non-existent.* In the Socratic dialogue near the very end there is the Lisaweta Iwanowna interlude in nuce: the artist's self-doubt, his sense of worthlessness and lack of virility, the desirability of detachment in art and the paralyzing impact of "knowledge." But most significant is the phenomenon of the sea landscape, the references and descriptions of which are like a leitmotif in the two stories. It is as if both heroes traveled to their vacation spots for no other reason than to contemplate and feast their eyes on the vast expanse of water before them. The sunrise on the sea, viewed from the hotel room in the very early morning, is an awe-inspiring experience which Gustav Aschenbach and Tonio Kröger both have in common.

Tonio's trip north has, to some extent, the same purpose as Aschenbach's journey. It too is a primitive attempt to make contact with life, but it is only a beginning. He is still too much dominated by the force of the repression which extinguishes the spontaneity

---

*Other parallels to Tonio Kröger are equally impressive; the artist frail of health, with smoothly shaven face, dark hair, and head inclined to the side; the life of solitude, the foreign and sensual mother, and the solid middle-class father (an official of the state); Tonio's pining sighs for the blonde Inge and Aschenbach's longing for the honey-haired Polish boy Tadzio; Hans Hansen dressed, like Tadzio, in a sailor's suit; the glass door of the hotel's dining room overlooking the sea through which Tadzio and his counterparts, Inge and Hans, enter; both heroes suffering silent martyrdom, "sitting in a corner," so to speak, and whispering their confession of love. Also it can be considered that Aschenbach's venture into sensuality is the pendulum of Tonio's extremes swinging back again. There is as well an indication of the same abhorrence of Italians and their lack of conscience in the allusions to official corruption in the city of Venice.

necessary for involvement. His problem has not reached the critical stage. He can thus enjoy the sea in a symbolic way as a sign of absolution, for the horror of his own death is not consciously a part of his thoughts.

Though Aschenbach's kinship with Tonio Kröger is extremely close, his overwhelming need for chastisement sets him apart, and in this he represents a kind of culmination of his artistic precursors. Nowhere else has Mann devoted so much space to self-motification as the necessary prerequisite for the artist hero's existence, to punishment as the means of rehabilitation and "self-control."

Aschenbach's credo is <u>Durchhalten</u>, "to the bitter end":

> Bearing the burden of his genius, then, upon such slender shoulders and resolved to go so far, he had the more need of discipline--and discipline, fortunately, was his native inheritance from the father's side. At forty, at fifty, he was still living as he had commenced to live in the years when others are prone to waste and revel, dream high thoughts and postpone fulfillment. He began his day with a cold shower over chest and back; then, setting a pair of tall wax candles in silver holders at the head of his manuscript, he sacrificed to art, in two or three hours of almost religious fervor, the powers he had assembled in sleep. Outsiders might be pardoned for believing that his <u>Maia</u> world and the epic amplitude revealed by the life of Frederick were a manifestation of great power working under high pressure, that they came forth, as it were, all in one breath. It was the more triumph for his morale; for the truth was that they were heaped up to greatness in layer after layer, in long days of work, out of hundreds and hundreds of single inspirations; they owed their excellence, both of mass and detail, to one thing and one alone; that their creator could hold out for years under the strain of the same piece of work, with an endurance and a tenacity of purpose like that

which conquered his native province of
Silesia, devoting to actual composition
none but his best and freshest hours.[36]

Aschenbach's agony of creation is reflected in
the type of hero which appears on the pages of his
works: Sebastian the saint who defiantly endures the
swords and spears which pierce his body. It is pain
for its own sake, an exultation in suffering:

> Gustav Aschenbach was the poet-spokesman
> of all those who labor at the edge of ex-
> haustion; of the overburdened, of those
> who are already worn out but still hold
> themselves upright; of all our modern
> moralizers of accomplishment, with stunted
> growth and scanty resources, who yet con-
> trive by skillful husbanding and prodigious
> spasms of will to produce, at least for a
> while, the effect of greatness. There are
> many such, they are the heroes of the age.
> And in Aschenbach's pages they saw them-
> selves; he justified, he exalted them, he
> sang their praise--and they, they were
> grateful, they heralded his fame. (VIII,
> 453-454)

At the beginning of the novella the acme of repression is described; but by comparison with his
prototype Tonio, Aschenbach has progressed a long way.
He needs far more drastic safeguards than those which
Tonio didactically imposed upon himself. So exaggerated is his stoicism that the life he leads is a caricature of the hero he writes about. He has come dangerously close to the breaking point. In emphasizing the
severity of the hero's self-mortification, a kind of
penitential exorcism to cleanse the soul of basic
urges, the author motivates with fine psychological
insight his final abandonment and degradation. Although Aschenbach's rigid asceticism contrasts violently
with his subsequent adventures in sin, it is nevertheless an indispensable condition for them. The more
severe the repressive force, the more violent the break
with propriety. In these terms, the impact the mysterious figure in the cemetery makes upon the hero is thus
comprehensible. Reality seems to be suspended by the
sudden arrival of this lethal figure; like an apparition,
he appears from nowhere. But rather than see this figure as standing outside natural law or as a symbol of
the uncanny as does Hans M. Wolff, we can interpret

him as lending greater force to the tension within
Aschenbach.[37] He exists logically as the figment of
the hero's repressed mind, and the chain reaction of
associations unleashed thereby, the vision of the
Asiatic landscape, is merely the extension of the same
hallucination. What Aschenbach sees is not dependent
on an external stimulus, but is rather the result of
forces at work within his mind:

> He had forgotten him the next minute. Yet
> whether the pilgrim air the stranger wore
> kindled his fantasy or whether some other
> physical or psychical influence came in
> play, he could not tell; but he felt the
> most surprising consciousness of a widen-
> ing of inward barriers, a kind of vault-
> ing unrest, a youthfully ardent thirst for
> distant scenes. . . . (VIII, 446)

The luxuriant dream jungle, raw, savage and chaotic,
represents the forbidden; it is a place where life runs
rampant, and as such, the source of decay and death to
the guilty artist. His reaction is drastic: "and he
felt his heart throb with terror, yet with a longing
inexplicable" (VIII, 447). The sight of this domineering and ruthless stranger in the cemetery who regards
him with such hostility triggers the fantasy of the
jungle which terrifies him. He is now conscious of
the fact that death is the reward for the liberation of
his tyrannized senses. This figure is also a prelude
to his coming fall and must precede the jungle vision
of life, for the expectation of death is the indispensable condition for the process of dissolution. It
provides the penitential factor and prepares the way
for the long-desired pleasure. In Aschenbach's mind,
as in the mind of every Mannian protagonist, sensual
gratification is associated with his own doom. Only
the threat of death could exert the strength needed
for him to maintain the prohibition against his clamor-
ing instincts. But now even this is insufficient. The
drive to experience becomes irresistible to him; the
immediate aim of gratification takes hold of him and
shunts aside the far-reaching considerations of dignity
and propriety. Already in the Munich cemetery it is
clear that it is only a question of time before his
intellect is powerless against the totalitarian claims
of his instincts. Aschenbach now acts impulsively;
more and more he interprets the world about him in
terms of an impatient inner necessity. Unlike Tonio
Kröger's, his decision to take a trip resembles a

flight into the unknown.

The shift in emphasis from Tonio Kröger to Death
in Venice, a change from exaggerated inhibition to
active engagement, is also reflected by the subsidiary
characters. The innocuous businessman whom Tonio met
on board ship becomes, in the spectral strangers Aschenbach encounters in Munich, on the steamer and in Venice,
frightening apparitions of imminent significance. The
red eyes they possess now assume a touch of menace, as
interpreted by Heinz Kohut, the inflamed anger of the
punishing father.[38] Tadzio also represents a change;
the perfection of the cool and phlegmatic Hans Hansen
has given way to the weakness of beauty; in his frailty
and carious teeth Tadzio symbolically no longer possesses the virility of Tonio's companion. And whereas
Tonio was perfectly able to casually dismiss both Hans
Hansen and the man on the ship, their counterparts in
Death in Venice, the strangers and Tadzio, come forth
as harbingers of doom.

Near the end of the story, Mann sums up the thesis
of Death in Venice by means of a Socratic dialogue.
Socrates discloses to Phaedrus the cruel impasse of
the artist who is hard put to expend his chaotic urges
without endangering his whole person:

> For you know that we poets cannot walk the
> way of beauty without Eros as our companion
> and guide. We may be heroic after our
> fashion, disciplined warriors of our craft,
> yet we are all like women, for we exult in
> passion, and love is still our desire--our
> craving and our shame. . . . So, then,
> since knowledge might destroy us, we will
> have none of it. For knowledge, Phaedrus,
> does not make him who possesses it dignified
> or austere. . . . It has compassion for
> the abyss--it is the abyss. So we reject
> it, firmly, and henceforward our concern
> shall be with beauty only. And by beauty,
> we mean simplicity, largeness, and renewed
> severity of discipline; we mean a return to
> detachment and to form. But detachment,
> Phaedrus, and preoccupation with form lead
> to intoxication and desire, they may lead
> the noblest among us to frightful emotional
> excesses, which his own stern cult of the
> beautiful would make him the first to con-
> demn. (VIII, 521-522)

Aschenbach's vivid artistic phantasy of the steam-
ing jungle is itself rooted in sexual tension. It is
thus hardly coincidental that he set out on his Munich
walk on a sultry spring day, because he is unable to
make any progress at all in his writing, powerless to
check those impulses connected with his artistic temperament. As his urges gain momentum, there comes the
realization that his artistic fantasy alone is, despite
its all-consuming consequences, inadequate to satisfy
his inner desire.

Under the influence of Eros, Aschenbach, in sight
of Tadzio on the beach at Venice, is once more involved
in pursuing his calling. He suddenly wishes to write.
The excitement which he feels is directed to the producing of the written word. The sexual ingredient is
the conditio sine qua non for his artistic creation.
Indeed, here as with Albrecht van der Qualen in the
earlier story, The Wardrobe, it is not fulfillment,
but free play of fantasy alone which yields the finished
work of art:

> Never had the pride of the word been so
> sweet to him, never had he known so well
> that Eros is in the word, as in those
> perilous and precious hours when he sat
> at his rude table, within the shade of his
> awning, his idol full in his view and the
> music of his voice in his ears, and fash-
> ioned his little essay after the model
> Tadzio's beauty set: that page and a half
> of choicest prose, so chaste, so lofty, so
> poignant with feeling. . . . Verily, it
> is well for the world that it sees only
> the beauty of the completed work and not
> its origins nor the conditions whence it
> sprang; since knowledge of the artist's
> inspiration might often but confuse and
> alarm and so prevent the full effect of
> its excellence. Strange hours, indeed,
> these were, and strangely unnerving the
> labor that filled them! Strangely fruit-
> ful intercourse this, between one body and
> another mind! When Aschenbach put aside
> his work and left the beach he felt ex-
> hausted, he felt broken--conscience re-
> proached him, as it were after a debauch.
> (VIII, 492-493)

Here there is still an element of the Tonio Kröger repression in the artist who numbs and attenuates his passions by the intellectual process of creation. But after Tadzio has once responded by a smile to the voyeuristic sallies of the hero, the latter's striving for beauty assumes the features of the perverse, culminating in the orgiastic dream:

> And one and all the mad rout yelled that cry, composed of soft consonants with a long-drawn u-sound at the end, so sweet and wild it was together, and like nothing ever heard before! . . . But the mountain wall took up the noise and howling and gave it back manifold; it rose high, swelled to a madness that carried him away. His senses reeled in the steam of panting bodies, the acrid stench from the goats, the odor as of stagnant waters--and another, too familiar smell--of wounds, uncleanness, and disease. His heart throbbed to the drums, his brain reeled, a blind rage seized him, a whirling lust, he craved with all his soul to join the ring that formed about the obscene symbol of the godhead, which they were unveiling and elevating, monstrous and wooden, while from full throats they yelled their rallying cry. Foam dripped from their lips, they drove each other on with lewd gesturings and beckoning hands. They laughed, they howled, they thrust their pointed staves into each other's flesh and licked the blood as it ran down. (VIII, 516-517)

The u-sound, a reference to the Polish pronunciation of the beautiful boy's name, Tadzio, is the lure to the depths of Aschenbach's fall and degradation. In his bacchanalian vision he achieves instinctual gratification, in essence the revenge of his repressed impulses. It is readily seen that love, normally associated with tenderness, is utterly lacking in this scene. The hero's ability to love has long since been severely crippled. What we find in his dream consummation of sex is sensual gratification with unmistakable elements of cruelty, aggression, and destruction. This dream offers convincing evidence of Aschenbach's ambivalence: in his mind the sexual is never dissociated from death. It also contradicts, in its brutality, the hero's professed love for the blond-haired Tadzio, to

155

be compared to Tonio Kröger's confession of affection
for the Nordic Hans Hansen in which hate and loathing
represented the guiding principle. Aschenbach's
Bacchanalia, the ultimate extension of Tonio Kröger's
and Klaus Heinrich's dance floor and Jappe's and Do
Escobar's combat arena, trenchantly reveals the stark
ambivalence in the Mannian hero. What to the average
citizen is a simple and prosaic step into the harmless
activities of life's dance, is felt by him to be both
a sacrifice to horror and a delicious thrill. But as
horribly degrading as his dream is, it is still the
logical consequence of the harsh stringency he has imposed on his drives. Degradation means for him a
measure of punishment and, as such, atonement. It also
weakens his carefully constructed prohibitions against
unrestrained behavior. Further, the frenzy of the
debauch points up the pleasures in store for him, if
he will outwardly let himself go. This is why the
dream shatters him; it represents an irresistible step
towards ruin, helps to pave the way for his death
through the plague, and at the same time gives further
sanctions to his burning transgressions.

After the dream orgy, Aschenbach wears foppish
clothes and lets himself be painted with cosmetics, in
order to become attractive to Tadzio. Aschenbach's
willingness to experience abasement shows us that he
is close to death. For in his self-imposed humiliation
he intentionally seeks out that which he fears in order
to allay the anxiety connected with his death. He
hopes thereby to prove that he is the arbiter of his
own destiny and not totally subject to unknown forces.
By arranging the humiliation himself, he dispels the
fear of the unknown.

The actual cause of Aschenbach's death is treated
so casually that the reader is apt to miss the terse
statements which describe his eating of the overripe
strawberries. Matter of factly and desultorily Aschenbach partakes of them on a stroll through the city.
The off-hand and brief manner of this presentation contrasts sharply with the minute history of his adventures
in Venice. Yet this description too fits the psychological needs of the hero. Though aware of the dangers
of pestilence, his haphazard and unthinking feast of
the moment sets aside his fear of falling directly a
victim to the plague. He does not reflectively dwell
on the possible consequences of his act, but rather
inadvertently stills his momentary and insignificant
need for refreshment. In this way, he prevents the

156

knowledge of his fate from being consciously apprehended by rational thought.

Only after he has exposed himself to the perils of disease can gratification occur. As is the case with Albrecht van der Qualen (The Wardrobe), who has only a few months to live, a decree of death has been handed down to him as the penalty for instinctual release. Only then are the ends of retributive justice satisfied.

In the final scene Tadzio is sadistically vanquished in a wrestling bout by his companion Jaschiu. Through this substitute symbolic contact is made between the lover and the beloved. Moments later Aschenbach dies. Consummation has exacted the final payment.

Nowhere else in his works has Thomas Mann given us such a look at the shocking results of unrestricted indulgence. Yet Gustav Aschenbach's passion for Tadzio is completely passive. Everything is at a distance. From afar he gazes longingly at the object of his love. Once he walks behind Tadzio and is overcome by the desire to touch him, but at the last moment he hesitates and successfully resists the urge. This is the closest he comes to putting his amorous designs into action. It is true that he destroys his dehors by letting himself be painted with cosmetics and that he shadows Tadzio through the streets of the city, but his love affair never progresses beyond the point of voyeurism. Consummation is all in his mind.

Though Thomas Mann creates powerful emotions which culminate in a brutish debauch, he manages at the same time to maintain his characteristic reserve and reticence in keeping with his other works. By means of symbolic references to death, Socratic dialogues, allusions to Greek mythology and classical figures of speech, the hero's passivity, and the dream which seals off the Bacchic revelry from the objective world, he achieves sufficient detachment.[39] And when he describes his hero, already debauched and with painted countenance, as the worthy artist who has renounced all sympathy with the abyss and who has rejected Bohemianism and all it stands for, he dissociates himself still further from this artist figure.

Erich Heller says: "Thomas Mann now tells the history of a passion with an economy and intensity unsurpassed in all his work."[40] The reason why we must immediately agree with Heller is because, unlike in

Mann's other works where disengagement may become an
end in itself or play too prominent a role, in Death
in Venice, great suspense is achieved by the intrusions
of irony and eloquence. The Socratic dialogues,
Aschenbach's procrastination and hesitation in Venice
--which contrast rigidly with his sudden flight from
Munich--and the other dilatory devices create a suspension of the mounting tension of the hero. Psychologically, they represent the attempt to reassert the Tonio
Kröger-like prohibition against the world of the senses,
for the life-long fear of consequences cannot be dispelled so easily by the hero. In this work where the
emphasis is on the relentless struggle in Aschenbach's
mind, in which the reader is never far removed from the
hero's thoughts and feelings, the total effect of these
stylistic devices is to prolong the tension, not to
resolve it. By retarding the action, they give the
reader time to participate in the protagonist's agony.
In letting his hero enjoy the situation and defer the
final payment, Mann perpetuates the state of the unbearable between anxiety and pleasure.

In Death in Venice, more than in any other major
work, the author dispenses with the external story-
situation and concentrates on the hero's psychic conflict. The tale represents the author's deepest penetration into the psyche of the artist figure and shows
us that Thomas Mann has few if any peers among psychological writers.

THE ARISTOCRATIC BEARING

Observations of a Non-Political Man

In <u>Observations of a Non-Political Man</u> Thomas Mann apparently steps out of character by stepping into the political arena, for despite the title of this work he tenaciously enunciates a political philosophy with all the self-righteousness, dedication and conviction of a lifelong chauvinist, proclaiming how the world will degenerate should the opposing forces take over:

> Where did the feeling come from that
> dominated me to the core at the beginning
> of the war, that I literally would not
> want to go on living--without having been
> a hero or the least bit eager to face
> death--if Germany had been defeated by
> the West, humiliated and its faith in
> itself broken to the point that it would
> have had to comply with and accept her
> enemies' philosophy of reason and ration-
> ality? Granted that that had happened,
> that the Entente powers had gained a
> quick and brilliant victory and that the
> world had been liberated from the German
> "nightmare," and the German spirit of
> protest, that the imperium of civiliza-
> tion had come into its own and now smugly
> reigned supreme with no opposition: the
> result would have been a special kind of
> Europe that would be a bit ludicrous, some-
> what dull and affable, trivial and perverse,
> feminine and elegant, a Europe already
> somewhat all too 'human' and somewhat
> intimidatingly persuasive and loudmouthed
> democratic, a Europe of the tango and two-
> step mentality,* a Europe of business

---

*Mann's description of what Europe would be like after a victory by the West echoes some scenes in his past works. The feminine-elegant world accurately re-flects the fastidious Thomas Buddenbrook. Tonio Kröger, like all Mannian heroes a lover of serious music, would hate the tango and two-step as he did his embarrassing prediciment on the dance floor as a young boy. The hero of <u>Tristan</u> expressed similar views. In his letter to the businessman Herr Klöterjahn, Detlev Spinell

and pleasure à la Edward the Seventh.
. . . an amusing Europe through and
through. . . .[1]

One wonders about such hyperbolic assertions,
especially since they originate from a person as
orderly and controlled as Thomas Mann. But these observations were not the result of a sudden burst of
passion; an enormous expenditure of research and effort
went into their formulation. Mann devoted nearly two
and a half years to this work, and from his son, Klaus,
we learn of the strain the author was under and how,
with bleak seriousness, he remained grimly confident
of Germany's chances for victory:

> He concealed his misgivings and qualms,
> if there were any, somewhere at the bottom
> of his heart.
> This wartime father seems estranged and
> distant, essentially different from the
> father I have known before and after those
> years of struggle and bitterness. The
> paternal physiognomy that looms up when
> I recall that period, seems devoid of the
> kindness and irony which both inseparably
> belong to his character. The face I visual-
> ize looks severe and somber--a proud and
> nervous brow with sensitive temples and
> sunken cheeks. Curiously enough, it is
> a "bearded" face, a long, haggard oval
> framed by a hard prickly beard. He never
> wore a beard, though except once in Tölz
> for a few weeks or months. However, this
> martial caprice must have considerably
> impressed me. The wartime father is
> bearded.[2]

According to Erich Heller, Mann conducts his argument in the Observations "with passionate pedantry,"[3]
and Henry Hatfield finds that the author obeys the
Goethean injunction, "know thyself," with painful and
almost embarrassing conscientiousness: "It is a repetitious, confused, wordy book, marked by that pseudo-
profundity to which German intellectuals so often in-
cline when they discuss politics, and by the reckless

---

called him dull and stupid and predicted that his son
would be tone-deaf.

manipulation of such antitheses as culture and civilization, nature and 'spirit.'"[4]

This 600 page polemic comes as a grotesque surprise to the reader who thinks of Thomas Mann as the chronicler of decadence, art and pathology. That Thomas Mann can also be the righteous, bitter and outraged political conservative who writes this book seems, at first, incredible; and one might well be inclined to pass it all off as a passionate and patriotic stage in his life. But such is not the case at all! This work was not the product of a momentary crisis or a flash of emotion quickly formulated and lacking in depth. It _is_ patently an extension of Thomas Mann's same attitudes regarding life and people as in the past and held with the same self-sustaining fervor. Essentially, his declarations here constitute an attitude reflecting the same inner tensions and hostilities of the Mannian artist in his relationship to the middle-class, unartistic world.

Written during the holocaust of World War I, the _Observations of a Non-Political Man_ are Mann's literary defense of Germany against the propaganda attacks of the Western Allies. In this prolix work Mann inveighs against the Western spirit of politics and democracy. The result is a violent tirade couched in broad stereotypes and generalities--Germany, France, England, Democracy, Progress--that possess little regard for differences within a whole nation. Royalist tendencies in France, for example, and socialistic trends in Germany are as blithely disregarded as is the fact that many French and English are sensitive artists with a deep appreciation of music and culture and that Germany has among her own people a vast number of philistines and insensitive materialists hostile to her art. The First World War is viewed by Mann as Germany's great struggle to preserve her individuality and freedom against the leveling forces of democracy: "This war is essentially a new explosion, the most magnificent perhaps, and, as some believe, the last of the ancient German fight against the mentality of the West just as the fight of the Roman world was waged against obstinate Germany" (XII, 48).

Mann feels it is not Germany's task or fate to realize political ideas: "The spirit of politics, contrary to the nature of the German, is by logical necessity anti-German because of its political nature" (XII, 30). The German people, Mann confesses with supreme conviction, will _never_ be able to flourish in a con-

161

trivance as unnatural and impersonal as political democracy: "He [the German] will never comprehend 'life'
in terms of society; he will never place the social
problem above the moral one, the inner experience. We
are not a social people . . ." (XII, 35). A social
people thinks in terms of political figures and forces;
but one is either concerned with the welfare of others,
that is, one is either a political person or one is
not, and the belief in the efficacy of politics is the
belief in the validity of democracy. However, such
thinking is not possible for the German who finds an
"eternally true antithesis between music and politics
. . ." (XII, 32). The German draws a distinction between spirit and politics: "Spirit is not politics.
. . . The difference between spirit and politics is
the same as that between culture and civilization,
soul and society, freedom and suffrage, art and literature; and the German character is culture, soul, freedom, art and not civilization, society, suffrage, litera
ture" (XII, 31). Mann looks at the Anglo-French concept of international democratic middle class with
bitterness and contempt, indignation and horror; he
finds it responsible for all the misfortune in the
world: "Germany's enemy in the intellectual, instinctive, pernicious and deadliest sense is the pacifistic,
virtuous, republican Rhetor-Bourgeois and fils de la
Révolution . . ." (XII, 32). Without mincing words,
Mann vents his anger at the republican's aggressiveness
and doctrinary intolerance in trying to promote humanity, liberalism and international brotherhood; he also
lashes out along the way with virulent obloquy and
denunciation against the Anglo-French conception of
reason, virtue, progress, freedom, equality, brotherly
love, Rousseauism, and Enlightenment. The author's
view of the United States is also interesting. Sharing Schopenhauer's opinion of America as an uninviting
place, he finds it to be an ochlocracy which, "not to
mention abject utilitarianism, ignorance, bigotry, con-
ceit, crudity and simple-minded worship of women, has,
as the order of the day, slavery and mistreatment of
negroes, lynch-laws, assassinations that go unpunished,
brutal gunfights, open mockery of justice and the law,
repudiation of public debts, revolting political ex-
propriation of neighboring provinces, an ever increasin
rule by the mob and then more of the same" (XII, 129).
The special term which Mann coins for the spokesman of
these "cultures" is the Zivilisationsliterat.*

In contrast to England and France, the nations of the Zivilisationsliterat, Germany is not a land of literature, but rather a mute and inarticulate country whose culture is musical, irrational, and inwardly oriented. Mann asserts that Germany does not produce men of letters or skillful debaters, but rather men in whom depth of feeling and musical experience replace beautiful phrases and oratorical brilliance.

Thomas Mann's great fear is that after a victory by the West the more profound culture of Germany will drown in the democratic flood-tide: "Whoever would attempt to transform Germany into a bourgeois democracy pure and simple in the Roman and Western sense, would deprive her of her best and weightiest quality, of her problematic character--which is the very essence of her nationality" (XII, 54). The mob is, to Thomas Mann, the greatest single threat to Germany, and if the Allies were to impose Western notions of progress and democracy on Germany, the result would be a mobocracy, a leveling of Germany's culture, and, above all, the end of music: " Finis musicae. . . . Progress from music to democracy . . ." (XII, 39). The only means by which to win out over this tendency lies in conservatism, which, according to Mann's definition, is this: "To be conservative means to want to keep Germany German" (XII, 262). Consequently, a truly European peace can only be won if Germany is victorious: "The peace of Europe should not be international, but supranational, it should be a German peace and not a democratic one. The peace of Europe can be based only on the victory and might of the supranational people, of the people who call as their own the highest, most universal traditions, the richest cosmopolitan endowment, and the most profound feeling of European responsibility" (XII, 207).

In addition to his main line of argumentation some peripheral points which Thomas Mann brings in for substantiation of his position border on the shrill and reveal the mounting anger he feels for his cause. He reminds us of the gladiator of God and righteousness, Hieronymus of Gladius Dei, who let his rage guide the

---

*This term has been translated in various ways: Ententophile intellectual, champion of civilization, progressive intellectual.

course of his argument. General Moltke, for example, is quoted in order to demonstrate that France under the guise of freedom, justice and humanity has been an aggressor nation throughout European history, especially where German territory is concerned. Reiterating his remarks from his article of 1914, Thoughts in War, Mann claims love of peace and warrior virtue are compatible traits in the German because his soldierliness does not originate in a mania for glory and is not an expression of an audacious, bravura-like desire to brawl or to attack, as is that of the French, who fundamentally are a much more warlike people than the Germans. Mann goes on to criticize the French mistreatment of German prisoners of war in the German colonies in Africa.

But the most embarrassing and incredible portions of the book are when Thomas Mann attempts to beatify the great bloodbath of 1914 to 1918: "Everyone knows and feels that there is a mystical element in war: it is the same element that belongs to all the basic forces of life, procreation and death, religion and love" (XII, 464). The First World War is viewed as a monumental event in human history and a time of greatness. It is "a time which has the same function as death personified: setting things right in spite of all confusion, elucidating and defining; a time which teaches us what we were and what we are and which grants us firmness and discretion under torment--Why should we not have a right to call such a time great!" (XII, 467-468). And the bloody sacrifices in this war will not have been in vain if one only insists on a glorification of war, death and ideals. One must insist on the great beauty of purpose in war, for it would not be "humane to take away from widows and mothers the consolation that those whom they sacrificed fell on the battlefields for a great cause" (XII, 466). Furthermore, Mann reports, the grim war in the trenches is not without its blessings: "I am again opening the letter of a young reserve lieutenant from the front in Flanders, otherwise a student and a poet, and glean from its contents something which staggered me so when I first looked at it. 'In the face of this immense predominance of death,' he writes, 'with this complete helplessness in the heat of combat for days and nights on end . . . the individual becomes joyful, not disheartened; one is so completely free of all cares, so free from the earth, hopeless, yet untroubled'" (XII, 458). Thus war, surprisingly, possesses an abundance of positive aspects--camaraderie, simplicity of pur-

pose, fulfillment; and it frees the mind of cumbersome
concerns and responsibilities. It is even responsible,
Mann reports, for a new appreciation of belles lettres:
"'Life,' declares my correspondent, had not left him
any time for the study of literature; only during the
war did he find the necessary leisure time for that.
War is indeed more humane and congenial to culture then
than 'life,' namely the professional life and a life
of peace" (XII, 462). Then, the author even goes so
far as to draw an invidious comparison between death
and the miracle of birth: "I have seen men die and
men being born and I know that the second event can
surpass by far the first in mystical frightfulness.
If the horrors of war make one's hair stand on end,--
well, so my hair once stood on end when there once occurred birth pangs of thirty-six hours of duration.
That was not human, it was hellish, and as long as
there are similar things, there can be war for all I
care" (XII, 464).

Mann's sentiment during the war should be compared
with his own short-lived and painful military career.
After having served approximately four months, he was
discharged at the end of the year 1900 on account of
a tendon inflammation in his ankle. The whole experience was, as his letters at that time attest, tinged
with irritation, disgust, gloom, and lamentation, but,
of course, Mann as a raw recruit was subject to the
tyranny of his superiors and, unlike his unbound of-
ficer-protagonists, in no position to play the role of
the aristocrat. At this point the reader may perhaps
recall that the artistically inclined army officer
appears a number of times in Mann's works: Tonio
Kröger, The Infant Prodigy, A Gleam, The Blood of the
Walsungs, and most important, of course, as René von
Throta in Buddenbrooks and Klaus Heinrich in Royal
Highness. These are certainly significant figures for
Mann as the militant author of this so-called "Non-
Political" work, but his position is not difficult to
comprehend if one accepts the soldier as an epitome of
stoicism, isolation, suffering, self-sacrifice or, in
short, as an image of the heroic artist himself. In
the author's mind at least the artist merges into one:
"Are they not completely symbolic connections which bind
art and war together? At least it has seemed to me that
it is not the worst artist who recognizes the portrait
of the soldier in himself."[5]

In tones rich in pathos Mann describes two casual-
ties of trench warfare whom he encountered on the

streets of Munich. One veteran had lost an arm, the
other his sight. The thought of being blind had always seemed to Mann to be the most horrible of fates;
it had always been incomprehensible to him how one could
bear to lead a life of blindness.* "Later, I learned,
to be sure, that my unlimited pity was exaggerated,
indeed, unsuitable. Blind people, I heard, were mostly
mild, composed, cheerful persons; deafness was a far
more embittering defect and deformed one's character,
whereas blindness tended to create the opposite effect"
(XII, 474). Thomas Mann actually makes a virtue of
blindness as he cites the remarks of the one who was
blinded while a middle-aged man:

> After a short period of grief, the man
> declared, his attitude had improved greatly,
> not only towards that time immediately
> following his blindness, but also towards
> the earlier time, the time before. He
> felt that the darkness was good for his
> nerves. He had gained peace of mind and
> harmony. . . . If he were to be honest,
> he would have to say: his misfortune also
> had its exceptionally light side, if he
> might express himself in such a way . . .
> to come right out and say it he had no
> desire to get his sight back.
>   That is, as I said, the actual utterance
> of a person who had lost his vision. Now,
> in the war, I have heard that blinded sol-
> diers are the merriest among all the patients
> in military hospitals. They scuffle with
> each other, they throw their glass eyes at
> each other. (XII, 475)

Finally, the reader of the Observations is en-
joined not to forget that the carnage of the great war
can be favorably contrasted to the horrors of peace
time. Before the war suffering and misery was a way
of life for a great number of people: Sicilian sulphur
miners and East-end slum children perished wretchedly,
shameless injustices went unpunished, the ordeals of

---

*In psychiatry, losing one's sight is symbolic
for castration; as the penalty for a sexual crime, incest, castration represents atonement without the total
destruction of the person.

illness, intemperance, passion, grief, old age and bitter death were daily phenomena. (XII, 476)

If we honestly visualize the horrible slaughter of the First World War, the glosses and glorification of war in the Observations come forth as a distorted, over-simplified illusion that simply defies the imagination. Such a sophomoric stand from a forty-three year old future Nobel prize winner in literature compels the critic to find an explanation for Mann's rigidly based attitude.

The task is not made easier by Mann's own bewilderment regarding this work: "this hard-pressed and painstaking artistic work, this slice of German thought, not scholastic philosophy, which I scarcely understood while I was writing it,"[6] is a statement that reveals only that the author was driven by a compelling desire to find his own values and wishes in the international cataclysm.

If we wish to find some rationale behind Mann's ponderous political moralizing, we must look at his most deeply held convictions. An important key to the understanding of the Observations is Mann's emphasized relationship to and association with music. For him, his homeland Germany had become the leading identification of the rapture and gratification he received from listening to music. Music was not something intellectually conditioned nor was it to be considered at any time a mild or indifferent experience, for music, we recall, created in him a high state of tension and turbulence which, in his works, acts as an automatic stimulus-response of incest and sexual excitement, parricide and sexualized hate.

When Mann thinks of music his mind is focused on one composer: Richard Wagner. His passion for Wagner's music crystallized for him as a young man: "I say 'passion,' because simpler words such as 'love' and 'enthusiasm' really would not describe the matter" (XII, 73). Mann characterizes this period as a "lonely and irregular youth, a youth seeking the world and death-- how it sipped the magic potion of these metaphysics [Schopenhauer's The World as Will and Idea], whose deepest essence is eroticism and in which I recognized the intellectual source of the Tristan music" (XII, 72). Wagner's Tristan and Isolde is the acme of all music. We learn from Klaus Mann that whenever his father sat down at the piano, he always improvised a motif from

Tristan.[7] This operatic work with its obviously sexual implications, both in story and melody, and its Oedipal love triangle continued, as did other works from Wagner's pen, to produce a hectic and skittish state in the author. In fact, Wagner's music, as articulated by Nietzsche, became the definitive and final word on art to Thomas Mann: "All my concepts of art and artistic greatness were forever determined or, if not determined, at least colored and influenced by it [Nietzsche's interpretation of Wagner] . . ." (XII, 74). "Even today, when a pertinent phrase, some fragmentary chord from Wagner's musical cosmos meets my ear, I am drunk with joy" (XII, 80). The agony of pleasure in music helps to explain how Mann makes the jump to politics, for he profoundly fears for the safety of German music in the event of a Western victory.

Germany is viewed by Mann as the soul of Europe, the focal point of music and culture. As such, it is allied, in Mann's own words, to the mother; and the author's attitude toward his homeland is akin to that of a son to his mother: "In Germany's soul the intellectual antitheses of Europe are decided in the maternal and rebellious sense" (XII, 54). France and England, by contrast, represent the non-artistic sphere of civilization which is oriented around business and materialism: "Speculation, the food profiteer--which mentality does he represent if not that of democracy which has set up money, profit and business as the highest values" (XII, 241). And Mann also speaks hopefully of a victory of the nobility of the soul over the spirit of enterprise (XII, 343). Germany, the sphere of the mother and art, is at war with the father world of business: England and France. The gauntlet had already been thrown down in Mann's earliest tales by Hanno against Thomas Buddenbrook, Hieronymus against Herr Blüthenzweig, and Detlev Spinell against Herr Klöterjahn. And from the following citation we are reminded of Tristan, where the impotent Detlev Spinell is confronted by the virile businessman's healthy baby, Anton Klöterjahn, Jr.: "For civilization and virility, civilization and bravery, after all is said and done, produce no antithesis" (XII, 463). The divided and suffering nature of the artist--and Germany--is not a part of the monolithic, unconscious, life-driven organization and progeny of the Western nations. Sexual potence is on the side of the Ententophile intellectual who affirms only one form of the elementary experiences of life--and that is sex: "Here his veneration, his liberality and tolerance are completely without limits,

168

one must acknowledge that. Sexual love and political philanthropy, that is, democracy, are ultimately connected within him" (XII, 465). Needless to say, the Zivilisationsliterat, like Thomas Buddenbrook, Herr Klöterjahn and von Beckerath, has no appreciation or understanding of Wagner's music--not a single note (XII, 122), for theirs is an uncomplicated fulfillment of the active sex drive in contrast to the forbidden and mysterious Oedipal theme found in Wagner's music and libretti.

Translated into such configurations of language and subjective purpose, we can see, without stretching the imagination, how Mann could find a positive side to the ordeals of war. In his pathetic explanation of the fate of the soldier blinded in war, Mann's sole concern was the preservation of the sense of hearing. Blindness could be tolerated, but the loss of hearing, which simultaneously meant being deprived of Wagner's exotic music, would be too great a cross to bear.

As far back as 1903 in Tristan Mann allows his heroes to state their preference for the dark; these figures stand in direct opposition to the people of the light (Lichtmenschen), the unproblematic types who are successful in their struggle for mastery in life. And we may also recall Hieronymus (Gladius Dei) who was likened to a shadow passing across the sunny sky, Lobgott Piepsam's (The Way to the Cemetery) threat to the crowd--to hurl them into darkness--, Detlef's (The Hungry) preference for the darkness, Tonio Kröger's distrust of the velvet blue sky of Italy,* and Gustav Aschenbach's feverish state in the fierce glaring sunlight of Venice.** The dark is thus a refuge, a sym-

---

*Thomas Mann's original intention was to call Hans Hansen, Tonio Kröger's boyhood friend and antipode, Tage. This relatively uncommon Scandinavian name represents an unusual designation for a German. Perhaps its real significance for Mann was that it also refers to the time when it is light, being the plural form for the word day in German.

**Aschenbach muses on the effect the sun has on him: "Has it not been written that the sun beguiles our attention from things of the intellect to focus it on things of the senses?" (VIII, 490).

bolic description of the death-wish, a furtive and clandestine sphere where the hero can let his fantasy soar to ever greater heights and can safely indulge in music, sexual play and self-gratification. Only the sense of hearing is indispensable. The people of the light, however, rely completely on their sense of sight for they are not the least bit musical.

Cum multis aliis, the representative of the Western powers is at home with high sounding rhetorical phrases. One recalls the nameless hero of Disillusionment, the prototype for the cultured German at odds with the Zivilisationsliterat, who complained bitterly about the great words which were a part of the pathetic atmosphere of pulpit rhetoric in his father's house.

But how is Thomas Mann able to make these associations on such a wide geographical basis? How can a Senator of Lübeck, which Mann's father was, be made a spokesman for countries at war with Germany? The answer lies in Mann's changed status as a renowned man of letters. In view of his new position as a leading and highly esteemed advocate of Germany's culture, it had become increasingly difficult for him now to direct his anger at the German middle class, as he did in his earlier works. Since, however, the hostility is still in force, he is compelled to shift ground in order to preserve his special dichotomy of intellect versus life. The German middle class, which now accepts the successful author, is no longer the immediate enemy. Consequently, the representatives of life are conveniently projected as images of Germany's war enemies; to justify the existence of remote hostile forces, he is forced to find a target beyond the borders of Germany as a necessary outlet for his feelings. The German middle class is thus assigned a peculiar and rehabilitated position in Mann's world. The renowned author is forced to count angels on the head of a pin so that he can prove the Germans are not philistines but rather a noble people essentially different from the bourgeois inhabitants of England and France (XII, 136-137). By associating the non-artistic businessman, the father, with the superficial French and English, Mann alienates him from the Teutonic maternal sphere of music and art in much the same way Detlev Spinell tried to come between Herr Klöterjahn and his wife Gabriele. Herr Klöterjahn, who has a penchant for English phrases, for example, also grew an English beard, and preferred English breakfasts. And in The Fight Between Jappe and Do Escobar, the puny Johnny Bishop came forth as an example of the braggart yet cowardly Englishman. Now, by associating the prosaic image of the father with the English, Mann gives vent to his resentment against those representatives of life who in their dilettantism hope to intrude into the sacred and inviolable maternal realm of art. Mann is frankly horrified at the possibility of German culture being encroached on by the prosaic forces of democracy that would pervade the maternal sphere with the bourgeois spirit of business, expediency, and practicality. Curiously, and cleverly, Mann now lands on familiar ground by equating the exacting standards of the German tradesman with a mirror image of the artist's own attitude towards his art. The German guild tradition is suddenly and soberly imbued with latent artistic qualities that characterize the whole German nation. The middle-class artisan's fidelity to his calling becomes symbolic of that paternal inheritance of guilt which exacts a toll of fulfillment and penance in the form of exhaustive toil. Thomas Buddenbrooks compulsive habits and Consul Kröger's stringent demands are now translated as external manifestations of the superior bourgeois-artist's need to work, suffer, and atone for his creations.

But in spite of his relentless attitude, Mann devoutly contradicts himself. He is not, as he repeatedly insists and as Tonio Kröger had categorically declared, a bourgeois manqué, but rather a proud craftsman above the middle class--an aristocrat to the core! What had been a rationalization for Tonio Kröger and other early protagonists becomes a parlor defense in the Observations. Mann engages in soaring mental gymnastics by his insistence on identifying himself, his culture, and his spirituality with the middle class of Germany that is now set apart and distinct from the commercialized, democratic bourgeoisie of the West.

Thomas Mann's own earliest recollections were of life in the upper class comfort of Lübeck. His family belonged to the patriciate of this Hanseatic city, and his father, Senator Mann, was among the foremost representatives of this aristocracy of wealth; and now in the Observations, Mann designates Thomas Buddenbrook, who was modeled after his father, as a co-regent of an aristocratic city democracy (XII, 72). The world which Mann knew as a child had a special existence removed from the crowd: "The bourgeoisie, and indeed the patriarchal, aristocratic bourgeoisie as a mood and feeling of life is my personal heritage" (XII, 139).

Another link in Mann's new claim to nobility is forged in his praise of Schopenhauer's philosophy, which he describes as a successful attempt to rescue the concept of guilt--an aristocratic concept (XII, 138). Mann also claims that Schopenhauer's loathing for democracy was based on his personal feeling of being an aristocrat (XII, 233). The aristocratic in the Mannian scheme of things is the principle of death (Todesprinzip) while the democratic originates in the forces of life.[8] And as the aristocratic attitude and sympathy with death is the guiding principle, so do cross, death, and the grave become its magic catchwords which lead, in turn to martyrdom, atonement and, ultimately, to a rebirth free of guilt.

Briefly, then, as self-styled aristocrats among men and nations, Mann and Germany are allied with death against the faithful followers of life, those unproblematic creatures who are able to live life without questioning it. The aristocratic attitude represents the withdrawal from the ties that bind, being the safeguard against submersion in the effacing flood of the abhorred masses. The aristocratic bearing contributes the means by which Mann and his protagonists are able to counteract feelings of worthlessness and alienation, engendered by a guilty conscience and temporarily cancelled by an assumption of superiority.

By his princely pose, Mann usurps an elevated aristocratic stature for himself while simultaneously debasing the image of the prosaic father. The aristocratic way of life with its good food, luxury, and leisure is never relinquished by Mann. His sensitive royal hero is carefully contrasted to the insensitive man of business just as the noble soul of Germany is compared to the coarse commercialism of Germany's enemies. Although Mann's own father was a highly respected Senator, he is unceremoniously lumped together with the unartistic middle class insofar as he was an elected representative of the people, and therefore, in no uncertain terms, a representative of democracy and a politician. But now the author confiscates from the father that aristocratic aspect of his background and brings it into harmony with his own lofty qualities as an artist. "The King is dead! Long live the King!" echoes through the work now. Mann both rejects and replaces his father; the artist is now king and the businessman has become an unwilling subject at the court of art. Thus, Tonio Kröger's claim as a bourgeois manqué has validity only in a symbolic way, not in the

external sense Mann would have us believe. True, the
wayward burgher who takes the path towards art has an
increased burden of guilt to bear, but the guilt incurred has its origins in father hatred, not in bourgeois transgressions. The artist abandons the bourgeoisie because he loathes it to the core; he flees
into the realm of artistic fantasy and the musical
sphere of the mother. By the same token, Mann general-
izes Germany as the profound musical realm of the
mother, the sphere of Liebestod, where sinful love and
blissful expiation of the concomitant guilt may be
experienced in an arpeggio of ecstasy; while the justifiable punishment, the final retaliation will be meted
out by the brutally powerful, paternal-like aggressiveness of the Western powers. And Germany, the essence
of beauty, "as expressed in me [Thomas Mann]" (XII, 31)
will be consumed in the purifying flames of a Götterdämmerung.

We can readily recall the implacable fury which
the early Mannian protagonists harbored against the
paternal representatives of life and yet how they desired punishment from the hands of these authorities.
A review of other works by Mann and his compounding of
earlier prejudices in the Observations demonstrates
that the overriding consideration in the author's
ambivalent attitude towards the bourgeoisie, whether
German, French, or English, is the wellspring of hostility which outweighs by far any feelings of genuine affection. From beginning to end, the object of his scorn
and derision is the massive, coarse, democratic-mercan-
tile world which constituted the sphere of the father.
Besides Buddenbrooks, where the revolution in the city
of Lübeck is described almost for the purpose of showing that the common people are basically ineffectual
and cowardly, or the scene in which the incredibly obtuse Grobleben (whose name means Coarse-life) acts
the embarrassing role of spokesman for the grain workers
at the christening of Hanno Buddenbrook, we have Baron
Harry in A Gleam, the gentleman with the spats in A
Railway Accident, Piero Medici in Fiorenza; Johnny
Bishop in The Fight Between Jappe and Do Escobar, the
common back-biting herd in Royal Highness, and the
narrator-hero's fear of the banal father world in the
sketch Death. But perhaps the best summation of Mann's
attitude is to be seen in his Picture Book for Well-
Behaved Children, which he and his brother Heinrich
composed for their younger siblings, Viktor and Carla
Mann, during their stay in Italy from 1895 to 1897.
This picture book contains numerous sketches with

MVTTER NATVR

DAS LÄBEN

174

accompanying text by the brothers. Two of them by
Thomas Mann, Das Läben (Life) and Mutter Natur (Mother
Nature), reveal that behind his attempt at humor there
is a deep-seated and uncompromising attitude. Although
written for their fifteen year old sister and six year
old brother, the picture book is really for grown-ups.
These sketches, so out of place in a book for young
children, demonstrate the early presence of Thomas
Mann's persevering antipathy to life. For here, as in
the Observations, he expends a considerable amount of
feeling for a dubious abstraction. In fact, the parallel between both works is striking, for it shows that
there has been no change in attitude at all from the
early malevolence towards life in the picture book to
the later declaration of hatred for life in the Observations: "It is impossible to be anything like a writer,
a fashioner of people, and thereby be indifferent to
people, unless it is that hatred and contempt of people
significantly become the creative principle" (XII, 448).

The World War, as analyzed in the Observations,
became just such a creative principle, carrying within
it vessels of form and content wich Mann could fill
with personal bile. It presented him with an opportunity for a sadistic release, an outlet for his pent-up
anger and resentment, and an excuse to return to the
open hostility of his earliest heroes. Their aggression, which was ever liable to focus indiscriminately
on an object, indeed, which tended to manufacture its
own victim, is paralleled in Mann's attack against
England and France. Under the guise of patriotism
Mann finds an outlet for his hostility by way of a
personal vendetta. His attitude again points up the
love-hate ambivalence, and his consistent inability to
love finds its corresponding fixation in sadistic aggression. What is indispensable in expressing this
conflict is a type, a stereotype, or a flat representation of a mental scheme. Thus, the whole culture of
the West and Germany is personified until it assumes
the form of something specifically tangible. The spade-
work for the artificial dichotomy of intellect versus
life and culture versus civilization had already been
evidenced in Mann's earlier works, in the splitting-off
process of character montage, and in the inability of
the hero to focus any genuine affection on an individual. In lashing out against a projected abstraction,
Mann is close in spirit to Lobgott Piepsam (The Way to
the Cemetery) who indiscriminately selected a vigorous
but unconcerned enemy in the person of the cyclist,
Leben; and then, without breaking stride, he blindly

and illogically turned his venom on the crowd which
gathered. For as one who was incapable of a permanent
human attachment free from doubt and cruelty, he found
it impossible to be thwarted in singing his hymn of
hate merely for lack of a victim.

Because of the author's pre-eminent concern with
death, he also views war as the special domain of the
creative writer. Consequently, he hails the outbreak
of the war with dithyrambic enthusiasm:

> How the hearts of poets immediately
> glowed when the war came about! And they
> thought they had loved peace. . . . Now
> they were singing of the war as if they
> were in poetic competition with each other,
> rejoicing with a deep surge of triumph.
> . . .
> Let's remember the beginning--those
> never to be forgotten first days when the
> great thing, that which was no longer
> thought possible, occurred! We had be-
> lieved in the war. . . . had in some way
> longed for it, felt deep in our heart that
> the world, our world, could no longer con-
> tinue.[9]

And Mann, as his reiterated assertions confirm,
feels equally buoyant and exultant at the collapse of
world peace, with which he was "fed up."[10] The war
was a "purging, a deliverance, and an enormous hope."[11]
It was an event in which Germany's entire youth and
beauty would enfold; yet, he simultaneously insists,
Germany had not wanted this war which had been unscrupu-
lously and shamefully instigated by business interests.[12]

The war becomes his personal and symbolic crusade.
While defending the profoundly, silent culture, that
is, while defending the quietistic and passive artistic
world against the national representatives of vigorous
life and practical affairs, he unleashes a fanatic attack on his opponents; and, as in the past, the provocation factor gains the upper hand in the passive artist
who goes searching for retaliation.* Mann's identifi-

---

*The author also sees in the world conflict the
end of an age, and in this respect his war confession
reiterates the spirit of Buddenbrooks, in which a

cation with war-time Germany drifts into the extremes
of masochism as he boasts of Germany's ability to suffer. Germany is a proud, even grateful, stoic for
whom suffering is an end in itself, and whom Mann,
paraphrasing the attitude of the Western powers, compares to a naughty child who will show goodness and
even gratitude for receiving punishment at the hands
of France and England (XII, 65).

Thus, The Observations are, à outrance, an exter-
nalized exposition of Thomas Mann's own inner conflicts
in the garb of political philosophy. Despite its apparent relevancy to historical events, this work is
little more than an apodictic extension of the repressed
fears and hostilities of Mann's previous fictional creations. With the advent of the great war, the fury that
lay bottled up within him (which since Tristan had only
found partial literary expression, as for example in
Gustav Aschenbach's dream orgy) finally encounters the
perfect climate for release. Though the hostility
against the father figure has been reversed by the repressive apparatus to a state of passivity and inac-
tion, it is all still there, concealed but at full
strength. The sexualized hate, welling up in all its
instinctual power, still demands an unmitigated degree
of satisfaction, destruction, and retaliation. For
this reason, there is still no real basis in his nature
for conciliation or reconciliation between the two
spheres of the artist and practical life. It all remains a one-sided struggle between Thomas Mann's subjectivity and the indifference of the father's world.

So the Observations of a Non-Political Man becomes
an outburst of fantastic proportions and one of Thomas
Mann's bitterest and most passionate works. But, it
should be added, Thomas Mann's rapture towards the war
was nothing unusual at the time; he was by no means the
only author to be swept along by the conflict. The
outbreak of the war was wildly and joyously acclaimed
by the foremost intellectuals and political leaders on
both sides of the conflict, among them Theodore Roosevelt. But whereas disenchantment with the aims of the
war soon affected most intellectuals, and they soon became disabused with assigning glory to the immense

---

pestilential death capped the dissolution of a world
which its hero despised.

slaughter, Thomas Mann managed to sustain his fervor during the entire conflict. Begun in November 1915, the Observations were only concluded in March 1918 and did not come out in print until a month before the end of the war. The next and obvious question concerns the long range effects of the convictions Mann set forth in the Observations. Critics are unanimous in the opinion that Mann's wartime book was essentially an isolated phenomenon and that he changed his mind, recanting his faith as he became more and more a friend of the West and its precepts of democracy. However, an examination of Mann's later works will put such critics' belief to the fullest test and will determine if we can truly ascribe such flexibility to an author who, in the prime of his life during the war, proclaimed his biased abstractions with such fanatic rigidity.

Frederick and the Grand Coalition

Mann's essay of 1915, Frederick and the Grand Coalition, is an artistic prelude to the Observations.* What Mann said in his great polemic on World War I is condensed in this portrait of the Prussian King. To Mann, the special problems confronting the artist and Germany during the First World War have their counterpart in those which Frederick and Prussia faced during the Seven Years' War. The author does not hesitate to draw the obvious political parallel between Saxony of 1756 and Belgium of 1914: "And Germany is today Frederick the Great. It is his fight, which we will wage to the end, which we have once again to wage. The coalition has changed slightly, but it is his Europe, the Europe allied in hate, that will not tolerate us nor him, the king."[13]**

Mann defends Frederick's invasion of neutral Saxony as he did Germany's violation of Belgium's neutrality--as a defensive measure to secure Prussia's

---

*The seeds for this essay had been germinating for a long time in Mann's mind; Aschenbach (Death in Venice) it may be recalled, was himself the author of a work on Frederick the Great.

**King August of Saxony stands here for Belgium's King Leopold, for his surprisingly stubborn resistance prevented a quick victory by Prussia.

flank in the war to come: "That Frederick began the war is no proof against the fact that it was basically a defensive war, for he was hemmed in, and he possibly would have been attacked in the early part of the following year."[14]

The resultant hue and cry, similar to the world's indignation at the rape of Belgium in 1914, is disposed of with sarcasm and even callousness by the author:

> Europe cried out as if from one throat, it was dreadful to hear . . . in its [public's] eyes the abrupt march into Saxony so to speak during the most profound period of peace meant such a shameless iniquity, an armed attack so unexpected and so repellent that no one could remain calm. To rape a neutral country, a good, guiltless country, one that was not the least bit aware of such brutality and which had quite recently reduced its military forces to a touchingly peaceful figure, to barely 22,000 men, so that [Count] Brühl could bewig himself even more and could buy himself more carriages and perfume bottles. It was intolerable, it broke one's heart, and it was not right that this snuff-taking Satan trampled with his jackboots everything called morality, justice, humanity, everything that ennobles life and the faith which is a necessity for an honest man. And Europe continued to scream, without catching its breath. . . . (X, 118)

Mann thus stands fully behind Frederick, the naughty child (X, 113), in the latter's opposition to the superior power threatening his Prussia. We recall Mann's belief in the <u>Observations</u> that a Western victory would result in an effeminate "tango and two-step" kind of Europe and that the land of the demonic, Germany, was engaged in a life-and-death struggle to prevent such a calamity. Well, so was the demonic "alter Fritz" ("Old Fred") who fought to the bitter end against the feminine century of the French (X, 92). For, as Mann points out, it is an age ruled by women: Madame Pompadour in France, Czarina Elizabeth in Russia, and Empress Maria Theresa in Austria. Yet the war is a time of greatness (X, 127) when the pent-up demonic forces are finally given the opportunity for a showdown struggle with the enemy. Frederick, we find, disdains the refined methods of attack and defense then current among the strategists of Europe in favor of "The battle at all costs! Force the enemy to fight! 'Battles are there to decide the issue.' Attack, Attack! Attaquez donc toujours!" (X, 86). His passion is the bayonet charge, a maneuver which he perfected: "Don't shoot indiscriminately, above all not too soon! At twenty, at ten paces from the enemy, 'give him a full salvo right in the face and follow it up at once by sticking a bayonet in his ribs'" (X, 86). Frederick, who apparently has war in his blood (X, 110), is close in spirit to Thomas Mann's Pyrrhic victors who wantonly provoked their adversaries. He is, in fact, really asking for trouble and probable defeat by insisting on starting the war against the advice of his generals; they are appalled at his insistence and simply cannot believe their ears.

Frederick, as developed by Mann, is a carbon copy of the ambivalent artist. He is a man of the night--as opposed to the Lichtmensch--who often gets up at a time when normal people might go to bed. Possessed by a fury to work and to accomplish, he leads an ascetic existence; Mann compares Frederick and his castle to a monk in a monastery. What the sanatorium Einfried is to Detlev Spinell, Sanssouci is to Frederick: a place of refuge from a natural life. The capricious age of French influences in which he lived could not understand his excessive misogyny (X, 90). He is fanatically reserved, has and wants no one to confide in, at times even toys with the idea of suicide. The opposite sex not only leaves him phlegmatic, but he hates, scorns and refuses to tolerate women in his presence. Yet, like Tonio Kröger in Italy, he descends as a youth into debauchery and sexual excess until, in typical all or nothing fashion, the pendulum of repression swings to the other side. As a very young man, Frederick declared that he only wanted to gain gratification from women, but as he grew older, he despised them. "Never once did he love" (X, 91). His choice of female, too, is typical: a forbidden woman, either intended for another or considered taboo. His love affair with Countess Orselska incurs the jealousy of King August II of Saxony, and his relationship with Baroness von Wreech is at the expense of her husband's feelings. Baron von Wreech later refuses to recognize his wife's child as his. Thus, both in love and war, "He had to burden himself with guilt, in order to be able to bring to light the guilt of his opponents . . ." (X, 117).

Frederick, who scribbled verse, played the flute, and furthered the arts, was boundless also in his hatred of the common herd. Although he fought and suffered in a superhuman way as he went year in and year out from one battle to the next, breathing the dust of his troops, he saw only the mob in people: "It remains incomprehensible why he, overwhelmed by contempt, continued to work so monstrously for this rabble . . ." (X, 133). "Cette race maudite" was Frederick's term for all humanity.

Frederick not only stands for the artist figure in royal disguise, but as the tarnished and highly unpromising youth who overcomes the opposition of the world he also represents the perfect exemplar of the ugly-duckling motif. This motif is clearly established at the beginning of Mann's work where the young Frederick, as a Crown Prince--at times elegant, occasionally dissolute, fearful, free-thinking, bourgeois, lazy, frivolous--becomes King. What were vices in the eyes of his father turn into virtues as soon as he is crowned ruler. And when he mounts the throne, he gains his revenge on a world that did not respect him and on a father who apparently despised him. To demonstrate how Frederick repudiates the oppressive world of his father, Thomas Mann quotes Shakespeare where Prince Hal repudiates the influence of the old roué Falstaff in Henry IV: "I know thee not, old man,"--to Mann "The most beautiful passage perhaps in all of Shakespeare's works" (X, 78). The fledgling prince of Prussia has now, as king, assumed the role of the omnipotent father. But he is not a revolutionary innovator. Instead, exactly like his father, he turns into a passionate soldier who would not think of weakening the military foundation upon which his father had erected a powerful state: "His conservatism goes so far that he even abstains from changing the positions in the line of command" (X, 79).

Frederick therefore becomes another of Thomas Mann's stoic heroes, a frail and oppressed figure whose triumph is made all the more remarkable by the extra suffering he needs to surmount his many handicaps. He is the heroic genius who faces a host of foes and wins despite overwhelming odds, a genius who "was not permitted to be a philosopher, but who had to be king so that the earthly mission of a great people could be fulfilled" (X, 135).

Just as Frederick duplicates by his talents and

daring the career of the Mannian artist, so does Frederick's struggle against the "monster alliance," as Mann calls the coalition of nations against Prussia, reflect the artist's and Germany's trials against the unholy alliance of the Western powers in 1914. How can this be the case, inasmuch as Austria, Germany's ally in the World War, was Prussia's foe in the Seven Years' War? Thomas Mann overcomes this disparity in the person of Prince Wenzel Kaunitz, Austria's foreign minister. In Kaunitz, besides Maria Theresa the only other prominent figure in the essay, we see the self-same characteristics that marked the antagonist of Mann's earlier works. Blue-eyed, almost English in appearance, Kaunitz is described as an eccentric and hypochondriac with a compulsion for cleanliness rivaling that of Thomas Buddenbrook. He is a slender, stiff, intense person who powders his wig with meticulous care in order to conceal the wrinkles of worry on his brow. Like Consul Kröger, who wears a flower in his buttonhole, Kaunitz adorns his coat with a diamond star. Mann's sketch of Kaunitz is not flattering. He is mean and petty, pedestrian and deceitful. But he is presented, nevertheless, as a noteworthy opponent--tenacious in his pursuit of plans and possessed by one single thought: to crush Prussia and the "evil" ruler in Potsdam. To accomplish this Kaunitz sets out to form an alliance between Austria and France--an ingenious and incredible idea, considering the antipathy and jealousy between these two powers at that time. In Paris, where he was chargé d'affaires, Kaunitz goes about his business with remarkable tact and perseverence (X, 105), in much the same way as every Mannian business man from Thomas Buddenbrook on has pursued his calling.* While fostering his intrigues against Frederick, he lives luxuriously in the company of several women. Even in this respect, the virile Kaunitz is contrasted to the ascetic and misogynistic hero of Prussia. Finally, Kaunitz's persistent whisperings find their way, with the desired result, to King Louis of France, and the grand coalition, which could have been baptized with the name Kaunitz, is put into effect. Thus the obnoxious characteristics of Kaunitz are aligned with the French in a preconceived Mannian image of the opposing world which posits a punishing prosaic father figure as

---

*The word "business" itself is emphasized by Mann in his exposition of Kaunitz's plot.

the unsavory coalition confronting Prussia.

England too, it turns out, is a questionable and weak ally, who pursues her own business interests in the New World and who, at a critical time, leaves Prussia in the lurch by cutting off her financial support.

Historically speaking, Empress Maria Theresa is Frederick's real opponent in the Seven Years' War, and although her hatred for the Prussian King is excessive and personal, as Mann shows, Frederick's own feelings toward her are an expression, for the most part, of his general deep antipathy towards all women. The animosity between these two is, as Erich Heller notes, somewhat toned down by Mann himself in his treatment of the Empress: "Of Maria Theresa, above all, Thomas Mann paints an exquisite miniature, forceful, humorous, and tender."[15] The implication is that Maria Theresa is a prisoner of the machinations of her chargé d'affaires. Although her hatred towards Frederick is pointed out, it is the Kaunitzian conspiracy to destroy the hero that is stressed in this essay.

The Oedipal triangular arrangement falls surprisingly well into place again in Frederick and the Grand Coalition, a work where one would least expect to find it. Frederick, Kaunitz, and Maria Theresa form the familiar triad: the business man and titled "father," the exotic Queen "mother," and the artist King Frederick who is closer to the Queen in station and affinity. When we consider that the World War represented a kind of sexual release for Thomas Mann, where combat was equivalent to the sex act,* then we have also in Frederick's war a symbolic expression of the father-son rivalry for the possession of the mother. At this point, we need only to recall the naked brutality and sadism in the culmination of the orgy in Aschenbach's dream in Death in Venice, where the war-like forces of sexual impulses are unleashed, not with a feeling of ensuing tenderness but with a degree of violence that transforms human sensibilities into animal force, death,

---

*Sexual union, we recall, was viewed as an engagement in combat in The Will to Happiness and, through reversal, in The Fight Between Jappe and Do Escobar.

and destruction.

A Man and His Dog

Of all of Thomas Mann's fictional works none seems to be less a part of the artist problem than A Man and His Dog, a simple but impressive description of a man's close relationship with his pet. Yet there are two distinct levels in this work, the graphic and animated depiction of a canine personality and a critical attitude toward the world. Behind the plot level one quickly senses an undertone of the ambivalence and evasive duality of the artist: "Extraordinary creature! So close a friend and yet so remote."[16] Throughout the story, the artist narrator expresses both a negative appraisal and a sentimental affection for his pet. The dog, Bashan, is thoroughly personified, endowed with human traits and behavior that affect his owner in a singular manner; in fact, it is the impact Bashan makes on his master that is central to the story. Clearly, Bashan is more than a dog. When because of a disease, he has to be kept in an animal hospital, the artist's reaction reaches a degree of emotional intensity usually reserved for two intimate friends: "My health suffered, gradually I approached the condition of Bashan in his cage; and the moral reflection occurred to me that the bonds of sympathy were probably more conducive to my own well-being than to the selfish independence for which I had longed" (VIII, 598).

But this tone of affection by the artist is more than counter-balanced by frequent negative and disparaging remarks about Bashan. An emphasis of the dog's inanities runs like a leitmotif throughout the story. Most of the time, Bashan's actions are characterized as comic or pathetic, light-headed, stupid, sometimes disturbing and unwanted. When he is first acquired by his master, he is the picture of wretchedness and an object for ridicule from the neighbors. His frenzied behavior, at times senseless, is nearly always ineffectual, and his clumsy and ungainly actions, especially on the hunt, nearly always climax in failure.

Representing life in all its banality, Bashan is an object of envy and disdain, even of repugnance by his owner. It is especially unnerving to the artist when Bashan meets another dog: "My excursions with Bashan have made me witness hundreds of such encounters, or I might better say, forced me to be an embarrassed spectator at them" (VIII, 554). Or: "Embarrassments

multiply when both of them are free of the leash. I
do not relish describing the scene: it is one of the
most painful and equivocable imaginable. . . . We are
now within twenty paces, the suspense is frightful"
(VIII, 556-557). The ensuing tumult when the dogs are
engaged in combat is beyond the ken of the owner: "I
speak of these things only to show how under stress of
circumstances the character of a near friend may reveal itself as strange and foreign. It is dark to me,
it is mysterious; I observe it with head-shaking and
can only dimly guess, what it may mean. And in all
other respects I understand Bashan so well . . ."(VIII,
558). The violence of the encounter and the reaction
of the artist take us back to the shattering dream orgy
of Gustav Aschenbach, who, like Bashan, is hypnotized
by the pull of his instincts. "He is under a spell,
he is bound to the other dog, they are bound to each
other with some obscure and equivocal bond which may
not be denied. We are now within two paces" (VIII,
557). In yielding to the intolerable pressure of his
drives, Aschenbach became a helpless victim of his
desires, and the result, the Bacchic orgy, resembled
a sadistic explosion of repressed forces. Similarly,
Bashan's violent fight with another dog becomes confused
to some extent in his master's mind with his concept of
sexual activity, pointing up to him, as it does, the
uncontrollable behavior of the lower class in its pursuit of sensual pleasure. The profound sense of uneasiness which strikes the artist on viewing his dog
in combat reminds him of the perils and the unsavoriness
of direct involvement with life.

The hunt is also viewed as a searching out of
sexual satisfaction. Bashan's frenetic pursuit of the
hare is felt vicariously by the artist as a sensual
experience:

> In it [Bashan's howl in scenting the hare]
> rage and rapture mingle, desire and the
> ecstasy of despair. How often have I
> heard it from Bashan! It is passion it-
> self, deliberate fostered passion, drunk-
> enly revelled in, shrilling through our
> woodland scene; and every time I hear it
> near or far, a fearful thrill of pleasure
> shoots through my limbs. Rejoicing that
> Bashan will come into his own today, I
> hasten to his side, to see the chase if
> I can; when it roars past me, I stand
> spellbound--though the futility of it

is clear from the first--and look on with
an agitated smile on my face. (VIII, 601)*

And when the hare escapes, the artist cannot resist
mocking and teasing Bashan about the futility of his
ridiculous exertions.**

Bashan's relationship to his master is consistent
with the dichotomy between the representatives of life
and the artist figures throughout Mann's works. Originally named Lux, Bashan stands for the Lichtmensch
and consequently, heralds the coming of the Zivilisationsliterat Settembrini, the Rhetor-Bourgeois and
ridiculous windbag of The Magic Mountain, who is referred to as Lucifer (Bringer of Light). Like the
serious-minded Consul Kröger, Tonio's father, with
the flower in his buttonhole, Bashan is similarly
adorned by a flower in his collar. His handsome appearance bespeaks virility, a characteristic which fits
the father figure and Rhetor-Bourgeois and sets him
apart from the Mannian artist. Especially small for
a proper pointer, Bashan represents the father cut down
to size, and, curiously enough, although a pointer,
Bashan is afraid of the water.*** And Thomas Mann also

---

*The narrator's pleasure in looking on at the
passionate activity of the representative of life reminds us of the many early voyeuristic heroes, but in
its present context, it anticipates Hans Castorp's
and Joseph's reaction to the uninhibited sexual license
in the sanatorium (The Magic Mountain) and in Sheol
(Joseph and His Brothers).

**On one instance, the master sarcastically calls
Bashan "My Hero!" The same remark was applied to the
ridiculous, but imperious delegate of life in The Railway Accident, the gentleman who wore spats. Just as
the master constantly gazes at Bashan, so too did the
narrator in The Railway Accident look at this gentleman:
"I could not look at him enough" (VIII, 418). Significantly, this gentleman with the spats is traveling with
his dog, an immensely handsome brute, whom he illegally
takes with him into his sleeping compartment.

***This attitude openly contradicts the immense
thrill the artist himself has when viewing an expanse
of water: "For my part, I freely admit that the sight
of water in whatever form or shape is my most lively

186

goes to great lengths to show Bashan's lack of stoicism in any matter dealing with a physical hurt, no
matter how slight.

The author's reflective experiences stand as an
opposing purpose to the egocentric world of Bashan.
When the narrator has a talk with Bashan, his words,
mostly the simple repetition of his dog's name, have
an electric effect on Bashan: "I rouse and stimulate
his sense of his own ego by impressing upon him--vary-
ing my tone and emphasis--that he is Bashan and that
Bashan is his name. By continuing this for a while I
can actually produce in him a state of ecstasy, a sort
of intoxication with his own identity, so that he begins to whirl round on himself and send up loud exultant barks to heaven out of the weight of dignity that
lies on his chest" (VIII, 560). The "intellect" and
the "word," Detlev Spinell's weapons in his battle with
Herr Klöterjahn, are again the means employed here to
transform life into a state of mind that reveals its
own mute, arrogant mediocrity. So the artist and
master assumes the responsibility of ennobling dull,
ordinary, commonplace life and gives it a sense of
eternity, by lifting it, as Mann has done here, into a
newly created world of symbolic unity.

When we read about a dog almost anywhere in Mann's
works, we are irresistibly drawn back to the tale,
Tobias Mindernickel, where the powerful tension between
love and hate built up to a dramatic climax of violence
and murder; but the present story of Bashan couches
the extremes of that early story in terms of a banal,
inevitable relationship. In muddying his master's manu-
scripts with his paws, Bashan symbolically reveals the
anti-artistic bias which dominated the businessman,
Thomas Buddenbrook. And he, like the Senator from
Lübeck, has sicknesses; one, hemmorhage of the mouth
and nose brings him to a state of hopelessness and
physical exhaustion. It is a time when he loses his

---

and immediate kind of natural enjoyment; yes, I would
even say that only in contemplation of it do I achieve
true self-forgetfulness and feel my own limited individuality merge into the universal. The sea, still-
brooding or coming on in crashing billows, can put me
in a state of such profound organic dreaminess, such
remoteness from myself, that I am lost to time." (VIII,
575)

last bit of dignity and distinction: "I went away,
after trying once more to rouse Bashan with renewed
calls and encouragement. In vain. He cared as little
for my going as for my coming. He seemed weighed down
by bitter loathing and despair" (VIII, 597). Bashan
is anaemic and nervous "as though he were the child of
some upper-class family" (VIII, 597). But Bashan, unlike the artist, lacks the heroism born of weakness.
He is not up to suffering as a way of life, and is
nearly shattered by an illness which reduces him to a
low mental and physical state. Yet, he, like Thomas
Buddenbrook with the reading of Schopenhauer, is unable
to grasp the significance of his great experience:
"He forgot. For Bashan, the ugly and senseless episode
sank into the past, unresolved indeed, unclarified by
comprehension . . . it was covered by the lapse of
time, as must happen sometimes to human beings" (VIII,
600-601). The owner, musing on the plight of his sick
companion, expresses sentiments similar to the feelings
of one possessed by his dog rather than vice versa:
"Perhaps I had taken him to the clinic only out of vanity and arrogance. And beyond that I may have secretly
wished to get rid of him for a while! Perhaps, I even
had a craving to see what it would be like to be free
of his incessant watching of me. . . ." (VIII, 598);
an interesting comment, indeed, one which more accurately parallels Hanno Buddenbrooks' feelings when his
father is taken away than one which applies to the feelings of a man who may rid himself of a dog whenever he
wishes. As a representation of the father, Bashan assumes the role of watchdog of his master's conscience.
The dog's master is a prisoner of the introjected
father as personified by Bashan, who in this story is
seen to be always vigilant and alert as far as his
master is concerned.

One of the more significant episodes occurs when
Bashan is on the hunt. A hare, beside itself with
fright, leaps right at the master and snuggles into
his arms. The master's reaction is one of excitement
and revulsion: "It [the hare] came to me, it clasped
as it were my knees, a human being's knees: not the
knees, so it seemed to me, of Bashan's master, but the
knees of a man who felt himself master of hares and
this hare's master as well as Bashan's" (VIII, 606).
The dog follows in full pursuit: "Bashan giving voice
in all the horrid throaty noises of his hue-and-cry.
As he gets within reach, he is abruptly checked by a
deliberate and well-aimed blow from the stick of the
hare's master which sends him yelping down the slope

with a temporarily disabled hind quarter. He had to
limp painfully back again before he can take up the
trail of his prey which by this time had vanished"
(VIII, 606-607). There was really no need for the
owner to hit his dog, for the hare had already escaped,
but it indicates in no uncertain terms who the master
is in this triangular conflict. In this scene, the
master proves to be the better hunter as well, for the
hare, personified like all the animals in this story,
comes to him for supplication and protection; or translated into human terms, the woman comes to the artist
figure while the father remains the unsuccessful and
smitten rival. Thomas Buddenbrook, we recall, was
similarly vanquished by Lieutenant René von Throta,
Hanno Buddenbrook's substitute.

The artist figure has, therefore, become the master
of life here. As he explicitly shows in describing
his pet's character, his association with Bashan is on
a feudal basis: "It is a deep-lying patriarchal instinct in the dog which leads him--at least in the more
manly, outdoor breeds--to recognize and honor in the
man of the house and head of the family his absolute
master and overlord, protector of the hearth; and to
find in the relation of vassalage to him the basis and
value of his own existence . . ." (VIII, 541).

An added dimension in the relationship between
the man and his dog can be gained from an examination
of the owner's comparison of Bashan with his former
dog, Percy. Percy, the model for Percival in Royal
Highness, was an aristocratic Scotch collie:

> First and foremost we must remember
> that Bashan was entirely sound in mind,
> whereas Percy, as I have said, and as often
> happens among aristocratic canines, had
> always been mad, through and through, a
> perfectly typical specimen of over-breed-
> ing. I have referred to this subject be-
> fore, in a somewhat wider connection;
> here I only want, for purposes of compari-
> son, to speak of Bashan's infinitely
> simpler, more ordinary mentality, expressed
> for instance in the way he would greet
> you, or in his behavior on our walks.
> His manifestations were always within the
> bounds of hearty and healthy common sense;
> they never even touched on the hysterical,

whereas Percy overstepped propriety on
such occasions in a way that was usually
quite shocking. . . .
    Bashan is coarser-fibred, true, like
the lower classes; but like them, also,
he is not above complaining. His noble
predecessor, on the other hand, united
more delicacy and a greater capacity for
suffering with an infinitely firmer and
prouder spirit. Despite all his foolishness, he far excelled in self-discipline
the powers of Bashan's peasant soul.
(VIII, 551)

Times have changed for Thomas Mann. Whereas the
inbred Percy takes us back to the theme of genetic
decline in Mann's first novel Buddenbrooks, A Man and
His Dog represents a new period in which a reversal
of roles has taken place: the son has supplanted the
father. Bashan is middle class in nature and spirit
compared to the artist figure who by 1919 has become
heir to and sole possessor of the aristocratic outlook.

As a study in canine psychology, without plot or
climax, A Man and His Dog is unique in its presentation;
but in part this tale offers an amazingly close parallel
to Death in Venice. Both stories begin with the advent
of spring, a long walk, and a trip that becomes a search
or hunt. In both stories, there is a constant flirta-
tion between two realms of existence: the one of restrained order and the other of subhuman, animal-like
urges. As we have seen, the description of the dog's
behavior is sexually tinged, just as Aschenbach's is
in Death in Venice. Aschenbach's pursuit of Tadzio
through the streets of Venice has its reversed counterpart in Bashan's continual stalking of his master.
Tadzio's physical flaws, like those of the dog, are
carefully enumerated and dwelled upon. The glass door,
through which Aschenbach gazes at the object of his
desires is also used in A Man and His Dog to show the
perpetually waiting Bashan separated from his master
at the writing desk.

Aside from characters and events, the description
of the park where Bashan hunts evokes memories of
Aschenbach's jungle vision and the images of decay in
Venice. Once a marshy wilderness with stagnant pools,
it is now luxuriously overgrown and choked with shrub-
bery in some places and yet it has the appearance of

a cemetery where wastelands or masses of green foliage
prevail. There is also a strip of ground enclosed on
both sides by water. The river flowing within this
whole area is compared to the swell of the ocean, and
there is even a beach with sand. Misshapen trees and
long-legged birds standing in the green water are
images that also occurred in Aschenbach's vision of the
jungle. Likewise, as in the vision, this description
of rank growth is paired off with destruction; the
swollen torrent of the river on a rampage, seething at
its base, whirls along old baskets and dead cats. There
are steps leading down to the river bed, a little foot-
bridge near which women kneel to wash their clothes,
and even a ferryboat and a house for the ferryman. The
description of this house would readily fit the home
of a Venetian gondolier: a kind of a villa with funny
little outcroppings of balconies and bay windows. And
the ferryman's rooster with his green <u>bersaglieri</u> tail
feathers hanging down behind, fixes the scene of Aschenbach's gondola ride in Venice even more vividly: He
sits beside the artist and measures him with a fierce
side-glance from his red eye. He is impressively
similar to the gondolier, an hallucinatory representation of the punishing father and the executor of
death, who became Aschenbach's menacing companion on
his fateful trip across the Venetian lagoon; but Bashan,
the symbol of <u>Leben</u>, remains on good terms with this
cock as they sit together on the ferryboat. Bashan's
gestures and the odd way he looks at his master here
are identical to the impressions made by two of the
repellent and threatening figures Aschenbach encounters
in Venice: "He . . . has a funny puzzled way of opening his jaws crookedly, shutting them again and running
his tongue around the corner of his mouth. It is not
a very refined gesture, in fact rather common, but
very revealing, and as human as it is animal--in fact
it is just what an ordinary simple-minded man might do
in the face of a surprising situation, very likely
scratching his neck at the same time" (VIII, 582).
Also, part of the hunting area is in a state of dilap-
idation and disuse: "The streets suit the signboards
and the signboards suit the streets--it is a strange
and dreamlike harmony in decay" (VIII, 569). Yet, it
is also a realm of art; the names, when legible, of
the street signposts are those of poets and writers.
Thomas Mann even steers us in the direction we are taking: "There is a tarry smell, a breeze off the water,
a slapping sound against the ferryboat. . . . Sometimes these things call up a familiar memory: the
water is deep, it has a smell of decay--that is the

Lagoon, that is Venice" (VIII, 581). Bashan's sickness, an editorial insertion in the description of the
hunt, brings him into an animal hospital. This realm
of the sick and the dying with its strong smelling
medicinal fumes conjures up the cholera plague in
Venice and its accompanying odor of carbolic acid. But
Mann is not yet content to let the parallels between
these two stories rest here. He even recounts a number
of details of Aschenbach's bacchanalia of sadism and
sexual perversion in A Man and His Dog. Once on a
walk, a sheep with an ordinary "sheepish face, save for
a narrow-lipped little mouth turned up at the corners
into a smile which gave the creature an uncommonly sly
and fatuous look" (VIII, 572), appears to be smitten
with Bashan's charms and follows him. A dairymaid,
holding a pitchfork in one hand and her breasts in a-
nother comes running, and together with the artist they
manage to divert the sheep away from the harassed and
embarrassed Bashan. This scene of Bashan's trial forms
part of Aschenbach's dream, with Tadzio rather than the
dog as an enticement to utter degradation.

The polemical spirit of the Observations of a Non-
Political Man is also reflected in this tale of a man
on a walk with his dog. When Mann describes Bashan's
encounter with a mother duck and her brood, we find that
Bashan's attack is decisively parried by the duck's grim
maternal devotion. The duck, aware of the infantile
nature of Bashan's desires, plays on his short-sighted
passions by leading him in a clever maneuver away from
her brood. Shortly afterwards, however, there occurs
an incident that is so painful to the artist master,
that it even gives rise to a measure of coolness between
him and his pet. A figure suddenly appears on the scene,
a rather rough-looking hunter with puttees and a knapsack who stands theatrically for a few moments on the
bank. Then in an operatic pose, he takes aim, fires,
and shoots a duck from the sky. Next, like a criminal
or a murderer in a melodrama, he retrieves the slain
bird and stuffs it unceremoniously into his knapsack:

> This was only the first half of the action.
> But I must interrupt my narrative here to
> turn the vivid light of my memory upon the
> figure of Bashan. I can think of large
> words with which to describe it, phrases
> we use for great occasions: I could say
> that he was thunder struck, but I do not
> like them, I do not want to use them. The
> large words are worn out; when the great

occasion comes, they do not describe it.
Better use the small ones and put into them
every ounce of their weight. (VIII, 613)

Bashan is so fascinated by the whole affair that
he is reluctant to start out for home and even refuses
to hunt on the way back. And finally, after Bashan
has impudently yawned and whined at intervals along the
way, it is the master who becomes irate and can no
longer tolerate his behavior:

> "Go away." I said. "Get out! Go to your
> new friend with the blunderbuss and attach
> yourself to him! He does not seem to
> have a dog; perhaps he could use you in
> his business. He is only a man in velvet-
> eens, to be sure, not a gentleman, but in
> your eyes he may be one; perhaps he is the
> right master for you, and I honestly rec-
> ommend you to make up to him--now that he
> has planted the idea in your head for you
> to seek your own kind of company." (Yes,
> I actually said that!) "We won't ask if
> he has a hunting license, or if you will
> both get into fine trouble some day at
> your dirty game--that is your affair and,
> as I tell you this, my advice is perfectly
> sincere." (VIII, 616)

Having already established some general principles
of relationships of this order in the Observations,
we can readily discern the symbolic meaning behind this
present episode. The duck stands for Germany with its
maternally oriented, quietistic culture (Ruhige Bildung), a culture which the raucous Bashan disturbs and
disrupts by his senseless barking, in much the same way
as all politically-minded people do. The hunter, out-
fitted like a soldier, with puttees and knapsack, acts
in a histrionic manner, perfectly befitting the Rhetor-
Bourgeois who prefers empty, high-flown phrases to
music, the exclusive possession of the German artist.
He kills the duck, a revealing act which is all the
more poignant now that Germany has lost the war. So
it is no wonder that the owner is put off by Bashan's
attitude and that he, in depicting this scene, does not
want to come down to the level of the Zivilisationsliterat by the use of grand and rhetorically bombastic
phrases himself.

Disorder and Early Sorrow

Thomas Mann's novella of 1926, <u>Disorder and Early Sorrow</u>, is the tale of a love between a young person and one much older. Here the situation is reversed from that in <u>Death in Venice</u>, in that a small child, Ellie, is infatuated with a grown-up, Max Hergesell. This story once again offers convincing proof of the Mannian thesis concerning the dangers of love and emotional involvement. It most dramatically confirms Tonio Kröger's belief that the one who loves the most is most doomed to suffer. But this time the actions and the trials of the one affected are viewed and analyzed by a third person: Ellie's father, Professor Abel Cornelius.

Who are the two people involved in this affair? Keeping within the framework of the typical Mannian scheme, we note that this love affair is again one-sided and lacking the sanction of reality; in fact, it is, as in earlier works, a forbidden liaison doomed to failure at the outset. The object of Ellie's desire, Max Hergesell, is, as his name indicates (<u>Geselle</u> means journeyman, comrade, or companion), a representative of life. An engineering student, clean-shaven, charming, good-looking, and, like Baron Harry in <u>A Gleam</u> and Hans Hansen in <u>Tonio Kröger</u>, he cuts a fine figure on the dance floor as he whirls about with the Ingeborg Holm type Miss Plaichinger: "Young Hergesell is a capital leader, dances according to rule, yet with individuality. So it appears. With what aplomb he can walk backwards--when space permits! And he knows how to be graceful standing still in a crowd. And his partner supports him well, being unsuspectedly lithe and buoyant, as fat people often are."[17] Max Hergesell's taste runs to popular music and to ordinary conversation. His nasal drawl is mocked by Ingrid, Professor Cornelius' eighteen-year-old daughter, who, with her brother, takes special delight in impersonating such stupid and commonplace people. We also learn that Max Hergesell has an extremely low tolerance of pain.

Ellie, whose eyes are underlined by what has come to be one of Mann's most dependable leitmotifs--bluish shadows or veins--can be compared to Hanno Buddenbrook. She loves and feels with an intensity that is almost too much for her delicate constitution; and she is precocious and aesthetically inclined, as her charming recitation of ballads shows. We are reminded here of

Hanno's saying the verses of The Boy's Magic Horn
in his sleep. Ellie is the picture of energetic frag-
ility: when a baby tooth has to come out, she pales
and trembles excessively. Hanno's harrowing emotional
ordeals in the dentist's chair come to mind here.

Ellie's brother, Snapper, is equally sensitive and
high-strung, often giving way to rage, tantrums, and
excessive suffering from remorse. He is convinced that
he is an irredeemable sinner who will surely go to "that
bad place" when he dies. By taking these two diminutive
characters together, we again have a montage of the infantile artist figure. Snapper complements Ellie and
the resultant superimposed portrait closely fits the
guilt-ridden and ambivalent hero of Buddenbrooks. Ellie
becomes involved with Max Hergesell on the dance floor
at Ingrid's and Bert's home party, and, like Hanno in
his indulgence in music, she becomes "sick" from the
overwhelming experience of dancing with Max Hergesell.
Though the musical aspect is of a secondary order, being of the popular kind, the intensity of Ellie's emotional suffering is so great as to allow a literal
comparison with Hanno Buddenbrook's whole apotheosis
of sin and atonement. Like the experience of Tonio
Kröger and Klaus Heinrich in Royal Highness, her adventure on the dance floor is perilous and her traumatic and shocking experience among the crowd of people
looms up threateningly as does every direct involvement
with life on the part of the sensitive artist.

The content of this story is given an added dimension by the reflections of Professor Cornelius, who
digests all the events that transpire and then analyzes
and interprets them to the reader. What the immature
and inarticulate Ellie goes through is clarified by her
father; and his feelings, no less than Ellie's, are
revealed as boundless. His love for his daughter has,
as he himself realizes, something not quite right about
it, for he loves her above everything else in the world:
"Ellie belongs to her Abel, so much hers because she
is so very much his; because she consciously luxuriates
in the deep tenderness--like all deep feeling, concealing a melancholy strain--with which he holds her small
form in embrace; in the love in his eyes as he kisses
her little fairy hand or the sweet brow with its delicate tracery of tiny blue veins" (VIII, 624). He reflects on this love of his and comes to the startling
conclusion that "His devotion to this priceless little
morsel of life and new growth has something to do with
death. It clings to death as against life; and that

is neither right nor beautiful--in a sense" (VIII, 627).
Just why his excessive devotion to Ellie should be
equated with death can only be derived from his attitude towards the life about him. His feeling for his
daughter is at the expense of his relationships with
other people, for Ellie's specially circumscribed
world, with its emphasis on omnipotent narcissism, is
removed from the sphere of an active give-and-take life.

Professor Cornelius is affected as much as Ellie
by the disaster on the dance floor. Informed of it
after he has returned from his evening walk, he attempts
to comfort her, but her submerged feelings stand beyond
help or healing. After Max Hergesell comes up to her
room and, by a few mundane words, transforms the sob-
bing, miserable creature into a radiantly ecstatic child
again, we read the following words: "Young Hergesell
leans over the bars of the crib and rattles on, more
for the father's ear than the child's, but Ellie does
not know that--and the father's feelings toward him are
a most singular mixture of thankfulness, embarrassment
and hatred" (VIII, 656). He is not really grateful to
Max Hergesell despite the latter's successful ministra-
tions, for to Professor Cornelius young Hergesell remains only an object of antipathy and scorn.

Through the eyes of Ellie and Professor Cornelius
we see the duality of opposing emotions, the love that
is coexistent with hate. The Professor and Ellie are
like one; what threatens her, endangers him as well.
At the end of the story there is a slight reconciliation
when Max Hergesell makes amends; but that is of lesser
importance than the lesson this tale teaches us: there
is danger in a sensitive soul's attempt to bridge the
gulf between itself and the representatives of life.
Life, indifferent to finer sensibilities, is not affected by such an encounter whereas the delicate artist
may be shattered by it. A fellow like Max Hergesell
will pass over such an experience with hardly a thought,
but the artist figure will suffer grievously and eternally by it.

As a mature artist figure, Professor Cornelius
reflects back on his own past which becomes more pronounced in the presence of Ellie, the daughter in whom
he finds the embodiment of innocence. She represents
to her father that sacred time when he himself was free
of guilt, when his own innocence was intact, unbruised
by the severe claims of life. The dependence between
father and daughter represents a kind of condensed

case history, telescoping, as it does, the inner bond
connecting infantile traumas with adult artistic attitudes. Professor Cornelius' hatred for life's representative, Hergesell, attains a high pitch in the
miniature tragedy which is Ellie's. Professor Cornelius' calling and interests lie in the dead past:

> He [Cornelius] knows that history professors
> do not love history because it is something
> that has come to pass; that they hate a
> revolution like the present one because
> they feel it is lawless, incoherent, ir-
> relevant--in a word, unhistoric; that their
> hearts belong to the coherent, disciplined,
> historic past. For the temper of time-
> lessness, the temper of eternity--thus the
> scholar communes with himself when he takes
> his walk by the river before supper--that
> temper broods over the past; and it is a
> temper much better suited to the nervous
> system of a history professor than are
> the excesses of the present. The past is
> immortalized; that is to say, it is dead.
> . . . It is this conservative instinct of
> his, his sense of the eternal, that has
> found in his love for his little daughter
> a way to save itself from the wounding in-
> flicted by the times. (VIII, 626-627)

So the professor of history attempts to capture a time
in the lives of men which is devoid of all the wound-
ing and shocking incidents involving life in all its
immediacy. Professor Cornelius ponders these thoughts
alone in the dark, for the dark is his sphere, as opposed to that of a "person of light" like Hergesell.

   Disorder and Early Sorrow is set against the background of the inflation in postwar Germany. There is
a great measure of resentment in Professor Cornelius
towards this new life in his mother country, for it is
the life of the new Europe, "a tango and two-step
Europe" which he no longer understands nor wants to
understand: "The Professor feels an involuntary twinge.
Uppermost in his heart is hatred for this party, with
its power to intoxicate and estrange his darling child.
His love for her--that not quite disinterested, not
quite unexceptionable love of his--is easily wounded.
He wears a mechanical smile, but his eyes have clouded,
and he stares fixedly at a point in the carpet, between
the dancers' feet" (VIII, 648). Little has changed for

197

the Mannian hero at this point except the external circumstances of life; he is still the insulated and violently "apolitical" man living in the vortex of ever-
changing times: "'And taking sides is unhistoric.'
And it could not, properly considered, be otherwise.
. . . For justice can have nothing of youthful fire
and blithe, fresh, loyal conviction. It is by nature
melancholy" (VIII, 650). Actually, Professor Cornelius
does take sides, and with a vengeance. The ambivalence
of his soul, however, holds back the hostility he feels
towards the unfair triumphs of life.

Although Disorder and Early Sorrow, with its emphasis on a society in dissolution, is consistent in
thematic background with Buddenbrooks, Royal Highness,
and Death in Venice, it also evinces similarities with
other works, directly with The Magic Mountain and generally with other stories to come. The events in this
tale are confined to a spacious private home into which
people from various strata of society come; the same is
true for the scene of action in The Magic Mountain--
the sanatorium Berghof. Some of these characters too
appeared, only slightly changed, in The Magic Mountain.
The nurse resembles Frau Stöhr, and Xaver Kleinsgütl,
who likes to frighten people by endangering his life,
stands for Herr Albin. The actor Ivan Herzl comes
forth as a prototype for the magician Cipolla in Mario
and the Magician, and Professor Cornelius himself, as
a passive on-looker at the activity about him, resembles
Hans Castorp, the hero of one of the most discussed
novels of the twentieth century.

AN INTERNAL TRIANGLE: THE MAGIC MOUNTAIN

Although The Magic Mountain is now old enough to
have produced its second or even third generation of
exponents, it has for the most part remained an enigma
in content and a somewhat amorphous entity in form and
structure.   In turn it has been labeled an allegory
between East and West, a realistic novel, and a philosophical study.[1]   Hermann Weigand insists that it is
a psychological Bildungsroman (educational novel),[2]
although others have been quick to point out that the
hero is much too inert or even stagnant in his development to be classified as a blossoming or emerging hero.
Indeed, a stronger case could be made for the prospect
of calling this novel an Anti-Bildungsroman, for in
spite of the seven years and his many experiences on
the magic mountain, the protagonist Hans Castorp is
essentially the same kind of person at the end of the
work that he was at the beginning.   Originally he flees
from life in general by taking up residence on the
mountain, and finally he flees from his new "hermetic"
life by searching out death on the battlefield.

But, as is to be expected, and in spite of certain
structural flaws of the work, the careful compilation
and artistic interweaving of facts and occurrences by
a writer as brilliant as Thomas Mann have won its adherents and captivated even a number of the negatively
inclined critics.   Since its initial appearance, the
novel has run the whole gambit of criticism from devoted
adoration to severe negative chastisement: from Erich
Heller's belief that The Magic Mountain is perhaps one
of the greatest novels ever written[3] to E. K. Bennett's
rebuttal that it is completely devoid of life.[4]   Yet
many critical differences might be resolved by testing
their validity against assertions about Mann's earlier
creations; for to an amazingly large extent Mann's
works are a variation on the same theme, and although
his figures in The Magic Mountain seem to cast longer
shadows, they are, just below the surface, similar in
size and shape to the earlier heroes.   Perhaps the
greatest similarity lies in Mann's tendency to dispense
with an involved story line in order to concentrate, as
he did in Tonio Kröger and Death in Venice, on the
hero's tendency to passively contemplate the world about
him.

While visiting his cousin, Joachim Ziemssen, in
the Swiss alpine sanatorium, the protagonist initiates

almost no action. He becomes ill and, although restored to health after a short time, he renounces his
ties to his home in the flatland and lingers on in this
isolated and ethereal world of sickness. During his
seven-year sojourn in the sanatorium Berghof, he reads
and studies, has a harmless affair with the "temptress"
Clawdia Chauchat, and becomes involved in long, pointless discussions with many patients, especially Settembrini, Naphta, and Peeperkorn. Only with the outbreak
of the First World War does Hans Castorp decide to leave
Berghof. The last pages of the novel show him in Flanders charging through a hail of bullets to meet, presumably, death on the battlefield.

Hans Castorp

    Hans Castorp seems at first glance to be an a-
typical Mannian hero. He neither appears to possess
any unusual talent in an aesthetic sense nor is he precocious intellectually.* However, his similarity to
previous heroes is seen if one takes the following
points into consideration: his North German patrician
origins and independent position in life, his early
exposure to the coffin and the baptismal font reminiscent of Hanno Buddenbrook's experiences, his inordinate
love of music, his natural reserve and propriety, his
ready tendency to exhaustion by ordinary work, his
passivity and inclination to daydream, his love of the
sea, his adolescent, exaggerated affection for a school
comrade, and his tarrying in a sanatorium long after
he has been cured--a way of life subscribed to previously by Detlev Spinell of Tristan. We also find other
patterns of autobiography in the old family mansion,
the hero's difficulties at school, including his failure
to be promoted, the family business, a wholesale enterprise, and its liquidation as the result of a death
when the hero was still young, the title of Senator
in the family, the hero's father who like Thomas Buddenbrook inspected warehouses and whose death called forth
a well attended funeral; and finally the sumptuous meals
of the Berghof residents--all reminiscent of Buddenbrooks.

---

    *Hans Castorp, like another hero, Klaus Heinrich,
is practically always named in full. In this respect,
his name assumes aspects of a title and provides overtones of the aristocratic image which Mann emphasizes
in the later heroes.

However, it is in the hero's extreme preoccupation with music that the most concrete connection can be made. Although the depiction of Hans Castorp is that of an essentially non-artistic young man, there is still strong confirmation of the same surreptitious and clandestine enjoyment which was a part of Hanno Buddenbrook's session at the piano: "He went to bed feverishly at a very late hour. . . . Then he remained in the lounge, or secretly returned and played music alone till deep into the night."[5]

Hans Castorp may be compared directly with Aschenbach of _Death in Venice_ who travels to an exotic place to recuperate from the pressures of life and finds before him the vastness of nature.* The symbolic similarity between an alpine panorama and an immense expanse of water is stressed in the novel itself: "Hans Castorp loved living in the snow. He found it related in many respects to life at the oceanside: in both realms the deep monotony of nature was similar; the snow, this deep, loose, spotless powder snow, played exactly the same role that the golden white sand did down below . . ." (III, 652).

In Berghof's specially delineated and circumscribed world of the dead and the dying, Hans Castorp, like Aschenbach in cholera-plagued Venice, carries on a long-distance love affair. He lies in wait for the object of his desires, Clawdia Chauchat, as Aschenbach previously pursued Tadzio on the streets of Venice. Even the glass door of the restaurant has a function in both works, but in _The Magic Mountain_ it assumes wider psychological overtones. By continually slamming this door, Clawdia Chauchat reveals her lack of restraint and her Bohemian-like nature; and the door shows essentially a one-sided relationship, a transparent wall that indicates both the hero's pathetic sense of isolation and his immediate need of security through distance. It is all a recapitulation of the unnatural love affair which took place in cholera-stricken Venice, even to

---

*As early as Mann's second story, _The Will to Happiness_, the artist, in his violent desire to be rid of the imperatives of duty and work, flees impulsively into an unknown or foreign climate where he imposes spiritual or physical isolation upon himself.

the point where Castorp associates his love for this woman with his youthful love for a young Slavic boy.

The author has again taken every precaution necessary to insure the segregation of the hero's emotions from the love affair itself, despite the assertion that Hans Castorp's passion for Clawdia Chauchat is devastating.[6] It is true that Mann steps into the narrative on more than one instance to announce the impact which the whole affair has upon the protagonist, as for example with the trite hyperbole: "Simply stated, our traveler was up to his ears in love with Clawdia Chauchat . . ." (III, 321). But it is not only such select statements that ring hollow but rather the total effect of the author's interference in asserting that a state of affairs very different from the obvious one predominates. Rather than being plagued by the uncontrollable desires and dreams of one in love, as the author claims, Hans Castorp is preoccupied with a feeling of playful detachment which becomes little more than a subject of adolescent-like teasing exchanges between himself and the foolish busybody at his table, Mrs. Stöhr. As a matter of fact the highly articulate "claims" of love on the author's part arouse the reader's suspicions and move him to ask for visible proof of the hero's tormented soul or of his irresistible desires. No, rather than themes of healthy hunger or of sexual desire, two leitmotifs are sounded to confuse each major appearance of the "loved one"--the Pribislav Hippe pattern and the theme of death.

The Hippe incident is established in the protagonist's mind as an inherent element in the aura that surrounds Clawdia Chauchat. Hans Castorp automatically associates Clawdia with an exaggerated and almost unnatural adoration he had in school for a fellow classmate (the same age, the same appearance right down to the haircut and the Slavic strain, the dress and composure as that of Tadzio in Death in Venice). The original incident, composed of Castorp's distant love for the lad and finally his surge of courage in asking the boy if he could borrow his pencil for an art class, is repeated at the apex of Castorp's conservative courtship of Clawdia Chauchat. The sexual symbolism of the pencil is actually too obvious. (Pencil is etymologically related to the Latin word penis.) The pencil is merely an excuse for Hans Castorp to approach first Hippe, and then Chauchat, but rather than providing for a direct encounter, it ironically draws attention away from the loved one. Invested with an aura of

solemnity and mystery, the trite matter of the pencil
becomes more memorable and important than the entire
emotional content of Hans Castorp's love affair. That
the Hippe incident takes place in school, once again
recalls Hanno Buddenbrook's helpless encounter with
the hostile forces of school and also Thomas Mann's
own equation of school and life in his <u>Observations of
a Non-Political Man</u>:

> He [Hanno Buddenbrook] fails altogether,
> he gives up, he relinquishes the life
> whose symbol and temporary expression is
> the school. Art--is it not always a
> critique of life, made by a little Hanno?
> The others obviously feel at home in life
> as it is, feel perfectly well in their
> element, just as Hanno's schoolmates do.
> The school itself, as mirrored in his ex-
> perience of it, is grotesque, tormenting,
> stupid, revolting. . . .[7]

What business does a lad have in school without
a pencil, or symbolically in life and love? Both Hanno
Buddenbrook and Hans Castorp have no recourse but to
be observers, onlookers who must reject any invitation
to participate and must resolve themselves for security's
sake to timidity and evasion of the actual. Why are
such seemingly trivial happenings even considered impetuous or foolhardy? "The actions of a man who is a
born observer will always be an unnatural, dreadful,
distorted and self-destructive activity," remarks the
author himself.[8] The second leitmotif that characterizes Clawdia Chauchat is death. The first time Hans
Castorp sees a dying man, Clawdia Chauchat smiles at
him, also for the first time. Immediately following
his nosebleed on his mountain walk, "his face white as
a sheet, his coat spotted with blood--he might have
been a murderer stealing from his crime," Castorp suddenly turns and sees Clawdia measure him with narrow
eyes (III, 124-125). His first extreme profession of
desire for her is accompanied by a feeling of terror
and dread, disease and panic, and the first time Hans
Castorp greets her directly, his temperature goes up
to a dangerous 104.4 degrees. The crescendo of Castorp's amorous outpourings consists of a constant confusion of the themes of love and death: "Le corps,
l'amour, la mort, ces trois ne font qu'un" (III, 476).
Just such incidents and exchanges mount and continue
until finally Hans Castorp kisses Clawdia, literally
over the dead body of her master and mentor, Mynheer

Pieter Peeperkorn.

Hans Castorp's behavior toward Clawdia Chauchat reveals more evidence of the nervous challenges and the guilt-ridden concerns of an anxious criminal or an embarrassed infatuated boy than it does the passions of a love-possessed young man. Either he perceives and dwells on one part of her body or on one character-istic movement (her arm or her hand up to her hair); or he recalls Clawdia most completely by regarding her X-ray photo, until Clawdia finally begins to take on greater significance as fantasy than reality.

The name Chauchat itself, literally "hot cat," reveals an ironic indiscretion which no author should bestow on a woman who is supposed to elicit a hero's genuine love and concern. Aside from the name, critics have come to the conclusion that between the conception and the delineation of this supposedly irresistible woman there is an ocean of difference dividing the as-serted ideal from the shadow. Hirschbach concurs that she is a two-dimensional figure: "She is 'the woman,' a symbol for all women, a representative of a type, just as Settembrini is 'the Western liberal' or Joachim is 'German youth.'"[9] But she is never _the_ woman who is capable of tempting beyond reason. Even when Hans Castorp confesses his love it is in French so that he may manage to preserve distance and reduce the danger of his true feelings. He is thus able, according to Thomas Mann, to utter things which he could never say in German.[10] But how did Hans Castorp develop such fluency in this language, a skill which throws him out of character as an average German youth? Weigand at-tempts to explain this away as having been the fruits of the hero's scientific studies; but Weigand himself is not fully convinced of his conjecture.[11]

So when emotion asserts itself and Hans Castorp must woo Clawdia Chauchat, he insists on doing so in a manner thrice removed—first in a foreign language which has neither the immediacy nor substance of one's native tongue; then in a cloak of ambivalence which asserts a willingness to pay for the gratifications of the body with death, and finally by emphasizing the anatomical relationship over and above responsible passions and spirit.

Hirschbach has noted an interesting aspect of the relationship: Hans Castorp waits seven months to talk to Clawdia and then he calls her _thou_ at the first

meeting.[12] Although his familiarity is a part of the
carnival spirit, it does assume a breach of normal
propriety, and may consequently be calculated to offend
and thereby, also, to protect in case of failure. Some
of Castorp's words are actually insulting and, in their
anatomical detail, they effectively curtail the emotional content of his confession of love--at any rate his
choice of themes and words belie each modicum of heartfelt expression or tender affection.* Fortunately, and
of necessity one must add, he is quite inebriated and
can therefore put his desires to the test with a mitiga-
tion of consequences. So he is scarcely set back when,
declaring his love on his knees, he is described as
babbling and Clawdia ultimately crowns him with a fool's
cap.**

The consummation of love is never fully stated but
certainly implied on several occasions in the second

---

*In Tristan the antagonist Herr Klöterjahn is
taken to task for expressing in English his affection
for his wife Gabriele when he could just as easily
and more naturally have used his native German.

**Like the buffoon the fool is, historically speak-
ing, a mythological figure, usually the inversion of
the king. Especially in performances or rituals of
sacrifice or assassination, the fool was often selected
as a substitute for the king. Whereas Hans Castorp
wants to be the man of first importance in Clawdia's
life, he is relegated to lowest position, for in court
the clown is always the last of the procession, the
king first!

And at the risk of pursuing the subject too far,
we point out again the general pattern of "hat" symbolism in Davos. Only those men who have recently arrived
from the flatlands wear a hat as a kind of a persevering of a bourgeois need to wear the acceptable and habit-
ual articles of clothing characteristic of their sex.
In this respect two points may be of some importance:
(1) Hans Castorp is given a paper fool's cap instead
of the "crown" of the king, husband or lover, and (2)
Peeperkorn, the antagonist and paternal rival, becomes
the only gentleman at the Berghof who continues to wear
his "crown" during his sojourn on the Magic Mountain.

volume of the work: "In any case the young man had
received those guarantees and consoling affirmations
before he had returned to room number 34; for the following day he didn't have a single word to exchange
with Mrs. Chauchat . . ." (III, 483). Thus the initial
unrest of the hero at the beginning of the novel ends
in the satisfaction of a passion which, taking place
behind the scenes away from the direct peril of exposure, withholds completely any emotional transference
for the reader.

Thus, despite the dramatic trumpeting of the love
and death themes, there is really no daring outbreak
of passion portrayed in this novel; the hero's phlegmatic disposition permeates the whole work and makes
The Magic Mountain a throwback to Royal Highness where
sheer weight of irrelevant detail dampens practically
all sense of vitality. We find a striking contrast
between Hans Castorp's incapacity to "let himself go"
and the otherwise frenzied sexual license of the sanatorium. Hirschbach discusses the special atmosphere
of Berghof: "The pleasure principle rules supreme. A
tremendous interest in one's own body and the gratification of its appetites is the only passion that never
fades. Vulgarity is the accepted mode of behavior.
. . . Occasionally, the general lasciviousness becomes
so wanton that emergency measures have to be taken.
. . ."[13] Other interpreters have referred to Berghof
as a Hörselberg or Venusberg.[14] But, on another level,
like school for Hanno, it is simply life in the raw
again.

The hero's reticence about the commitment of his
feelings is again in keeping with the conditions of
ambivalent love of Mann's previous artist figures.
Love, disease, and consequent exposure to death go hand
in hand for them, and posit in essence life's goal as
a Liebestod. Like others before him, Hans Castorp
fails to exclude death from his love. For him, love
is not simply a fulfilling emotion and a release from
tension; it contains within itself a kind of retributive
justice that summons up self-destructive tendencies.
Instead of purging inhibited instincts and thereby im-
proving one's health and state of mind, this sense of
guilty love demands self-immolation with each emotional
involvement. Hans Castorp, like his artist brothers,
Hanno Buddenbrook, Johannes Friedemann, Gustav Aschenbach, and Adrian Leverkühn (Doctor Faustus), finds in
"love" the dissolution of the will to live.

206

The concept of sickness is assigned a dimension in The Magic Mountain which Mann expands into a well-defined credo in Doctor Faustus, where again it is linked directly to the hero's involvement with the heroine. What for Hanno Buddenbrook and Gustav Aschenbach was a symbolic representation of their sense of guilt, is for Hans Castorp inseparably associated with a relationship to a specific woman. We remember Hanno Buddenbrook's atonement by typhus for his intensely erotic and hectic release at the piano and Aschenbach's flight into a disease-ridden sphere as a sine qua non for his compulsion to find gratification. But for these two heroes the function of disease was still symbolic. For both, a fatal sickness was the price they had to pay for the liberation of pent-up desires. Aschenbach's questionable behavior culminating in his orgiastic dream was atoned for by his accepting a self-imposed fate as a victim of cholera, and Hanno's remorseless death by typhus occurs at the heels of his self-indulgent pleasures and passions at the piano. But for Hans Castorp a glance or a word from Clawdia Chauchat is sufficient to cause his temperature to soar dangerously. Here illness is a direct extension of the hero's fantasy, the end result, seemingly, of corporealization or omnipotence of deeply-rooted and frightening Oedipal thoughts.

Settembrini

A substantial part of The Magic Mountain deals with Hans Castorp's friendship with Settembrini, Naphta and Peeperkorn.* It has been argued that Settembrini

---

*Two other prominent figures are Hofrat Behrens, the chief doctor and surgeon of the sanatorium, and his assistant Dr. Krokowski. Behrens is characterized as a diamond in the rough, and, except for Joachim Ziemssen, he is on closer terms with Hans Castorp than any other figure in Berghof. Hans M. Wolff accurately sums up his person: "He is not only shown to be an important doctor, who above all renders great services in the field of surgery, but he is also a true judge of people and an expert of life as well as of death. . . . Mann lets us see that kindness and a well-meaning attitude are concealed behind his rough exterior, for by appealing to a dying patient's sense of honor and by admonishing him to pull himself together, Behrens softens the suffering person's ordeal of death. . . . The reader's

and Naphta constitute conflicting forces that fight for
the soul of Hans Castorp who, so the argument runs,
eventually comes to advocate a philosophy favorable to
life and close to Settembrini's point of view.[15]   However, a close examination of the part played by these
two and of Hans Castorp's relationship to them makes
their actual influence on him doubtful. The same is
true for Peeperkorn who supposedly occupies a larger
than life position as a caricature of the Dionysian
man,[16] or who is characterized as having a humanizing
effect on the hero and on the other residents of Berghof.[17]   But a thorough look at these people shows them
as familiar forces in Mann's works and establishes Hans
Castorp's behavior as consistent with that of Mann's
other heroes.

    Next to Hans Castorp, Settembrini plays the most
conspicuous part in the novel. His role is essentially
symbolic: he stands for a set of abstractions which
prevent him from appearing as a vitally convincing
character. On several occasions his allegorical function is explicitly defined: "But Settembrini was a
representative--of things and powers that were worth
hearing about . . ." (III, 582). Hans Castorp expresses
the same thought directly to the Italian: "You are not
some person with a name. You are a representative,
Mr. Settembrini, a representative at this place and at
my side. Yes, that is what you are . . ." (III, 458).
To Erich Heller there is evidently no doubt about

---

sympathy for Behrens is further increased by the knowledge that the latter himself is shown in chapter six
to be suffering from ill-health and that he is one who
has undergone severe trials and for that reason possesses a full and complete understanding of the misery
of his patients" (pp. 58-59). To a certain extent he
embodies some specific virtues of the Mannian hero:
dedicated service to his calling combined with a tolerance for suffering and the correct attitude towards
death. In contrast to him stands the questionable
figure of Dr. Krokowski who, with his lounge suit,
pierced sandal-like shoes, Bohemian impression, yellow-
ish teeth, foreign and drawling accent, and phosphor-
escent pallor, assumes a somewhat sinister aspect and
closely approaches the conception of the abhorrent
Bohemian. Wolff is probably correct in assuming that
Krokowski is a caricature of the founder of psychoanalysis or of a Messianic follower of Freud (p. 59).

Settembrini's role, for he dispenses with him as one-dimensional, too obvious, and without mystery.[18]

We learn from Thomas Mann himself that it is not wrong to regard Settembrini in this light. He admits that his main characters were not created to live as people but to promote ideas: "They are only exponents, representatives and messengers of a conceptual realm, principles and worlds. I hope that they are not, because of that, shadows and wandering allegories."[19]

Settembrini's lectures possess a progressively more unreal quality. He sounds like a preacher or a textbook in nearly every discussion, and it is stated that his words convey the taste of a Sunday sermon (III, 86). Settembrini cannot help but preach, moralize, and "enlighten" his listeners. On his visits to the convalescing Hans Castorp he turns on the light to banish the powers of darkness; and he repeatedly warns the hero of the dangers of Berghof and tells him, unrealistically, to leave--the first time after Hans Castorp has just arrived and naturally could not comply out of deference to his cousin, and the second time when he is quite literally sick. Settembrini has a natural antipathy towards Clawdia Chauchat as a possible representative of the irrational (by implication, a victory for her is a defeat for his concept of reason). Settembrini's words on carnival night when the hero sets off to borrow a pencil from Clawdia Chauchat reveal him to be a spokesman for the forces of reason but hardly a credible depiction of a flesh and blood character: "Engineer! Wait! What are you doing? Engineer! A little reason, you know! But this boy is crazy!" (III, 462).

As the exponent of rationality and clarity of thought and as a political champion of progress, democracy and enlightenment, Settembrini is obviously a reincarnation of the Zivilisationsliterat or Rhetor-Bourgeois against whom Thomas Mann vented his spleen in the Observations of a Non-Political Man. Nicknamed Lucifer (Bringer of Light), Settembrini comes forth as a shallow utilitarian who finds in education and reason a panacea for the ills of the world, a superficial refusal to acknowledge the existence of death, and a naive and unquestioning affirmation of the world. Obviously taking sides, Mann lets Settembrini promote beautiful catch-words and empty phrases and reveal himself to be remarkably fatuous for such an erudite

person.* Settembrini is proud of his dedication to
politics: "We admit that we are political, admit it
openly, unreservedly. We care nothing for the stigma
attached to this word in the eyes of certain fools--
they are at home in your country, Engineer, and almost
nowhere else. The friends of humanity cannot recognize
a distinction between what is political and what is
not. There is nothing that is not political. Everything is politics" (III, 711).

Continuing where he left off in the Observations
of a Non-Political Man, Thomas Mann characterizes Germany as the "unliterary land" and the Germans as people
who subscribe to "a musical way of life." Settembrini,
in keeping with the Zivilisationsliterat of the war
book, and like all Lichtmenschen or exponents of the
father world of commerce, possesses a deeply ingrained
aversion to music. To him it is "politically suspect."
He is quick to detect in Hans Castorp a serious disposition towards this insidious art so contrary to the
spirit of commerce, and, concerned, he immediately
warns him of its inherent dangers: "With music alone
the world would get no further forward. Frankly, it
is a real danger. For you, personally, Engineer, it
is beyond all doubt dangerous. I saw it in your face
as I approached" (III, 161).

But Settembrini's significance moves beyond the
image of the Zivilisationsliterat as he assumes, more
and more, the role of a parent. He exhorts Hans
Castorp to leave Berghof to take up a useful calling
in the flatland, and continuously treats him as if he
were a docile schoolboy, tirelessly admonishing him to
turn his back on the powers of darkness and embrace
the enlightened precepts of Western civilization.

After having made a case for the simplicity of
Settembrini's character, we must insist that the picture is not quite so simple. For in essence there are
two Settembrinis in the novel. Hans Castorp's initial
encounter with the Italian is certainly decisive for
approximately two-thirds of the work; and this impres-

---

*In contrast to the grand phrases, i.e., große
Wörter (great words) of the Zivilisationsliterat,
modest turns of speech or kleine Wörter (little words)
come from the mouth of the German hero Hans Castorp.
See Weigand, p. 123.

sion established at the onset lasts with only slight modification up to the chapter entitled "Snow," after which a basically new Settembrini who borders on the unusual begins to take shape. When Hans Castorp is first introduced to the Italian, he thinks of him as an organ grinder and windbag; and these depreciative designations continue to be applied to Settembrini, who, as an organ grinder, turns out a monotonous and platitudinous melody of words.

For the most part Hans Castorp is depicted as rejecting Settembrini in some fashion: "But I hope we don't meet Settembrini again. I'm not up to any more learned conversation" (III, 118). In Hans Castorp's dream Settembrini is envisioned as his enemy, and also, on more than one occasion he purposely provokes the Italian to anger. In deliberate defiance of Settembrini's wishes Castorp visits and comforts the sick.

By the time Naphta arrives on the scene the author has successfully undermined Settembrini's position, although, strictly speaking, he has not been able to dissociate the Italian's personality from his philosophy. The ground has been paved for Naphta's dark outlook of devaluation to easily carry its full weight. Settembrini, during the ensuing discussions, thus becomes an easy mark for Hans Castorp and Naphta. With facility they repudiate the cherished virtues and beliefs of the democratic humanist, and as long as the verbal battles continue we find that Settembrini is no match for the Jesuit Naphta. Though Mann later makes short shrift of Naphta, there is certainly no mystery as to where the hero stands in relation to these two; he tells us frankly that Naphta's arguments are right!

After the "Snow" chapter Settembrini gradually emerges with traits which he did not possess before. In contrast to the beginning, where he is incapable of spontaneous mirth and is critical of Hans Castorp's merriment, he becomes more disposed to laughter and cheerfulness. He assumes a more intimate tone with the hero and even begins to yield slightly in discussions towards the end of the novel, and Hans Castorp himself finally gives up referring to Settembrini as a windbag.

With the arrival of Peeperkorn, Settembrini's and Naphta's importance to the hero is gradually reduced until it seems to vanish behind a myriad of disconnected activities, although in the last thirty-five pages of the novel the process of Settembrini's rehabilitation is sharply accelerated and he actually becomes a different person. Confronted by the Jesuit's bitterness, he tends to lean over backward. And when Naphta and he fight a duel near the close of the novel, the loquacious Italian, having a chance to live up to his words, does make a brave humanitarian gesture; this act comes as a surprise if we recall Hans Castorp's earlier doubt that Settembrini would ever have the courage to face certain death (III, 535). Finally, when the hero leaves to go to war, it is Settembrini who relents, becomes humanly emotional, and addresses him by the familiar thou--a contrast to his rigidity during the carnival, a time when everyone but he fell into the spirit.

Naphta

Hans Castorp's second "teacher," Naphta, is also characterized inconsistently. As the novel progresses, the Jesuit is increasingly characterized as malicious, malevolent, icy and offensive, and Hans Castorp does not hide the fact that he finds his unpleasantness pathologically tinged. It is Naphta who insists on fighting a duel; it is he who refuses to yield to reason, and it is he who insanely proposes to make the duel a veritable suicide. Yet, Mann obviously felt close to Naphta, for in one sense Naphta is assigned a superior position in the work: from beginning to end no one is able to refute Naphta's arguments, and yet, in spite of the convincing force of his arguments, his life terminates with the act of complete frustration-- suicide.

Here and elsewhere we detect in the figure of Leo Naphta a previous character of Mann's works: Raoul Überbein in Royal Highness. Their spiritual similarity is striking, both in biography and disposition. The revolutionary and aristocratic Naphta and Überbein uphold certain class distinctions, although both are nihilistically inclined and question all values. The following words of Überbein exemplify their extreme position: "I am fundamentally not much for humanity. I speak of it disparagingly with the greatest of pleasure. . . . For the spirit, Klaus Heinrich, the spirit is the tutor that presses inexorably for dignity; yes, that actually produces dignity. It is the arch-enemy and the distinguished foe of all human satisfactions."[20]

Raoul Überbein, like Naphta, is filled with a contempt for people and is opposed to the general frater-

nity of mankind based on shallow sentiment in Settembrini's sense of the word. In Roger Nicholl's opinion, Überbein stands for certain Nietzschean principles
which Mann no longer took seriously.[21]

Leo Naphta and Raoul Überbein are to a large extent lifeless abstractions. They represent either the
destructive influence of Nietzschean philosophy or the
extreme and hostile aspect of the artist's own personality; on the surface, it can be argued, their violent
deaths symbolize a repudiation of their philosophy,
the heroes' attempt to throw off their imminent authority and consequently to turn towards an alternate
position in life.

Peeperkorn

Undoubtedly the most striking and most controver-
sial character in Thomas Mann's novel is the Dutch
planter Mynheer Pieter Peeperkorn. To Weigand, he is
a "weird figure,"[22] and to Erich Heller he is "a big,
inarticulate tottering mystery."[23] In the opinion of
Joseph Warren Beach, he supplies that something which
is essential to a true philosophy of life,[24] while
Wolff claims that the real significance of Peeperkorn
lies in his caricature of the dionysian-like person.[25]
In R. H. Thomas' words, "Beside this phenomenon the
analytical disputes of Settembrini and Naphta appear
lifeless indeed. Peeperkorn is no mere intellectual
observer of existence and its problems. He is life
itself."[26]

And Thomas Mann himself, rather than shedding light
on the subject, contributes to the mystery of the figure
by candidly revealing that he used his friend Gerhart
Hauptmann, the poet and the dramatist, as the model
for Peeperkorn.[27] It may well be true, as S. D. Stirk
claims, that Mann concentrated on certain of Hauptmann's
external traits and exaggerated them almost beyond recognition,[28] but this observation does little to establish this character's raison d'être within the purview
of the novel.

Mann's portrayal of his friend is not only unflattering but hostile, for a close inspection of "this
grand old man" discloses a disconsolate and pathetic
figure. Although Thomas Mann editorializes to achieve
an aura of eminence around Peeperkorn, his continuous
reference to him with attributes such as "kingly,"
"regal," "majestic," "broadshouldered," "weighty person-

ality," succeed only in making us suspicious of a
character that must be styled out of descriptive em-
bellishments rather than out of intrinsic comportment.
Peeperkorn's outrageous choler--three times at the
banquet scene he strikes the table with his fist--is
paralleled only by the obnoxious fury of the gentleman
with the spats in the story, The Railway Accident. The
latter's lordly manner and particular utterance bordering on childishness--"He used the term 'Jackass'--a
manly expression, a virile expression and a cavalier
expression, stimulating to hear,"[29]--is comparable to
the author's mocking comment on one of Peeperkorn's
inappropriate expressions: "'Judgment Day'--how well
those words fit his image!" (III, 784). And in the
following teasing words beginning the chapter entitled
"Mynheer Peeperkorn (continued)" we note a strong
parallel tone to the introductory paragraph of The
Railway Accident:

> Mynheer Peeperkorn remained in the Berghof
> throughout the winter--what there was left
> of it--and on into the spring; and among
> other memorable events an excursion took
> place (which Settembrini and Naphta attended)
> that led to the waterfalls in the Fluela
> valley. That happened towards the end of
> his stay. End? So he remained no longer
> then? No. He went away? Yes,--and no.
> Yes and no. How then, yes and no? Please,
> no prying into secrets. We shall understand
> it all in time. We do know the Lieutenant
> Ziemssen died, not to mention other less
> honorable dance partners of Death. Old
> inarticulate Peeperkorn was carried off
> then by his malignant tropical fever?--No,
> he wasn't. But why the impatience? That
> not everything can be seen simultaneously
> is a condition of life and of a narration;
> and one certainly doesn't want to rebel
> against the God-given forms of human knowl-
> edge! (III, 795-796)

Mann began The Railway Accident in the same tone,
with a series of rhetorical questions designed to aug-
ment a mood of sarcasm and derision for the representatives of life in the story. There, as here, the purpose was to reveal the dichotomous characterization of
a visibly forceful, aggressive representative of life
whose total composition constituted little more than
a thin, exterior shell.

The lavish meal which Peeperkorn ostenatiously orders and then imperiously dismisses, is, in its senseless waste and extravagance, hardly conducive to increasing the reader's respect for the Dutch planter; and ironically, just a few pages later, the great personality makes an appeal for the simple life, thereby managing to effect a contradiction of the first magnitude.

The manner in which the other residents of Berghof react to Peeperkorn calls to mind the devoted attention which Prince Klaus Heinrich's subjects inevitably paid to him for one bit of trivia after the other.

Peeperkorn is unreflective in his remarks, democratic in his interests (he treats each bit of trivia with the same gusto and abundant energy), and questionable in his relationships with the inhabitants of Berghof:

> He made love to each and every woman within reach, without discrimination and without consideration of person. He even made such propositions to the dwarfish servant girl that that crippled figure broke out with grinning lines to cover her aging, oversized face. He paid Mrs. Stöhr compliments of such a type that made the vulgar creature press her shoulder forward extravagantly and become almost senseless with adoration. He begged for--and received-- a kiss on his thick, chapped lips from Miss Kleefeld. He even flirted with the hopeless Mrs. Magnus--all of this without offending the delicate homage he paid to his traveling companion, whose hand he often pressed to his lips with gallant thought. (III, 793)

When we bear in mind the Mannian hero's rigid aversion towards overt expression of his feelings, especially in such a commonplace fashion, we cannot help but be astonished at the blatant irony or even coarse duplicity with which Mann handles this character. Hans Castorp's tone, beneath his apparent affection for the patriarch, repeatedly assumes a derisive and hypocritical quality, as if he were consciously baiting a buffoon with undeserved praise. Castorp is openly described as a rascal and a wag who knows how to be impudent with a great personality like Peeperkorn and yet be able to extricate himself unharmed. And the author himself, even while commenting on the hero's sympathy towards Peeperkorn, indirectly disparages the old man: "[some people would prefer] that our hero should hate Peeperkorn, avoid him and had spoken of him only as an old jackass and a cowering old drunkard. Instead we see him at Peeperkorn's bedside when he was attacked by fever . . . allowing himself to be taken in by the personality . . ." (III, 797).

Sometimes the ridicule is even more direct and this man of "Format" takes on more the role of a lamentable figure, as he is designated as a stupid old man and a domineering zero. Hans Castorp imitates him, as he previously had mocked the utterances of Settembrini, and in the same breath he is certainly equivocal in defending the Dutchman when Settembrini calls him stupid (III, 807-808). Nor are Peeperkorn's stature and bearing always considered imposing; when he is outdoors he looks much less than majestic, and in one description he even appears as a feeble old man (III, 806). But the most telling proof of Peeperkorn's rejection is to be found in Clawdia Chauchat's evasive and ultimately negative answer to Hans Castorp's question as to whether she loves the Dutch planter or not.

Peeperkorn's inarticulateness, more than any other aspect of his personality, is emphasized. This inability to finish a single sentence is pointed up continuously, and the high point of the caricature is reached in Peeperkorn's grotesque oration before a thunderous waterfall, an oration which no one hears. What could be more absurd than the sight of an inarticulate person trying to outshout a thunderous waterfall? Indeed, the arrogance and foolishness of someone trying to accomplish this in earnest indicates only the predominance of blind will over good sense. It recalls the many statements of one of Mann's mentors, Arthur Schopenhauer, who repeatedly set out to show how the myopic, willful force of life, untempered by intellect, dramatically and repeatedly reveals its own shallowness. In varying his old theme of the hollow affirmer of life, of the assertive, uninhibited personality who, though paying total homage to life and appearing fully equipped for survival, fails miserably and is found to be ludicrously deficient, Thomas Mann paints the ultimate portrait, nearly ad absurdum, in the person of Mynheer Peeperkorn. The composition of The Magic Mountain takes a new turn by this commanding and royal figure, for now Settembrini and Naphta, more philosophical repre-

216

sentations than corporeal characters, become less important and central to the narrative. Hans Castorp is
no longer interested in the abstractions of East and
West; what commands his attention at this time is the
figure of life, Peeperkorn, the paternal rival in the
Oedipal situation.

The Eternal Triangle

    Hans M. Wolff's belief that Peeperkorn is a cari-
cature of Gerhart Hauptmann and basically something
external is undoubtedly correct.[30] Whatever the resemblance to the German dramatist, the fact remains
that Hauptmann was certainly not inarticulate and was
highly thought of by the author; yet Thomas Mann made
little or no effort to conceal the identity of the
figure, and Hauptmann recognized himself immediately
in the character of Peeperkorn. How is one to explain
this violation of taste and decorum, especially in view
of Thomas Mann's reputation for propriety and form?
And if neither Thomas Mann nor Gerhart Hauptmann could
find a reason or purpose for this all too obvious and
yet pointless caricature, then it is not too bold to
assume that Hauptmann's role is a subterfuge to mask
a specific attitude, to camouflage an inbred antipathy
towards a life force that blindly dominates the scene.

    Hauptmann was insulted rather than flattered by
the Peeperkorn portrait, and with good reason, although
Peeperkorn is praised and admired by both Hans Castorp
and the author himself in his commentaries. To be sure
Hans Castorp drinks Brüderschaft with Peeperkorn and
seeks out his company as often as possible, but if
friendship and fraternity with this "true representative" of life is submitted as evidence for the hero's
kinship to life, then the evidence rides only on the
surface, for the hero's guilt still has a deep-seated
position in his soul. Have things really changed from
the stark attitude expressed in Thomas Mann's letter
(to his brother Heinrich) of January 3, 1918?: "I
didn't want this life on earth. I detest it. One must
live it to the end as well as he can."[31] The total
Peeperkorn episode, as well as other aspects yet to be
discussed, speaks strongly against such a transformation. If Peeperkorn is praised on the one hand as "a
great personality," he is diminished on the other as
energy without substance, as a vacuous spirit plagued
by nameless anxieties and impotency. But what at a
glance may seem so odd, namely that Hans Castorp submits to him consciously but never totally, begins to

217

assume logical meaning if we relegate Peeperkorn to the dominant position of the father and reduce Hans Castorp to the unequal role of the child. With Clawdia Chauchat as the maternal influence we once again establish the familial triangle of Mann's Buddenbrooks and other intervening works. And the mere weight of external evidence should be sufficient to convince us of the set role which Peeperkorn, Chauchat, and Castorp play within the total context of this novel: Peeperkorn is a businessman, plantation owner, and tycoon like Samuel Spoelmann in Royal Highness, who, incidentally, also came from an exotic land. Like Thomas Buddenbrook he has two palatial houses and is ailing. In a similar manner to Hanno, Hans Castorp witnesses the death of a father. (Peeperkorn is constantly calling Castorp his child and in Castorp's description of Peeperkorn we see a child's ambivalent conception of his father--strong, majestic, domineering, and unpredictably inclined to anger, but at the same time impotent, sickly and afraid of life.) In scenes paralleling Hanno Buddenbrook's relationship with Thomas, Peeperkorn is rendered impotent and ineffectual--and at the end he is a sorry and pitiful figure whose death is as unheroic as was Thomas Buddenbrook's. One describes Peeperkorn as tall and broad, giving the impression of being robust, but it is only an impression: he has a wrinkled face, there is no color to his eyes, and he is twice described as a doddering old man.

Recalling that previously (in the chapter "The Dance of Death") Hans Castorp was the only one among all the patients, and despite opposition, who instituted the practice of visiting the moribundi (those patients on the point of dying), we must find it exceptionally significant that he now sees fit to sit at the bedside of Peeperkorn when the old man becomes merely ill. Is Hans Castorp, suspecting that the Dutchman is going to die, endowed with prophetic vision? At any rate, his vigil at Peeperkorn's bed, having been prepared for in the earlier chapter, can now be conceived of as a kind of culminating duty. We know that Hans Castorp's visits to the moribundi gave him as much pleasure as it did the patients, for his anticipation of their death was a constant source of morbid pleasure and relief for him. He now awaits Peeperkorn's death with fascination. But for all the professed devotion Hans Castorp displays no real emotion when Peeperkorn dies! In fact, Peeperkorn's death may be construed as Hans Castorp's triumph: "over Peeperkorn's dead body," he kisses Clawdia Chauchat!

Peeperkorn's suicidal death poses an additional
problem that extends in significance far beyond itself.
After his death, Hans Castorp feels that life is not
worth living: "Hans Castorp looked about him. Everywhere he saw the uncanny and the malicious, and he knew
what he was seeing: life without time, life hopeless
and without care, life as depraved and assiduously
stagnating, dead life" (III, 872). This attitude--so
contrary to his famous avowal of life in the chapter
"Snow"--develops immediately after Peeperkorn's death.
Why should Hans Castorp feel this way unless it is a
reflection of some deep inner emotional turmoil? For
what conceivable reason should Hans Castorp no longer
wish to live because the old man has died? Again, the
whole Peeperkorn episode only makes sense when viewed
as a father-son relationship within a family situation.
Witness, for example, Hans Castorp's recalcitrant
schoolboy behavior as he contradicts the threatening
father figure, provoking him one time, deferring and
agreeing the next, submitting then to the superior
force of his personality, but ultimately trying to retain his individuality and the father's good graces.

In spite of her seductive name and the apparent
passions which surround her, Clawdia Chauchat reflects
the cold nature, yet tempting qualities of the Mannian
mother figure in general. She does not love her sur-
rogate husband, Peeperkorn. One also fails to see any
indication of any real deep love for Hans Castorp. She
mechanically accompanies Peeperkorn for some incomprehensible reason which is never explained;* and she submits to Castorp only with an air of flattered but indifferent concession. Such a relationship of a woman
to two men is an odd one at best, but an incomprehensible one at worst if not perceived as an involvement
with maternal overtones. The stuff from which Thomas
Mann has cut the material for Clawdia Chauchat has a
familiar pattern. She often appears disheveled as
Consuelo Kröger did, and like all Mannian heroines she
is cold and has strange dark shadowed eyes, bluish in

---

*Compare Spinell's carping on this issue in
Tristan! There too the assertion is made that the
marriage between the Klöterjahns is completely unnatural
and ill-advised. Indeed, Spinell even goes so far as
to refuse to recognize the fait accompli and stubbornly
wishes it out of existence.

tint. She is somewhat histrionic in her gestures, although her relationship with others can only be defined as subdued, stand-offish, or perfunctory. She is, once again, foreign born, exotic, tempting and yet terrifying; for, of course, a very conspicuous element of danger is involved: Hans Castorp, like most Mannian heroes, can only become excited about a forbidden married woman.

If, as the author suggests, there was sexual consummation between Clawdia Chauchat and Hans Castorp on the evening after the carnival, then their unnatural indifference to one another and their exaggerated concern for Peeperkorn, become doubly puzzling. Why does Hans Castorp now expend all his energies trying to ingratiate himself with Peeperkorn rather than win Clawdia back again? Why has his former "passionate love" suddenly turned so cold? Hans Castorp's relationship to Clawdia is striking only in its inconstancy and insensibility (similar to that of Spinell's lackluster reaction to Frau Klöterjahn in Tristan once he gained what he had sought). His real aim was to vanquish his rival, and once he accomplished that, he was no longer interested in a relationship with her--certainly not in a permanent one. He prefers to listen to phonograph records and fantasize his pleasures rather than assume unnecessary risks.

But let us return again to Hans Castorp's preoccupation with Peeperkorn and point out how and why his professed affection for the man does not ring true. If Hans Castorp has been waiting in Berghof for Clawdia's return, as in fact the author insists and the critics agree he does, then what a terrible shock it must be to have her return under the protection of a powerful and vindictive father figure. How is he to react in the face of possible retribution by such an imposing person? He realizes that to hate such a powerful adversary openly is to court disaster. Only one alternative seems open to him--to make a virtue out of necessity and curry favor with this mentor and protector of Clawdia Chauchat. The undeserved praise and affection which Hans Castorp lavishes on Peeperkorn reflect the confused inner state of one trying to win the favor of a person he fears to have as an enemy. Like a child sensing the possible anger of a father, Castorp cajoles Peeperkorn while nervously attempting to retain a feeling of integrity--although not at the price of provoking him--and finally submitting in all encounters of will. To retain some modicum of dignity he must con-

vince himself of the strengths and virtues of this man
and dare not admit that he is cowering to some intellectually inferior being against whom he has transgressed. The focus of his behavior is set on deceiving
Peeperkorn, convincing him of friendship, while almost
as if by practice and design he leads Peeperkorn to his
death. The discussions, for example, on death and poi-
sons between the two are as suggestive as they are
informative. When Peeperkorn finally commits suicide,
and Castorp receives the kiss from Clawdia Chauchat,
it is a formal kiss of victory. The kiss contains no
passion, for the final psychic battle which Hans Castorp
waged was not so much one of desire for Clawdia as it
was one based ultimately on hate and fear of an ominous
figure of life and of retaliation. Hans Castorp's
total being was committed to ridding himself (at least
on the uncontrollable level of fantasy) of the threatening figure of the father. And when it finally happens
as he had so ardently wished, then the effect produced
must be understood as one of mordant guilt rather than
relief--and the guilt is of such a nature that it
evokes, in turn, two additional responses: (1) an
involuntary repression of the natural emotions of love
and hate that results in a persistent state of apathy,
and (2) a desire for punishment in kind, in retribution
for the fantasized crime of leading Peeperkorn to his
death. Both effects are in evidence in the novel, and
both precisely determine the conclusion of this momentous work.

The Education and Death of Hans Castorp

By and large critics agree that The Magic Mountain
is the gathering place of current thoughts, disciplines,
philosophies, and histories, and that the story of the
novel is essentially the story of Hans Castorp's fascination with these ideas and concepts. The most usual
explanation for the Settembrini-Naphta conflict is that
they are two vocalized philosophies fighting for the
possession of Hans Castorp's soul; for it is certainly
true that their disputations comprise the material bulk
of the work. Hans Castorp supposedly receives an education as a result of his sojourn in Berghof (for the
most part from Naphta and Settembrini), an education
which is the result of an eclectic selection of elements
that affirm life but nevertheless recognize fully that
it also has its dark side.

The attainment of this ultimate clarity takes

place in the chapter entitled "Snow," which Weigand characterizes as "the spiritual climax of the whole novel."[32] On his near fatal journey into the snowy landscape of the Alps, Hans Castorp has a vision of a Mediterranean landscape in which dwell <u>Sonnenleute</u>, people of happiness. But behind the surface happiness of the children of the sun (<u>Lichtmenschen</u>) lurk the inescapable horrors of life and the senselessness of existence. The view shifts abruptly from the idyllic and sunny surroundings of these people to an unlit temple with a horrible scene in its center: two execrable hags in the act of dismembering and eating a child. After he awakes from his dream-like state, Hans Castorp slowly formulates the end result, presumably, of his education in Berghof: "For the sake of love and goodness, man shall not concede mastery over his thoughts to death" (III, 686). <u>In nuce</u> this sentence, the only one in spaced type in the whole work, represents the high point of the novel. But what is especially striking about the hero's newly acquired knowledge is its triteness, a judgment which we base on the fact that this idea, so conventional in the writings of Mann, is suddenly proclaimed with a vehement claim to freshness. With a kind of spiritual revelation that can only be considered a substitute for genuine clarification, Hans Castorp grasps an idea, already bland in the scope of Mann's early writings, as the epitome of wisdom. But it is a wisdom that is entirely counterfeit--for it dwindles rapidly (showing its evanescence), and, as an insight, it has essentially become used up.

It would be repetitious to compare this apparent rejection of death's powers with the words of Tonio Kröger's claim of love for life. But the need of both to assert that thoughts of death will no longer control their lives betrays certain inherent doubts. In fact, Hans Castorp's statement of affirmation is made twice during the snow scene. Mann's insistence on spelling the idea out so palpably is doubly suspicious in view of the short-lived effect it has upon the hero. Just several paragraphs later, after Hans Castorp has escaped death in the snow and returned to the Berghof dining-room, we read: "At dinner he took sizeable helpings. What he had dreamed was already beginning to fade. What he had thought out he no longer understood that very evening" (III, 688). Hirschbach concludes from these words that "Snow" <u>is</u> "a glorious episode without consequences. . . ."[33] In the same way that Thomas Buddenbrook's experience of <u>death</u> à la

Schopenhauer did not take hold, so, too, is Hans
Castorp's vision of <u>life</u> devoid of any lasting quality;
for he does in fact permit death to hold sway over his
thoughts to the very end.

After Joachim Ziemssen's death, Castorp's interest
in Settembrini and Naphta dwindles; and when the two
debaters return to the center of the stage after a
prolonged absence, their arguments, aside from one
meager paragraph of rebuttal by Settembrini, are in
indirect discourse, indicating their lack of vital import for the hero's further enlightenment. At times
Hans Castorp is patently bewildered by his friends'
rambling exchange of words, as if it were now a hopeless task to follow them. His interest wanes steadily
and occasionally he is annoyed by both men. At the
end of it all, the two litigants' bickerings have little
relationship to the implied aim of winning Hans Castorp's
soul. Thus, as far as the representatives of East and
West are concerned, the hero's education is essentially
complete with "Snow," although in point of time Hans
Castorp's sojourn in Berghof has only reached the half-
way mark. Four and one-half years are still left out
of the seven, certainly time enough for him to get
back into life if that is really what he wishes. But
the "new" Hans Castorp's actions are puzzling, to say
the least. Frank Donald Hirschbach, rightly concerned
about the hero's behavior, sums up the contradictions
as follows:

> That Hans Castorp becomes thoroughly pre-
> occupied with death prior to his excursion
> into the snow is an obvious fact. That he
> turns away from the side of death and that
> he decides to take a renewed interest in
> life, is also a fact. But the reader might
> look at the remaining 334 pages which fol-
> low the snow scene and ask: How does Hans
> Castorp express his new interest in life?
> Does he make any attempt to burst the chains
> that hold him? Does he engage in activities
> or find new interests which express a more
> positive attitude toward life? The answer
> to all these questions must be negative.
> Between "Snow" and "The Thunderclap" lie
> almost five years of continued lethargy.
> During this time his health improves to
> a point where Doctor Behrens himself can
> no longer explain the causes of his high
> temperature. The causes for his deten-

tion, the tubercular spots on his lung,
are gone. During these five years, he
has three great experiences: the acquaintance with Mynheer Peeperkorn, music and
the seance. The Peeperkorn affair lasts
about six months, his musical infatuation
perhaps another six months, and the seance
one night. Between these experiences lie
years and years of dullness, infertile
periods during which Hans Castorp merely
vegetates. Why does he stay?[34]

As a supplement to these remarks we should also
remember that the hero has no real friends among the
patients of Berghof, except perhaps Settembrini who,
however, wants Hans Castorp to return to the flatland.
The inhabitants of the sanatorium are a shallow, frivolous and brainless lot who have nothing in common with
the hero. Their way of looking at music contrasts significantly with Hans Castorp's all-consuming passion
for it. Countless references to the vulgarity and
stupidity of Frau Stöhr, the most memorable of the minor
actors, becomes an obvious leitmotif. Other, perhaps
more important representatives of the commonplace,
Ferge and Wehsal, also fail to touch a responsive chord
in the reader, even in the duel near the end; and at
times they are pilloried mercilessly: Wehsal with his
ludicrous and gushing pathos and Ferge with his colossal
ignorance. (The latter is only capable of perorating
on the manufacture of rubber boots in Russia.)

It has been argued that the hero's reason for
lingering on in the sanatorium is the end result of his
intense love for Clawdia Chauchat. At least this is
the rationalization of Hans Castorp himself. But how
convincing is a passion which is carried on for the
most part from a distance and which is, in a sense,
climaxed by indifference or even by hostility: "In
a word: Hans Castorp saw no more than a holiday adventure in his passive relationship to this slovenly
member of the patients up here, an adventure which
could make no claim for sanction before a tribunal of
reason or of his own enlightened conscience: principally because Mrs. Chauchat was, after all, sick, in-
dolent, feverish and tainted within, a condition which
was closely connected to the disreputability of her
entire way of life and was vehemently concerned as
well with Hans Castorp's reservations and feelings of
caution" (III, 203). We must agree here with Hans
M. Wolff's explanation of the hero's vegetation in his

224

sanatorium retreat: "To be sure, even his fruitless waiting is in the final analysis only a pretense, for the actual reason for his lingering on is not his love for Madame Chauchat, who, precisely like Tadzio, is strictly speaking only a symbol, but rather this sensitive latecomer's fear of life."[35] Thus, all told, six years and three months elapse between "Walpurgisnacht" and "The Thunderclap" with the Peeperkorn interlude which strikes the reader as episodic, filling in probably no more than half a year.

Just as mystifying as his prolonged stay is the hero's sudden decision to leave. His complete lack of patriotic feelings, his unconcern for the other patients who may have left for war, and his almost total indifference to the fate of his relatives in the flatland show convincingly that there is nothing in the world below to motivate his departure or his desire to take up the dangerous life of a soldier. In a conversation with Clawdia Chauchat he says, "To whom should I write letters? I have no one. I no longer have any feeling for the flatland; I have lost it entirely" (III, 823). Hirschbach's conjecture is that as a result of his apathy in life, Hans Castorp seeks death on the battlefield as an honorable form of suicide, an observation that is completely consistent with the hero's distaste for life after the death of Peeperkorn.[36] And to Hatfield as well, Hans Castorp's departure signifies that he has rejected any avowal of life: "Mann has been blamed for this resolution: Castorp's entrance into the battle can be read as a repudiation of the vision in the snow; death, dialectically defeated, is historically victorious."[37]

The ending of the novel is, however, not simply a paradox but rather a logical characterization of the guilty Mannian hero. Hans Castorp, who, like his brother artist figures, has hardly been exposed to life rejects it categorically in his longing for an end to his worthless existence. The paean of life epitomized in the snow scene is overshadowed by a longing for death. If on the surface the battle of philosophies and the suicide of Naphta have resulted in a rejection of darkness, then underneath there continues to lurk in Hans Castorp a deep aversion towards the perpetuation of his guilty life.

The fabric of conflict, guilt, and resolution in which Hans Castorp is imprisoned and from which he cannot liberate himself is like the web that entangled

Tristan and Isolde,* and most of Mann's earlier heroes.
Applying the schema of the medieval epic Tristan and
Isolde to The Magic Mountain, we conclude that a bold
and terrifying change of plot has taken place--King
Marke dies! Theoretically, at least, this should leave
the lovers a free path to happiness, as one might have
believed when he still stood as an obstacle between
the two; but one soon discovers that the death of a
king is a double-edged sword. A great figure who has
been the center of all concerns, loyalties and fears,
hate and love, disdain and admiration, has vanished
from the scene; and along with him disappears a primary
vortex of life, making the hero's return to life "flat,
stale and unprofitable." Peeperkorn is dead and, consciously or unconsciously, Hans Castorp has led the
supreme Moribundus up to death's very door, playing
the part of the loyal subject while looking forward
with a feeling of pleasure and relief to his liege's
death. But once the death occurs, powerful feelings
of guilt arise to prevent any flow of emotion that
might again draw him into some similar painful involvement. The result is a complete rejection of any contact with aspects or agents of life, and all expressions of vital existence are now made to look either
ludicrous or abhorrent. By guilty necessity then,
Hans Castorp becomes the personification of a person

---

*After Clawdia returns with Peeperkorn, a scene of
some tenderness does take place, one which exhibits
many of the conflicting difficulties in the courtly
concept of keeping troth. When Hans Castorp asks
Clawdia if she loves Peeperkorn passionately, she replies, "He loves me . . . and his love made me proud
and grateful and devoted to him. . . . His feelings
forced me to follow and serve him. What else could I
do?" (III, 829). And Hans Castorp agrees that her
loyalty is certainly owed to him, to Peeperkorn; but
all the while this tender conversation on obedience,
trust, and fidelity is going on, the two are sitting
"knee to knee," "pressing each other's hand," and
finally: "she kissed him fully on the mouth. It was
a Russian kiss, the kind that is exchanged in that
vast, spiritual land, at high, religious feasts, as a
seal of love" (III, 831). Only by pretending loyalty
to Peeperkorn can Castorp delude himself that he may
kiss Clawdia Chauchat again.

dégagé, occupied only with a few impersonal and aimless
pursuits or with the self-gratification of voluptuous
music.

Once Peeperkorn is dead, Hans Castorp's feelings
of guilt prohibit him from taking the lady as his prize.
Indeed, he does not even seem to feel any attraction
to her any longer, as if the battle had been concerned
only with outlasting the enemy rather than in taking
the spoils. But the repercussions of the competition
go much further. Dwelling on thoughts of death that
cause apathy and despair does not mollify to any great
degree Castorp's burden of guilt. His love and involvement in life ended with an adversary's death and
now he must pay for that death with his own life.

The degree of pleasure which Hans Castorp derives
in seeking out his own death on the battlefield borders
on blissful apotheosis. He is fighting for nothing but
his own destruction, and he presses forward to find it
with a feeling of frenetic, gleeful exultation. One
would be hard pressed to find a more succinct glorification of the horrors of war than one finds in the description, on the final pages of this book, of the
tortured, blood-stained soldiers: "Here they lie, their
noses in the fiery filth. They are glad to be here--"
(III, 992). As Hans Castorp gouges his hobnailed boots
into the hand of a fellow comrade, we find him singing!:
"What, singing? Yes, that is how he uses his breath,
he sings unaware, staring straight ahead" (III, 993).

Only now, in immediate anticipation of dying, can
Castorp feel lighthearted and relieved of his oppressive
sense of guilt with its deadening impact. Only now, as
he faces punishment by death, can he charge aggressively
into the fray, totally involved, glad and singing. Why
is his pleasure so supreme in this carnage? What has
he done within the whole scope of this novel that might
cause him to seek out death so gleefully on the field
of battle? He had rejected the voice of good sense
(Settembrini) and taken possession of Clawdia Chauchat;
he had professed loyalty and fraternity to Peeperkorn
and yet taken his hidden pleasure in "the great God's"
death; for as Clawdia remarks at his demise, his suicide was "'. . . une abdication,' she said. 'He knew
of our folly?'" (III, 867). Of course, he had guessed
at the truth of their relationship, Castorp answers her.

His crimes of conscience were of no less magnitude
than that of breaking troth, seduction, and (at least

in the realm of fantasy) murder! Rather than ars
vivendi, the art of living, we find ourselves confronted
in The Magic Mountain with a book which is essentially
a description of ars moriendi. The Peeperkorn-Chauchat
experience yields the final crystallization of the
death desires which Hans Castorp had already brought
to the mountains with him. This delicate child of life,
as he is called, possesses a quality congenital to all
of Mann's heroes; Hans Castorp is cast in the old Mannian mold, for his sickness began long before he as-
cended the Magic Mountain. Already in the flatland he
was not attracted by the challenges of life: "For
some reason it [my profession] did not draw me. I admit this openly, even if I can't explain the reasons
for it other than to say that they are veiled in obscurity, the same obscurity that envelops the origin
of my feeling for your [Peeperkorn's] traveling companion . . ." (III, 847-848).

If Hans Castorp's threatening involvements in an
affair of the heart constitute a dangerous journey for
him, then the nature of the danger must be a recollection from childhood--for nothing really happens in the
whole scope and sequence of The Magic Mountain which
can possibly be interpreted as a major crisis or justification for suicide on the battlefield. Castorp was
soured on life even before his arrival on the Mountain,
and now the fairly harmless replay of the Oedipal situation is enough to tilt the scales in favor of punishment and death. In Berghof, Hans Castorp finds nothing
new--he merely confronts an old specter and acts out
the subconscious phantasmagoria that he has brought up
to the sanatorium with him!

Essentially, Hans Castorp remains unaffected by
the struggle between the enlightenment of Settembrini
and the terror of Naphta; he does not really heed their
arguments, nor does he learn anything from all the
other patients, but rather he listens only to the
inner voice of guilt. Despite their length and com-
plexity, the experiences and disputes are only superficially meaningful for the hero's existence.

How untenable, then, seen in the present light,
are the conclusions of Heinrich Mann, the author's
brother, who finds affirmation in this novel: "Der
Zauberberg too teaches us only how to live,"[38] or to
Lydia Baer, who claims that this work represents a new
humanism, a manifestation of Mann's "growing friendliness to life."[39] Mann himself uses the term "humanity"

to define The Magic Mountain[40] and endorses the view held by these two critics: "It is a book of good intentions and resolve, a book of imaginary renunciation of many things that I loved, of many a dangerous kinship, enchantment and seduction . . . a book of farewell . . .; a book to serve life, its purpose is health, its goal the future."[41] But in this case we must draw on the adage that the author is at times the poorest judge of his own work! If we were to believe Thomas Mann here, we might also be compelled to believe his equally indefensible and incredible statement that The Magic Mountain is a humorous novel.[42]

Time and Regression

Along with Hans Castorp's waning involvement in life in the splendid isolation of Berghof, time loses its meaning, stands still, or expunges itself for him. His rejection of time, the yardstick of responsible activity, is tantamount in the final analysis to a flight from reality; his attitude stands in direct contrast to the activities of the conscientious citizen for whom time is equivalent to work and money. The hero literally "kills time" to achieve a suspension of purposes, for time, in order to be felt as a real element, must be invested with emotions and activities in a human context. In the hermetically sealed society of Berghof the hero manages to freeze his sense of time along with his emotions, and to nullify the past and present of its imperatives of duty. Thus, existence in a time vacuum is what ultimately defines Hans Castorp's hermetically enclosed life in the Alps. Berghof, like Detlev Spinell's "monastic" sanctuary in Einfried, remains a place where risk of exposure is held to a minimum, despite Hatfield's comment that "this very hermetic quality makes it an unequaled if perilous place of education."[43] There is actually a high degree of safety in this disease-ridden world that does not possess the immediate challenges of life. The give-and-take, which is life, is not at all present in this refuge from the responsibilities of the flatland. Therefore, the designation of The Magic Mountain as a Bildungsroman that develops the hero in a sequence of time, is in need of qualification for the simple reason that all previous models of this genre in German literature, from Wilhelm Meister on, have been concerned with the hero's education in the environment of a real world, not on a "magic" mountain.

The patients subsist in a constant state of iso-

lated play just like children who lack an acute sense
of time. Because of illness, they are not held strictly
liable for their actions, for a grim retribution has
already been paid to them in the form of sickness, and
their stringent conscience is enfeebled inasmuch as
the evasion of duty carries no penalty. They have no
real work to do or duties to fulfill, and so for them
every yesterday, today and tomorrow become the ever-
present now. They are not able to project into the
future or to forge plans that control their destiny;
and the distantly past traumas, insofar as their mind
can retain the memory of them, appear to have happened
only yesterday. In Hans Castorp's case, as with all
of Mann's heroes, time, the metronome of his conscience,
is initially felt to be closely linked to discipline
and duty and therefore a race against the clock. Up
until his trip to the Magic Mountain, there was a
frantic need for him to order life into manageable
units of time. His compulsion towards time in finish-
ing his studies, going to work, etc., reflected the
Mannian hero's unbearable pressure of his obligations
and conscience, but that is suspended in the Berghof's
world of disease and death. Liberated from his ties
of conscience in the land of the dead and dying, he
is also liberated from his relentless sense of time,
and for the while, Hans Castorp succeeds in achieving
the tranquillity of innocence as he reverts to what
is basically a child's conception of time.

While in Berghof Hans Castorp really exists in a
vacuum, for the element of meaningful emotion has been
withdrawn from his behavior and his attitude towards
time has become devoid of purpose and progress. Indeed, what kind of direction is possible for Hans
Castorp as he vegetates in a hermetically sealed realm
where personal problems are held to a minimum and where
he can, like a naughty boy, bring self-indulgence to a
high state of perfection; where he can disclaim all
necessity for an active life and let his fantasy assume
supreme control?

As Hans M. Wolff says, "The enchanted inhabitants
of the mountain have no ambition, goals or obligations
at all and are only excited about one single desire:
to enjoy themselves insofar as their illness will permit it."[44]

And Hans Castorp attempts to justify his juvenile
morbidity in the oft quoted lines which he addresses
to Clawdia Chauchat: "But unreasoning love is spirit-

ual; for death . . . is the <u>spiritual</u> principle . . .
for love of it leads to love of life and love of humanity. . . . There are two paths to life; one is the
regular, direct, honest. The other is bad, it leads
through death--that is the <u>spiritual</u> way!" (III, 827).

But, as it turns out, this famous citation from
<u>The Magic Mountain</u> is a hoax. The hero's preoccupation
with death does not lead him to a love for life or for
people. In fact, this is perhaps the most fraudulent
statement in the novel, if not in world literature.
What humanity, love, or even humane attitude is there
in Hans Castorp's attitude towards his fellow patients,
or, for that matter, where it is abstract and entails
no risk, for even mankind as a whole? In Berghof he
lives for himself, pretending tolerance only where it
leads to his own gratification; and on the battlefield
at the end he dies only for his own needs, looking forward to death as self-punishment and pleasure. At
best, Hans Castorp tolerates the people in Berghof, but
even here, as in Frau Stöhr's case, tolerance is lacking.

Is Hans Castorp's disavowal of time not, therefore, commensurate with a rejection of life? Over and
over again he speculates and theorizes on time, rather
than invest his energies and emotions in it. And what
is the "magic" of the mountain if it is not its "timelessness" and its removal from the normal flow of life
and events? The source of pleasure for Hans Castorp
lies in his comfortable and depersonalized sojourn outside of time. But now one may also quite honestly ask
what pleasures really exist outside of time, for that
is, in truth, "the stuff that life is made of." Mann's
answer to such a question is the work itself, for it
is a complete study in suspended emotion, aimless
existence, encapsulated triviality--a study in the willful withdrawl from life. Why? If life is the bearer
of pleasure, it is also the purveyor of pain; but both
may be experienced only insofar as a person is able to
engage his emotions in life's events and entities. But
that is an investment which Hans Castorp cannot make.
Life had long ago turned painful for him; somewhere in
the scope of his experience, emotional commitment had
become too terrifying. Something had hardened his emotions, made him involuntarily repress and control his
feelings, or, in the words of Tonio Kröger, "put them
on ice." A major transgression was made, remorse felt,
punishment feared, at first--and then desired. And
now Hans Castorp patiently awaits his fate, his final

release--death.

Is not Hans Castorp's preoccupation with death and his removal from time the result of his own deep-seated sense of guilt? His brooding and speculation about death in the abstract masks his personal problem of death, momentarily detracts and glosses over the thought and horror of his own doom. But at the same time there is a wonderful sense of sadistic gratification in this suspicion of his--about what he wishes to believe: that death <u>really does</u> hold sway over life and that the destruction or decay of the father world is actually only a matter of time.

The Magic Mountain as a Bildungsroman

A number of critics agree with the author himself when he describes his novel as a <u>Bildungsroman</u>. Roy Pascal claims that "Castorp gains a philosophy of life, love of men and tolerance, and with it returns to the real world, the world engaged in a death-struggle. . . ."[45] Weigand is the most articulate in applying this concept to the novel and defines it as an affirmative attitude towards life as a whole.[46] Elizabeth M. Wilkinson is typical of the many critics who agree with Weigand, for she too believes that Hans Castorp really embraces life: "Thomas Mann's great <u>Bildungsroman</u>, <u>The Magic Mountain</u>, . . . is the story of Everyman who, in his journeying through life, learns to become an artist of life, learns to use that two-edged sword, the imagination, so that it turns outward to fruitful living and not inward to self-destruction."[47] One of the few dissenters is Jean Fougére who appropriately calls <u>The Magic Mountain</u> a parody of a <u>Bildungsroman</u>.[48]

Although we have dealt with this topic in other sections, it was in passing; and other arguments which speak strongly against the designation, educational novel, must now be presented to bring the subject into sharper focus.

Aside from the absence of an affirmative attitude towards life which Weigand states as a precondition for the educational novel, the term <u>Bildungsroman</u> is further called into question by another look at Hans Castorp's so-called teachers. If, as it has been generally agreed upon, Naphta as a foil to Settembrini were really responsible to a great extent for the hero's education, then why did he make his entrance into the novel so late? He first appears on page 517 (the work embraces

232

994 pages), and his actual influence extends over only slightly more than 100 pages. As Hans M. Wolff points out: "The second part of the novel came into being at the time of the Treaty of Rapallo, when the question of the day was whether Germany was to make common cause with the democratic West or the communistic East."[49] The Treaty of Rapallo was formally signed on April 16, 1922, two years before the novel appeared in print, and the first mention of Naphta's existence and function in the novel is in a letter of June 2, 1922: "Leo Naphta . . . has appeared and is continually involved in sharp disputes with Herr Settembrini which one day will lead to a pedagogical duel."[50] If Naphta's role as an exponent of terror with leanings toward the left were truly dependent upon this actual event in Germany's foreign policy, then his function and influence were inserted in the novel as an afterthought and forces one to ask if Mann himself had been aware of his original intent.

In the beginning Mann's interest was directed towards the Rhetor-Bourgeois Settembrini: "When Mann sketched his plan of the novel in 1912, he saw Settembrini exclusively as the representative of 'Virtue,' this word to be understood in the sense of the Observations of a Non-political Man. . . ."[51] Certainly, then, Mann was not thinking of writing a Bildungsroman in 1912, for it is asking too much to expect Hans Castorp, the music-loving German, to truly heed the words of a Zivilisationsliterat, that is, a loud-mouthed politician and tedious fighter for democracy. Historically and psychologically, in fact, it defies credence to view Settembrini as a mentor of the hero at all! To accept such a proposition would mean dismissing the whole of the Observations of a Non-Political Man as a meaningless interlude in the author's life. It would infer that this immense outburst of speculation and writing which consumed the author's energies and seared his soul for the length of the war touched him only lightly or was perhaps meant to be a five-finger exercise. For Thomas Mann to renounce the strident argument of the Observations of a Non-Political Man as a futile and frustrating endeavor once postwar inertia and misery settled over Germany is one thing, but for him to embrace in a convincing and authentic way the anti-musical, father-world of Settembrini is quite another. Such an interpretation would presume a genuine reconciliation between the hatred father and the artistically oriented son whose whole nature is supercharged with murderous fantasy. Although Thomas Mann claimed in 1950 that he had dissociated himself from the Observations of a Non-Political Man as soon as it was finished,[52] the truth is that he was still laboring under the same illusions of the war book shortly before and after the appearance of The Magic Mountain. In a letter of 1920 the tone is that of 1914 to 1918;[53] in another of 1922 the author denies that he disavowed his polemic of the war,[54] and in 1928 he states his position with even greater firmness: "For I do not renounce the Observations, and I have not done so with any words which I have written after its completion. One does not disavow his life, his experiences, or that which one has gone through, because one has gone through it. . . ."[55] And it was not until 1922, less than two years before the date of publication, that Thomas Mann referred to The Magic Mountain as a Bildungsroman. We do not know what inspired the author to apply such a designation at this late time, but it certainly appears doubtful that this appellation had much to do with the essence of the novel itself.

If asked to pinpoint the sum and essence of the hero's attainments in Berghof, one would certainly be hard pressed to come up with an answer. What is, after all, so special about Hans Castorp's education? His sympathy for the coffin and predilection for the grave was something he had acquired very early in life in the flatland, and here his attitude contrasts strikingly with that of Dr. Behrens. One can readily appreciate the value of the education Behrens receives from his life of dedicated work and service in Berghof, so similar in many respects to the devoted creativity of Gustav Aschenbach before his trip to Venice. By comparison, Hans Castorp's curiosity about the moribundi is pathologically tinged, he being less interested in an intellectual and scientific probing of the problem of death than in flattering his morbid inclinations and in savoring the pleasures of self-indulgence. It has been said that Hans Castorp gained a higher degree of freedom through sickness, in that it liberated him from the ties of life. But how illogical and contrary is such a view! Hans Castorp's behavior has in reality an infantile cast, his life in Berghof unquestionably resembling a regressive, dreamy, narcissistic paradise. Hans Castorp, it must be acknowledged, actually enjoys his self-inflicted incarceration in the sanatorium. In this respect he is practically a duplicate of the immature Detlev Spinell who found in Einfried a refuge from the crucible of life. Conspicuously missing from Hans Castorp's education are the truly formative ex-

234

periences of the adult personality. What has he learned
about hardship, love, or parenthood that he could not
more easily have acquired in the flatland? For that
matter, what real intellectual challenges has he been
exposed to in all those countless daily exchanges of
opinion? Settembrini, the delegate of life, is flatly
rejected; Naphta's rigid views are hardly to be taken
seriously, and Peeperkorn is simply unable to communi-
cate.

Hans Castorp's decision to stay on the "Magic
Mountain" is a commitment to death just as surely as
Gustav Aschenbach's flight from his work in Munich is
a renunciation of life. For each protagonist, the
"decision" represents an irrevocable step which terminates development rather than promotes it.

If not a Bildungsroman then, what did Thomas Mann
have in mind when he wrote The Magic Mountain, aside
from the depiction of a hero who yields to his morbid
tendencies and yearns to court the dangers of the
abyss? If anything, The Magic Mountain, minus the
political overtones of the Zivilisationsliterat, has
as much similarity to Royal Highness as to any of Mann's
other works. In order to demonstrate this theory it is
necessary to look more closely at the role of Joachim
Ziemssen, Hans Castorp's cousin, for it is in this
figure that the hero's inner-isolation is surmounted,
at least in part. Of all the inhabitants of Berghof,
including even Clawdia Chauchat and Peeperkorn, only
Ziemssen really ever has the confidence of the hero.
And after Ziemssen's death, which takes place immediately after "Snow," the novel takes on a fragmented
appearance, and thus it is at this point that there
occurs a definite break in the conception of the novel.
Once again, two figures, Hans Castorp and his cousin,
combine to form a montage of the Mannian artist. Descended from the patriciate of a Hanseatic family on
the wane, Joachim Ziemssen is called by Behrens the
Pollux to Castor(p). As Hans Castorp's only confidant,
he, by his silent and omniscient presence in the story,
can be called the corporeal conscience or alter ego of
the hero. In his extreme reserve, dedication to service of the state, and his penchant for the military
uniform, Joachim is a duplicate of Prince Klaus Heinrich
and thus an artist figure in his own right. His "purely
formal existence," the leitmotif of the hero of Royal
Highness, is continually alluded to, and he literally
reenacts a scene that took place at the beginning of
the earlier work when he, as a tyro officer, was saluted

for the first time by a soldier (III, 689). In his
letters he also mentions taking part in social functions, affairs which play such a dominant role in
Royal Highness. But by no means is Joachim Ziemssen
a bourgeois in the conventional sense. His life in the
service of form, which reechoes Tonio Kröger's obsession
with depersonalized art, makes him unfit for a real
existence in the flatland. Ziemssen dies of inadequacy,
for strict form leads to sterility and paralysis. He
is a reincarnation of the old Klaus Heinrich who, under
Überbein's influence, had qualms about expressing his
feelings and had crawled into a protective shell before
the arrival of Imma Spoelmann. Joachim, for example,
does not dare to address the laughing and exuberant
Marusja, and he never even meets her halfway until it
is too late. His death, like Überbein's suicide, is
supposed to confirm that the hero really has an independent hold on life. And he is just as determined in
his opposition to Madame Chauchat as Überbein was to
Klaus Heinrich's marriage to Imma Spoelmann.

But what is the significance of this montage?
Ziemssen is a model of repressed desires and the voice
of the hero's conscience; his death, right after the
"Snow" episode in which Hans Castorp is supposed to
find clarity of mind and love for life, corresponds to
the ending of Royal Highness where Klaus Heinrich finds
through his marriage a new--but unconvincing--lease on
life. Überbein's suicide, coinciding with Klaus Heinrich's marriage, gives sanction, presumably, to that
hero's newly acquired stake in life. Ziemssen, like
Überbein, is unable to live; and, unsuccessful in his
attempts to bridge the gulf between his purely formal
existence and the common people, he is likewise eliminated as an influence on the hero.

Ziemssen's death and the "Snow" experience represent the first of the dubious but familiar Tonio Kröger
affirmations of life which we found at the conclusion
of Royal Highness. The second occurs when life's advocate, Settembrini, gives Hans Castorp his blessings just
after Naphta shoots himself and thus supposedly loses
the battle of philosophies. Settembrini, we recall,
assumed a new function and personality in the last third
of the novel as opposed to his role of the detested
Rhetor-Bourgeois in the beginning; he changed character
to become, obviously and unjustifiably, more than a
match for the inflexible and pernicious Naphta. Sal-
vaged at the end to give Hans Castorp a push into life
in the flatland, Settembrini helps to neatly tie the

loose threads of the narrative and therefore to deceptively make a case for a positive affirmation of life.

The duplicate ending of The Magic Mountain is reflected in its composition, in that "Snow," the climax of the novel according to the critics, does not lead directly to an organic conclusion and appears to be functionally separate from the more than 300 pages which follow. As the high point it remains especially undramatic and shows in reality that Thomas Mann was obviously dissatisfied with the direction the work was taking after World War I when the duel between the music-loving German Hans Castorp and the loud-mouthed politician of the West Settembrini was bound to lose its sting. But, more importantly, the whole political conception of the novel, the original impetus of the work, was destined at the very outset to become a blind alley for Thomas Mann's art. The Rhetor-Bourgeois could not hope to sustain the author's artistic fervor--as, indeed, he did not--, even if the events of post-war history had not caught up with and passed by the questionable political abstractions which Mann had so heatedly formulated during the war. The conception of Settembrini was from the very beginning not the stuff of drama. As a purely political manifestation he could now have no direct bearing on the love-triangle situation which is and always has been the nucleus of Mann's belletristic writings. The author's resentment towards the Western politician could not bear artistic fruit, because the relationship between hero and antagonist was completely one-sided. Settembrini's characterization as a Western spokesman and foolish windbag precluded any and all tension in terms of a dramatic conflict. That is why Thomas Mann felt the need to shift the spotlight from Settembrini to Peeperkorn and thus to retard the ending after the climax "Snow." Retardation, a virtue in Death in Venice, therefore assumes its lengthy proportions in The Magic Mountain. Peeperkorn, the afterthought "inspired" by Gerhart Hauptmann, belatedly makes his entry and becomes the tie that binds. With the introduction of the Dutch planter, Mann takes the ending of The Magic Mountain out of the realm of the pure abstraction of the Observations of a Non-Political Man and returns it to a direct confrontation with an Oedipal situation where the dichotomies of Germany and the West no longer have any measure of artistic validity. Peeperkorn becomes the necessary catalyst for the author whose writings gained their strength and intensity from the eternally recurring Oedipal conflict.

237

The abstractions of culture and civilization which during the war provided Thomas Mann with an outlet for his deep-seated ebullient impulses were now no longer adequate as far as his immediate creative spark is concerned. Once the symbolic pressure of war had abated, the prime mover of Mann's passionate fury vanished with it. Peeperkorn thus supplanted the spokesman for the West, Settembrini, and the fascinating Oedipal theme once again became the relevant question and vital problem for the author.

Conclusion

In the case of The Magic Mountain Mann is scarcely the best critic. It is simply impossible to reconcile his words of affirmation with the morbid behavior of his hero; or, for example, to take the following words of the author seriously: "Yes, certainly, the German reader recognized himself again in the straightforward but 'cunning' hero of the novel. . . ."[56] In the first place, the two adjectives, straightforward and cunning, contradict each other; in the second, these words do not describe Hans Castorp nor convince most readers. Throughout the novel, Hans Castorp reveals clearly that he is not "straightforward," "cunning" nor even a "hero" in the usual sense of the word, but rather that he tends towards inner isolation and has little in common with anyone except Mann's own passive and crippled protagonists. Hans Castorp's main concern is a preoccupation with death that exceeds mere scientific curiosity and becomes an end in itself; actually from beginning to end his back is turned on life and his stand remains unmodified.

One wonders if the great international success of The Magic Mountain did not come as a real surprise to Thomas Mann who, after having written the greater portion of the novel under the spell of his war polemic, was perfectly willing in the twenties to pass over the Observations in silence, as he knew all too well that his political cause was not only dead but potentially damaging to his popularity as a writer. He could hardly have predicted that the critics would discover more in the novel than he himself dreamed of. To the critics it is, among other things, a microcosm of Europe before the First World War, a saga of Western man, a commentary on the crisis in Europe's culture, a great analysis of the age, a document on the psychic condition of Europe, a work about the twilight of the European bourgeoisie, and a novel whose hero is modern European man. These

statements fail, of course, to take the original conception of the novel into consideration: that it was
Thomas Mann's controlled, malevolent hatred of the
Zivilisationsliterat that determined the basic content
of the work. Consequently, it is safe to say that The
Magic Mountain is no more a microcosm of Europe than
Spinell's Einfried. Further, it is a tenuous proposition to equate the tuberculosis sanatorium with the
Europe on the brink of war, especially since it is not
at all certain whether Mann (who had the "Snow" chapter
as the ending of the novel in mind) had at all intended
to bring in the war at the end of the novel. If the
novel had been completed before the great war broke
out, then there would certainly be some validity to the
above statements by the critics, and Thomas Mann himself would have gained a deserved reputation for his
prophetic vision.

But regardless of what position one takes toward
this work, one cannot deny that The Magic Mountain is
a milestone in Mann's career. Henceforth Mann becomes
almost exclusively a writer of long works of fiction,
and with their greater length Mann frequently, and
unfortunately, thins out all the more genuine expressions of affect and neutralizes the passions of his
heroes. Irony and distance, his stock in trade, become even more pronounced, and his disengagement, so
similar to Tonio Kröger's gospel of frozen art, enables
Mann to stand aside from his creations instead of running the risk of being overwhelmed by their conflicts.
The doctrine of irony, an extension of Thomas Mann's
proverbial urbanity, becomes his new life preserver
in an ever changing world, reflecting not only the
resignation of defeat but also the loss of belief and
value. It resembles both a loss by default, in that
he does not bother to show up for the game at all, and
a victory over the mental anguish which is sure to follow from decisive involvement. The result is that Mann's
art takes on a self-consciousness that often results in
an all too arbitrary manipulation of plots and protagonists. He also develops a tendency to play with the
critics by feeding them what they want to devour; and
as a result, some artificial incongruities are posited
to give cause for speculation. When Mann's ex post
facto opinions conflict with the text of the work itself, the poor critic is really caught up in a dilemma,
for if one wishes to come to grips with some subtle
problem in the text, he often has to clear the way to
the problem with a refutation of the author's opinions.

In gaining distance by such various and sundry means, Mann becomes more detached from his hero's travail, while his own goal becomes the unassailable position of being above it all, one from which he may look down on life's activity. Mann's previous heroes, though just as passive, at least stood in a dramatic conflict with the threatening antagonist--one need only compare the Peeperkorn episode with the agonized tension between father and son in Buddenbrooks to comprehend the difference in approach. From now on--and with The Magic Moutain--the hero prefers to tilt with abstract windmills, and, as a result, Mann appears to gain stature as a philosophical writer, as he, ironically detached, expounds on the questions of life in complete safety.

Yet, after all critics have had their say, The Magic Mountain stands incontestably as one of the most widely read novels of the twentieth century. At times it is difficult to say why, for there have been very few novels as popular as The Magic Mountain with such pale shadows for characters. And the popularity of this work, we believe, certainly does not stem from Mann's avowed purpose in writing it! Its acclaim seems to reside in an attitudinal stance which the author strikes early and succeeds in preserving throughout the novel. The hero's superficial attachments and passive explorations in a world devoid of measurable time may, in the manner of a placebo, satisfy readers with its apparent plethora of forms and events that simulate but never impose on him the frustrating conflicts of real life. In addition, Mann also proves himself here to be an insatiable scholar and a master of digression as he wanders almost uncontrollably at times through one special area of knowledge and another: medicine, psychology, politics, sociology, philosophy, botany, and music. But for all that, Mann's genius for ensnaring the reader in a unified web of details sounds chords, rhythms, and a melody for a morbid dance of death that will undoubtedly continue to exert a fascination on the literary mind as well as on the general public for some time to come.

JOSEPH AND HIS "FATHERS"

The years of political fermentation prior to World War II presaged for Thomas Mann the creation and growth of enticing but personally threatening forces, which, in more ways than one, find anxious expression within the production period of Joseph and His Brothers. Two of Mann's most politically colored works, Mario and the Magician and The Tables of the Law, were the result of voluntary interruptions in the writing of his monumental Joseph tetralogy. The first of the two novellas was published in 1930, and in Mann's own words, "deals with the psychology of Fascism and of 'freedom.'"[1] The latter, written on conclusion of the first three volumes of the Joseph stories, is described by Mann as "the polemic against Nazism on behalf of human morality."[2]

It should, however, be remembered that between and beyond both these novellas, before, during, and after World War II--at home and in exile--Thomas Mann was constantly occupied with the creation of his Joseph tetralogy. As the forces of history increased in intensity, Mann was uprooted but submitted stoically to necessity, simultaneously recording the urges of his artistic imagination with Biblical symbolism, defensive irony, and transposed time. But in spite of the surface scenery which embellishes these works, we must still insist that the author's choice in arrangement and exposition rests solidly on the same psychological needs that conjured up the earlier Mannian fables and heroes.

Mario and the Magician

Simply stated, Mario and the Magician is the story (told within the frame of a first-person narrator) of a sadistic hypnotist who, during a stage performance at an Italian seaside resort, humiliates and provokes the young Italian Mario to kill him. With Cipolla as the magician of the title representing the power and fascination of a Fascist dictator, this story may readily be interpreted as an allegory of the political situation of 1930. But even where the political elements seem clearly obvious, they are, on examination, still subordinated to the theme of the artist who, in his isolation from life, hostility towards the world, and deficiency in the sexual sphere, is compelled to force the issue in order to gain relief from his inner drives.

The narrative, which in Hatfield's opinion falls

into two disparate parts, first treats the story-
teller's impressions of the hotel, the beach crowd and
then the fatal performance of the hypnotist Cipolla.
Though Cleugh has labelled the initial events "pleasant
anecdotes,"[3] Hatfield convincingly shows how these apparently harmless anecdotes possess real significance
by adding dimension to the second part.[4] And the fact
of the matter is that they are not pleasant at all.
The narrator is highly incensed at the annoyances and
high-handed behavior of the Italians in general, and
he obtains no sense of comfort in his stay at the resort, actually becoming bitter about ordinary people
for their naive misuse of power and sycophantic corruption.

Like Tonio Kröger and others, the narrator finds
the middle-class natives a pleasing breed to look at,
but is plainly disturbed by the mob's mediocrity. He
is further distressed by the harsh voices of the women
and disgusted by the ill-breeding and repulsiveness
of a particular young boy who is unable to endure even
a modicum of pain. In the narrator's attitude of disgust and admiration towards the middle class we detect
the familiar ambivalence of the Mannian heroes. Also
like Tonio Kröger, he is detained by the authorities
for a harmless reason: they take offense at the nudity
of his small daughter on the beach. Offended here, and
later in disgust, the narrator moves from his hotel
into a more refined atmosphere of the Pensione Eleonora
(in honor of Eleonora Duse, the artist) which harbors
a sense of the past and the artistic. Hatfield is quick
to point out how the international and somewhat aristocratic atmosphere of this residence is devastatingly
contrasted to the lower middle class vulgarity of the
resort.[5]

The oppressive atmosphere, the sirocco air, and the
official corruption recall <u>Death in Venice</u>. Like
Aschenbach the narrator tarries too long, almost against
his will, in the town as well as at Cipolla's performance. And again in this story, there is a poetic depiction of the sun's aesthetic effect on the expanse
of water.

But it is the figure of Cipolla that stirs memories
of other works. Again, a montage effect reveals the
various aspects of the artist's personality. Like
Naphta in <u>The Magic Mountain</u> Cipolla can be seen to
embody that particular side of the artist's nature which
constitutes a dangerous threat to his precarious exist-

ence, for it is this side of the artist's existence which gains the upper hand when repression is no longer successful. Savonarola, Aschenbach, Überbein, and Naphta all gave way to excess, the destructive release of extreme repression, and Cipolla likewise behaves drastically. He needlessly and contemptuously provokes his audience and like Naphta perishes from a bullet. It is certainly consistent to assume that Cipolla's affronts are calculated to elicit retaliation and punishment which the guilt-burdened artist figure secretly desires. With his hunger for dramatic retaliation, for a Götterdämmerung in which he is the principle god, and with his provocation of the fates and the furies, Cipolla reminds us of Mann's essay on Adolf Hitler where he compares the dictator with the artist. Mann sees in Hitler the artist in all his repugnance: his bad conscience, guilt-feelings, shameful laziness, uselessness, and his compensatory reaction of fury and hate.

Cipolla and Naphta are like identical twins with their unpleasant nature, unpopularity, piercing voices, sharp manner, arrogance, lack of humor, icy and mocking tone, elegance of dress and poor state of health. The detestable side of both is stressed practically in the manner of a leitmotif; yet, in spite of a negative characterization, Hans Castorp's and the present narrator's initial fascination for their respective adversaries is undeniable. The demonstrated fascination must lie deep below the surface, for both Cipolla and Naphta must be considered reprehensible. Both represent a totalitarian point of view, the cornerstone of which is a devout contempt for any human individuality. Both demonstrate, the one by incisive logic, the other by his hypnotic power, the inability of reason to confront the forces of darkness. Cipolla vanquishes all ordinary opponents with ease and occasionally he sounds in spirit like the Jesuit: "The ability to surrender oneself, to become a willing tool, to obey in the most unconditional and perfect sense of the word, was only the reverse side of that other power: to will and command; commanding and obeying were one and the same ability; together they formed one principle, one indissoluble unity. . . ."[6]

Although the story emphasizes the contrast between the decent Mario and the repugnant and cruel Cipolla, the true hero of this tale is the hypnotist. It is he who actually possesses the greatest measure of the author's sympathy, just as Naphta appealed more to Hans Castorp than Settembrini did. In fact, it is Cipolla whom Thomas Mann directly identifies himself with; Mann himself was called the "Magician" by members of his family, by friends and even by a number of critics. Cipolla does make people sit up and listen, just as every Mannian artist figure transforms the dull and banal life about him by dint of his special demonic powers. Hatfield points out the accomplishments of the magician: "By flattery, tricks, intimidation, and above all by hypnotic powers, Cipolla subdues almost the entire audience. Even the aristocrats, including an army officer, a lady of cultural pretensions, and a 'long-toothed Anglo-Saxoness' fall under his spell. The spectators, it is worth noting, have never liked the magician, and generally show sympathy for his victims."[7] Cipolla's opponent, Mario, is a thick-set, dreamy lad of twenty. Again, it is Hatfield who touches the relevant by pointing to the republican associations connected with the name and the quality of his decent demeanor: "Though he is destined to kill, he is without a trace of brutality. He has been trained to obey; he has no desire for a clash with Cipolla, and tries to escape from him before the crisis occurs. Mario strikes only when the magician, in his <u>hubris</u>, humiliates him beyond endurance; he acts from some instinctive sense of personal dignity."[8]

Cipolla's faith in terror and cruelty echoes in each sadistic remark as well as in his outright animosity towards the audience in general. He never tires of making fun of a handsome local youth; and in playing on the spectators' supposed success with the fair sex, he betrays a genuine ground for his antagonism. As we detect the sexual element behind the artist's guilty personality, we find that Cipolla, like Mann's other artist figures, is different from and hostile to the person who is able to love. What he lacks in himself, he blames in others. In his overcompensation for crippled virility he, like Savonarola, substitutes aggressive fanaticism and hatred for the potential to love, while his deformity identifies him as a cursed artist, or in familiar terms, a "marked man."

The whip which Cipolla cracks continuously is symbolic of violent force, and its appearance coincides with a draught of cognac, calculated to stimulate and enhance his demonic powers. The contrast to Tonio Kröger, the epitome of repression, is striking. Tonio's cup of tea must not be too strong, otherwise it might lead to overstimulation and consequent dire results, whereas Cipolla, the dark artist, impulsively desires alcohol to help speed him on his reckless collision course.

Aside from the political overtones, the people and the locale serve Mann's central purposes. Italy in this story is a magic land; a place where the unbridled conscience of the animal-like Italians reigns supreme, a place where sexual virility is on constant exhibition. The magician Cipolla, like Aschenbach, confronts the rampant forces of life and attempts to master them, but for all his efforts he is finally destroyed for his excessive presumption.

In both stories, <u>Mario and the Magician</u> and <u>Death in Venice</u>, the hero attempts to bridge a gulf between love and hate with bitter hostility and death gaining the upper hand. Aschenbach's safe and passive glances of love towards Tadzio were more than counterbalanced by his dream orgy of lust and cruelty. Here too, Cipolla, while giving overt proof of his love, creates an opposing impression. His kiss, rather than being a true sign of affection, is designed to humiliate and destroy the bourgeois dignity of the hypnotized Mario. "'Kiss me!' said the hunchback. 'Believe me, it's all right. I love you. Kiss me here.' And he pointed with the tip of his index finger to his cheek, near the mouth. And Mario bent and kissed him" (VIII, 710). This is another pregnant example of the protagonist's attempt to love life (or claim of the same), couched again in peculiarly perverse terms so that the opposite impression is thoroughly conveyed, defeat is guaranteed from the very beginning, and retribution for the guilty act becomes an inevitable consequence.

The narrator is an artist-aristocrat, not at all happy among the mob: "The beach, as I have said, was still in the hands of the middle-class native, a pleasing breed to look at . . . and among the young, we saw much shapeliness and healthy charm. Still, we were necessarily surrounded by a great deal of very average humanity, a middle-class mob, which, you will admit, is not more charming under this sun than under one's own native sky" (VIII, 665). The author hears the harsh and hideous voice of a mother calling a spoiled brat whom the author especially dislikes: in fact that cry is indelibly printed on the narrator's brain, in the same way the cry <u>Tadziu</u> reverberated through Aschenbach's dream orgy. But here the image of the young boy is thoroughly debased and devoid of beauty: "The cry was addressed to a repulsive youngster with disgustingly raw sores on his shoulders from a bad sunburn. He outdid anything I have ever seen for ill-breeding, refractoriness, and bad-temper . . . and besides this he was a great crybaby, putting the whole beach in an uproar by his outrageous sensitiveness to the slightest pain" (VIII, 665).

Mario resembles the father figure, a member of the mob and a believer in political power; especially if we take Hatfield's word that his name stands for Marius, the republican champion and leader of the lower classes of ancient Rome. Mario, as serious and nebulous as Thomas Buddenbrook was in his dreaminess, is simple if not dull in obedience to his calling in life. Beckoned to the stage by the hypnotist, he is forced to come right to Cipolla, like a dog to his owner. The whole episode parallels in tone the parable of a master (the artist) who tames and manipulates life as a man does his dog. Interestingly, Cipolla says he has known Mari for a long time and, alluding to the latter's success with women, continues to prod him in a familiar way: "I know what you are thinking; what does this Cipolla, with his little physical defect, know about love? You are wrong. He knows a lot about it. . . . Your charming Silvestra! What! Is she to prefer any young gamecock to you, so that he can laugh while you cry? To prefer him to a chap like you, so full of feeling and so sympathetic?" (VIII, 709). And then at the end Cipolla assumes in the hypnotic scene the role of Silvestra to complete the identification of the artist her with the woman in the possession of the representative of life. With arrogance, animosity and magic, he not only forces the audience to bend to his will but also wrests from them a measure of acclaim. "Life" is made to dance to the tune of the magician as Cipolla on stag appears to lash out in revenge on the people for the in convenience and suffering they caused the narrator of the story, the artist's brother.

Although Mario shoots the exponent of force and darkness, Mann's sympathies still lie irresistibly with his artist hero, as the powers of darkness continue to exert a tremendous fascination on the author. The artist hero, often loveless and unloved, crippled by impotence, has to bring his peculiar kind of love affai to a climax, even though it becomes the basis for his own destruction. In his act of ultimate involvement with life, so similar to the goal of Mann's earliest protagonists, his main concern is to appease a tortured libido. Unconsciously he acts out the game of provoca-

tion and defeat in order to achieve the ultimate in
pleasure and punishment.

There is, in contrast to Mario, the young gentleman from Rome who makes a heroic bid to resist Cipolla's
command to do a dance on the stage: "'Balla!' said he
[Cipolla]. 'Who wants to torture himself like that?
Is that your idea of freedom, forcing yourself? Una
ballatina! Why, your arms and legs are aching for it.
What a relief to give way to them--there, you are already dancing! That is no struggle anymore, it is a
pleasure!' And so it was. . . . In a way it was a
kind of consolation to see that he was having a better
time than he had had in the hour of his pride" (VIII,
702-703). This young gentleman, an aristocrat--as
opposed to Mario, who, as one among the common herd,
is putty in Cipolla's hands--puts up a heroic fight.
But once his strength of purpose wavers and he yields,
even he finds himself in a state of bliss. The dance
is his prelude to the delights of the sexual and the
demonic, and indirectly reveals the young Roman's secret
longing. By forcing these members of the audience to
dance, the Mannian artist hero triumphs over the representatives of life in the glare of the stagelights,
but Cipolla's victory on the "dance floor" (the arena
of the tango and two-step), the first clearly defined
occurrence in Mann's works, is all too brief. The
atonement which must follow such conspicuous aggression
is symbolically realized by the bullet Mario fires at
him.

Projected on to the political events of the day,
Mario and the Magician, a reverberation of the Observations of a Non-Political Man, expresses the view that
the real opposition to Fascism will have to come, impulsively and spontaneously, from the politically-
minded citizens of the West. Not too much can really
be expected from the holder of the aristocratic outlook, for aristocratic sympathies, his own included,
are compellingly and inextricably aligned with the
forces of darkness.

Joseph and His Brothers

In his re-interpretation and expansion of the
Biblical tale of Joseph, Thomas Mann created a work
which by virtue of its style and tremendous scope, must
fall, as Mann himself says, into the category of the
fantastic. From his initial conception of the idea to
the final recording of finis operis eighteen years

passed during which the author explored the depths of
Bible history, theology, comparative religion, archae-
ology, geography, and cultural history. Mann's ac-
quisition of academic data was commingled with invented
narrative to yield a tetralogy of nearly 2000 pages
that oscillate between the extremes of presumed fact
and captivating fiction.

The Old and the New: Parallels with Earlier Works

To begin with, Mann was not content to concentrate
on his protagonist's tribulations alone but had to develop the work, like Buddenbrooks, into a genealogical
excursion into the past. The first volume of the tetralogy, Joseph and His Brothers (Genesis 27 to 36),
deals with the adventures of the hero's father: Jacob's
theft of the birthright from his brother Esau, his
flight to the house of Laban, his marriages to Rachel
and Leah and the birth of his children, his escape and
his covenant with Laban, his reconciliation with Esau,
and the rape of Dinah followed by the massacre of
Schechem. Volume two, Young Joseph (Genesis 37), is
the account of Joseph's quarrel with his brothers,
their mistreatment of him by casting him into a pit,
and their selling him to the Midianite merchantmen on
the way to Egypt. In volume three, Joseph in Egypt
(Genesis 39), Joseph serves as a slave in the house of
Potiphar, a wealthy Egyptian, until the latter's wife,
Mut-em-enet, frustrated in her attempts to seduce Joseph, falsely accuses him of improper advances and has
him thrown into prison. The last volume of the tetralogy, Joseph the Provider (Genesis 38 and 40 to 50), is
the story of Joseph's salvation: how he correctly
interprets the Pharaoh's dreams, takes charge of the
country's affairs, saves it from the famine, and is
again united with his father and brothers.

Yet, despite the author's incredible exhibition of
historical sources, the Joseph story is, as Hamilton
Basso points out, once again that of the artist: "The
fabric of his story, furthermore, is largely woven with
the strands of certain preoccupations which have gripped
Mr. Mann ever since he wrote Buddenbrooks and which are
most apparent in the short story Tonio Kröger, where,
in what amounts to a self-portrait, the author explores
a theme that is identical with that of the Joseph series
--the relation of the artist, or the man of unique endowment, to the world at large."[9]

In Joseph, as in Hanno Buddenbrook, we detect the

dreaminess and introspection inherited from the mother. In his furtive worship of the moon, bordering on an ecstatic or trance-like state, the memory of Hanno's evasive practices at the piano is called forth. Music, as we have seen, constitutes a forbidden enjoyment much akin to Joseph's forbidden adoration of the moon. Our initial encounter with Joseph shows him to be hopelessly preoccupied with ancient moon worship--a feminine and maternal symbol as Mann indicates--; he is presently approached and admonished by his father Jacob who tells him to "clothe his nakedness." But after Jacob leaves, Joseph cannot restrain himself: he again returned to the well, "anointed himself and then performed with the moon the somewhat decadent ritual of wooing at which his ever-anxious father had surprised him."[10] Later, while indulging again in self-abuse and pleasure, he is reproached by his father for his "lack of care for health, lack of modesty, and religious backsliding" (IV, 99).

Also, we readily detect another major theme: with their crude ways and gross values, Joseph's brothers can be said to represent "life" in all its unthinking banality. To Jonas Lesser, "Joseph's brothers are what Thomas Mann's first teacher called 'the manufactured goods of nature'--average mediocrity in contrast to the brilliant exception, the extraordinary person, the genius who is marked and distinguished at the same time."[11] The brothers' treatment of Joseph is all out of proportion to his sins and in some measure reminiscent of the discomforts and cruelty which life meted out to Mann's early heroes: Lawyer Jacoby, Tobias Mindernickel, Lobgott Piepsam, Tonio Kröger, and the protagonists of The Clown and The Railway Accident.

But more significantly the hero's attitude toward the involvement of his emotions decisively demonstrates his similarity to previous guilty heroes. Joseph's love affair in the wealthy household in Egypt closely resembles Hans Castorp's amour in Berghof. Like Peeperkorn, Potiphar represents a rival to the hero for the favors of the desired one and is likewise a middle-aged patrician, a plantation owner, and sexually impotent (Potiphar has actually been castrated). Behind the epithets which are continually applied to Potiphar --noble, towering, aristocratic, captain of the guard-- is unmercifully revealed a preposterous and grotesque man totally lacking in virility. Thomas Mann goes to great lengths to reach a balance in ambivalence in portraying, by means of sham respect, the unreality and

hollow pretenses of Potiphar's life. With silky glib-
ness Joseph adroitly manipulates the lonely Potiphar
in much the same way the sly and devious Hans Castorp
employed equivocation to deceive and control Peeperkorn. Joseph is also calculating and left-handed in
praise of his master, casting doubt by means of appro-
bation upon the latter's ability as a horsetamer and
hippopotamus-hunter: "Joseph had known how to flatter
his master by making these exploits appear as the es-
sense of masculinity; but actually they were sicklied
and forced . . ." (V, 1087). Thus, Joseph's friendship
with the father figure, the representative of life,
acquires sinister overtones expressing deceit and contempt more than sincerity. Charity is almost wholly
lacking at the outset--unpityingly and mockingly Mann
states the hollowness of this eunuch's attempts to play
the virile role of captain of the guard: "Poor Potiphar! For a cipher he was, in all the splendor of his
fiery chariot-wheels and his greatness among the great
of Egypt. His young slave Osarsiph [Joseph] had a
cipher for a master" (IV, 876).

Though a zero in form and substance, Potiphar commands the loyalty and the respect of his whole house-
hold--the respect of slaves--in much the same way
Peeperkorn dominated the residents of Berghof, and,
like the Dutch planter, he is essentially charitable
to the hero and appears to be aware of the latter's
superiority. But Mann denigrates Potiphar even more
than he did Peeperkorn for the Egyptian is described
as totally ridiculous in appearance. In a number of
instances when Potiphar's tremendous obesity is under-
scored there are also references to his appearance:
fat with tiny head, hands and feet--the description of
either an infant or a strange animal-like character.
He leads a sedentary existence; his physical life consists in eating to support his huge bulk, his mental
in having books read aloud to him (as one would for a
young child). If Mann intended his caricature of Potiphar to be that of a baby, then we are witnessing a
complete reversal of roles in the father-son conflict.
In the earliest tales it was the hero who often bore
unmistakable traces of an infant: in Tristan the hero
flees at the sight of the antagonist's masculine productivity, the baby Anton Klöterjahn, Jr. Thomas Mann
is now, at the height of his career and lionized by
the world, in the best possible position to reduce the
stature of the ever threatening paternal figure by
transforming him into a harmless and inert mass.

Nevertheless, despite the inversion, several of Potiphar's features and attributes could be suitably applied to Senator Thomas Buddenbrook. The Egyptian only possesses the good name and titles pro forma, fan-bearer on the right hand of the king, captain of the Pharaoh's guard, head executioner and commandant of the royal prisons; they are empty honors, for a substitute actually handles the serious responsibilities of office. In fearful solicitation about the dignity and security of his household, Potiphar's efforts are almost exclusively concerned with maintaining his self-esteem; the same anxieties dominated and nearly overwhelmed Hanno Buddenbrook's father. Joseph is immediately aware of Potiphar's pathetic loneliness and the hollow front put up by the members of the inner circle: "Therefore they [members of Potiphar's household] strove more to strengthen by all this tact and courtesy each other's self-respect. If in this house of blessing there reigned an atmosphere of uneasiness which even had its comic side, in this it consisted; if there was a weight of care, herein it lay. It gave itself no name, but Joseph guessed it: the dignity was a sham" (IV, 842). And the parallels continue to grow. Frequent references to the splendor and opulence of Potiphar's house and its delicate aesthetic marriage, so similar to Thomas Buddenbrook's nominal relationship, is based, as we learn from the chapter entitled "Husband and Wife," as much on animosity as tenderness. Potiphar himself is imbued with a feeling of life weariness. Like both Peeperkorn and Thomas Buddenbrook, the exponent of life ultimately proves himself to be its most pitiful example of vitality. As a result of this loveless and impossible marriage, there will be no descendants to carry on the name of Potiphar; the marriage between Thomas Buddenbrook and Gerda, which infused decadence into the last male heir, likewise insured the decline of the patrician family of Lübeck. That it was Thomas Mann's intent to superimpose, to a great extent, the theme of Buddenbrooks on his Biblical tale by concentrating spiritual qualities in the last heir or "son," is revealed in the following passage:

> But something else rejoiced him [Joseph]
> even more: a more pervasive atmosphere
> in this world to which he had been trans-
> planted. He detected it as he sniffed
> for advantage or disadvantage with that
> pretty if rather thick-nostrilled nose
> of his, and it was an air in which he was
> as much at home as a fish in water. For

the prevailing atmosphere--to put it into
an old phrase--was fin de siècle. It was
that of a society composed of descendants
and heirs, already remote from the patterns
of the founding fathers whose victories
had put their successors in the frame of
mind to regard the conquered as elegant.
It appealed to Joseph, for he himself was
late, too, in time and in his soul, a very
good specimen of a descendant, volatile,
witty, difficult, and interesting." (IV,
835-836)

Other parallels to The Magic Mountain, aside from
the Mut love affair, which we shall soon discuss, are
present, though incomplete, in the subsidiary figures
of Joseph in Egypt. Mont-Kaw, the steward of the Potiphar household, closely resembles Hofrat Behrens, the
chief surgeon in Berghof. Each is shrewd, rough-hewn
and muscular, and with florid features. But behind the
rough exterior there shines a benevolent twinkle. And
though unsentimental, each has eyes which are continually filled with tears. Both are stoical in that they
have been silently suffering from illness. Both are
efficient, conscientious and dedicated to serving, as
overseers, the management of their respective establish-
ments. Both determine that the heroes are to stay in
the particular surroundings, and both act as mentors in
initiating them into the concepts of their profession;
the two heroes, Hans Castorp and Joseph, turn out to be
apt pupils, the one in medicine and the other in business administration. Beknechons, the fanatical high
priest, embodies the beliefs of Naphta in that he, as
an advocate of rigid conformity to a system and to
terror for its own sake, is incapable of pausing for a
minute on mundane details but immediately passes over
into more exalted spheres, haranguing the four quarters
of heaven as he holds forth on the problems of state.
Beknechon's disciple Dûdu, the hostile dwarf, carries
the figure of Naphta one step further as he becomes a
caricature of Adolf Hitler: his arrogance, pompous
strutting, implacable hatred against the Hebrew protag-
ónist based completely on irrational grounds, and, last
but not least, the renowned thatch on the upper lip help
to make, considering the time when Joseph in Egypt
appeared in print, a reasonable case for such a caricature. His counterpart in size, Bes-em-heb, the good
dwarf, bears a more than accidental resemblance to
Settembrini: he cuts a comic figure, takes an immediate
interest in Joseph and assumes a protective attitude

towards him, especially where Mut is concerned. His
furious quarrels with Dûdu recapitulate to some extent
the interminable arguments of Settembrini and Naphta;
and at the end of the novel when Joseph's death seems
to be imminent, Bes, like Settembrini, becomes sentimental and by clinging to Joseph's coat even runs the
danger of sharing his friend's fate.

Despite the exotic setting or, perhaps because
of it, Mut is very little different from preceding
heroines: exotic, musical, untamed, even unkempt or
Bohemian in appearance; cold and austere, stern and
haughty, nunlike yet smouldering with sensuality; repellent in the view of the Mannian hero and attractive
at the same time with the familiar fatal shadows about
her eyes. Ultimately, of course, her involvement with
the hero results in his banishment or symbolic death,
for to love this woman is equivalent to tempting a dire
fate. And as usual it is the woman who makes the first
overtures. Joseph's affair, like that of Hans Castorp,
proceeds from a distance, likewise through gossip and
hearsay in the beginning. Further conspicuous resem-
blances are present in Joseph's remarks to Mut about
the decay of flesh, remarks which correspond to Hans
Castorp's grotesque anatomical discourse to Clawdia
Chauchat; the final showdown even occurs amid the merry-
making of carnival time, where in both cases the hero
has imbibed more than usual. Also, the chapter "How
Long Joseph Stayed with Potiphar" has its exact parallel
in "By the Ocean of Time" of The Magic Mountain where
Mann playfully speculates about the meaning of time at
that point in the novel when he introduces his hero to
the arbiter of time, the threatening father figure.

In the relationship between Mut and Joseph, Thomas
Mann dispenses with the customary masquerade and insists
on spelling out the Oedipal conflict. During the course
of the love affair the heroine's passion is often described as maternal longing, until Mut, whose name means
mother in Egyptian, finally exclaims to Joseph: "How
like a foolish boy you answer in your fear, which as
your mistress in love I must break down! With his
mother each man always sleeps--the woman is the mother
of the world, her son is her husband, and every man
begets upon his mother--do you not know, must I teach
you these simple things?" (V, 1175). And at the climax
of the novel when Mut attempts to force the seduction
of Joseph, he is deterred from willing compliance only
by the vision of his father:

253

> Her desire had discovered in him a
> manly readiness; and the forsaken woman
> alternately tore at and caressed the
> garment which he left in her hands--for
> we know that he left his garment behind
> him--in anguish. The Egyptian woman's
> cry, repeated over and over again was
> <u>Me'eni nachtef</u>! I have seen his strength!
> Something enabled Joseph, in that
> uttermost extremity, to tear himself away
> and flee; that something was his father's
> face. He saw his father's face. . . .
> Not an image of settled and personal linea-
> ments. . . . Rather he saw it in his mind
> and with his mind's eye: an image of memory
> and admonition, the father's in a broad
> and general sense. For in it Jacob's
> features mingled with Potiphar's fatherly
> traits. . . ." (V, 1259)

And that parricide is inseparable from Oedipal
passion is unequivocally allowed to be stated when Mut
proposes that Joseph murder Potiphar, a proposal that
Joseph is slow in condemning: "How I hate his lazy
flesh, since my love for you has lacerated my heart
and made my own flesh to a vessel of love--I cannot
say, I can only shriek it. So, sweet Osarsiph, let
us make him cold, for it is a little thing. Or is it
something to you, to knock down a fungus with a stick,
some foul tindery mushroom or puff-ball?" (V, 1173-
1174). Despite the triumph of chastity, and his solemn
pledge to Mont-Kaw to serve and love his noble master
Potiphar, Joseph's guilt is difficult to deny. He
continually eggs Mut on, so much so that Bes is aware
of Joseph's real feelings: "But the wise little dwarf
had been right when he had seen in Joseph's pleasure,
in his freedom of choice between good and evil somethin
very like pleasure in evil itself, not only in the free
dom to choose it" (V, 1155).

Joseph's pedagogic plan to arrange the events of
his life in accordance with the greater and divine plan
serves less to prove his fortitude and strength than
his delight in the tempting and provocative situation,
his painful pleasure in retarding the onrush of desire,
and the bliss of savoring the death of Potiphar. And
when at the last Mut shouts that she has seen Joseph's
manhood, Joseph secures a moral, but sweet victory over
the castrated father.

Challenge and Response: The Game of Repression

Joseph's relationship with Mut represents the culmination of a theme which began very early in the creations of Thomas Mann: passive feasting of the forbidden
and passionate enjoyment without fulfillment.   Voyeuristic teasing and repression bordering on the perverse
sustain themselves in this prolonged account of three
years of emotional intensity.   The tension in the Joseph
in Egypt volume mounts slowly but steadily to reach a
final pinnacle of frenzy which calls to mind the rampant
expression of the basic drives in Aschenbach's Venetian
dream orgy.   A self-contained narrative, the Joseph-
Mut story could be studied in detail as a psychological
case history on frustration.   Hirschbach compares Mut
to the hero in Death in Venice, both of whom are over-
powered by sensual urges and give way to excess after
years of repression.[12]   Although dissolution and degradation occur not to the protagonist but to the object
of his desire, the atmosphere has not changed.   Joseph's
heart pounds like Aschenbach's as he tempts fate by
failing to heed the inner voice of warning, even though
he is definitely aware of the potential danger.   For
Bes-em-heb, the good dwarf, warns him openly of the
possible consequences of his entanglement with Mut,
advice which parallels Settembrini's admonition to Hans
Castorp concerning Clawdia Chauchat; and even Dûdu, the
licentious dwarf and would-be pander who is treated
harshly by Potiphar, serves as a foreboding to Joseph
not to yield to temptation.   Martyr-like and stoically,
Joseph rejects the lust of the flesh while simultaneously stimulating new excitement--preserving chastity
but achieving an even greater measure of masochistic
pleasure.   Although the fear of direct involvement is
the source of peril, Joseph is still more than willing
to risk terrible punishment by toying with Mut's passion
despite the fact he has no intention of surrendering to
her amorous onslaughts.   And in reality, besides enticing Mut, Joseph is provoking punishment--the second
pit in the prison of Zawi-Re.   It is as if the problem
of chastity were subordinate to the need to make his
guilt manifest and assuage his conscience through imminent punishment.   But conjecture on this point may
be curtailed here for Mann himself breaks into the narrative to speculate on the reasons for Joseph's deliberate self-exposure to danger:

> Why did he disregard the whispered warn-
> ings of his pure-hearted little friend,

who already saw the pit yawning, and make
friends instead with the phallic-minded
manikin who played Lothario and mumbled
out of the corner of his mouth? In a
word, why did he not avoid the mistress
instead of letting things reach the pass
they did for him and for her? Yes, that
was coquetting with the world, it was
sympathy with the forbidden thing. . . .
And it had a savor of arrogant self-
assurance, of a notion that he could
venture into danger and retreat whenever
he liked. . . . It was a willingness to
take a dare, an ambition to face the worst
and run the risk, to push matters to the
uttermost in order to carry off a greater
triumph--to be a virtuoso of virtue and
thus more precious to the father than a
more restricted and an easier trial would
have shown him. Perhaps, even, it was a
secret knowledge of his own course and the
line it took, the suspicion that its next
lesser round was to complete itself and
bring him to the pit, which was inevitable
if all that was to be fulfilled which was
written in the plan. (V, 1145-1146)

The extent of the affair with Mut and its crescendo of passion would be unique in the works of the
mature Thomas Mann if there were no mitigating factor.
But once again as in Death in Venice and The Magic
Mountain the author felt compelled to tone down the
stark confrontation of sexual cupidity and lessen the
horror which accompanies passion in the guilty hero.
We see in the previous quotation the insulation which
the author achieves with his editorial comments on the
hero's adventures. The effect of constant interjected
comments becomes at times one of almost clinical detachment. For example, the author goes to great lengths
to catalogue the reasons for Joseph's chastity. When
Joseph is directly propositioned by Mut, his reaction
is depicted as follows: "And Joseph? He sat and ran
over his seven reasons in his mind, conning them for-
wards and back. I would not assert that his blood
did not rise in a wave to beat on the shore of his
soul. But it met the wall of his seven reasons, and
they held firm. To his credit be it said, that he did
not turn harshly against her or treat the witch with
contempt . . . but was mild and gentle to her . . ."
(V, 1164).

256

And when the culminating event leading to Joseph's downfall occurs, the intense crisis of his long, drawn-out temptation, the author decides to extract it hygienically from its raw but real human elements. He coldly interrupts the story to say that he prefers to draw a veil of delicacy and human feeling over the whole climax!

Mann's treatment of Mut is not radically different from his depiction of Joseph. Her feelings and thoughts are analyzed by the author directly. He insists that she is more the victim than the instigator of her violent urges and goes to great lengths to uphold her reputation. He denies outright that she is base, a harlot or a nymphomaniac. And in order to lessen her infamous proposition to Joseph, the author has Mut bite her tongue so severely that her words come forth as parody: "Thleep with me!" (V, 1164); but, interestingly enough, this does not prevent Mann in the least from painting Mut finally as a hag-like creature under the spell of passion. The motifs of passion and physical deterioration recall the Mannian law of ambivalence: for every expenditure of passion there is a corresponding amount of decay. Therefore, in Joseph in Egypt, the reader is once again confronted with the primary relationship underlying all of Mann's works: erotic urges lead irresistibly to dissolution and death.

Among the arguments Joseph uses to resist Mut's blandishments is his concern for his destiny in history. He tells her that her story could easily become history and literature and that she might become known to posterity as the mother of sin if she persists: "You have little pity for your legend, one must admit, for you give yourself the name of mother of sin for all future times. But remember, that we are perhaps, yes, very likely, in a story, so pull yourself together!" (V, 1174-1175). The anachronistic, ironic unreality of Joseph's words helps again to take the edge off the sharpness of the deep-felt and dangerous experience.

Recourse to such protective devices does not end with the third volume, for in spite of its artificiality, it actually increases in frequency in the last volume of the tetralogy. On one occasion Joseph remarks about a plan of action by his lieutenant Mai-Sachme: "Of course, because it [the plan] is the only right one and as good as written down already. In fact, this whole story is written down already in God's book, and we shall read it together between laughing and tears" (V, 1596). Later, and with even greater irony, he realizes that Mai-Sachme's advice to confuse the hero's brothers by placing money in their grain sacks is a natural suggestion since it belongs to the Joseph tradition. He admits that he had almost overlooked this important detail of his own story. And at the very end of the novel Joseph advises his brothers not to be troubled about obtaining his forgiveness. Their alarm signifies to him that they have missed the meaning of the story they are in, but of course he cannot really blame them for not knowing nor understanding the story which they are acting out. Such extreme emphasis on ironic devices has as wide a significance for the author as it does for the hero; for like romantic irony its use provides a psychological escape from the challenges and entanglements of the story. It thins out the involvement and displaces uncomfortable concerns with levity, a usual device for shifting focus from the disturbing feelings of guilt-laden heroes!

The Psychology of Theocracy

Joseph's feelings of being alive primarily for the sake of a story parallels his uncanny ability to predict the future. His foreknowledge of his total role is at once derived from and extended beyond the powers of his forefathers. Actually, the basic link between the four volumes is provided by this binding relationship which synchronizes familial history with teleological theology. The result lends Joseph a kind of supernatural aid and comforts him in any situation he encounters, as he, in every instance, stands above the claims of his particular environment.

Passing by the mountains of his homeland on the way to Egypt, Joseph rejects any attempt at flight on his part as running counter to a higher plan. He is certain that he is being snatched away to some great purpose, that some omnipotent intelligence has conceive great designs for him; and consequently, he feels that to kick against the pricks of fortune and to shrink from affliction would be a great sin. The sense of higher mission protects Joseph from the uncertainty of the possible fate of toiling misery which awaits a slave in Egypt. Indeed, Joseph is virtually immune to the consequences and terrors of what life has in store for him; and even the fear of immediate death affects him in an uncommonly trivial way:

He had wept and wailed when big Ruben
had given his voice that they should
throw him into the pit; yet at the same
time his reason had laughed as at a joke,
the word used was so laden with allusions:
'Bor' the brothers had said. And the mono-
syllable was capable of various interpretations. It meant not only well, but prison;
not only prison, but the underworld, the
kingdom of the dead; so that prison and the
underworld were one and the same thought,
one being only a word for the other. Again,
the well, in its property as entrance to
the underworld, likewise the round stone
which covered it, signified death; for the
stone covered the round opening as the
shadow covers the dark moon. . . .
It was the abyss into which the true son
descends, he who is one with the mother and
wears the robe by turns with her. . . .
The kingdom of the dead, where the son becomes the lord, the shepherd, the sacrifice,
the mangled god. (IV, 583).

As reflected in this passage, Joseph's faith and
fantasy allow him to meet any situation without qualms.
With the advantage of the supernatural, he emerges from
the pages of the novel almost de-humanized, a person
not endowed in a real sense with mortal weaknesses.
For the most part Joseph remains less real than mythical, one who belongs to a legend, following as he does
in the footsteps of his ancestors as did his father
before him. As a result, Joseph, along with a number
of other characters, often strike the reader as mechanical figures acting under the bidding of historical
necessity and expectations extrapolated from other,
previously-lived lives.

Although nothing unique in the conception of the
modern novel, this ability of the hero to go beyond
the strictly human and to make thereby his existential
fate a matter of colossal indifference to himself leads
Käte Hamburger to observe within the framework a new
approach to the art of the novel:

Indeed, it is a method based on reservations which finds its application in this
novel, and it forms, to be sure, the greatest conceivable contrast to that identifi-

cation--"of being down among the characters"
--which traditional aesthetics demand of a
novel in general and of the historical in
specific. But Thomas Mann knew what he was
doing when he made "reserve" his method of
realization. "Resolution is beautiful.
But the really fruitful, the productive and
hence the artistic principle we call reserve . . .," so he says at the end of his
great essay Goethe and Tolstoy. It is a
principle which "plays slyly and irrespon-
sibly--yet not without benevolence--among
opposites and is in no great haste to take
sides and come to decisions." --and that
is for Thomas Mann an ironical principle.
For irony is to him the specific attitude
of reserve, namely the principally free
bent of the mind which does not lose itself
in the characters nor is merged with them,
but rather is always raised again above
them and creates a distance from them.
And even if the method of ironic reserve
dominates more or less pronounced in his
other works, it is still nowhere so decisively exalted as a principle of presentation as in the Joseph novels.[13]

But what Hamburger ascribes as positive to the
novel--the depersonalization of the hero and his insulation from certain crucial emotional experiences--
is, in reality, the necessity behind Mann's art, for
it is essentially in conjunction with the hero's passions that his ironic reserve originates. If the
Joseph novel is to be consistent with past creations,
then, we must regard this irony as a device by which
the hero may subdue his raw emotional surges in various
and ingenious ways. From this point it is only a half
step to the assumption that the "freezing" of Joseph's
personality by means of ironic measures is in direct
proportion to the length and intensity of his affair
with Mut, which, aside from Fallen and The Blood of
the Walsungs, represents the most extensive and starkly
sexualized relationship thus far described on the pages
of Mann's books. Elaborate personal passion and involvement compel Mann to develop an equally elaborate
scheme of detachment, to follow, so to speak, in his
own footsteps so that he may again disengage himself
from a threatening human situation replete with guilty
associations.

Mann's critics are by no means united on the merits of the exaggerated irony he applies in Joseph. What Hamburger evaluates as positive, Hatfield, for example, reproaches as lacking human genuineness. He notes that with deliberate retardations, the narrative becomes increasingly ironic and that the long asides compare unfavorably to "the genuine power of the recognition scene" and "the bestowal of the blessing."[14]

From Thomas Mann's need to separate himself from the sustained tension between Joseph and Mut has come, as we have seen, the ramification of basic themes throughout the whole novel. Thus the track motif, i.e., Joseph walking in his ancestors' footsteps, is employed to lend a logical basis for Joseph's foreknowledge of his destiny. It also prepares the way for his special and unique position, with its divine implications, as the supposed recipient of the blessing. But despite the elaborate preparation to assign Joseph a special supra-human position in the novel, the motif of the blessing leads into a blind alley as far as his role in the genealogy of the Messiah is concerned. Though Joseph is exempted from ordinary conditions of fate, consciously and unconsciously repeats the pattern of the myth, and is considered, or at least suspected, by his brothers as being the next holder of the blessing, it is not he, but Judah, who becomes the chosen one and whose heirs are to culminate in the Savior. It is true that Mann is given an assist by the confusion or disparate authorship in the tradition itself (in the Biblical text account of Joseph's "near" blessing), but the author has made this theme and its ramifications wholly his own and in the final analysis dependent on the Mut affair.

As Hamburger notes it was not until the appearance of the final volume that the question of Mann's intent was fully ascertained: "Joseph's story had been presented as an allusion to the myths of the Gods, who were supposed to return one day in spiritualized form in the miracle of Christ. Up until the appearance of the fourth volume, this connection made the question inevitable whether Thomas Mann intended to depict Joseph as a Savior figure. . . . Thomas Mann transforms . . . the original Christian meaning of salvation of this tradition into a humanistic one."[15] In order to prepare Joseph for the denial of the blessing and to juggle his tale to fit the needs of the fourth volume, Joseph the Provider, Thomas Mann characterizes him as more

human. Now that the crisis of the Mut affair is passed
Joseph loses his protective, god-like power. In Erich
Heller's words: "With unobtrusive care and subtle art
Thomas Mann divests Joseph's 'ego,' as he rises to
power in Egypt, of bond after bond of the 'mythic collective.' The more he becomes a god in the eyes of
the world, the more human he becomes to himself and the
more humorously he 'acts.'"[16]

The Myth of Death

Joseph's living mythically is more than externally
involved with his descent into the "pit" and later im-
prisonment, for he gladly goes to Scheol or Egypt, the
land of the dead, in order that his resurrection to
greater heights will take place and that his people wil
follow him there according to legend. The personal
embrace of the myth becomes an analogue for his close
affinity with death and gives the motivation for Joseph's acceptance of his fate while effectively concealing his real attitude. Like Hanno Buddenbrook,
Gustav Aschenbach, and Hans Castorp, Joseph actually
finds the solution to his inner problem in the endorse-
ment of death. From the very beginning the "underworld
attracts him; he worships the moon by the well, symbolic of the powers of night and death. His laughter
after being thrown into the well, his refusal to escape, and his change of name to Osarsiph in honor of
the god of the dead also characterize his morbid predilection. What for Jacob at Laban's was an escape
from adversity is for Joseph in Egypt a procrastination
among the moribund.

The parallel to Hans Castorp's life in Berghof is
extremely close. The rarified journey up to the Alpine
sanatorium finds an echo in the trip across the desert,
and if we think of the forbidding fortress of Thel,
Egypt is no less insulated than the hermetically sealed
Berghof. The similarity to the sanatorium is made complete in terms of licentiousness. Sexual frenzy runs
rampant in the ancient kingdom of the Nile, customary
freedom appearing as sexual promiscuity to the non-
Egyptians. This contrast in viewpoint points up strikingly the familiar clash between the lax Berghof patients and the more virtuous people of the flatland.

Joseph's mythic life conjures up a profoundly lost
sense of time. Not only Egypt but the entire tetralogy
is inhabited by people who do not quite know when they
live or who they are.[17] The past becomes like a dream

and events both recent and far-off flow inaccurately
into each other. Hirschbach remarks that when a person
keeps walking in circles, he soon loses count of the
number of revolutions. In the same manner, the members
of Jacob's and Joseph's families have little sense of
time, both past and present. They have lost sight of
the number of generations which have come and gone
since Abraham, and the farther they move away, the
closer the distance Abraham-Isaac-Jacob seems to become.[18] As a momentous spirit of the past, Abraham,
the arch-father, becomes the ever-present specter of
the present and flows inescapably through the thoughts
and actions of the living.

Joseph feels truly at home in the loose world of
the dead, for although the dead may symbolize his
punishment as everyman's fate, they also issue a pass-
port to license. As we shall see, the proximity to
the danse macabre liberates Joseph, as it did Albrecht
van der Qualen, Gustav von Aschenbach and Hans Castorp,
from the categorical imperative to behave in a responsible manner. Egypt, a mecca of sexual freedom and a
place "far down on the map," exerts a compelling fascination on the hero, just as Italy, the land of sensuality and conscienceless inhabitants with an animal-
like glance in their eyes, attracted the repressed hero
of Tonio Kröger. Tonio, as the vehemence of his con-
demnation--the true measure of his fascination--betrayed,
keenly felt the pull of this land.

"What concerns us," says the author in the first
volume of the tetralogy, "is time's abrogation and dissolution in the alternation of tradition and prophecy"
(IV, 32). The word timeless is a key word that represents a kind of parable to the Mannian artist, a world
within which the restricting bonds chaining the artistic
imagination are broken. The artist whose fantasies
are timeless may be encouraged here to create independ-
ently of reality in an eternal present. In those rare
moments when he momentarily perceives the passing of
time, he is upset and irate at being reminded of something unpleasant and intolerable. More and more Joseph feels the need to resort to dreams in order to
place himself outside of the father realm of subservience to time. The Joseph story therefore becomes a
succession of dreams, beginning with fantasies that are
sinful and criminal and then passing on to a sense of
guilt and a need for punishment which his forbidden
dreams have called forth. But living in the land of

dreams and death permits Joseph, so to speak, to continue to sin, to be punished (by the three pits and
exile), and yet to still prevail as a victor. The
world of forbidden fantasy becomes a perfect, if illogical, world in which the sequence of sin, punishment, and death does not end in tragedy but in new
life, in rebirth. In Joseph the Provider the hero
succeeds beyond all his dreams, or perhaps better
stated, because of his dreams. As if in a dream, the
figures in the novel walk in circles, and the circular
motion equals the process of renewal and rebirth.

With the eternally recurring, Mann condenses eons
of time into a scheme where only the now exists; and
by pervading his whole tetralogy with this sense of
timelessness, he manages to keep his hero in a perpetual state of childhood. The infant in his fantasy
would neither acknowledge reality nor recognize the
necessity of time, and the loss of time conceptuality
enables the infantile protagonist to dispense with
time's harsh stringencies and win out over the adversity of his guilty past. He thus has it both ways:
there is no penalty without time because the future
with its consequences will never come, but there is,
nevertheless, plenty of time to repeat life and start
afresh in a state of innocence. By walking in the footsteps of his parents the hero demonstrates both his
regression to an infantile state where time is absent
and also his advancement to the father's role as the
enforcer of his conscience. In his essay Freud and
the Future (1936), Thomas Mann makes the following
acute observation about the father's role in the shaping of the child's conscience:

> The mystery of the metaphysician and
> psychologist, that the soul is the giver
> of all given conditions, becomes in Joseph
> easy, playful, blithe--like a consummately
> artistic performance by a fencer or juggler.
> It reveals his infantile nature. . . .
> Infantilism--in other words, regression
> to childhood--what a role this genuinely
> psychoanalytic element plays in all our
> lives! What a large share it has in shaping
> the life of a human being; operating, indeed,
> in just the way I have described: as myth-
> ical identification, as survival, as a
> treading in footprints already made! The
> bond with the father, the imitation of the

father, the game of being the father, and
the transference to father-substitute
pictures of a higher and more developed
type--how these infantile traits work
upon the life of the individual to mark
and shape it.[19]

What Mann means by the eternally recurring is simply
a perpetual revolution about the same theme: the incestuous yearning for the mother and the coming to
terms with the father.

This line of reasoning runs counter to R. H.
Thomas' view: "The innate qualities of one 'who so
sorely needed education' are heightened and intensified
in his 'death' in Egypt as in a hermetic retort. When
Jacob believes him dead, he imagines him 'preserved'
and 'unchangeable.' But Joseph was not 'removed from
time.' He 'grew and matured,' preserving his 'pattern
of form.' In Egypt he 'became a good deal more manly'
in 'death' more intelligent."[20] Like Frank Donald
Hirschbach and others, R. H. Thomas therefore sees in
Joseph a Bildungsroman, a continuation of the process
which Hans Castorp undergoes.[21] But the same objections
which applied to this designation of The Magic Mountain
are valid here in respect to Joseph, who almost godlike
and conscious of playing a role or being in a story,
stands above and beyond the crucible of life, those
forces which shape and form. Fear of consequences does
not concern him in a meaningfully human context. In
dispensing with risk he eliminates the strain on his
feelings, he freezes the life situation, and he is fully
sheltered against the awful finality of a misstep.

The Genesis of Joseph

Originally Mann conceived of the Joseph story as
a series of three novellas dealing with the history of
religion, Spain, and Germany. But, as in the case of
his first novel, the manuscript grew far beyond this
original conception to include the lengthy essay and a
detailed exposition of the generation that gave birth
to Joseph. Thus, like Buddenbrooks, it became a genealogical novel which elaborates on numerous and color-
ful adventures as a kind of preparatory stage for the
appearance of a talented and exotic hero. The question
that we posed for Buddenbrooks is also a proper concern of Joseph: Why did Thomas Mann dilute his concentration on the artist protagonist to take up the
involved picaresque exploits of Jacob and his family?

Our answer, too, is the same: both the prelude and Jacob's trials and tribulations, serving the same purpose as volume one of <u>Buddenbrooks</u>, are simply there to shift the weight from the third volume where the hero openly revels in the secret and forbidden ecstasy of a sado-masochistic Oedipal relationship. The whole tetralogy is really concerned with father-mother-son relationships, and actually the title of the entire work, <u>Joseph and His Brothers</u>, is a misnomer; more pertinent would have been <u>Joseph and His Fathers</u>.

Among the author's earliest statements concerning his plans to write a Biblical epic is the one revealing that he was not thinking strictly in terms of historical accuracy but rather along guidelines firmly established in the past. We learn from Monika Mann that the model for the figure of Joseph was not a person from the Middle East, neither Arab nor Jew, but her school friend of Spanish descent who thus harmonized Mann's earliest memories and profoundest interests with South America.[22]

Hatfield offers two explanations for the creation of <u>Joseph</u>: Mann's decision was "to combine the mythical element with a highly rational, sophisticated psychology, to treat a 'dark,' primitive subject under the aspect of reason and light."[23] Hatfield states later that the intention of the novel was less to recreate a period of the past than to show typical and timeless figures against a more or less distinct background.[24] But, as we know, the writing of <u>Joseph</u> led Mann to undertake an elaborate program of scientific research into the sources of the Joseph legend and to digest works on Egyptology, Orientology, comparative mythology and religion as well as Freudian and Jungian psychology.[25] He even took a trip to Egypt and the Holy Land. Yet, the end result was by no means an historical reconstruction of Biblical events, nor more than a faint-hearted step into the well of the past.* At any rate, a number of critics are dubious about his success. Joseph Wood Krutch doubts that Mann himself knows what the dream-

---

*Whether the Joseph legend is exclusively a myth or a documented piece of history, Mann runs counter to its tradition by placing his hero in the time of Amenhotep IV, approximately two centuries later.

like meaning of this novel is.[26] Elmer Davis is of the opinion that the method of accounting for doublet traditions is both clumsy and unscientific.[27] To one critic the myths are bewilderingly intermingled, not living art but art in a museum.[28] To another, Joseph in Egypt is no more than an archeological dream of characters stilted in their conversation, vaguely allegorical, semi-philosophical, and pseudo-archeological.[29] And C. O. Cleveland feels that in Joseph in Egypt Mann has not fused his sources into an organic whole, the epic's chief weakness being the excessive weight of unorganized knowledge.[30]

But did Thomas Mann ever really consider the historical perspective as an end in itself? Did he truly set out to attain insights that are eternally valid for all ages and climes, as Weigand feels he did? "For that is really the sense of Joseph, that in it the past and present ages, their religions, politics and ways of thinking are fused into prototypes and ideas. In the final analysis it is not concerned with the unique, locally conditioned tensions of ancient Egypt, but rather with the tensions and expressions of life which, in transmuted forms, recur in every cultural age and every cultural realm."[31] But despite these words of Weigand, when the tetralogy is finally weighed in the balance, the author's actual achievement consists in taxing his work to the utmost by an excess of polymathic knowledge. And in achieving this aim, Mann really succeeded only in attaining the more stringent and compelling goal of blurring the focus on the starkly sexual content of the Mut-Joseph relationship. Thus, although Mann expended an enormous amount of effort on reconstructing the mythical past, his theme is still the one dearest to his heart: the family story with its typical concentration on the hero's exclusive problem of sin and atonement, self-sufficient fantasy, and narcissistic withdrawal from life.

Mann deceptively stated that he had lost his interest in the bourgeois concept of art: "I had been in readiness to feel productively attracted by a subject matter like the Joseph legend because of the turning of my taste away from the bourgeois toward the mythical aspect."[32] But regardless of Mann's assertions, the story of Joseph is again the story of the artistic pariah amid hostile, bourgeois, crude entities and at odds with his parents or a parent substitute. Buddenbrooks is a testimony to the decay of a bourgeois family;

The Magic Mountain deals with the dissolution of a circumscribed society; and Joseph has at its heart the
collapse of an ancient Egyptian but still bourgeois
household.

Not content with his first explanation, Thomas
Mann shifts ground to state in a lecture that Joseph
depicts the birth of the ego out of the mythic collective: "In short, we see how the ego in the process of
its emancipation soon becomes an artistic ego, attractive, delicate, and--endangered. . . . In Joseph the
ego flows back from arrogant absoluteness into the collective, the common; and the contrast between artistic
and civic tendencies, between isolation and community,
between individual and collective, is fabulously neutralized. . . ."[33] But how dubious this statement
appears when we examine the "ego" of Joseph. Joseph
has no real home, no resting place, and psychologically,
it should be kept in mind, his narcissism isolates him,
as it did Hans Castorp, in extreme passivity. In his
timeless existence and free-floating fantasy there is
no reality. It has been annulled so that he can mentally dominate his environment heedless of objective
interference. From his first entrance he succumbs to
his indestructible fantasies, and his story, a continual walking in circles, self-contained and impervious
to deviation, is a perpetuum mobile where the artistic
already exists fully developed at birth. Mann never
really withdraws from the twentieth century in his attempts to depict the dawn of the artistic ego in history. He has instead called all too heavily on the
forces of darkness of the recent past and concludes
by placing Joseph on a par with his hero's artistic
brothers in previous works. In this respect, Philip
Blair Rice's words about Joseph in Egypt aptly apply
to the whole tetralogy: "Joseph is really in the pit
all the time, a slave in the house of death. His rise
is illusory. He is no part of this polyglot Egypt,
which is both a symbol and a counterfeit of the human
race. He walks through it in the detachment of a
dream."[34]

Mann also confesses that his aim was to take the
myth away from the Fascists by investing it with psychology and, by humanizing it, give it a new function.[35]
Again, we are compelled to ask if this is the actual
reason for the author's preoccupation with the mythical.
We also feel the need to ask what the myth of National
Socialism or Italian Fascism has in common with the

mythical story of the ancient Hebrew family of the
Bible. How does Mann usurp the myth from the Nazis
by telling the story of Egypt under the pharaohs?
The myth of racial superiority and anti-semitism as
promoted by the leaders of the Third Reich has only
the most tenuous connection to a world antedating even
that of ancient Rome. Perhaps Mann is merely wooing
the sensibilities of his critics? The fact that his
remarks about wresting the myth from the hands of Fascists were not made until 1941, approximately half a
decade after the completion of Joseph in Egypt leads
us to ask if he was really thinking of this goal at the
beginning of his work on the Joseph novel, a time when
the Nazis were not at all considered a serious menace
by Germans. In answer we cannot help but wonder if
the author is not again whispering coquettishly into
the ears of reviewers and literary historians.

Another assertion by the author that one must con-
tend with in dealing with the genesis of Joseph and His
Brothers is that the work was intended as a comedy. At
least a dozen times in his critical remarks he makes a
claim for humor: "Its [the novel's] task: to prove
that one can be mythic in a humorous way."[36] But the
sense of fun which Mann invests in the Joseph novels
makes unfair demands on the reader. One would have to
search long and hard to find the prelude, "Descent into
Hell," amusing, and there is little evidence to prove
that within the story itself Thomas Mann has succeeded
in bringing together the natural incongruities in characters or situation that might illustrate the fundamental absurdities of human nature. Needless to say, most
critics are more in agreement with the author's own
doubts about the humorous qualities in Joseph in Egypt:
"Oh, the old book has, I fear, frighfully pedantic
lengths. . . ."[37] Some reviewers find it dull and pre-
tentious,[38] and another goes so far as to advise the
reader to skip the opening 242 pages.[39] Even as careful a scholar as Hermann J. Weigand finds the story
overburdened with atmosphere and exposition; he questions Mann's penchant for names and allusions that place
such an unnecessary strain on the reader, and he predicts that many would sooner give up reading the novel
altogether than put forth the effort to keep step with
it.[40] He also deplores the incredibly slow pace of the
work: "It seems to us as if the magician [Mann] at
times were overtaxing his art, as if pure form were
running rampant, as if he were particularly unsuccessful in giving lifeblood to the transparent phantoms
which he has conjured up from the depths of the ages."[41]

269

Certainly the reader has some right to complain when, after working through more than a thousand pages, he is told by the protagonist that he should not get too involved because this is all merely a part of the story. To be sure, some playful notes are struck within the limits of the total work, especially in the protracted scenes of the hero's involvement with Mut. Hatfield notes that the theme of Joseph in Egypt, masculine chastity, is in itself a subject for comedy.[42] But Mann's attempts at humor are as dubious as they are effective, and though we may question the success of it, we shall certainly not doubt the need! It is here in Potiphar's house that the presence of humor is required, for incest has always been an intensely serious preoccupation of the author. Against the familiar background of forbidden activities Mann felt bound to call on devices which would help him gain some relief from the tension of the Mut affair. Dangerous but immense pleasure is derived by the hero merely by being the focus of Mut's attention; although actually innocent of the crime of which he is accused, Joseph is most certainly guilty of willfully inciting the mother figure. And, we recall, if in fantasy consummation has taken place, then, as a matter of course, the imagined murder of his rival also occurs and there follows a subsequent need for self-mortification. Joseph's ambivalent mentality is caught up in the implacable love-hate situation, and conflicting forces neutralize each other as the repressive device of irony cushions every output of incestuous feeling. Wolff also interprets the light tone at this point in the novel in the same manner: "The tendency expressed here, to treat the dark regions of human nature with a smile, perhaps in the hope of making them less perilous by employing mockery, is characteristic of all the late works of Mann."[43]

To Käte Hamburger the Joseph novel promotes the idea of humanity; she sees in Joseph Thomas Mann's ideal being, one in whose person and history the concept of humanity is especially pronounced. She finds that Joseph's path parallels that of Hans Castorp in The Magic Mountain; both must go through the realm of dissolution and death before they attain their humanity: a friendly attitude towards life which, however, takes its dark side into consideration.[44]

While it is true that Joseph takes positive steps as the provider for his people--steps which entail very little sacrifice on his part--the paean to humanity, or

even the friendliness towards life which Hatfield feels
to be axiomatic, seem on close examination to be for
the most part incidental, certainly less central, than
the reunion with the father and brothers.[45]

Since the concept of humanity, as we shall see,
cannot be considered an organic development of the total
work, it must therefore assume a less significant position in evaluating the meaning of the last volume,
Joseph the Provider. Based for the most part on coincidence and luck, Joseph's rise to become the bene-
factor of the people has little to do with true atonement and sacrifice. It simply goes to prove that everything is possible in the realm of fantasy, for as Hatfield remarks, Joseph's stay in the penitentiary after
Mut has denounced him must be considered "one of the
most gemütlich imprisonments in literature."[46]

But a study of the genesis of the Joseph tetralogy
is not complete until we examine its scheme of composition. The first three volumes appeared successively
in 1933, 1934, and 1936.* But Joseph the Provider,
the last volume and the one which treats, supposedly,
the concept of humanity, was not published until 1943,
during which time two other major works, The Beloved
Returns and The Transposed Heads, came into being. The
intrusion of these works suggests that the final volume
of the Joseph tetralogy was exposed to the danger of
not being written at all; at least it shows that Mann
had lost an all-consuming interest in it. In the middle
of his labor on Joseph the Provider Mann complained of
exhaustion and weariness with the theme of antiquity,[47]
a feeling he undoubtedly did not possess while engaged
in work on Joseph in Egypt, the story of Mut and her
impact on the hero.** With the termination of that

_____

*The slight delay in the appearance of the third
volume can be attributed to the political events of the
day. Although Mann finished volume two, it is believed,
in the middle of 1932 his concentration was inhibited
by the rise of the Nazis and his subsequent self-imposed
exile.

**When Mann first intended to write The Beloved
Returns it was clear that he needed a considerable
amount of reading in order to familiarize himself with
the historical figures in this Goethe novel. His method

story, the author's interest flagged and the basic
motive for the entire conception was satisfied. Mann
himself admits that the highpoint of the tetralogy was
Joseph in Egypt and that the fourth volume came as an
anti-climax.[48]

In one sense Joseph the Provider has nothing to
do with the volume it belatedly followed, for in this
book Joseph behaves as if the immediate past, as recounted in Joseph in Egypt, did not exist at all. He
never bothers to reminisce, reflect on, or digest the
remarkable upheaval in his soul that his relationship
to Mut and Potiphar brought about. He exists essentially in a vacuum, independent and unencumbered by the
past; in his mind the true test of the meaning of emotional involvement lies exclusively in the momentary
ecstasy of gratification. Once his relationship with
Mut becomes a closed book, Joseph, as reflected in
Joseph the Provider, seeks again to perpetuate his timeless self. Except for the reunion with his family,
Joseph acts as if there had been no struggle to rise
from a slave to a high position, but behaves as if he
had actually been born an Egyptian nobleman.

---

of creating was to first assimilate, arduously and
intimately, every aspect of the new subject matter.
This was especially true of Joseph: "To begin is always terribly difficult. Until one feels himself master
of a subject, until one learns the language it speaks
and can reproduce it, much courting and laboring, a
long inner familiarization are required. But what I
planned was so new and unusual that never did I beat
about the bush longer than this time. There was the
need of establishing contact with a strange world, the
primitive and mythical world; and to 'make contact' in
the poetic sense of the word signifies something very
complicated, intimate--a penetration, carried to identification and self-substitution, so that something can
be created which is called 'style,' and which is always
a unique and complete amalgamation of the artist with
the subject" (Works, XI, 659). Mann had already finished the legwork for Joseph with the completion of the
third volume, but now he found it easier to work his
way into the new realm of Goethe than to rekindle the
spark of the Joseph legend. We therefore conclude
that the subsequent adventures of his protagonist after
the showdown with Mut were simply not vital to his
artistic endeavors.

Within the verifiable framework of the Biblical
tradition, Mann has, frankly, not told the Joseph story.
In the Old Testament, the protagonist's stay in the
house of Potiphar takes up only fourteen verses of
Genesis 39 (7 through 20), while Joseph's rise to greatness in Egypt and his reconciliation with his family,
as recounted in Joseph the Provider, span twelve chapters: Genesis 38 and 40 through 50. Joseph's affair
with Potiphar's wife is told in passing in the Holy
Scriptures and her name is not even mentioned. What
is truly the point of the Biblical story is the family
reunion. But in Mann's telling of the tale, an incidental sidelight grew into the largest single volume,
and the central part of the Biblical version very
nearly failed to get beyond the planning stage.

The Significance of the Political

Critics have not failed to notice that Thomas
Mann, during the writing of the Joseph tetralogy, became a noteworthy player in the arena of world politics.
One should not overlook the large number of speeches
which Mann wrote and personally delivered for radio
transmission to Hitler's Germany. In America he became
the spokesman pro tempore for all that was still great
and eternal in German culture. Several times while in
America the Manns were even guests of the President in
the White House; and Thomas Mann not only admired
Franklin D. Roosevelt intensely but also felt a degree
of gratitude to him, believing that he was partly responsible for the honorary doctor's degree which he
received from Harvard University in 1935. It is no
wonder, then, that Hans M. Wolff draws a parallel between Joseph's position as advisor to the Egyptian
ruler and Thomas Mann's role as counselor and mediator
of German life and letters in America: Joseph's warn-
ings of danger and his pleas for preparedness in the
face of the pharaoh's aversion to political realities,
especially to foreign entanglements, reflect the role
Mann to a certain extent played while in the United
States.[49] And Franklin D. Roosevelt was probably the
model for Joseph the Provider, as Hatfield hints.[50]
In any event, Mann depicted his hero as an aristocrat
possessing enormous political power and functioning,
like the patrician of Hyde Park, as an administrator
par excellence of the country.

Joseph the Provider takes up where Mann's essay
Frederick and the Grand Coalition left off. Here we

have the return to the ugly duckling motif, where the
outcast is transfigured into the indispensable man of
the hour, superior in wisdom and beauty. Joseph and
his elevated career in Egypt reflect Mann's own up-
surge from ignominious disrepute in the Third Reich
to a position of national acclaim and honor in a new
land. Already as a youth Joseph had been preparing for
just such a noble role.[51] As an enlightened patrician
and practical manipulator of mankind's destiny, Joseph
receives carte blanche to dispense benevolence and remake society. He also has the real power which both
Jacob and Potiphar never possessed, and at the end
Joseph even has Jacob come to Egypt (the licentious
place abhorrent to the latter) and from his lofty position reunites with his father on his own terms. Thus,
the great Mannian dream is realized. The son has surpassed the father. The son has gained possession of
real power and genuine honor.

A general review of Thomas Mann's political life
after the appearance of The Magic Mountain is revealing.
In the face of the social unrest and increasing anarchy
in Germany after the First World War (together with his
own growing literary reputation in the world) Mann
gradually lost the ultraconservative image and the a-
political posture he had constructed in the Observations
of a Non-Political Man. The more international his
fame became, the more he spoke out regarding contemporary happenings. From the middle of the twenties on
he became a familiar cosmopolitan figure who traveled
to various countries of Europe, to both the eastern
and western part of the continent, to receive high ac-
colades and give speeches before distinguished groups.
The culmination of his literary career came in 1929
when he received the Nobel Prize for literature, and
the extraordinary honors continued during the thirties
and later in America where he was given an honorary
degree from Harvard University, invited to hold a
series of lectures at Princeton University, and asked
to become the voice of free Germany in BBC radio broad-
casts to his homeland during the war. And the light of
his new role illuminated a number of his essayistic
writings; primarily those on Lessing, Freud, and his
Appeal to Reason are eloquent testimony to his blossoming concern with politics.

However--and this is an extremely curious however,
--as energetic as Mann was in his efforts to combat the
Nazis, a careful evaluation of the author's political
development does not yield ready-made conclusions which

are immediately obvious. While it is apparently true
that Mann placed himself in the camp of reason and enlightenment, it is equally true that his ironic temperament would not permit him to embrace its principles
without qualification, especially where they touched
his subjective feelings of pleasure and offended or
disgusted his finer sensibilities. When we remember
the intense rhetorical passions of the Observations of
a Non-Political Man, the sheer equivocation of Hans
Castorp with regard to the Lichtmensch, or the supercharged hostility of the magician Cipolla toward the
mob--what Heinz Kohut would call the ferociousness of
the hero's hatred against the father image[52]--, we feel
the need to take a second look at Mann's apparent conversion to the principles of the West.

The modern political allegory to be found in Joseph
in Egypt--a deliberate infusion of twentieth-century
ideologies into this tale of early mankind--raises the
obvious question of its significance for Thomas Mann's
own political convictions. Unlike the time of World
War I when the non-political author found in politics
a perfect fusion of his artistic passions, he was in
the Nazi period placed in a position where his defense
of Germany could no longer be sanctioned by the world
at large. The Observations of a Non-Political Man,
harmonizing political attitudes with literary effusions,
represented no contradiction nor ambivalence; the tar-
gets of his scorn in his war book were only a half step
removed from the objects of his heroes' hostility in
his literary creations. But in the thirties Mann was
driven into a corner by the Nazis' successful usurpa-
tion of power. The maternal fount that Germany represented could hardly be defended as it had been justified
previously. Nevertheless, the traditional dichotomies
with which Mann had operated over the years did not
change radically, and it only takes a routine probing
to reveal that the concerns and obsessions which plagued
him before are still strikingly in place in the mythic
land of the pyramids. The father figure Potiphar is,
like the Rhetor-Bourgeois of the Observations of a Non-
Political Man, a liberal and a cosmopolitan with a
loose tolerance for foreign ways, not at all averse to
the possibility of the leveling of the superior indig-
enous culture of Egypt. We also remember Mann's identical concern in his World War I book about the pernicious
influence of Western notions on Germany's profound
music-cultural heritage. Potiphar's religio-political
creed even has its source in the West, a remarkable fact

275

considering that the geography of civilized ancient Egypt was conditioned solely by the South-North flow of the Nile. And, like the representative of the occidental West, Potiphar refuses to face the facts about the dark instinctive side of human nature, unwilling to believe Dûdu's truthful charges against Joseph.

Opposed to Potiphar's views are those of Mut, Dûdu and the Naphta-like priest, Beknechons. The latter, the first prophet of Amun, is a rigid personality, a strict defender of the sacred and the traditional, the embodiment of patriotic conservatism, and a believer, like Naphta, in "terror." Both Mut and the evil, phallic-minded dwarf Dûdu are fanatical followers of the reactionary Beknechons; Mut herself is a moon priestess belonging to the aristocratic order of Hathor whose home is the temple of Amun.* In fact, she is known as the harem-wife of Amun and, being excessively musical, teaches the other women of the harem how to sing. The name Dûdu, we learn from the author, was taken from a figure in Nietzsche's Thus Spake Zarathustra; but this figure, a caricature of Hitler in Joseph, appeared in Nietzsche's work as a lewd female and later became the model for the professional ladies of the Cologne brothel in Doctor Faustus, among whom is the leading maternal figure, Hetaera Esmeralda.** But perhaps Mann was in reality inspired by the similarity in sound between Dûdu and Dodo--the nickname of his mother.[53] A number of critics have found parallels in Beknechons' aggressive cult, backed by lance-bristling temple troops, to National Socialism with its storm troopers and bodyguards. Wolff points to the following citation from the novel, where Beknechons' program is set forth in words, as a direct reference to the doctrine of faith of the National Socialists: "The old must become lord in the new, the strict and sinewy be set over the kingdom that looseness not go too far and the reward of strictness be lost" (V, 957).[54] The cult of Amun, the God of the South, presents in its followers a real and powerful menace to the God of the North whose superiority exists only in the realm of morality and must

---

*We recall young Joseph's furtive and guilty worship of the moon, a serious activity of night people.

**Nietzsche got the name from history; there was a high officer of Amenhotep IV named Dûdu.

therefore rely on diplomacy and conciliation.* Mut herself embodies the violence and intolerance of the Amun creed. After her final attempt to seduce Joseph fails, she denounces him before the whole household, an outburst which Malcolm Cowley calls a "Jew-baiting" speech.[55] The modern tone of her speech before her servants in the courtyard is readily apparent: "'Egyptian brothers!'--They were her brothers all of a sudden; it went through and through them; they found it thrilling" (V, 1262-1263). Slochower goes even further, claiming that her speech is not only a direct and pointed reference to Fascist demagogy, but is also "a kind of pre-enactment of the Nazi Putsch of 1933, in which Joseph's coat is the 'sign' for which the Reichstag fire was made to serve."[56]

But it is hardly surprising to us now that the maternal sphere should be linked to the forces of terror and evil. The Observations of a Non-Political Man demonstrated long ago how the political, yoked to the sexual, called forth an explosion of fury against the followers of reason; and we have also noted the identification of the artist figure with the sadistic and hypnotic spellbinder in Mario and the Magician. What could have been more natural for Thomas Mann than to find, contrary to the obvious, a real and compelling fascination in the National Socialists with their veneration of Richard Wagner, their contempt for parliamentary democracy, their emphasis on German romanticism, their susceptibility to provocative cruelty, and their proclivity for sado-masochistic satisfactions. In his essay Brother Hitler, Thomas Mann left no doubt about the nature of his kinship with the dictator. Hitler is depicted as a replica of the artist figure, endowed with the same mental attitudes and behavior as

---

*Historically, Amun, also spelled Amon, Ammon, or Amen, had already been the traditional and most important god in Egypt for two centuries before the religious heresy of Amenhotep IV, the pharaoh in Joseph the Provider. Amun had not only become the chief god of the country but also the tutelary deity of the empire abroad. The real usurper of the status quo was therefore the pharaoh himself with his attempt to create a monotheistic religion at the expense of Amun and other gods.

Mann's early misfit heroes.*

On the surface Mann appears to have softened his
contempt for the Western representative. Considering
America's acceptance of Mann, it is no wonder that its
literary embodiment, Potiphar, is now depicted as fair-
minded, tolerant and decent, although inconsequential
in the grand scheme of things. Potiphar, the symbol
of a leveling but open-minded democracy, naturally ad-
heres as a <u>Lichtmensch</u> to the party of Amenhotep III
who favors the sun deity Aton-Re, a god whose horizon
is general, nondescript, broad and all-inclusive. But
the fact remains that Potiphar is covertly betrayed
by Joseph, and according to the latter's own subconscious rules even vanquished by him. This representative of the West, this flabby and political-minded
mass, this bulwark against the demonic, is cuckolded
in spirit by Joseph who, in masochistic ritardando
while remaining perversely chaste, attains the acme of
pleasure by prolonging his deep-seated and dubious
liaison with Mut. By no means does Potiphar's benevolence prevent Joseph from breaking his solemn promise
to Mont-kaw: to serve his master with love and loyalty,
in the same true manner in which Mann served the Western Powers. Joseph is certainly honest in saying
"Poor Potiphar," for where he is concerned, there is
no justice left. Despite his sense of fair play,
Potiphar is made the laughingstock of his own house
and deceived by Joseph in that deep realm of sexual
competition where he is completely vulnerable. Contrary to appearances, Thomas Mann has not let clemency
guide his pen. In his depiction of Potiphar, he once
again has been most deeply motivated, not by any love

---

*Mann's conception of Hitler in this essay was
certainly not completely appreciated by his contempo-
raries; and because of the objections of Gottfried
Bermann Fischer, the author's publisher, this work was
left out of the intended collection of essays entitled
<u>Europe, Beware!</u> Mann's own subsequent comment expressed
a veiled but ambivalent dissatisfaction: "That 'the
Brother' had to be omitted, troubled me, and to me it
was somehow a defeat because it was the first time,
that I was not able to bring before the world a work
containing my agony, hatred and mockery" (<u>Thomas Mann
Briefe1937-1947</u>, ed. Erika Mann [Frankfort on the Main:
S. Fischer, 1963], p. 70).

or concern for the father or what he stands for, but rather by the hero's insatiable psychological needs. And as Joseph related to Potiphar, so Mann relates to the nations of the world that symbolically fall into the light or dark sides of life.

Potiphar's own parents, Huia and Tuia, serve as additional evidence that in this father-son relationship we are on the same ground as in past works. These two bizarre figures are aged duplicates of the twins of The Blood of the Walsungs, Siegmund and Sieglinde. As twin brother and sister they too possess names that go together, commit incest, continually hold hands, are elegant, spoiled and experts in good taste, in short, extreme decadents. Huia defines their incestuous union, the fruit of which was Potiphar, to his sister-wife Tuia: "For we, male and female, begot in propriety, but we did so in the dark chamber of our sister-brotherhood. And the embrace of brother and sister--is it not after all a self-embracing in the depths and so not far removed from the brewing mother-stuff, hated by the light and the powers of the new order?" (IV, 864).

In honor of Amun, the God of darkness, Huia and Tuia monstrously sacrificed their son by emasculating him. When Tuia expresses concern because her son's attitude to his sexless fate is "negative" (!), Huia becomes angry: "That . . . would be grumbling against the exalted parents in the upper story! For his duty is to reconcile us with the age, it was for that we dedicated him; and what he gets in return is enough to make everything good, so that he need not find fault or pull a long face" (IV, 868). All the while Joseph is listening intently to every word of their fond nostalgia, savoring and reliving vicariously their unnatural conversation about pruning a son for the sake of some kind of exaltation. No less than Siegmund who by his incestuous union with Sieglinde vanquished and thereby "exalted" (sexually displaced) his despised rival von Beckerath, Joseph relishes the ultimate satisfaction of sexualized hate.

From the high level of both honor and sensual pleasure, which Joseph enjoys in Potiphar's house, we are able to understand more clearly Thomas Mann's actual attitude towards the momentous political upheavals of his time and to surmise what urged him to denounce the National Socialists so vigorously. In the same way that he and his heroes passionately lashed out against the

Bohemian type of artist in his earliest works, Mann ambivalently castigates Hitler now, his own particular sense of guilt still forcing him to deny what fascinates him the most.

The external reasons for Mann's condemnation of the Nazis are common knowledge. Their heavy-handedness and obvious crudity left Mann, along with other persons, little or no choice. And it took no great insight on Mann's part to realize that his Jewish wife and relatives by marriage would face a brutal and intolerable situation in Hitler's Germany. However, the internal associations of a lifetime are still at work reflecting his ambivalence more than any fundamental change toward new political liberalism. On the one hand he desires exactly that which places him in extreme jeopardy, and, on the other, he abhors that which he is compelled to embrace. Because of this ironic and agonizing position between the two extremes there was even a period of hesitation after his emigration from Germany. For a while after Hitler's rise to absolute power Mann, wishing to keep in contact with his German readers, abstained from waging a verbal war against the new regime, with the desired result that his books not be banned.

Mann's embrace of the democratic spirit of the West contains a question mark, a pale one to be sure.* His prejudice, which he is unable to dissociate from the father-world symbolically residing in the Western rational Lichtmensch, is continually in force. A partial solution is to combine the two worlds, at least figuratively, in his novel. He does this in The Tales of Jacob by investing the common people with blind and unreasoning force. Joseph's brothers, all antitheses to the artist-type, take cruel and destructive revenge on the

---

*The following remark of the author offers us an interesting sidelight to his attitude. On a speaking tour in the United States in 1940 Mann made an observation about the population of San Antonio, Texas, which he found to be greatly mixed with Mexicans: "an often very attractive type and a relief after the eternal world of the Yankees" (Bürgin and Mayer, p. 145). Here is a hint of his lack of real comfort among the kind of Northern people Tonio Kröger would have found to be simple and dull. The Latin type, his maternal inheritance, on the other hand, will never lose its direct appeal to him.

town of Schechem after their sister Dinah has been abducted by a Schechemite. And in Brother Hitler the dictator's phenomenal success is equally ascribed to his mastery of the medium of politics as well as his gift for that field which heretofore had been the exclusive property of the father-world.[55]

Joseph and His Brothers is less an historical novel than it is, aside from the standard Mannian tale of incest, a personal allegory of the author's own role and position as an exile from Nazi Germany. It represents, in essence, a kind of symbolic biography of Thomas Mann. This is especially true for the last two volumes of the tetralogy that were written when the struggle between Fascism and democracy became a matter of greatest urgency. In the ancient land of the Nile Joseph becomes the uncompromising target of the Hitler-like Dûdu who is bent on destroying him. But even though Dûdu's attitude is so implacably menacing to him, Joseph's true desires and inclinations are closer to those of this spiteful and pompous dwarf brother of darkness than they are to those of his charitable protector, the enlightened man of the West, Potiphar. His sympathies tuned to vibrate only in the maternal artistic sphere to which Dûdu belongs, Joseph is incapable of achieving real and intrinsic pleasure except in the sado-masochistic course which demands two victims: the rival paternal figure and the hero himself. And so, as a master of equivocation and double-dealing and despite his basic position with regard to Potiphar and Western liberalism, Joseph, like Thomas Mann himself, emerges at the outcome as the man of the hour, the beholder of real political power, and the possessor of honors.

SEQUELS AND INTERLUDE: THE BELOVED RETURNS,

THE TRANSPOSED HEADS, AND THE TABLES OF THE LAW

Before the complete Joseph tetralogy came into
print, two shorter works of some significance had ger-
minated and flowed from Thomas Mann's pen with another
that followed immediately afterwards. Only by stretching the imagination can one find a snug category in
which to group them. Chronology probably offers the
best way out, embracing, as it does, the final elapse
of years taken to complete Joseph the Provider. The
Tables of the Law and The Beloved Returns, almost in
contrast to The Transposed Heads, still fit the schemata
of Joseph by presenting an artist-hero of God-like
quality: one, Moses, the sculptor of a new society and
writer of the commandments; the other, Goethe, the cultural giant and advisor to the throne in the duchy of
Weimar. Though Mann stated that The Transposed Heads
was a "metaphysical jest" or experiment, it still can
be brought under one roof with the other works. All
three (four if we include Joseph the Provider) seem to
have as their goal the attempt to demythologize a myth,
to remake it in accordance with vital principles of
human behavior. In all these works the line dividing
mythology and psychology is a hazy one that erratically
drifts first into one realm and then into the other.
The three may also be placed beside each other as possible responses to the exigencies of world history. As
long as the magnetically seductive and diabolical dictator, the Bohemian artist Hitler, held firm control
over Germany, Mann could hardly resist the temptation
on the one hand to reflect on the so-called "leader's"
machinations or, on the other, to escape them.

The Beloved Returns

To what extent Thomas Mann's portrait of Goethe
in The Beloved Returns (1939) corresponds to reality is
less important for our purposes than the question of
what problems in this work are peculiar to Thomas Mann.
Although apparently quite remote from Joseph, The Beloved Returns is still in close keeping with the biblical, historical narrative. It, too, is a fusion of
psychology and myth, and again Mann busies himself with
a careful study of a vast number of documents that
terminates with the creation only of another typical
Mannian-type artist figure. For all his efforts in
research, fresh discovery and new insight, Mann is left

283

with little more than an old Tonio Kröger or a decrepit Joseph.

The beloved in <u>The Beloved Returns</u> is Charlotte Buff-Kestner whom Goethe was infatuated with as a young man and whom he had rendered immortal as the heroine of his Storm and Stress novel of 1774, <u>The Sorrows of Young Werther</u>. Her sentimental visit to Weimar in 1816 when Goethe was at the height of his success, becomes the framework for an analysis of the artist figure's personality. But before the widowed Lotte has a chance to meet Goethe, she encounters three leading personages of Weimar: Adele Schopenhauer, the sister of the philosopher; Friedrich Wilhelm Riemer, Philologist and Goethe's secretary; and August von Goethe, the poet's son. Each of them engage Lotte in a long conversation in which various sides of Goethe's personality as well as his convictions and attitudes are both set forth and illuminated.

That Mann's Goethe portrait is analogous to that of Joseph is revealed by the following words of Hatfield: "He can regard Goethe as another paradigm of the artist: the poet not as outcast but as a figure of state, holding a position in his little duchy not dissimilar to Joseph's in Egypt."[1] This view receives further support from Mann's own essay, <u>Fantasy on Goethe</u> (1948), in which the similarities of the two protagonists are compared. But the parallel goes far beyond these works. Alone, the obvious and general points should be sufficiently convincing to let us place Goethe in the rank and file of preceding heroes: his compulsion to work, his meticulous toiletries, his distance from the masses, his incapacity to love one individual person, his illness and suffering, his lack of normal warmth and consideration, his withdrawal from life, and his preoccupation with death--in itself the motivation toward the aristocratic status which Goethe has acquired. Such status as a direct expression of death stands out clearly if we interpret literally a passage from Mann's <u>After-Dinner Speech in Amsterdam</u> (1924) as a basic part of the artistic soul:

> I have been most seriously concerned with the concept black as being an expression of nobility.
> Is not black the color of death? And is it not proper that man instinctively connects the idea of aristocracy with that of death?. . . .

United in our hearts with death and
devoutly joined to the past, we should not
let death be master of our head, of our
thoughts. The pathos of freedom must be
opposed to that of piety, the democratic
principle of life and the future must
counterbalance the aristocratic principle
of death, so that that which is solely
and exclusively aristocratic might arise,
so that humanity might come into being.[2]

With special delight Mann voices in his essays,
both early and late, Goethe's own words, "We Frankfort
patricians have always considered ourselves equal to
the nobility."[3] And more than once he makes note of
Goethe's "innate merits"[4] as a man of genius, natural
nobility, and invention. But, once again, the very
qualities which distinguish him also separate him,
rendering him cold and distant in the eyes of the people. In fact, the emphasis throughout Mann's various
essays and novel about Goethe is placed on his aloofness, coldness, malevolence, his disdainful lack of
feeling or even his contempt for the masses.* Indeed,
Goethe's deprecation of the citizens exposed to the
Eger massacre hardly seems appropriate for such an occasion as the formal dinner in honor of Charlotte:

"Citizens of Eger!" cried the narrator.
So then he amounted to something and had
been splendidly recompensed. He had lost

---

*Another favorite quotation concerns Goethe's re-
sponse to the question about the kind of life he would
have lived, if he had been born in England instead of
in Germany: "'If I had been born in England I should
have been a duke, or better still, a bishop with rev-
enues of thirty thousand pounds sterling.' Very fine.
But suppose Goethe had not drawn the big prize in the
lottery but had instead drawn a blank. To which Goethe
replied: 'Not everybody, my dear friend, is made for
the big prize. Do you think I would have done such a
foolish thing as to draw a blank?'" (Goethe as Representative of the Bourgeois Age [1932], Works, IX, 321).
It goes without saying that Goethe, as Mann sees him,
hardly comes forth as a true representative of the
bourgeois age but rather as the exclusive property of
the aristocracy.

his wife and children, his friends and
relatives, all his property and posses-
sions, his whole society, not to speak of
the suffocating effect of the dreadful
hours he spent up the chimney. He stood
there naked as he was born, but he was a
citizen of Eger, and after all he was proud
of it. Human beings, that is the way they
are. Give way with gusto to the impulse
to commit the cruellest deeds, and after
their heads are cool again, enjoy quite as
much the large gesture of repentance with
which they think to pay for the crime. It
is laughable--and touching.[5]

But the poet's anti-democratic bearing and pronouncements do not stop here. Goethe's reference to
the people as "the vile and vulgar herd" stands at
the end of a series of similar statements that are put
into his mouth by the major characters who precede him:
"Must we not rejoice . . . when the common herd, contemptuous as it is by nature of the things of the mind,
is yet compelled to venerate the mind in the only way
it can understand, by seeing that it serves their
interests?"(II, 407); "You think you can teach me
about the mob, and the all too crass motives of their
curiosity, which at bottom have pathetically little to
do with mind" (II, 477-478); "I have always noticed
that society, especially our German society, actually
takes pleasure in bowing down . . ." (II, 486);". . .
enthusiasm is beautiful. But not without enlightenment.
When hysterical, narrow-minded citizens revel meta-
phorically in the shedding of blood, because the his-
toric hour has given the rein to their evil passions,
the sight is painful to behold" (II, 535).

Bernhard Blume, in a major study on Mann and
Goethe, forcefully sums up the attributes of Goethe
which Mann puts into Riemer's mouth, attributes which
again recapitulate to a greater or lesser extent the
character and attitudes of all previous Mannian heroes:

But he puts even more into his mouth,
namely, Thomas Mann's own words, those
previously mentioned observations about
Goethe's destructive equanimity, his
characteristic coldness and indifference
which "remains totally uncommitted," his
lack of faith, his irony, his mischievous
spinelessness as a poet, in a word: his

nihilism. Riemer emphatically dwells on
Goethe's "complete skepticism," which
shows no respect for people and does not
believe in ideas; he enlarges upon Goethe's
increasing tendency towards solitude, towards ossification, tyrannical intolerance,
pedantry, strangeness, and weird mannerisms;
he enlarges upon his sullenness, his disgust
and his hopeless silence, his mysterious
embarrassment. . . .[6]

The contempt for the people is expressed and repeated in excess throughout the novel. Considering
the frequency of the denigrating comments from the
mouths of practically everyone who is given a separate
speech in the novel, the conclusion must be drawn that
that "hate of the masses" extends beyond Goethe and
even beyond his satellites to the author of the book
himself. Yet, what a strange emphasis to insert in
novel by an author who is the honored guest in America,
a land which in his mind is the very epitome of the
burgher-citizen, the democrat, and the concept of freedom. "Freedom for what?" Goethe inquires, implying
that the masses have no need of anything beyond the
satisfaction of their basest drives. In a truly ironic
and ambivalent manner, his hate for the masses is set
off against an excessive love for a dictator, Napoleon,
in many ways the prototype of the tyrant who drove
Mann from his homeland.

In spite of his forced visit to this democratic
land and his serious attempt to play lightly and ironically with the human substance of his host country,
Mann could only see in the masses of people in America
the common world of the father. Once more his distant
attitudes toward his own father work symbolically to
determine Mann's relationship to a whole nation.

From behind the heroic stature of creative genius,
the destructive side of the artist's nature (as seen
in Naphta, Cipolla and the miniature sketch of "Brother
Hitler") truly exposes itself. Goethe's coldness and
callousness towards his fellow humans notwithstanding,
Mann attempts to make a virtue out of Goethe's death
by saying: "They claim his last words before he passed
away were, 'Let more light in.' That is not completely
certain. But what he really said, his actual last
words, words against death and for life was this: 'At
the end it's only appropriate to move forward.'"[7] In

denying the prevailing belief concerning Goethe's last uttered words, Mann insures that the poet will not reveal attributes of the <u>Lichtmensch</u>.

In the hero's attitude towards life we detect the usual contempt the hero feels for the world about him. Nevertheless, Mann still tries to make a strong point in his Goethe essays, as he did in <u>Tonio Kröger</u>, of Goethe's "friendliness to life" (<u>Lebensfreundlich-keit</u>).[8] How strange the expression "friendliness to life" is--as if the love of life were not a matter of course. How insufficient in essence must this surface remark appear, more like an afterthought, a catchword which runs totally counter to the hero's basic attitude and actions. Once more the familiar ambivalence of past works is demonstrated; the compulsive desire to palliate the inner doubt of life contrasts strikingly with the measures adopted to shield the self from the life experience and with the carefully chosen words to broadcast the contempt that is felt.

Goethe's collecting mania, referred to more than once in Mann's essays, points up the kind of self-erected barriers he establishes between himself and his fellowmen. At the dinner party, for example, Goethe is embarrassed when he is unable to readily locate the silhouettes of the youthful Charlotte and her family. By contrast, his memory of inanimate objects, such as coins and rocks, is astonishingly vital compared to the things which he has invested with his deepest feelings. Thus, Goethe, with his imposing superior wall against candidness and direct expression is seen as the "unification of the refined and the demonic,"[9] not too far removed from the earlier Mannian heroes who found a similar defense in studied propriety. And, just as they did, so too does Goethe lead a life entirely sufficient unto himself and frigidly divorced from the emotional demands around him. Charlotte frankly labels him a parasite who uses and sacrifices people--Riemer, August, and Ottilie--for his own ends, just as he did the women of his youthful love affairs. In the act of sacrifice there is a special kind of emotional involvement; artistic aims are served without the hero being trapped in his own feelings. There his love does not overwhelm to the exclusion of all else, for an inner degree of doubt with hostile overtones safeguard his deeper, unmanageable instincts. But to reinforce and implement controls he must, whenever he is able to, disengage himself. Goethe, no less than Tonio Kröger, must remain chaste and detached for his art, for as he himself is fully aware: "Every poem is to a certain degree a kiss which one gives to the world. But kisses alone do not beget children."[10] Art is a by-product of a chaste form of love which the artist selects for himself through denial and renunciation; but even as it produces no vital progeny, neither does it pose any emotional challenges.

The renunciation of love in all its inherent perils once again becomes the guiding principle for the Mannian hero; and Mann, as Bernhard Blume has also noted, safely links up Goethe's youthful passion for Charlotte Buff with its counterpart in old age, his relationship to Marianne von Willemer. By "falling in love" with the wife or beloved of another, the protagonist Goethe repeats the Buff-Kestner experience and walks in the footsteps of preceding Mannian heroes, who, almost without exception, expose themselves to the resignation of a hopeless love: a type of love-affair which must by nature be doomed to failure on the one hand and to an increase of frustration and denial of the value of life on the other. Mann, in his essay Goethe and Tolstoy (1921), attests further to this mutual fraternalism that forms the deep bond between the Promethean hero and his own earlier artist figures:

> But where he loved so that lofty poesy was the result, and not merely a Venetian epigram ticked out in hexameters on a maiden's back; where it was serious, the romance regularly ended in renunciation. He never actually possessed Lotte or Friederike, nor Lili, nor the Herzlieb, nor Marianne, nor even Ulrike--and not even Frau von Stein. He never loved unrequited--unless in the immensely painful, absurdly shattering affair with little Levetzow. Yet in all these cases resignation was the order of the day: either on moral grounds, or for the sake of his freedom. Mostly he bolted.[11]

From Goethe as Representative of the Bourgeois Age we find other features of Goethe that complete the portrait of the typical Mannian protagonist: the poet's concern for his dehors, for his elegance of dress, his cleanliness and neatness and his love of good food and drink.[12] Also, according to Mann, Goethe fought a continuous battle with his health, and therefore, he is revealed here as a stoic sufferer--he takes care

that Charlotte does not become aware of his sore arm
during the social function. His stoicism is further
contrasted with that of his opportunistic secretary,
John, who appears unable to put up with adversity or
pain without complaining. In fact, there are even
paeans of praise to the value of suffering for its own
sake: "To be a hammer seems to everyone more praiseworthy and desirable than being an anvil, but yet, what
it doesn't take to endure these endless, eternally recurring blows!"[13] Suffering with an overtone of self-
commiseration as a way of life for the artist hero is
also implied in the simile of the burning candle: the
creative artist consumes himself in his art just as
disease, the necessity and the punishment behind his
art, ravages and consumes. Thus, the artist, in narcissistic loneliness, is left to himself, burning as
the candle in a slow kind of death.

That the Mannian hero's characteristic relationship to music is also in force in the figure of Goethe,
is convincingly demonstrated by Bernhard Blume who
points to the manner in which the author has changed
Sulpiz Boisserée's 1815 account of Goethe's romance
with Marianne Willemer. One of the discrepancies from
Boisserée's source occurs at the end of Goethe's remarks on the concept of time: "'Here we have music.
It has its dangers as far as clarity of mind is concerned. But it is a magic means to contain time, to
expand it, and to give it its peculiar meaningfulness.'
And now there rises before him the image of the singing
Marianne. The words which Marianne speaks and which
Boisserée reports are reinforced even more by Thomas
Mann . . . '[he] said: love and music, the two are
pleasure and eternity' is immediately revealed to be a
special slant and interpretation according to the spirit
of Thomas Mann's concept of art as a dichotomy."[14]
Blume's remarks are well taken, for as in the past, it
is music which binds the erotic with the taboo. Mann
gives his own emphasis to Boisserée's report, the emphasis of Wagner's music which is the wellspring of
the artist's unchecked feelings and sexual desires.

Goethe would like nothing better than to disregard
time altogether, like Albrecht van der Qualen and Hans
Castorp who were without a time sense and therefore
devoid of any feeling for responsibility. This controlled "maternal patience" (as Mann designates the
neglect of time in Goethe as Representative of the
Bourgeois Age) must eventually shatter and give way
to the time concept of Tonio Kröger or of Gustav von

Aschenbach before his trip to Italy. For them time signified an implacable sting of conscience, a compulsive and painful inheritance of penitence in the fatherworld. Time is transformed into a torturous regime of self-willed punishment; it becomes a means of atonement through self-imposed work against the clock, as well as a guaranteed bulwark of repressive measures against timeless, destructive instincts. Time, as life, must therefore be borne with persevering courage as well as with a good deal of evasion because it constitutes a mass of painful suffering for the guilty hero. We are told how this ambivalence affects Goethe: "It reaches down into his moral existence, into his relationship to _time_, for example, which is partly a powerful _taking-one's time_, a waiting, a postponing, yes a humdrum, a vegetating passive trust, and then again, with all that, it is truly a cult of time, the most exact watching, retaining, exploiting, cultivating of the gift of time. . . ."[15]

The concept of time ascribed to Goethe conveys the conflict and tension inherent in the Mannian protagonist: an evasion of the responsibilities and commitments implicit in measured time paired off with a compulsive observance of each second and minute. Mann himself reveals the importance of this camouflage in an unguarded statement by Goethe: "Enough craziness left in me, too, underneath all the brilliance! If I had not inherited the knack of order, the swing of saving myself, a whole system of protective devices--where should I be?" (II, 656). By the same token his stoicism and his tyranny, his isolated withdrawal from all immediate involvement, and his poetic license to study and see (voyeuristically) life and love from afar constitute a refined system of rationalizations which are passed off with conviction as a total expression of a great, individual genius. In actuality, however, Mann in his portrait of Goethe is again making a heroic virtue of necessity, clothing his necessities of repression in sublime, artistic garments. Anyone of the many revealing items that decorate Goethe's person may be traced to their source in repression and guilt, but let us, for now, select the great poet's attitude towards women.

Adele Schopenhauer says: "In his attitude to the feminine there is something overbearing, I might also say coarse--a masculine prepossession that would deny us access to the lofty realms of poetry and intellect" (II, 489). Her statement is later borne out by Goethe's own opinion: "Cruelty is one of the chief ingredients of love, and divided about equally between the sexes: cruelty of lust, ingratitude, callousness, maltreatment, domination. . . . What sweet love is, is itself put together out of nothing but sheer horrors, and the very purest just a compound of shadinesses we dare not confess to! Nil luce obscurius?" (II, 636). The roots of such statements grow deep in the soul of the Mannian artist whose antagonism can be traced back to deep affinity and desire for the mother and to a fear of the father. So rather for his own needs than for Goethe's, Mann traces the poet's artistry and sensual qualities back to the mother's side of the family, the mother's mother, born Lindheimer. From her Goethe got "his skull and mouth and Mediterranean skin" (again the maternal southern, exotic influence on the Mannian protagonist): "The husk, outward features, they were there a hundred years ago, with no more significance than just a female, a buxom, clever armful of a brunette. In my mother it slumbered, she became the shape and person of that which I am. Took on an intellectual significance it never had before and never needed to get" (II, 656-657). This idealized picture of a fertile Mediterranean woman, undiluted by intellect represents a simplified prototype rather than a reality which Mann's Goethe seeks in all women. How simultaneously attractive and forbidden the image becomes! The idealized, gifted, and desirable mother stands as an eternal attraction which might be attained except for the threatening presence of the father. Goethe's description of his ancestors reminds us of Buddenbrooks and the roles played by Thomas and Christian: "My father was a shady character, late-born child of elderly parents, his brother definitely out of his mind and died an imbecile --as did my father, too, in the end" (II, 655). Goethe also tells us that his father was much older than his wife, unhappily married and a pedantic hypochondriac.

In the omnipresence of the ever-threatening father and the irresistible mother, what recourse do we find for the Mannian protagonist in his Oedipal dilemma but escape through repression glossed over with the deception of fantasy: "Life could not be borne unless we glazed it over with warm, deceptive feelings. Yet beneath it always lies the icy coldness. You make yourself great, make yourself hated, telling the ice-cold truth. And anon do penance and appease the world by merciful, heartening lies" (II, 655). In summa, the Oedipal conflict again determines the total nature of

the protagonist's behavior, his renunciations and excesses, his ambivalent love-hate of a tyrannical dictator and his people.

The qualities that make the protagonist Goethe
a vehicle for the author's emotional autobiography are
by now apparent. The protagonist and his author both
organize their lives by virtue of the repressive mechanism: they maintain their distance and composure at all
costs, politically they keep their philosophical distance from a world that is collapsing around them, they
stoically resist (and take secret pleasure in) the pain
and suffering that is visited upon them, they are both
fascinated and disturbed by a dictator who contributes
only to their discomfort, they are looked on as traitors
to their country, and both feel themselves to represent
the grossly misunderstood but genuine spirit of German
culture.

The instances of Goethe's and Mann's castigation
of the Germans in their state of blind and perverted
patriotism are too numerous to mention, but for a conclusion of this discussion, let us quote one of Goethe's
longer speeches and defy the reader to insist that it
is not rather the speech of the bitter and defiant
writer, Thomas Mann, in exile in America:

> So they [the Germans] mistrust your German
> soul and you; they feel it an abuse, your
> fame is a source among them of hate and
> anguish. Sorry existence, spent wrestling
> and wrangling with my own blood--yet after
> all it is my blood, it bears me up. It must
> be so, I will not whine. That they hate
> clarity is not right. That they do not know
> the charm of truth, lamentable indeed. That
> they so love cloudy vapouring and beserker
> excesses, repulsive; wretched that they aban-
> don themselves credulously to every fanatic
> scoundrel who speaks to their baser qualities,
> confirms them in their vices, teaches them
> nationality means barbarism and isolation.
> To themselves they seem great and glorious
> only when they have gambled away all that
> they had worth having. Then they look with
> jaundiced eyes on those whom foreigners love
> and respect, seeing in them the true Germany.
> No, I will not appease them. They do not
> like me--so be it, I like them neither, we
> are quits. What I have of Germany I will

keep--and may the devil fly away with them
and the philistine spite they think is
German! They think they are Germany--but
I am. Let the rest perish root and branch,
it will survive in me. Do your best to fend
me off, still I stand for you. (II, 657-658)

The Transposed Heads

Thomas Mann's "metaphysical jest," The Transposed
Heads,represents not only his stay in the world of
mythic timelessness but an escape into a realm where
the harsh realities of the political present have no
force. In bringing this weird and fanciful tale into
harmony with his past creations, Mann illustrates, as
he does in Joseph, The Beloved Returns, and The Tables
of the Law,that his sources, no matter how remote in
time or theme, are no more than the necessary raw
material out of which he fashions old themes into new
works. Here he again invests an abstract Hindu legend
with his very own special brand of psychology, placing
his peculiar stamp on a traditional theme.

The Transposed Heads is the tale of two rivals for
the affection of Sita, Shridaman and Nanda, who in self-
sacrifice, frustration, and despair decapitate themselves. However, Shridaman's wife, Sita, with special
intercession from the Goddess Kali, is permitted to
replace the heads; but alas, in her excitement she
places the two heads on the wrong bodies. The result
is a vexing confusion in identity and a painful uncertainty in the personal relationships of each figure as
to his correct role. Mann is certainly at his most abstract in this story in which his two chief characters
do not exist as real human beings but rather as obvious
symbols of intellect and of life. Mann's selection of
(and departure from) the traditional motifs and leitmotifs of the Indic myth provide an exotic framework
for a story of fantastic love and horror that seems to
give full expression and detailed examination to certain
minor, almost peripheral episodes of former stories,
such as Aschenbach's dream and vision in Death in Venice
or the narrator's nightmare in The Fight Between Jappe
and Do Escobar.

The hero Shridaman, the Brahman son of a wealthy
merchant of near noble lineage, is emphatically contrasted to the goat-nosed smith and cowherd Nanda, a
son of the people whose family, it is told, "were

quite distinctly members of human society."[16] Not the
least bit interested in things of the mind, the simple
and blithe Nanda is accustomed to the noise of the
market-place where the crowd has the contemplative
individual at its mercy. He "with the laughing eyes"
has no use for words other than as a vehicle for practical communication. Crude and unproblematical, he
considers his body the basis of life. In keeping
with the pleasures of his virile state, he rejects
every ascetic mortification of his physical self as
he thrives on undivided banality, sentimental concerns,
and maudlin responses. Shridaman, on the other hand,
is a learned, good-looking, sensitive and tender man
whose fine lips and soft beard hint of precocious,
child-like immaturity or even arrested physical development. The head is the significant appendage for
Shridaman who is indifferent to his brittle, flabby,
and weak body. And with artistic precision the articulate Shridaman strives continually for the mot juste,
pedantically correcting Nanda's diction and pronunciation. In attempting to explain the aesthetic way to
Nanda, he calls to mind Tonio Kröger's scornful doubts
about the dilettante lieutenant who, by his embarrassing recitation, hoped to pluck a leaf from the laurel
wreath of art:

> After all you are actually a child of
> Samsara and thus completely taken up with
> life . . . you do not belong among the
> souls who feel the need to emerge above
> the frightful ocean of laughing and weep-
> ing as lotus flowers rise above the sur-
> face of the stream and open their cups to
> the sky. You are perfectly at home in the
> depths, where such a complex profusion and
> variety of shapes and forms exist. You are
> well off, and that is why one feels good at
> the sight of you. Then you suddenly get
> the idea in your head to meddle with Nirvana
> and talk about its negative condition and
> how it cannot be called hushed nor cozy,
> and all that is funny enough to make one
> weep, or, to use the word made on purpose,
> it is touching, because it makes me grieve
> for that well-being of yours that is so
> good to see. (VIII, 720)

Cursed by insidious self-doubts, Shridaman demands
repudiation of the senses and, by extension, of his own
life. The guilt that has long slumbered in him makes

him deny the pleasure-laden moments in his marriage to
Sita. In opposition to the natural ebb and flow of
life, he analyzes every experience to the detriment of
feeling and the ruination of pleasure. Spontaneity
cannot be a part of him; all sensations must be filtered
and denatured by his fantasy and intellect. In fact,
his intact imagination is more meaningful to him than
the fulfillment of all his physical yearning. Captivated at first sight by Sita's voluptuous attractiveness, Shridaman, like a naughty child, guiltily watches
as Sita bathes nude in the river.* And once his imagination has been stimulated he finds himself in an
agitated state of urgency that dominates him as it did
Herr Friedemann and other early protagonists. While
Nanda can take each moment as it comes, and, in the
spirit of carpe diem, participate fully in its attrac-
tions, the artist-hero must once again postpone the
enjoyment of the present, disavowing the immediate
temptations of the senses until his fantasy kindles an
intense degree of passion. But then, once inflamed,
he is compelled to rush headlong into a fateful union,
to possess Sita in all haste, even if it means narrowly
skirting the edge of the abyss. But his course is
strangely and ultimately motivated by the knowledge
that Nanda had known Sita before and had "swung her up
to the sun" (VIII, 727). Chosen as sun maiden of her
village at the feast of the sun,** Sita was pushed in
the swing by Nanda's powerful arms "so high in the
heavens that one could hardly hear her screams" (VIII,
728). With quivering voice and flushed cheeks the
brooding and melancholy Shridaman impulsively reproaches
his companion for this act of familiarity as well as
for the latter's indifference to the real charms of
the girl: "This familiarity seems to have made her
entirely a material being in your eyes and dulled your
gaze for the higher meaning of such a phenomenon. Otherwise you would not have spoken with such unpardonable
coarseness of the fine shape it has taken on" (VIII,
731).

---

*The woman Sita possesses a name similar to Gerda
again.

**Again, like the previous Mannian heroines, Sita
is the center of the social whirl in her village.

Nanda's act recalls Potiphar's religious adherence to the sun-god as well as the belief of all of Mann's Lichtmenschen in a world devoid of darkness.* Shridaman is openly jealous of the cowherd and the thought of Nanda's swinging Sita becomes an unbearable thorn in his side. Shridaman's reaction to the swinging literally leads the reader to a sexual interpretation of the relationship between Nanda and Sita and thus to a story of a family conflict. Nanda, a child of the sun, vulgar, illiterate, unimaginative, and maudlin, is the third person in the familiar love entanglement. His eternal presence in the life of the hero even after the latter's conquest of the woman, places this tale, despite, and because of, the strangely erotic and bizarre mantle in which it is wrapped, within the typical Mannian framework of Oedipal rivalry. We remember that both Siegmund (The Blood of the Walsungs) and Hans Castorp continually referred to the omnipresent specter of their rivals when making their own declarations of love. Nanda had known Sita before the hero became acquainted with her; or, in more precise terms, the father had possessed the mother before the son did. What now seems to spur the hero on to take Sita as his wife is a sadistic spirit of competition rather than an all-consuming consideration for her as a person. So Shridaman's friendship for the representative of life, continually undermined by the need to vanquish, is scarcely as striking in its affection as it is in the underlying enmity of a love-hate competition.

Yet, when Shridaman gains possession of Sita, he becomes overwhelmed by a feeling of life-weariness and indifference to his newly acquired wife, who provided only a brief reprieve from the dark substratum of his thoughts. On his trip to the home of his relatives, the hero, walking open-eyed to his own destruction, finally puts an end to the dolorous mental burden he bears. Obeying an impulse of the heart--an act of spontaneity--, Shridaman enters the shrine of the fearsome Kali, the dark mother, to find a mirror reflection of his tortured mind in the grotesquely satisfying and gruesome paintings flanking her image:

---

*Once married, Sita sees Nanda by day but spends her nights in the arms of her husband.

> Visions of life in the flesh, all jumbled
> together, just as life is, out of skin and
> bones, marrow and sinews, sperm and sweat
> and tears and ropy rheum; filth and urine
> and gall; thick with passions, anger, lust,
> envy and despair; lovers' partings and
> bonds unloved; with hunger, thirst, old
> age, sorrow, and death; all this forever
> fed by the sweet, hot streaming blood-stream,
> suffering and enjoying in a thousand shapes,
> teeming, devouring, turning into one
> another. And in that all-encompassing
> labyrinthine flux of the animal, human,
> and divine, there would be an elephant's
> trunk that ended in a man's hand, or a
> boar's head seemed to take the place of a
> woman's. (VIII, 746)

This frightful description of questionable necessity,
calculated to prove in a Schopenhauerian sense the
enticing nothingness that is the sum and inner substance
of life, reminds the reader both of Hans Castorp's
vision of horror in the Greek temple (an artistic,
religious shrine) and of the grim, repulsive and life-
shattering orgy which haunts the dream of a degenerate
Aschenbach. Transfixed in the spell of the All-Mother,
Shridaman stands before the sacrificial alter:

> This was She, the Deathbringer-Life-
> giver, Compeller of sacrifice--her whirl-
> ing arms made his own senses go round in
> drunken circles. He pressed his clenched
> fists against his mightily throbbing
> breast; uncanny shudderings, cold and hot,
> surged over his frame in successive floods.
> In the back of his head, in the very pit
> of his stomach, in the woeful excitation of
> his organs of sex, he felt one single urge,
> driving on to the extremity of a deed against
> his own life in the service of the eternal
> womb. . . .
> "But let me enter again into thee through
> the door of the womb that I may be free of
> this self; let me no more be Shridaman, to
> whom all desire is but bewilderment, since
> it is not he who gives it!"
> Spoke these darkling words, seized up
> the sword from the floor, and severed his
> own head from his neck. (VIII, 747-748)

Shridaman's precipitate act of masochistic destruction takes us back to Mann's earliest stories
where the hero impulsively and frantically rushed to
achieve the ultimate gratification of his pressing
sexual urges by means of release through self-immolation, but never before has the obsessive, forbidden
lust been articulated so clearly. And Nanda, the father
figure, simply cannot understand his friend's suicide;
death and its meaning are to him as they were to Thomas
Buddenbrook, utterly beyond his ken. Though he must
follow Shridaman in self-murder in accordance with the
Hindu legend, Thomas Mann arbitrarily invests him with
unthinking behavior and questionable insight.

The plot of The Transposed Heads revolves, therefore, around two apparently unmotivated suicides. But
if there is madness in the method, the opposite is also
true. By means of his friendship pact with Nanda,
Shridaman succeeds in ridding himself of the person
who seems to plague and threaten his entire existence,
this person whose continual presence robs him of all
his peace and spontaneity. His wish that the world be
rid of him "who swung Sita" is granted. Symbolically,
and in this story, actually, the protagonist Shridaman
in his self-murder succeeds in killing the introjected
father, the physical representative of life. Kali,
the goddess herself, proves the timeless nature of the
Oedipal wound by sanctioning the deep-rooted disaffec-
tion in the soul of Shridaman, whose self-sacrifice
was carried out first to remove the threatening father
figure, but finally to appease and possess the eternal
mother. But the results of his act also prove that
there can be no true and permanent victory in a triangular love affair that is based on equal amounts of
hate and love. Every triumph over the despised rival
demands atonement through the mechanism of guilt, and,
therefore, once the heads are restored by mistake to
each rival's torso, nothing really changes; there is
no subsequent conquest of the eternal ambivalence.
Shridaman's suicide as a symbolic attempt to start life
afresh, unburdened by the weight of Oedipal transgressions, results in failure. For the act of self-murder
only serves to compound the deep-seated sense of guilt.

The transposing of the heads onto different bodies
brings this tale even more conclusively into an incestuous relationship with its consequent transposition
of nuptial partners than it does a rebirth in innocence.
And the double suicide resembles more an act of dismembering the father, inasmuch as Shridaman carries

off, for the moment at least, in the exchange which
follows, the body of the father figure with its inherent strength and pleasures: the mind wins out over
life, for the body turns into a tame appendage of the
head. But, ironically, the body of each reverts back
in the following years to the same shape it had before;
Nanda's head converts his new weak frame into an athlet-
ic and powerful torso, while his former muscular body
becomes a flabby imitation under the influence of
Shridaman's intellect.

In the original Hindu legend Sita becomes the
property of Nanda, for according to the holy man and
judge, Kamadamana, one reaches the right hand to the
bride in marriage and the hand belongs to the body.[17]
But in Mann's solution the head is the highest limb,
and thus it is Shridaman who emerges victorious. Nevertheless, no satisfactory relationship ever prevails in
the mental scheme of the Mannian hero. Like Faust
after his pact with the Devil, Shridaman has the best
of both worlds; but also like Faust, his own nature
compells him to subvert every measure of happiness.
The pervasive doubt of the self assumes dominance, and
the age-old inhibitions become manifest as Shridaman's
new-found life turns out to be only another Pyrrhic
victory. The following words indicate how every triumph
of the Mannian hero carries within itself its own defeat:

> Shridaman, son of Bhavabhuti, had by
> mistake been given a beautiful, sturdy
> body to accompany his noble head, where
> love of the beautiful reigned. And his
> intelligent mind straightway found something
> sad in the fact that the strange had now
> become his and was no longer an object of
> admiration--in other words that he was
> now himself that after which he had yearned.
> This sadness unfortunately persisted through-
> out the changes which his head suffered in
> combination with the new body; for these
> changes were such as go on in a head that
> through possession of the beautiful more
> or less loses the love of it and therewith
> its own spiritual beauty.
> The question remains open whether this
> process would not have taken place anyhow,
> without the bodily change, simply because
> Shridaman now possessed the lovely Sita.
> (VIII, 793-794)

Yearning is still the ultimate goal of the artist figure, and no tangible, earthy satisfaction can satisfy the hunger to calm the spirit. As in the early novella The Wardrobe, where the flow of artistic inspiration was cut off whenever the hero Albrecht van der Qualen insisted on embracing his beautiful visitor, there remains for Shridaman, a degree of permanence only in the unreal dependence on fantasy. Dreams and visions that suspend reality provide the only food by which the artistic spirit is nourished. The concrete substance of actual possession with all its daily, crabbed demands must prick the bubble of illusion for the guilt-ridden artist.

The renewed marriage between Shridaman and Sita is of short duration, lasting only four years after the birth of their son, Samadhi, who is the epitome of beauty and perfection. Having served its purpose, this union becomes boring for Sita who leaves her husband of questionable virility to seek out Nanda, the only one who is able to gratify her physical needs. When Shridaman in his subdued jealousy follows, there can be only one way out of the dilemma. His final solution, a suicide on a funeral pyre built for three, finds an echo that reverberates throughout the whole scheme of Thomas Mann's works: the end of an age as mirrored by the decline of a family. The Buddenbrooks' misfortunes sum up Mann's attitude as does the following statement of Detlev Spinell in Tristan: ". . . it not infrequently happens that a family with sober, practical bourgeois traditions will towards the end of its days flare up in some form of art" (VIII, 234). In reviewing the totality of Mann's works as a study of artistic production and in keeping with the symbolism of this tale, we witness Shridaman's attempts to come to terms with life and also with his pressing need to kindle the creative spark. The latter result takes form in his progeny Samadhi, who in his attractiveness and aesthetic interest can stand for the finished work of art--the product of sensitive intellect and life. Samadhi, a symbol of artistic perfection, lives on as a record of his family which has died out because of internal disintegration, just as the novel Buddenbrooks survived the family conflict to become the chronicle of a scattered Hansa family.

Behind the trappings of Hindu religion and the self-sacrifice couched in the inscrutable language of the mysterious East, the Mannian hero is revealed in his most morbid state. His gruesome act on the altar

301

of stagnant blood and gore identifies this work as a
chilling expression of a morbid psyche. Mann, to be
sure, attempts on several occasions to brighten the
noxious mood somewhat when he, for example, lets the
Goddess Kali scold Sita and commiserate at the sight
of the headless victims, in the manner of an irate
fishwife, but one has to admit that the author has
failed miserably in relieving the perverse and pathological feel of this tale. One is forced to shake his
head in bewilderment as to where the point of Mann's
"metaphysical joke" is to be found or how and by what
stretch of the imagination Karl Kerényi, who calls
this story "The Golden Parody," is able to discover
something golden or even slightly burlesque in this
work.

The Tables of the Law

        Thomas Mann's journey into the dawn of history
did not come to an end with the completion of Joseph
the Provider in 1943. The very day following his
champagne celebration of the final lines of the tetralogy, he began preparations for The Tables of the Law,
a novella about Moses as the liberator of the Hebrews
from Egypt, the founder of Israel's theocracy, and its
first lawgiver. Although originally requested only
to write a preface to The Ten Commandments, a work in
which ten internationally famous authors were to share
in writing, Mann volunteered to make a greater contribution by writing a new story about the first command-
ment.* The initial purpose of a war-time anthology of
this nature was to combat the perverted values of Fascism by asserting the vital presence of human ideals
and by upholding the concepts of traditional morality.
Mann explains his decision to contribute as follows:
"I had long been asking myself why I should contribute
only an essayistic foreword to the book of stories by
distinguished writers--why not an 'organ prelude,' as
Werfel later put it? Why not a tale of the issuance
of the Commandments, a Sinai novella? That seemed very
natural to me as a postlude to the Joseph story; I was
still warm from the epic. Notes and preparations for

----

        *In the English anthology Mann's story is entitled
Thou Shalt Have No Other Gods Before Me.

this work required only a few days."[18]

What now transpires in Mann's presentation of the Moses legend, however, is less a study in morality than the re-creation of the familiar career of the God-like artist who, despite the adversity of popular distrust and misunderstanding, successfully triumphs over his handicaps to give guidance and dispense charity to the multitude. Moses is another Joseph the Provider or Goethe in Weimar, only not as easy-going, sympathetic, or passive. Rather than let himself be buffeted by the winds of fortune, Moses self-consciously and relentlessly drives himself like a demonic figure who, humorless and choleric, has supreme confidence in his mission to mold and elevate his people. Moses, the Mannian artist, combines again in typical fashion the dichotomies of purity and sin, violence and philanthropy in his own person, displaying first of all the attributes of a marked man:

> His birth was irregular. Therefore he passionately loved order, the violable, the bidden and the forbidden.
> Early he killed in a frenzy; he thus knew better than the inexperienced that, although killing is delectable, having killed is detestable, and that thou shalt not kill.
> He was sensual, therefore he longed for the spiritual, the pure and the holy-- the invisible--for this alone seemed to him spiritual, holy and pure.[19]

Similar to so many of Mann's heroes, Moses, his nose flattened in a death struggle with an Egyptian overseer, bears the outward disfiguring sign of a murderer wherever he goes. His lewd and aristocratic mother lusts after a Hebrew slave, seducing him into becoming the protagonist's father.* This union between the hero's parents again lacks the ingredient of real love (the usual case in Mann's works), and Moses' father is immediately killed on order of the royal mother as soon

---

*Moses is later sent away to a private school where his misery as a misfit echoes Hanno Buddenbrook's unhappy life as a schoolboy.

303

as she, an Egyptian princess, satisfies her sexual
hunger. The author's version of Moses' ensuing birth
is at variance with the Biblical source which has Moses
the son of exclusively Hebrew parents, Amram and Joch-
ebed. But Mann, seemingly as he must, again presents
the two opposing strains that unite in the hero.

Here, as in Joseph in Egypt, the exotic mother
world is linked to the powers of darkness and political
oppression, while the father-people, the Hebrews, work
as slaves under the tyrannical lash of the Egyptians.
Moses never loses his taste for exotic women; his wife
Zepporah is not from the Midianite tribe, nor is, of
course, the Ethiopian girl he takes to his bed. And
even the musical mother appears in this tale: Miriam,
who, according to Otto Rank, is a mother-substitute in
the Biblical verson, is noted for her musical inclinations and later contributes to dissolution by leading
the licentious orgy around the golden calf.[20]

As Moses grows beyond receiving comfort and protection from his mother, he begins to take refuge in
the invisible God Jahwe with whom he ultimately identifies. Viewed in terms of the past, in Joseph and
before, Jahwe represents for Moses the spirit of darkness, the unseen and magic God as opposed to the visible
deities of the father or the Lichtmensch. To the unthinking and plodding Hebrews, Jahwe is simply another
deity to whom they thoughtlessly make their sacrifices
just as they do to their visible gods; while for Moses,
Jahwe the invisible is the sole object of all devotion.
Moses' purpose, then, is to impose the concept of Jahwe
on his father's people, and to this end he works tirelessly, an outcast of a higher calling pursuing an
entirely unnatural and dedicated life. Jahwe thus resembles more a patron saint of the artist figure or,
as Hans M. Wolff interprets the relationship, this
deity is identical with Moses himself.[21] In these
terms, Mann is therefore asserting the same concept in
The Tables of the Law as he did in Joseph and previous
tales: the mother-darkness, the medium of the artist,
signifies and honors the inexpressive and mute banality
of das Leben, the father-concept, paradoxically enlightening life by the means of darkness, just as Potiphar was "enlightened" by his transformation into the
sexless shadow of a man.*

---

*Among the rules Moses imposes on his father's

The father's people come forth as a miserable lot and Moses' goal of molding them into a higher state appears to the very end to be a well-nigh impossible task. But the Mannian artist thrives on superhuman challenges. When Mann describes Moses' legislative efforts as a kind of Michelangelo-like creativity in carving out the divinely inspired, legal tablets in stone, he means literally to apply this image to The Tables of the Law, with the Hebrews representing the basic carved out, raw material.[22] The people of the father as an uncut block of stone, out of which the artist with his divine inspiration must fashion humaneness, morality and beauty, becomes the most consistent leitmotif in the story.* Coupled, however, with the repeated references to the sculptor shaping his material are the scenes of the people displaying themselves in the worst possible light. In pronounced contrast to their unflinching and self-assured leader, they are revealed as the whimpering, spoiled and formless dregs of humanity. Their prolonged grumbling and wailing, self-compassion, and childish embrace of the commonplace--as demonstrated by the "Great Words" they employ to describe the drowning of the pursuing Egyptians-- all serve to heighten the difference between them and the stoically suffering and inwardly-turned artist figure. Moses, by no means a Rhetor-Bourgeois, is never given to long speeches or useless talk. To reach his goals, Moses resorts rather to practical trickery and fraud. And just as Joseph acted out his adventures in accord with the knowledge of a pre-ordained divine plan, so too does Moses as Jahwe, a deity

---

people are restrictions against love and lust, and when during his absence they slide back into an abandoned state of shamelessness with dancing, and, of course, music, the protagonist punishes them with a vengeance. Mann has finally allowed his hero to win the battle on the dance floor, transforming him from an intended victim of the swirling crowd to the grim judge and jury of the same.

*Michelangelo is further alluded to in the hero's battered face; the Italian sculptor's nose was also broken during a fight in his youth. See Thomas Mann, Das Gesetz, ed. Käte Hamburger (Frankfort on the Main: Ullstein, 1964), p. 101.

in control of his own destiny, fall back, as one critic notes, on pragmatic legerdemain and deception in order to carry out his task: "Unusual events recounted in Scripture are easily passed off as tricks or as coincidence. There is the trick of the magic rod, there are the coincidences of the plagues. It appears that the Israelites leave Egypt and cross the desert by virtue of an unbroken series of propitious coincidences of winds and waters and an edible fungus called manna."[23]

But in spite of all the efforts, anxieties and dedication, there is no love lost between the protagonist and the crude embodiments of life which are his father's people. Moses must keep perpetual vigilance over his flock, even being forced to play the role of a sanitary engineer, for the Hebrews in Mann's view are clods, more like animals than human beings, unaware even of basic rules of cleanliness. They in their obtuseness are not only likened to cows ruminating on the meadow, but are on one occasion actually described as filth. A monumental, even heroic undertaking confronts the artist hero in his aim to bring this ignorant pack onto a higher level of humanity, and Moses' struggles against their stupidity literally cost him blood--the pigment used to paint his stone tablets of laws. Again, only through suffering can the Mannian hero live the role of the creative artist.

As a work whose ultimate purpose was a polemic against National Socialism, The Tables of the Law possesses a curious if not bizarre touch. Of all the contributions to the anthology The Ten Commandments, Mann's is the only one which has no direct bearing on Nazi tyranny. Only his is displaced in time, from the contemporary scene to ancient Canaan, and only his can be said to lack direct polemical reference to the Third Reich. It is a paraphrase of the Biblical book of Exodus, containing the accomplishments on Mount Sinai with their immense judicial significance for the development of humanity, but it does not really represent an attempt to contrast the Mosaic Law to the inhuman violations of the twentieth century. If anything, it gives the reader the exact opposite impression from the other selections of the anthology which depict the brutality of the National Socialists, for Moses, as the inventor and upholder of the law, resorts exclusively and successfully to totalitarian methods to gain his ends. And, therefore, as Mann renders this hero to modern view, the tale of ancient Hebrew legislation becomes just as readily a vindication of the

Führerprinzip as it does an attack on the Nazi dictator-ship.

Although the author's story remains essentially faithful to the overt Biblical account of the Israelite Exodus, it is amazing how closely the career, problems and behavior of Mann's Moses resemble those of the Füh-rer of Nazi Germany. Like Hitler, Moses is a fanatic who leads an irregular and suspect life, a man who pos-sesses an overwhelming belief in his own destiny, a mass psychologist who does not fall short of the dia-bolical on his way to triumph, and a visionary with an astonishing tenacity of will who remains undaunted in the face of every setback. Even Hitler's attempt at self-deification is paralleled by Moses' relationship with his personal god Jahwe. Wolff's thesis that the personalities of Moses and Jahwe are indistinguishable receives convincing corroboration from Käte Hamburger who shows that the Bible itself, as interpreted by a number of famous men of letters, leads to this very same conclusion; and Jahwe, therefore, in terms of this narrative, simply becomes a fantastic device by which the hero can successfully insure that his people will heed his commands.[24] Moses is revealed as a divine Provider, Messiah and Savior of his people, similar in his position to Hitler, who laid claims on the German people as their redeemer and spiritual leader. Like a successful dictator, Moses is endowed with an intuitive perception of the will and the needs of his people, who, the author stresses, have no ability to decide for them-selves what is good for them. They bring with them from Egypt a slave mentality which their Führer tyran-nically exploits in order to obtain great sacrifices from them. Authoritarian, cynically contemptuous of the mob, and by no means squeamish, Moses emerges, therefore, from the pages of this work as a spiteful Prometheus and an inveterate confidence man. In his use of deception as a means to an end we are reminded of the dictatorial magician, Cipolla, who ruthlessly and remorselessly manipulated his fellow citizens. Given to outbursts of fury, Moses also cajols, woos and threatens the crowd with clenched fists and sudden anger that characterize his intense and fanatic pent-up nature. While Moses is somewhat above the phrase-mongering of Hitler, he still remains a raging and despotic phenom-enon to his people. Both men are also leaders of a "chosen people," for the traditional Hebrew concept of God's favored children ironically and paradoxically co-incides with the Nazi ideology of racial superiority.

But the closest Mann comes to identifying Moses
with Hitler is during the battle of Kadesh. Here the
Israelites conquer and drive out the inhabitants of
this place--in the language of the nineteen-thirties:
Germany's irredentist claims on land which once belonged
to them. As long as Moses keeps his arms raised as he
surveys the fighting in the valley below, his people
gain the upper hand; the reverse is true when he, in
his fatigue, must lower them. The forces of Jahwe become victorious only when Moses' helpers come and support his upraised limbs, a parody, certainly, on the
Nazi salute. But Mann's playful treatment of this
scene, illustrating as it does a victory for the Führerprinzip, by no means cancels out the kinship between
Hitler and the artist hero.

Finally, in this implacable moralist who attempts
to purify as well as transform the apolitical, apathetic
and shapeless mass, we find a man with a double standard
of morality. For Moses the end always justifies the
means employed. Concrete force and trickery are the
true measure of the hero's success while justice becomes merely a device for consolidating the organization-
al gains he has made. To achieve his objectives, Moses
dispenses with open discussion, in modern terms, with
parliamentary procedures, and very early becomes dis-
enchanted with conciliation as an effective instrument.
When his people slide back into their old, free, and
licentious ways and worship the golden calf, Moses calls
on the militant Joshua to settle accounts with these
renegades. The chilling phrase, "After the executions
were carried out," comes as a real shock to the reader
who expects to find a pervasive spirit of humanity and
charity in this tale.* Joshua is one of the more significant figures in the story, the hero's right arm and
avenging angel who backs up his leader by force after
the latter's words fail to persuade. Training a band
of young toughs, Joshua with his unquestioned loyalty
employs strong-arm methods to help his Führer carry out
his policies. It is he who is responsible for the
tenth plague to visit Egypt, a calamity which turns out

---

*Hatfield calls Moses the spokesman for Thomas
Mann himself and the Hebrews (who dance about the golden
calf) a symbol of the deluded Germans under Hitler. See
p. 121; see also Das Gesetz, ed. Hamburger, p. 106.

to be a vicious bloodbath in which all the firstborn of the Egyptians are killed. He and his young follow-ers enthusiastically greet Moses' (or Jahwe's) decision to break off negotiations with the Pharaoh and commit a "wicked vesper" in order to gain permission to leave Egypt.

> One has to note the difference between
> Jahwe and his destroying angel. It was
> not Jahwe himself who went about, but his
> destroying angel, or more properly, a
> whole band of such, carefully chosen.
> And if one wishes to search among the many
> for one single apparition there is much to
> point to a certain straight, youthful
> figure with a curly head, a prominent Adam's
> apple, and a determined, wrinkled brow.
> He becomes the traditional type of the
> destroying angel, who at all times is glad
> when unprofitable negotiations are ended
> and deeds begin. (VIII, 827-828)

By describing his characters in such a manner, Mann divests the narrative of divine guidance or revelation, passing the action off as psychological needs or inner voices. Jahwe becomes for Moses and his black band a rationalization for authority to carry out the actions and deeds he was in any case inwardly compelled to do. And by emphasizing the leadership principle Mann dis-places what was unique in early Judaism, "monotheism" with invisible presence and inner communications. This is precisely the point one critic, W. G. Kümmel, makes in his article "Das Mosesbuch Thomas Manns und die Bibel":

> . . . according to Thomas Mann the God
> which Moses invokes is not discernible
> from Moses' own inner self, and the pleasure
> which Moses takes in the people is that
> "of not being indistinguishable from God's
> at all, but actually one and the same with
> it." With that, however, the basic fact
> of the religion of the Old Testament, that
> God in grace and mystery confronts his
> people of His own choice, is abolished for
> the sake of a religion of passion which no
> longer knows the difference between God
> and the world, between God and the people.[25]

The final implication is that Moses is using the people
totally to satisfy his own needs. As Friedrich Schiller,
Mann's protagonist in A Weary Hour, punished himself
by creating, so it is again with Moses who cries out
"What need have I of this?" At the same time he knows
that no other path to life would even be possible. He
needs this mass of slaves as an outlet for his hostilities and compulsions; as a result, he measures his
success only in the degree to which his anxieties,
hates, and ambitions become those of the people. But
one need not look only at the dramatic moments for confirmation, for the means with which Moses brutally goes
at his work can be verified on every page of the story.
From the moment he murders the Egyptian, acting out in
fact the guilt he previously felt, he hesitates at no
crime and flinches at no inhuman punishments to bring
the totality of his people around to his own way of
thinking--actions of cruelty based on deceptions which
only lead the reader to question repeatedly Mann's
characterization of this supposedly great human hero.

In his preface to The Ten Commandments the German
political analyst, Hermann Rauschning, explains Hitler's
war against the Moral Code as a murderous assault on
every form of higher human culture: "It concerns all
of us, Christians, Jews, and freethinking humanists
alike. It deals with the deliberately planned battle
against the dignified, immortal foundation of human
society; the message from Mount Sinai. Let us name
it clearly and simply: Hitler's Battle Against the
Ten Commandments."[26]

The purpose of this book, as expressed by Rauschning and by the editor's foreword,--"to help open the
eyes of those who still do not recognize what Nazism
really is"--can scarcely be advanced by Thomas Mann's
Moses-contribution. The Tables of the Law serves as
perhaps the worst possible example about which to
polarize an anti-Nazi viewpoint. There is nothing of
the Judeo-Christian doctrine of love and charity in
the way Moses sets about his task of enlightening his
fellow Hebrews. His attitudes and behavior smack more
of a Nazi conceived philosophy than they do of the
ideas which Hitler strove so flagrantly to destroy.

The Biblical tale of Moses, if anything, offered
Thomas Mann the opportunity to give full expression to
his ambivalent attitude towards the political events
of the day. Among the "chosen people" of the Nile

delta he finds the Germans of the twentieth century, beguiled and blindly following a fanatic, cunning leader; and in the person of Moses, Thomas Mann sees his Bohemian, opportunistic artist figure in the guise of a dictator, a magnetic personality that cows the rabble. Ever ready to embrace passionately what he seemingly hates, Thomas Mann finds in Moses a wrathful, relentless and sadistic god-like figure. Like a number of highly respected and intellectual Germans who were in some measure deluded by National Socialism (men such as Gerhart Hauptmann, Gottfried Benn, Rudolf Binding, Martin Heidegger and Ernst Jünger), the author of the anti-Hitler polemic (?), The Tables of the Law, was unable to divest himself completely of the thralldom which the demonic magician and high priest of the Nazis exerted on him. Mann's efforts to sublimate his profound conflicts were not always possible. And so it should not come as a complete surprise that the fabulously successful dictator whose power to hypnotize the masses has perhaps never been equaled also wove a spell on a man who struggled all his life against contradictory obsessional forces raging within him. As long as Mann could personally conceive of Hitler, the single-minded, dreamy artistic misfit, as a kindred soul of his own literary projections, it was only a short step to viewing him as the magician who prevails over the forces of the authoritarian father to become the sole possessor of maternal Germany.

Myths, Past and Present

In setting out on "his journey into the dawn of mankind in order to explore and humanize the myth," Mann creates the impression that he is embarking on a new adventure whose finding will probably effect the most embracing concepts of human understanding; but in reviewing the extent of Mann's arduous travels from the beginnings of Joseph to the trials of Moses, we are forced to recall Kant's definition of understanding as "the realization of something only to the degree it is sufficient for our needs or purpose." Beyond the works in question, Mann claimed to establish an ultimate goal for his endeavors--"to humanize the myth,"--a claim which in itself is in need of examination, for it serves as the conceptual mover for the bulk of his production during the Joseph period. In examining this intention in the larger context of Mann's total production, we are led to ask if some qualitative change or shift in direction has taken place, or if, in reality, merely the old forms, values and emotions have been rebottled with new labels. This question is obviously a rhetor-

311

ical one, considering that we already have the endless
number of similarities between the Joseph series and
earlier works; but the evidence notwithstanding, the
question still requires some clarification. Certainly,
Mann did not write the Joseph tetralogy, nor do we
read it, to study the facts of religious history, for
they can easily be found (and more accurately) elsewhere. What does interest us here, however, is the
question of how these facts are altered to fit the
principles of symbolic creation in the author's own
heart and soul.

Adhering to patterns and associations of observations already enumerated in the study, we submit that
the author's commentaries as well as the works themselves originate in the framework of infantile fantasy.
What Thomas Mann has called "demythologizing," we
have chosen to point out as the author's constant need
to uncover and expose the personal weakness and falli-
bilities of the representatives of the father world.
Over a period of forty years and thousands of pages of
literature, we have in fact followed the author in his
attempts to destroy the "hallowed myth" of the father!
Therefore, the concept of humanizing becomes now another
weapon of retaliation against the father: "humanizing"
reduces him in status and stature in Mann's context
and exposes him to ridicule and scorn by pointing up
his weaknesses.

Thomas Mann's time-consuming investigations and
amazing assimilation of remote ages lead less to a re-
interpretation of an historical period than to a medium
by which he can again express his pre-eminent fascination with the interplay of love and hate. His scientific exactitude in researching his subject matter often
gives way to a glib and arbitrarily facile manipulation
of the material: it is not the sources themselves
which sway him but the purposes to which he can put
them to use. History, the ancient and near past, serves
Mann's artistic ends by enabling him to construct the
frame on which to hang his creative genius. And the
more pressing and painful the chaotic present, the
greater the necessity for a detached artistic haven.

The Hitler period in Thomas Mann's creative scheme
(the production period of The Beloved Returns, The Transposed Heads,The Tables of the Law, and Doctor Faustus)
is characterized in general by two opposing tendencies:
a tremendous output of polemical energy to combat Fascism publicly and provocatively, and an alternative

displacement of the present in his fictional works to
find a sanctuary from the highly charged political scene.
Mann, we feel, becomes more involved in World War II
than he did in the First World War out of which sprang
the dubious abstractions he formulated so cooly and yet
enthusiastically in the <u>Observations of a Non-Political
Man</u>. But in gauging the author's real state of mind,
one must carefully examine his serious productions in
the realm of <u>literature</u>, where, in contrast to his
rhetorical attacks against the Nazis via radio broad-
casts, he remains as addicted as ever to the opiate of
hatred and violence. The truly striking fact about
Mann's fictional works of the Nazi period is that he
does not leap artistically into the fray as he did in
World War I with his <u>Observations</u>, an aesthetically
oriented work. Having painfully learned his lesson from
the <u>Observations</u>, he does not now attempt to combine
art and politics into one major production. Instead he
divorces himself artistically from the upheavals of
this time, ambivalently taking two positions as he
simultaneously becomes a political publicist and a
creative producer of allegorical fiction. Whereas the
<u>Observations</u> represented a true expression of his artis-
tic passion during World War I, he writes for two audi-
ences during the Second World War: for himself and for
the West. From a letter of the author we obtain indirect confirmation that the attitude expressed in his
fictional works is the most intrinsic and meaningful to
him:

> For about a decade my essayistic and cultural
> critical attitude had been emphatically
> rationalistic and idealistic, but actually
> I have come to take this attitude only
> under the pressure of an irrationalism
> that is contemptuous of every balanced
> humanitarianism and of a political anti-
> rationalism that has gained ground in Europe
> and especially in Germany. Do you know
> Antigone? This young girl originally wor-
> shipped both types of the deity in the
> same way: the underworld and the lucid;
> but because of the shallow overestimation
> of the upper powers on the part of her op-
> ponent Creon, she comes to overemphasize
> the powers of Hades. In my own case the
> opposite and yet related thing holds true.
> It is characteristic that the rational-
> idealistically humanitarian is almost only

> expressed in my critical essayistic, and
> polemical writings, but hardly in my poetic
> works where my original nature, which seeks
> a balance in the humane sphere, finds more
> clearly by far its true expression.[27]

Here in The Tables of the Law one would expect
Thomas Mann to eschew the promulgation of force or, at
least, to avoid endowing the great Biblical lawgiver,
for example, with passionate, uncontrollable or even
fanatic impulses; for as the literary lion of the hour,
Mann had every reason to be unequivocally committed to
the triumph of democratic institutions. But the habits
of a lifetime must of necessity prevail against even
the dramatic tendencies of the moment; and where necessity forces a new imposition of attitudes, they must
perforce remain like a thin veil that only obscures but
does not change the contents of one's vast store of
values and emotions. The recurring refrain of friendliness to life in The Beloved Returns and in the Goethe-
essays, for example, is blatantly contradicted by
Goethe's cold and controlled hostility against the
German burghers. As a benevolent despot, the artist
hero, marked by an incapacity for object love, can find
no real frame of reference for genuine affection for
the father-people. Rapport between them and the hero
is practically non-existent, manifesting itself only
in the feudal relationship based on the fixed distance
of a fief to the lordly and all-powerful protagonist.
Thomas Mann's attitude towards "plain people," now his
allies in the life and death struggle against National
Socialism, never undergoes any fundamental transformation. The charity and concern his heroes shower on
those beneath cannot be claimed as the issue of a sincere and eloquent love of humanity but rather as the
triumphant expression of cold superiority. Moses'
accomplishments in the field of legal justice are not
motivated by a feeling of shared struggle based on
mutual understanding and cooperation with his people.
No sense of comradeship, spirit of altruistic philanthropy, or even responsible human tolerance are to be
found in his actions. One even begins to wonder why
he feels the need to exert himself at all in their be-
half--unless, ultimately, he leads them for the sake
of personal needs and self-aggrandizement. Though
extreme and justifiable pride in accomplishment desig-
nate the titanic efforts of this artist, the satisfaction he gains is actually rooted more in hostility
against the embodiment of life than it is in his de-

sire to spread moral edification. In a mood of great
irritability and arrogance Moses brings about the
betterment of his society, but only after he has caused
his people a great measure of suffering and forced his
tyrannical will upon them. The Mannian hero's friendship for life again resembles a game which he is determined to win at all costs, one which he cannot lose for
the simple reason that he may play it according to
subjectively inspired rules which change on the spur
of the moment, and which, in the face of all verity and
logic, carry the hero irresistibly to the goal he has
staked out for himself.

CAVE MUSICAM

Of all the works we have examined thus far, none surpass Doctor Faustus in pathological conception, in frigidity of presentation, or in stoicism of execution. Mann's earliest works certainly placed heavy stress on morbidity, and often waded knee-deep in gloom; but compared to the sang-froid and stark nihilism that find expression in this narrative, they can be studied as sketches of humane sympathy and compassion. Nowhere else among Mann's creations do we encounter such a paean to self-immolation or such a veritable Lethe of suffering as we do in this highly autobiographical novel, Dr. Faustus.

A preliminary and natural question for the casual reader might well be how this work relates to Goethe's Faust, for any modern work carrying a reference to Faust in its title must perforce stand somewhere in the shadow of Goethe's monumental work. But the answer (if one does exist) to such a question would have to be based on contrast, reversal, or inversion rather than on any assumed similarity. True, the fascinating nucleus of both works revolves around a pact with the devil, but what for Goethe's Faust was an agreement to end his separation from the world of immediate experiences and to submit himself to the intense pleasures and pain of life and love, is for Adrian Leverkühn, the hero of Doctor Faustus, a very opposite, calculated, self-imposed withdrawal from human warmth, a voluntary renunciation of love, and a willful, self-incarceration in an isolated, unhuman world of abstract forms. And although elements from the lives of a good number of well-known artists and thinkers have been incorporated into the welding together of the character of Leverkühn, Goethe makes no conspicuous contribution.

The Anatomy of Nihilism

This is a novel of the life of a musician and composer, but of equal significance to music per se is the strange and uncanny way the hero relates to the world and people around him. From early childhood estrangement of life to the last days of grotesque existence, Leverkühn lives alone in a philosophy based on psychological necessity, personal pride, and artistic stimulation. The total result, however, suggests the life of the philosopher, Friedrich Nietzsche, rather

than any other artist. Many critics have made note
of the parallels in the lives of these two figures who
both lived unmarried and apart from their fellow men,
who were interested in music, and for a time in theology, who at the age of fifty-five reached the end of
their lives on the twenty-fifth of August after approximately ten years of mental illness in the care of
their mothers. Both lived at an early age in a town
on the Saale river and both suffered from migraine.
More specifically, Adrian Leverkühn's marriage proposal
through an intermediary recapitulates Nietzsche's asking for the hand of Lou Salomé through his friend Paul
Ree, and his behavior in visiting a house of prostitu-
tion corresponds exactly to Nietzsche's in a similar
situation, where he rushes over to a nearby piano and
strikes a chord. The cause of Leverkühn's insanity is
syphilis, and Nietzsche too is supposed to have collapsed from paresis.

Mann never makes any effort to conceal the borrow-
ing from Nietzsche's life. But as intrusive as these
Nietzschean biographical features may appear, they are
of only superficial significance for the novel as a
whole, representing more a tedious and elaborate smokescreen on the part of the author than an attempt to
make Doctor Faustus a novel about Nietzsche. For
Mann's poetic embroidery does not stop with Nietzsche;
there are also parallels to the lives of Mahler,
Tschaikovsky, Hugo Wolf, and Beethoven. Arnold Schön-
berg, believing himself impersonated by Adrian Leverkühn, even became involved in a bitter controversy with
Thomas Mann. But Mann reveals much of himself in Doctor
Faustus; in Erich Kahler's words, "this book is in part
more openly autobiographical than any other this author
who had already scooped in abundance material from his
one life."[1] That Kaisersaschern, Leverkühn's boyhood
home on the Saale, is to be identified with Mann's
own birthplace, Lübeck, is convincingly demonstrated as
follows by Bengt Sorensen: "Not to be overlooked is
the similarity of birth places, the identity of Kaisersaschern and Lübeck, which goes so far that Mann literally takes the description of Kaisersaschern from
Doctor Faustus for Lübeck over into his lecture 'Germany
and the Germans,' and he does so even without calling
attention to the fact."[2] From Wolff, among others, we
learn that Adrian Leverkühn's stay in Italy corresponds
precisely with Mann's own sojourn there: the same local-
ity, the same address, Via Torre Argentina, as well as
the hero's same indifference to the Italians.[3]

The autobiographical reaches extensive proportions during the hero's life in Munich. A comparison
of the text with Mann's own A Sketch of My Life and
his brother's (Viktor Mann's) autobiography, There Were
Five of Us, reveals another close affinity between
fiction and fact. In Munich Adrian Leverkühn becomes
a lodger with Frau Rodde, who, like Mann's own mother,
was once wealthy and a widow of a Senator from North
Germany. Frau Rodde soon assumes familiar prominence
in her resemblance to the "mothers" of the earliest
works: she is morally lax and suggestive in both behavior and dress, an excellent pianist and at the same
time a questionable gypsy type. When Adrian, who,
incidentally, like his creator enjoys cycling, moves
to his retreat at Pfeiffering--which according to
Hans M. Wolff, was Mann's own distance from the Munich
Bohemian and artistic world--Frau Rodde, curiously,
follows him and takes up quarters close by.[4] That the
town of Polling, where Mann's mother lived, is meant
by Pfeiffering, is also enhanced by the fact that it
is the place of the suicide of Frau Rodde's daughter
Clarissa. This incident, in its details, is practically
a verbatim account of the description in A Sketch of
My Life of the death of Carlotta Mann, the author's
younger sister, even to the way in which Leverkühn con-
soles the distraught Frau Rodde. Julia Elisabeth Mann,
Mann's other sister, also committed suicide, and therefore, comes in for consideration as the model for the
other daughter, Ines Rodde, for both figures, fictional
and live, were married and gave birth to three daughters
including a set of twins. Julia Elisabeth Mann's self-
inflicted death can also be equated with the homicidal
outburst which Ines Rodde surrenders to. And now, if
we superimpose Frau Schweigestill, Adrian's landlady
in Pfeiffering and another mother figure onto the hero's
actual mother, we find that the combined number of
children these two women bore, equal that of the Mann
family when the author was a child. Frau Schweigestill's
son, Gereon, with his agricultural training, was obviously modeled after Viktor Mann, who learned farming
in Polling from a certain Schweighart family.

Whereas Joseph had more than its share of "fathers,"
Doctor Faustus is a return to the "mothers"; for this
novel is provided with a number of mother figures, all
of whom illustrate the necessity of a continual recurrence of the eternally maternal for this Mannian protagonist who must completely immerse himself in the
sinful pool of music. One of the most obscure maternal
figures is the hero's patroness, Frau von Tolna, who

avidly follows and furthers his career. However, we
never see her face. All we know of her is that she
lives as an invalid and widow on the estate of her late
Hungarian husband and that she is exceedingly wealthy.
But it turns out that she is none other than the prostitute herself, Hetaera Esmeralda, as Victor A. Oswald
has convincingly demonstrated by ingeniously uncover-
ing the hidden references and etymologies relating to
her.[5] We are thus placed back into Adrian Leverkühn's
boyhood surroundings, the home of his father, for it
was Jonathan Leverkühn who first told his son about the
tropical butterfly Hetaera Esmeralda. This insect
which, significantly, "in transparent nakedness loved
the dusky gloom of the forest's shade,"[6] is actually .
no figment of the author's imagination, but it is
known to exist in Brazil, the birthplace of Thomas /
Mann's mother.[7] Reducing, therefore, Mann's filigree
of references and allusions to the essential, we find
the debased mother, similar to the lewd Consuelo Kröger
of Tonio Kröger, in the person of the syphilitic whore
Hetaera Esmeralda combined with the patrician, wealthy
and exotic maternal attraction, the mother-darkness,
in the Hungarian noble lady Frau von Tolna.

    The sinister servant who guides the hero to the
bordello is a reincarnation from Death in Venice; his
red cap, protruding lower jaw, garbled speech--broken
bits of bad English and French--and his diabolic manner
remind the reader of those apparitions whose presence
warned Gustav Aschenbach that inhibitionary release or
letting go would be lethal. But now inside the bordello
the hero seems to realize that a bond exists for him
between music and sinful adventure; he rushes over
and strikes a chord on a nearby piano while the prostitute Hetaera Esmeralda (as Adrian calls her) brushes
his cheek with her arm. Later Adrian feels compelled
to seek out this woman, to consummate his passion, even
though it means a long journey to the city of Pressburg.
Although this woman warns him of her diseased body, he
is not to be dissuaded and he voluntarily and with grim
determination infects himself with syphilis. Only after
this experience does Adrian turn creative in his music.
In fact, this carnal relationship even becomes the
dynamic factor in his art. Adrian's musical compositions deal with forbidden sexual motifs more than any
other single theme; wanton women play a prominent role
from the "Oh, Sweet Girl, How Bad You Are," (a song
which recapitulates the hero's own relationship with
the prostitute who infected him) to the loose Rosaline
of Love's Labor's Lost, the tales of the Gesta Romanorum

concerning immoral wives and incest, and the Whore of
Babylon in the _Apocalypsis cum figuris_. Significantly,
as is clear from these themes, it is not love in any
real and tender sense but its distortion, its emphasis
on failure and self-centered gratification which determines the artistic interest for the composer. Every
composition that flows from his pen alludes to Hetaera
Esmeralda through some arrangement of the notes B, E,
A, E, and E-flat.* Thus Adrian's relationship with
this debased maternal figure, this mother of darkness,
becomes the profound experience of the hero (one could
say the _only_ experience) and conditions every phase of
his life. Later in the narrative Adrian learns from
the Devil himself that his pact with the representative
of hell to gain perfection in his art had really been
concluded six years previously with the contraction of
venereal disease. Even so the Devil hands down as the
basic clause of the pact that Leverkühn must not love,
demonstrating again that tender love is not a deter-
mining factor in an affair with a woman or in the making of music.

Every allusion to music, then, is really a reference to sex. Adrian's first contact with music, it is
revealed, was through the milkmaid of his boyhood
home, Hanne, a bosomy creature who smelled of her animals and whose feet were always caked with dung. The
animal nature of music to the hero is shown even more
directly by his statement: "Music has so much warmth
anyhow, stable heat, bovine heat that it can stand
all sorts of laws to cool it off" (VI, 94). And the
human voice, Adrian adds, possesses more animal heat
than any other.

The lure of music is equal to the spontaneous
pull of the libido, as we see in the words of a student
friend of Adrian: "The demonic--we call that in German
the instincts or drives" (VI, 167). Adrian Leverkühn's
equation of music and the sexual act has its parallel
in Hanno's rapture at the piano and the ensuing onslaught of typhus. The consequences for both are
grievous, agonizing and ultimately fatal. But the

---

*H is the letter used in German to denote the
seventh tone of the C major scale, i.e., English B;
and ES stands for E-flat, thus giving us in German,
H, E, A, E, Es.

similarities and parallels between these two works, divided by almost a half century of time but practically by no change in content or conception, are too startling to pass over so quickly. If one of the theses of this whole study is to be that Mann does not develop perceptibly in depth of psyche or scope of content from his first works to his last, then perhaps a careful comparison of Hanno Buddenbrook and Adrian Leverkühn, their worlds, and those of other early works, are in order here without risk of digression.

Hanno and Adrian certainly carry a sleek and encompassing identity: both are decadent and suffer early in life from migraine; both are musicians and own a harmonium on which they make their first musical attempts; both obtain their first instruction from the cathedral organists of the city: Pfühl in Buddenbrooks and Wendell Kretschmar in Doctor Faustus, two men who like to expound on music and its history.[8] Mann's first epic work also presents a detailed description of social gatherings, a focus on the hero's disdain for his schoolteachers, decline through heredity, and sickness as preparation for art. Both heroes have a dark, exotic mother; and the nervous, unstable and semi-talented Christian Buddenbrook is recreated again, as Hirschbach shows, in the amiable, popular and entertaining Rüdiger Schildknapp.[9] There is also the same fusion of the sexual with music and doom by means of the fateful piano: Hanno's musical prelude to illness and death, Adrian's striking the keyboard when touched by the prostitute Hetaera Esmeralda, and at the end of the novel, his mental breakdown at the music instrument.

Leverkühn's regression to his childhood in Pfeiffering, the description of which is minutely identical with his original home, points up the early period of life in which he, like Hanno, participates without restraint in music only to be crippled by it for life. The presence of his mother at Pfeiffering reminds us all too directly of the maternal derivation of Hanno's talent, and the description of her dwelling and furnishings also refreshes our memory of the family novel. And the image of young Hanno Buddenbrook is also reawakened in the figure of Echo who precociously recites from literature while going to bed and who is mercilessly carried off by a horrible and ravaging disease.

In Adrian Leverkühn one sees the life of Hanno Buddenbrook carried with logical consistency to its very end. Had Hanno lived to become a full-fledged musician, he would have undoubtedly acted out his existence crippled by guilt in precisely the same manner as the hero of Doctor Faustus. The irresistible attraction which music has over both heroes can only be measured by its effect of horror on them; and the explanation for that lies, no less with Adrian than with Hanno, in the inner core of the instincts. Indeed, a review of the composer's life vanquishes all doubt as to the intimate link between the sexual and his art. Only the force of the basic drives would suffice to weave such a hypnotic spell of ecstasy and doom over the hero as well as elicit a compulsive desire for continual gratification. Thomas Mann's words in his Schopenhauer essay come to mind here: "Creativity is nothing else and in him [Schopenhauer] too it was nothing else than spiritualized sensuality and ingenious intellect derived from sex."[10]

We learn from The Story of a Novel (the author's account of his ordeals while writing Doctor Faustus) that Mann at the conception of Doctor Faustus was also thinking of some never realized plans for a novel from the Tonio Kröger period.[11] Close similarities exist between these two works. Jeanette Scheurl, the lady novelist friend of the protagonist, is reminiscent of Tonio's platonic relationship to Lisaweta Iwanowna. Adrian, like his forerunner, makes a program out of his inability to achieve genuine emotions; the diabolically imposed "thou must not love" as a basic condition for the composer's art takes us back in time and space to Tonio's "frigid art." And again it is not difficult to detect the same rationalization, in that the concept of warm and felt experiences as being banal and useless for art is first derived from an inner necessity and only afterward made to appear as the true criterion of art. Like Tonio, Adrian has no choice; the slightest giving way to his real feelings is capable of shattering him by setting free the lurking chaos within.

Without question we find in Adrian Leverkühn the culmination of all the self-sacrificing and morbid tendencies of previous works. His loneliness, isolation and utter coldness are so pronounced that they run like a leitmotif through the whole novel. "He is also the artist, a sort of Tonio Kröger in reverse who does not regret his isolation, but looks down with cold contempt on the bourgeois and the ordinary."[12] As a mature man he has no ties to his family and no close

companionship with anyone; his familiarity with Serenus
Zeitblom, his biographer, and Rudi Schwerdtfeger is of
a very dubious nature at best, and his friendship for
the theology students of the University of Halle is by
no means close, based, as it is, on abstract, unemotion-
al discussions. His refusal to say du to Rüdiger Schildknapp and Rudi Schwerdtfeger is pointed up in the course
of the novel, although he eventually makes an exception
in the case of Schwerdtfeger. Adrian is repeatedly
described as a man of disinclination, avoidance, reserve
and aloofness; a man for whom physical cordialities are
impossible and whose handshake, even, is infrequent and
hastily performed. One of the few times that he is
able to retain both a person's first and last names is
when he presumably falls in love with Marie Godeau.
His indifference is so great that he is hardly aware
of what goes on about him or of what company he is in.
It is not surprising, then, that he, whose heart is
dead and who cannot love, is not interested in the
world at all--and Marie Godeau is no exception. At best
Marie Godeau represents a faint spark of passion. Zeitblom finds Leverkühn's use of an intermediary to court
Marie Godeau forced, devious, and uncomplimentary, and
also suspects that Adrian had to some extent foreseen
what the probable outcome would be. In any event, it
would be the height of presumption on the part of the
syphilitic Adrian Leverkühn to be serious about contracting a marriage with her. The only place where
there is a flicker of warmth in the chilled life of the
hero occurs with the visit of his nephew Nepomuk
Schneidewein or Echo who was modeled after the author's
own grandson. But even here one cannot resist ascribing a narcissistic tone to Adrian's behavior, for the
fate of young Echo symbolically embodies the relentless destiny of his own once innocent self. Adrian
laments the lost state which his nephew's affliction
(the fatal link between disease and art) reflects as
a physical expression of early traumas. It is also
significant that the calamity which befalls the little
Nepomuk, a precocious child and destined, probably, to
become an artist, is spinal meningitis, a disease of
the meninges or pia mater which, according to the Devil
himself, is the focus of artistic syphilitic virulence.
Leverkühn feels remorse and a sense of having failed
this young soul-mate, his Echo, before madness sets in,
as he vicariously relives in him the symbolic atonement
which Echo's dream represents.

    To protect himself from the carnage which is feel-
ing itself, Leverkühn flees to the solitude of Pfeif-

fering, a place in spirit much like a monastery cell, a hermetically sealed atmosphere, a place where the ascetic tendencies of the hero reign supreme. The withdrawal to Pfeiffering is an infantile gesture, a regression (as has already been pointed out) to a specific realm of his own past. The symbolic attachment to his parental home and to his earliest, outlived childhood, especially since his ties to the members of his family are now virtually non-existent, elicits a perspicacious comment from Zeitblom: "Was that artificial 'return' simply a whim? I cannot think so. Instead it reminds me of a man of my acquaintance who, though outwardly robust and even bearded, was so highly strung that when he was ill--and he inclined to illnesses--he wished to be treated only by a child specialist" (VI, 40).

Like Albrecht van der Qualen, he hides from the world and his refuge is a kind of furtive concealment where he can indulge unmolested in his art. Over and over again he is described as living in a state of high tension in his retreat. But although the hero is now damned as a marked man, the final effects of first contact with Hetaera Esmeralda, he is essentially no different than before he contracted syphilis. As Bernhard Blume sees it, "The uncanny coldness which flows from the devil into Adrian, and which is mentioned again and again, is nothing but the coldness of Adrian's own nature. . . ."[13] Adrian is just as cold at the beginning as at the end. Signs that he was already a crippled soul were apparent very early, for only a guilt-ridden mind could have motivated such a desire for self-infection.

When he was very young, Adrian possessed the disposition to mockery; he was already reticent and aloof towards people--to Lucia Cimabue, the employee in his uncle's instrument warehouse, for example--and he displayed diffidence even to Zeitblom. His schoolmasters thought him arrogant. But it is with his inclination to laughter that a truly morbid part of his personality is revealed. (To Thomas Mann laughter was a dubious phenomenon for it meant spontaneous expression of himself.) In Adrian Leverkühn this element is strikingly valid. His laughter is hardly ever appropriate, neither in its intensity nor in given situations. He literally shakes with helpless laughter at the objective report about nature's tricks of survival among certain species of tropical butterflies. Later, his convulsive laughter about the old Roman legends of parricide and incest patently reveals his exultation in the pleasures of sadism originating in repressed, psychic conflict.

Adrian Leverkühn punishes himself with the deadly spirochete. And the question may well be asked at this point why he still finds it necessary to take up such austere protective measures as utter seclusion and withdrawal from real human contact; also why the Devil feels the need to insist that the hero must not love, inasmuch as he is incapable of this emotion anyway.[14] The answer is that although he has paid the total cost in advance by means of disease, he is still unable to wash away the corrosive acid of doubt which plagues him. Like Thomas Buddenbrook with his obsessional ceremonials, Adrian must pay continually for his transgressions. Chronic doubt demands chronic sacrifice. His conscience is like a racketeer who cannot stop extorting from his victim. Though disease ultimately represents the supreme penalty, the pressures of the instincts are not so easily appeased. Adrian must continue to reinforce the inner prohibition against the world of the senses in any form, for music suffices by itself to threaten his whole person and to overwhelm him with total ruin. Every impulse of spontaneity is stifled by his dread of the consequences and by his expectancy of disaster, no matter how remote they are from reality.

Of analogous interest to this bond between disease and the demonic and instinctual is Thomas Mann's account of Dostoevsky's attack of epilepsy, a disease so intimately connected to the Russian's genius; which in Mann's opinion "is definitely rooted in the realm of the sexual; it is a wild and explosive manifestation of sex dynamics, a transferred and transfigured sexual act, a mystic dissipation."[15] The author elaborates upon the symptoms of this disease to demonstrate the aftermath effect of prostration before life which music exerts on the hero of Doctor Faustus:

> Two symptoms, according to his [Dostoevsky's] description, are characteristic of the falling sickness: the incomparable sense of rapture, of inner enlightenment, of harmony, of highest ecstasy, preceding by a few moments the spasm that begins with an inarticulate, no longer human scream, and the state of horrible depression and deep grief, of spiritual ruin and desolation, that follows it. This reaction seems to him even more symbolic of

326

the nature of the disease than the exaltation that precedes the attack. Dostoevsky
describes it as a rapture so strong and
sweet "that one is ready to exchange ten
years of life or even life itself for the
bliss of these few seconds." The subsequent, terrific hangover, however, according to the confession of the great invalid,
was marked by a feeling of being a criminal,
by the weight of an unknown guilt, by the
burden of an awful crime.[16]

For Adrian Leverkühn disease is inseparably bound
up with his musical endeavors. Music, as the non plus
ultra of his deepest desires, would be unbearable unless neutralized. It is disease which counteracts this
ecstasy and, as the instrument of punishment, acts as
the safeguard of his vengeful conscience. Unable to
endure the anxiety which is part and parcel of his pursuit of music, Leverkühn deliberately forces the issue,
brings about the desired punishment by infecting himself with syphilis, and attempts by means of voluntary
suffering to buy off his pitilessly cruel conscience.
By such a maneuver he feels he preserves himself from
the dread of imagined retaliation, that is, from a
nameless dread of the Oedipal punishment threatening
to overwhelm him. By incurring syphilis with methodical
and relentless premeditation he strives to make resti-
tution to his conscience in advance. And in making a
virtue of necessity, illness becomes not only a means
of inner redemption through atonement for the hero's
crushing sense of guilt, it also becomes, rightly, the
cornerstone of new inspiration. The luetic malignity
in Leverkühn represents more than masochistic salvation, for the hero's imagination, freed to a certain
degree from the sense of immediate transgression, may
now grow vivid and reach new heights.

There Is Music in His Madness

In order to give some credence to the spirit of
mockery and parody in his musical creations or (in the
case of one of them, The Lamentation of Dr. Faustus) to
the mood of abject melancholy and sorrow, Adrian calls
on the realm of literature. There is hardly a work of
his which does not depend on the text of some poetic
masterpiece for assistance in demonstrating the particular distinguishing marks of his music. And it comes
as no surprise to learn that his musical compositions
are invariably permeated with a spirit of intense

327

negation or devaluation; The Marvels of the Universe, for example, is an orchestral work whose essence is mockery and leaves Adrian open to the reproach as one whose art is antithetical to the artistic mind, blasphemous and nihilistically sacrilegious. In the Apocalypsis cum figuris, which makes Zeitblom think of an open abyss into which one must hopelessly sink, the distinguishing marks of parody and mockery reach a crescendo. With misgiving Zeitblom hears the Apocalypsis cum figuris: "This Gehenna gaudium, sweeping through fifty bars, beginning with the chuckle of a single voice and rapidly gaining ground, embracing choir and orchestra, frightfully swelling in rhythmic upheavals and contrary motions to a fortissimo tutti, an overwhelming, sardonically yelling, screeching, bawling, bleating, howling, piping, whinnying salvo, the mocking, exulting laughter of Hell" (VI, 502). With the composer's last work, The Lamentation of Dr. Faustus, the revelling in pain and the wallowing in sorrow and despair attain a climax. It is a lament of gigantic proportions, an "Ode to Sorrow" which reverses the ninth symphony of Beethoven and recants all that is goodness, joy and hope: "No, up to the very end this dark tone poem does not permit one iota of consolation, reconciliation or transfiguration" (VI, 651).

Music attains a new dimension in Doctor Faustus. Here Thomas Mann extends his conception of music beyond its previous confines, seeing in it a universal force, capable by itself of conveying a mood of total negation and evoking the depths of dejection and despair. But by assigning these attributes to music, Mann leaves himself open to a serious objection, for his readers may well question the validity and significance of these descriptions of music as inconsolably pessimistic, destructive or dangerous. For music to be objectively terrifying to the beholder as exemplified in the Apocalypsis cum figuris the sounds would probably have to resemble outright noise or pandemonium. And one wonders if a listener could really detect mockery and irony, as Zeitblom maintains, in any composer's works, much less in the hero's whose compositions are chiefly atonal. The more discordant the music, the more difficult it must be to ascribe conventional emotions to it; and only by first establishing moods can one subsequently parody them. Without a basis of contrast it would be virtually impossible under the twelve-tone system to determine where one begins and the other leaves off. In the final analysis, then, it is highly questionable, without abandoning the artistic and the aesthetic, that concepts of mockery, irony or parody can be applied at all (except perhaps in the most general way) to the pure sound of music, no matter what forms, conventions or texts are employed. Zeitblom, a serious judge of music in his own right, can only describe Leverkühn's magnum opus as noise, crescendo and sardonic damnation, but certainly not in subtler terms.

A further point is that in the twelve-tone system it becomes virtually impossible to assign established moods or mutual emotional responses to a configuration of notes. Indeed, it is the purpose of the twelve-tone system to leave conditioned conventionality behind and work with sounds, as Leverkühn is prone to do, as if they were in the cold, hard realm of pure mathematics.

Like Tonio Kröger with his "frigid art," Adrian Leverkühn feels the need to eliminate conventional emotions from his art, for, as we have seen, the full force of the instincts lurk behind his musical inclinations. In this respect the hero is no different from his creator as we see in Germany and the Germans (1945) where Mann states his own peculiar definition of music:

> Music is a demonic realm. . . . It is Christian art with a negative prefix. Music is calculated order and chaos-- breeding irrationality at once, rich in conjuring, incantatory gestures, in magic of numbers, the most unrealistic and yet the most impassioned of arts, mystical and abstract. If Faust is to be the representative of the German soul, he would have to be musical, for the relationship of the German to the world is abstract and mystical, that is, musical--the relationship of a professor with a touch of the demonic, awkward and at the same time filled with arrogant knowledge that he surpasses the world in "depth."[17]

What to Thomas Mann is highly subjective and the extreme in personal danger is and has been to the world at large something entirely different. This is brought out by Hans Egon Holthusen, who takes issue with Mann on this point:

> Music therefore, which the author still
> loves passionately, now as in other days,
> is in league with the Evil One. Music,
> of which Luther said that "Satan was very
> hostile" to it; music, to which men have
> always ascribed the power to calm, make
> blissful, bear them upward; music, which
> the most ancient wisdom and mythology of
> mankind has quite decidedly associated
> with the spirit of joy, with piety and
> love, with the "harmony of the spheres,"
> with the cosmogonic Eros. Was not music
> always the smile of the soul? Were not
> even the wild beasts calmed by Orpheus?
> Did he not move the underworld, "humanize"
> it, make it responsive to his amorous com-
> plaint?[18]

However obvious Mann's position on music is, it
is equally obvious that the rationale behind his attitude is his all-embracing rapture in sexualized music
and that artistic considerations alone did not dictate
such a unique and baneful proposition.

Thomas Mann subsumes the whole of German culture
under the heritage of German music. His subjectivity
is not a limited passion for music but ramifies to
penetrate the other arts as well as segments of society
and finally the German nation as a whole. He openly
claims for the German a profundity which is superior,
for example, to that of the French or English. In the
same essay, Germany and the Germans, but with words
echoing a spirit which reaches back into the remote
past of 1918, into his Observations of a Non-Political
Man, Mann defines this depth which he claims Germans
possess: "What constitutes this depth? Simply the
musicality of the German soul, that, which we call its
inwardness, its subjectivity, the divorce of the specu-
lative from the socio-political element of human energy,
and the complete predominance of the former over the
latter."[19]

Thomas Mann's willingness to ascribe artistic
depth of soul to a whole nation, an attribute which only
attains its full strength in individual artists, is
really only explicable in terms of the heart-rending
impact which music makes on him. Mann is guilty here
of incredible projection as he invests the whole German
soul with his own ambivalent attitude towards music:

something intensely pleasurable and something demonic-
ally evil.

But seen more closely, Mann's idea of German music
is surprisingly incomplete. When he speaks of German
depth in regards to music, his thoughts are invariably
turned toward a very specific aspect of German culture,
and that is romanticism: "German Romanticism, what
else is it but an expression of that most beautiful of
German qualities--German subjectivity?"[20] Just why
it is German romanticism which fascinates Mann so completely is readily seen in his remarks in praise of
Nietzsche: "For the romantic is the song of homesick-
ness for the past, the magic song of death and the phenomenon called Richard Wagner which Nietzsche loved so
infinitely and which his soveriegn intellect had to
overcome; it was nothing more than the paradoxical and
eternally interesting phenomenon of a world-conquering
intoxication with death."[21] Richard Wagner certainly
had long been one of the profoundest forces in Mann's
life; his music, almost to the exclusion of all other,
even forms the backdrop of a number of Mann's narratives
with a musical theme. In it Mann found an overwhelming
power capable of moving him heart and soul: "My passion for Wagner's enchanting works began as soon as I
became aware of them, began to make it my own and penetrate it with my understanding. All that I owe to him,
of enjoyment and instruction, I can never forget: the
hours of deep and singular bliss in the midst of the
theater crowds, hours of nervous and intellectual transport and rapture, of insights of great and moving import
such as only this art grants. My zeal is never weary,
I am never satiated, with watching, listening, admir-
ing. . . ."[22]

Inasmuch as Mann's conception of music is inseparable from the erotic, it is natural to expect that the
pull which Wagner's music exerts on him is bound up
with sexual pleasure. We learn this from his essay on
Wagner where he openly states that Wagner's art is essentially sensual: "Sensuality, enormous sensuality,
mounting into the mythical, spiritualized, depicted
with the extreme of naturalism, sensuality unquenchable
by any amount of gratification. . . ."[23] Wagner's
music, which knows no "pathos of distance" is conceived
as "the highest intellectual kind under the guise of
an orgy of the senses. . . ."[24] Elsewhere in this
essay Mann discusses the Liebestod music of Tristan
and Isolde, the erotic-demonic in Siegfried and the
seductive figure of Kundry in Parsifal. Mann finds

Tristan to be saturated with Schopenhauer's erotic
philosophy and the Sehnsucht motif itself "is Schopenhauer's 'will,' represented by what Schopenhauer called
the 'focus of the will,' the yearning for love."[25] Not
fulfillment, but sexual yearning and the free play of
fantasy in the dark characterize Mann's favorite piece
of music: "Its cult of the night, its execration of
the day, are what stamps the Tristan as romantic, as
fundamentally affiliated with all the romantic aspects
of emotion and thought. . . . Night is the kingdom
and home of all romanticism, her own discovery, always
she has played it off against the empty vanities of
the day, as the kingdom of sensibility against reason."[26]

     Thus, what is German for Mann can be reduced in
the final analysis to the subjective influence of a
narrow field of German romantic music, specifically the
music of Richard Wagner. Even Beethoven, whom Mann
considers less a classicist than a romantic, is of
secondary importance. Virtually neglected in the
author's cultural scheme are Bach, Handel, Gluck,
Haydn and Mozart; although by ignoring this whole
spectrum of German music (a period of creation which,
in productivity at least, was far more prolific than
the romantic) Mann weakens and colors--even cheapens--
his argument. This major omission from his considerations of culture is conspicuous, and his emphasis on
Wagner at the expense of these earlier masters would
undoubtedly draw forth a plethora of objections from
serious musicians everywhere. And such an incredibly
narrow interpretation of an extensive and intricate
phenomenon can only find justification in his extremely
personal preference and needs.

     One may ask, quite frankly, what makes Wagner
loom so large in Mann's eyes that his music so completely consumes the author's soul and, to his mind,
embraces the heart of a nation as a kind of universal
principle. The answer, psychologically at least, must
be that the substance of Wagner's music fulfills a vast
emotional need for Mann and satisfies a profound spiritual hunger. And what is the stuff that Wagner's operas
are made of--forbidden love, excessive desire, guilt,
and rapturous atonement in the flaws and passions of
a Liebestod. In short, it is the incest motif which
is the heart of Wagner's libretti and the core of his
music that churn Mann's emotions with passionate longing and forbidden gratifications. For Mann, as for

332

Wagner, such dreams and commitments constitute the ultimate truth. But in Germany as elsewhere, a plurality of people, motivated predominantly by other needs and faculties, must find equivalent or even higher "truth" and satisfaction in the compositions of Bach, Mozart, Handel, or Haydn. Undoubtedly, Germany's greatest contributions to world-wide pleasures are to be found in her musical treasures; and their universal appeal lies less in the romantic agony of Richard Wagner, as Mann would have us believe, than in the works of a number of his predecessors whose mastery of the various genres of music surpassed by far the one-sided greatness of the opera composer, marvelous though he was in his command of the orchestra.

But in all fairness to Mann, it must be stated that his knowledge and love of music extended far beyond the realm of Wagner's operas. And like Adrian Leverkühn, he was especially taken by German Lieder, for which, one must add, there is biographical precedence. In A Portrait of My Mother Mann describes the long and happy hours he spent listening to his mother play the piano.[27] Though he does mention Mozart and Beethoven, he includes Chopin and stresses the late romantic masters of the German art song: Schubert, Schumann, Robert Franz, Brahms, and Liszt.

The Disposition of Disease

There are no indications of happy hours with music in Doctor Faustus. The desperate and difficult tones of Leverkühn's music reflect only the hopelessness and nihilism of his life and of a career that was, symbolically at least, conceived in syphilis. As we have shown elsewhere, Leverkühn's contraction of the disease is no more than physical confirmation of a lifelong degeneration process that was already well underway beforehand. But why syphilis and not cancer or some other horrible disease? The "beautiful" and simultaneously morbid answer for Mann is that venereal disease originates in the sex act and therefore the moment of pleasure may immediately be blended with a guarantee of pain, retribution, and death. Thus, Adrian has in fact the proof he seeks, Oedipally at any rate, that sex is the source of endless suffering and final destruction, evidence and confirmation which his anxious soul has secretly been seeking and yearning for since childhood. And one may witness the presence of this Oedipal mechanism at work in each and every one of Thomas Mann's stories, from the first to the last. But

one must accept this as a fact rather than as an explanation and then make further assumptions and posit new
propositions that may clarify and explain the nature of
Mann's works. How else can one, for example, come to
terms with Mann's factual but naive preoccupation with
illness, suffering, and death?

Mann was fascinated by disease all his life. In
his presentation, For the Reception of Gerhart Hauptmann in Munich (1926) Mann states: "Health is idi-
ocy."[28] That this simple, if not naive, equation is
to be taken in the literal sense of the word is explicitly manifested in the context of the novel itself.
But are we to ascribe profound insight to this tightly
held conviction? Are we actually dealing with a case
of a deep thinker at work in this instance, a genuine
commentator or an accurate observer of the great human
comedy as Heinz Politzer unswervingly claims for
Mann?[29] Or must we stress the obvious? Honest observation of victims of paresis, cancer, mutilation, or even
lesser forms of suffering will surely not lead to the
same conclusion as that of the author. For the real
fact of the matter is that disease is simply wasteful
and devastating, that severe illness distorts or limits
creativity, and that great minds can still create
great works amid good health and relatively happy circumstances. Rather than accept Mann's view at face
value as Politzer does, it is far more reasonable to
see it as an offshoot of his fascination with death
and his loathing of life. Certainly, a strong case
can be made for aesthetic inspiration as a derivative
of neurotic impulses, as Mann's own artistic creations
amply and convincingly testify. Albrecht van der Qualen
and Gustav von Aschenbach are exemplary instances of
the intrinsic connection between sexual impulses and
creative fruits. But is this what Mann is talking
about in Doctor Faustus? Let us examine his proposition
more closely.

In Doctor Faustus one finds no distinction between
mental conflict and bacterial infection, and actually,
the further along the disease progresses, the greater
(supposedly) Leverkühn's music becomes. Adrian's destructive malady is contrasted to that of Baptist
Spengler, the painter; for him the spirochete, inasmuch
as it attacks only his vitals and not his brain, proves
to be non-productive in an artistic sense. But in
Adrian Leverkühn's case the creative process is directly
attributable to the actual toxic effect of cerebral

334

syphilis. And again Mann confirms in his essay on Nietzsche that this allusion is to be taken literally: "People have widely criticized the physician Möbius for writing a book in which the story of Nietzsche's development is authoritatively presented as the story of a progressive paralysis from an expert's point of view. I have been unable to take part in the indignation over this. The man has said, in his way, the incontestible truth."[30] Nietzsche's illness (to Thomas Mann unequivocally a luetic infection) literally becomes the driving force behind his creative fancy: "A typical symptom of paralysis, presumably due to hyperemia of the affected cerebral parts, is the surge of an intoxicating sense of bliss and power and an actual--though medically, of course, pathological--intensification of productive capacity. Before it clouds its victim's mind and kills him, the disease grants him illusory (in the sense of sane normality) experiences of power and sovereign facility, of enlightenment and blissful inspiration. . . ."[31]

It is really striking that as late as 1946, Thomas Mann is willing to assert such a dubious proposition so dogmatically. That he does not hesitate to claim for syphilis, this profoundly ravaging and devastating disease, a property capable of artistic inspiration, causes us to confirm our initial statements and to search for additional implications of Mann's position. For example, equally startling is the appropriateness of the above citation when applied to that mad political genius, Adolf Hitler, whose heroically dying Germany forms the background and frame for the story of Doctor Faustus. We have yet to discuss the role of politics and war in this novel, but even there we shall find a high correspondence between its significance and that of music, where, in both cases, Mann's stand is less than objectively honest or logical. But even emotionally, music extends far beyond simple pleasure or gratification to a devastating and obsessive sense of guilt. Like all of life, the pleasures of music for Mann rest in a treacherous ambivalence of love and evil, desire and destruction. And just such ambivalence generated the all-consuming tension that conditioned the whole of Thomas Mann's life, causing him, finally, to view entire cultures and a world conflagration through the split vision of a disjunctive psyche.

Serenus Zeitblom: The Protagonist's Other Half

Because of the frightful dangers inherent in music,

Thomas Mann felt it necessary to insert an intermediary between himself and his hero. The author frankly admits that the frame device was the result of a bitter necessity in order to achieve a certain humorous leavening of the somber material, to make its horrors bearable to himself as well as to the reader by having the demonic strain pass through an undemonic medium. The device also helped reduce the burden of personal exposure and enabled him to escape the turbulence of all the direct, personal and confessional elements which underlay his creative conception. [32]

Serenus Zeitblom (by his name one who is not torn within and thrives, therefore, in tranquillity) can be likened to the god Apollo, and for Mann, "Apollo, god of the Muses, he who shoots his arrows from afar, is a god of distance, of space, not of pathos and pathology or involvement, a god not of suffering but of freedom. He is an objective god, the god of irony. . . ."[33] Zeitblom, although always involved in the story as the narrator, remains above and beyond it. He is free to comment, judge and interject without restrictions. And as a result, his moods and irrelevant observations consume suspense and often delay or obscure direct confrontations with the substance of the story. The result is heavy going for the reader. Pickard comments as follows:

> We find we are not allowed to race on with the story; the chronicler interrupts with surprising determination in a great variety of ways. Long before incidents are due, he tells us what will happen, as if to prevent our pursuing outward events. He draws parallels between the life of the individual genius and the genius of the country as a whole, as if to floodlight an otherwise invisible link between individual and community. He makes us bear in mind a number of different periods or stretches of time, as if to wean us from a short-sighted immediacy to a long-sighted, global concept of the influence on our lives of this fourth dimension. [34]

To Erich Heller such devices are parody, specifically self-parody, and are, presumably, a virtue of the novel,[35] but other interpreters are not so charitable. Henry Hatfield and Hamilton Basso both deplore the slow pace and the lack of life in the central figure.[36]   J.

C. de Buisonjé finds that Mann has not sufficiently motivated and prepared the life-long impact which the shadowy figure of Hetaera Esmeralda makes upon the hero.[37] The need for Zeitblom to further slow down or subdue the action must evoke surprise, considering that Thomas Mann had already succeeded in cooling down everything emotional in the novel. Adrian Leverkühn, with Zeitblom's help, becomes so dehumanized that he is hardly credible; in fact, he is only believable in terms of an extreme clinical picture that may carry academic interest but utterly fails to convey the electric quality of life. And Hans Egon Holthusen's violent objection to Erich Kahler's interpretation of Doctor Faustus as "one of the most shattering love stories of world literature"[38] needs little confirmation beyond the recognition that little warmth and no real love can be identified in this prodigiously repressive work.

But while Serenus Zeitblom, the chronicler of the life history of his musician friend, unravels the intricate fabric of this narrative, he also assumes the role of a counterbalance or contrast to the hero. More than one commentator has seen in this narrator of the hero's life an extension of Mann's own autobiography in that Zeitblom represents another aspect of the author's own nature. To Erich Heller, the hero and the friend "represent the 'two identities' of their author";[39] to Erich Kahler, "he is probably the other half of the author, he is probably the Overbeck of the Adrian Nietzsche, he is probably the outward, ironic reaction of the normal to the abnormal again. . . ."[40]

But Zeitblom can also be considered, as Charles J. Rolo maintains, as playing the role of the expatriate Thomas Mann cut off from his homeland:

> After Germany's defeat, wondering whether to return to teaching, Zeitblom writes "I fear that the youth of my land has become too strange to me . . . Germany herself . . . is strange to me." This is surely Mann, once potentially the cultural "Provider," speaking; Mann who journeyed to Europe a year ago and was deeply reluctant to set foot on his homeland. Zeitblom goes on to ask: "Did I do right when I drew back from Germany's sins and hid them in my seclusion?" And he adds: "Did I actually do that?" (My italics) Zeit-

blom's loyalty to the artist Leverkühn,
symbolic of Mann's devotion to art, seems
to him a species of loyalty to Germanism.
Here is the final flourish on the "Brother
Hitler" theme. Is not Mann saying that
no German artist is free of the "migraine"
inherited from a Kultur which includes
Nietzsche as well as Goethe, Wagner as
well as Bach? Is not Doctor Faustus an
anguished confession that, whatever Mann's
public personality, the artist has never
really left home?[41]

To Rolo, Zeitblom is "a masterly parody of certain
Mannian traits (that pedagogical bent and rather ponderous playfulness) and, more importantly, of the bourgeois aspects of Thomas Mann: son of a wealthy Lübeck
merchant, father of six, man of regular habits--work
every morning, a walk at noon, reading and correspondence after luncheon, visitors for tea, preferably music
in the evening."[42] Jonas Lesser remarks: "His [Zeit-
blom's] position in August 1914 is precisely the position of Thomas Mann, as it was in his rejection of
National Socialism. . . ."[43] In fact, only by regarding Zeitblom as one aspect of the hero's split personality can there be motivation sufficiently credible to
explain Zeitblom's attachment for Leverkühn. Although
he fully realized that Adrian never once returned the
feeling, Zeitblom confesses that he loved him with
tenderness and terror, with compassion and devoted admiration. He shrinks back in horror at the news of
Leverkühn's first visit to the prostitute Hetaera
Esmeralda, and for days after the hero's encounter with
her Zeitblom feels the touch of her flesh on his own
cheek, just as if she had also brushed him with her
hand.

Zeitblom is, without exaggeration, that repressive
side of Mann which seeks to deny the diabolically artistic nature with its highly charged criminal impulses.
The serene humanist Zeitblom, like Settembrini, the
advocate of enlightenment in The Magic Mountain evinces
unrequited affection and concern for the hero, and yet
at the end it would be Settembrini who would finally
write Hans Castorp's epitaph just as it is Zeitblom
who chronicles the death of Adrian Leverkühn here.
Zeitblom rejects with dread the demonic forces in Leverkühn which might break out in destructive excess at
any time. As P. M. Pickard has shown so cogently, the
threat of forces breaking out of control is everpresent

338

in Zeitblom's biographical account: "This breaking through to consciousness of unconscious or repressed forces."[44]

But the concept of breakthrough, so very terrifying for Zeitblom, becomes an exciting possibility for Leverkühn himself, who extracts great delight both by probing and holding back: he prolongs his inevitable fate to increase the conclusive explosion of forces, and he searches relentlessly for the breakthrough that triggers both creation and destruction. Darkness is precisely what Leverkühn wants, and his continual migraine which forces him to avoid the light of day and seek the dark serves him well. The entities of the day, the forms and movements of the vital world remind him of the source of his inadequacies, fear, and guilt. It is therefore not without reason that Adrian often prefers to receive Zeitblom (the Licht-mensch) in the darkened room where one can hardly distinguish the other's form. And, Leverkühn realizes, fantasy thrives on darkness. Even the prohibition of love which the cold and dark Devil imposes on the hero restates the fact that fantasy is superior to fulfill-ment. Adrian's total love-life consists in narcissistic self-indulgence in fantasy, for his imagination is everything--completely self-sufficient. Even the crimes for which he pays with his life are nonexistent although through omnipotence of thought they may be tantamount to the heinous deeds of the Nazis, as we shall now see.

Mann, Mania, Literature, Politics

In A Sketch of My Life, written in 1930, Thomas Mann prophesied that he would die in the year 1945, at the age of seventy as his mother had. In a sense that prediction came true, for, as Mann tells us in The Story of a Novel, his life had, biologically speak-ing, reached a low such as he had never known before.[45] But the following year produced an even greater re-duction in the state of Mann's health, one that corre-sponded not only to the predicted fatal age for his mother but also to the demise of his "maternal" Germany. The collapse of Germany in 1945 found the author half-way in time through his novel about the musician and his musical country, and his identification with his hero was no less than his identification with his home-land. Germany and Adrian Leverkühn were symbolically one and the same, and music was their common bond. The equation "Adrian Leverkühn equals Germany" is reflected in every facet of the hero's life with the events of his career corresponding minutely with those of recent German history. Henry Hatfield points to some of the significant dates affecting both hero and country:

> Zeitblom . . . draws a "symbolic parallel" between one of the composer's attacks of illness and the hectic condition of his country after 1918. At times, the deliberate rebarbarization of German culture is paralleled in Adrian's work . . . the composition [Apocalypsis cum figuris], like the theories of the Nazis, gives an effect of "exploding old-fashionedness." Just as Faust, even in Goethe, has something Mephistophelean in his nature, both Adrian and Germany are Satanic as well as Faustian. The concept of "breaking through," one of the central themes of the whole work, applies equally to the German thrust for world power and to Adrian's desperate efforts to create a new music. . . .
> His [Leverkühn's] final collapse is described at the time when the Allied armies are overrunning Germany. In the final sentence of the novel, Zeitblom's words: "God have mercy on your poor soul, my friend, my fatherland" reassert the fundamental parallel with the finality of a great chord.[46]

Almost everything in Mann's novel is in essence an allusion to something peculiarly German and, consequently, something alien to the West. The story of Mann's hero therefore represents the author's personal conception of the history of Germany in this century, a Germany sundered not only by its political but also by its demonic strain.

Thomas Mann's very own special concern for his homeland as well as for his excessively guilty protagonist transcended, as was to be expected, the confines of his normal solicitation about his works. Indeed, the torment Doctor Faustus cost the author in energy and health was truly immense and unique even for Mann.

Doctor Faustus, the work which itself became the

subject of another book (<u>The Story of a Novel</u>), represents in certain respects the pinnacle of Mann's creative intensity. We read in this novel of a novel, this
chronicle of physical pain, that <u>Doctor Faustus</u> literally became a matter of life and <u>death</u> to the author
himself. In a commentary, <u>On Doctor Faustus</u> (1947),
Mann again sums up the feelings which make up the physical content of his novel:

> It is a biography of almost criminal
> pitilessness, a strange kind of figurative
> autobiography, a work that cost me more
> and gnawed more deeply in me than any
> previous one (the Joseph tales were an
> absolute lark by comparison) and whose
> inner excitations, I believe, still come
> through where it is most boring. . . .
> Really, one can indeed call it an excep-
> tional event, that a person of seventy
> years writes his "wildest" book. It was
> also no coincidence that I became danger-
> ously ill in the middle of it, and then
> like a young man made an astonishing re-
> covery so that I could finish it.[47]

We are forced to take Mann at his word in both
this passage and in <u>The Story of a Novel</u>. His repeated
illnesses and moods of depression which culminated in
a grave ordeal by surgery were a truly remarkable
phenomenon of inner turmoil and passion. Though the
element of self-commiseration, if not exaggeration, is
present in the detailed account of his tribulations,
the actual sufferings, which his aged frame had to
undergo truly reveal themselves as a stoical achievement. As one critic says, "No doubt--this 'work of
suffering' saved the life of its creator. Without
<u>Doctor Faustus</u> there would have been no <u>Holy Sinner</u>
and no <u>Felix Krull</u>, not only in the spiritual sense of
the word but also in actuality."[48] But whether or not
this novel saved or endangered the author's life, the
fact remains that its creation undoubtedly represented
an incredible personal experience in Mann's seventieth
year of life.

The sweat and tears expended in the formulation
of this work spring from its autobiographical foundation
and is eloquently supported by Mann himself as he answers
his own rhetorical questions about this work and protagonist that stand closest to his heart:

The Faustus novel was the costliest work
for me, simply because I paid the highest
price for it, because it cost me the greatest measure of life blood, because to this
work of my seventy years I gave the greatest
part of my life, my most personal self with
a kind of wild disregard for consequences
and a kind of an inner turmoil that I shall
never forget. Earlier and later things by
me, Joseph or The Holy Sinner, for example,
may be happier, more cheerful and more attractive in an artistic sense, but I cling
to this work as to no other. I do not like
anyone right off who does not like it. Whoever reveals himself to be sensitive to the
high psychic tension under which it exists
will receive my complete gratitude. And
as far as its hero is concerned, this Adrian,
I have thus admitted in the small volume,
The Story of a Novel, that I have never loved
an imaginary figure as I did him, neither
Thomas Buddenbrook, nor Hans Castorp, nor
Aschenbach, nor Joseph, nor the Goethe of
The Beloved Returns. In writing this work
I literally shared the feelings of the
good Serenus Zeitblom for him, was anxiously
in love with him from his arrogant schoolboy days on, was foolishly fond of his
"coldness," his distance from life, his
lack of "soul," of means of conciliation
and reconciliation between spirit and emotional drives; I loved his unhumanness and
desperate heart, his conviction of being
damned.[49]

Mann emends this statement in The Story of a Novel
to admit one exception: Hanno Buddenbrook--the only
other protagonist of his who surrenders himself to the
lures of music. Hanno, the author tells us, no less
than Adrian claimed Mann's full sympathy and affection.
But most readers, German and American alike, have seemed
unable to share Mann's ecstatic regard for a work in
which the coldness of the protagonist certainly does
block out all qualities of human warmth, enthusiasm or
even interest in many cases. And one must certainly
wonder about the rabid praise which Mann lavishes on
his most admirable hero, especially after he enumerates
the reasons that literally induce the author's "love":
arrogance, coldness, distance from life, lack of soul,
inhumanity and doubt, and conviction of damnation. Yes,

one must certainly wonder and question the nature of such a "love," just as one must doubt Mann's statements about the book's dramatic, passionate reconciliation between "spirit and emotional drives."

After struggling through a morass of allusions and inert personalities, the reader will also find his credulity strained by Mann's designation of Doctor Faustus as his "wildest book." In the words of André von Gronicka, "No other major work of Mann equals it in depth of analysis, in intensity of feeling, none is so much the product of personal experience surcharged with emotion. . . . There is here a directness of purpose, a severity and seriousness never before equalled in Mann's creations."[50] But if no other work is, for Mann, so heartfelt, there is also no other work which contains so many heavy-handed allusions, obscure puns, pedantic references, deliberate asides, and tedious retardations. If, indeed, as Victor A. Oswald has said, Doctor Faustus is the work "richest in the use of allusions, of veiled references, of cunning innuendos,"[51] then one wonders again about their purpose. All these devices really fail to impress themselves upon the normal reader as anything but wearying annoyances which detract from the work, rob it of life, and permeate it abundantly with denatured phantoms. Has Mann himself become as dry as his narrator Zeitblom? At least Hanno came to life fully from the pages of Buddenbrooks; but Adrian Leverkühn lacks all of Hanno's youthful intensity, authentic anxiety, and poignant suffering. As a matter of fact, the only place in this novel where the author tries to touch the existence of such real emotions--the Echo episode-- is in itself of questionable value in an aesthetic sense.

One may read with disbelief and a shake of the head in The Story of a Novel that actual tears were shed over Echo's death by friends and members of the author's family.[52] Conversely, it is interesting to compare the exaggerated sentimentality of the Echo-episode with Thomas Mann's impatience to dispatch this little creature: "I do not believe I have ever worked with more eagerness."[53] Mann actually seems to take great pleasure in making a ritual victim or sacrifice of the young boy. Apparently dissatisfied with his own denial of love, the artist now proceeds to kill it off wherever it tends to appear. But if Echo is present in form, he is hardly present in life, composed as he is of all the good, beautiful and precocious clichés which Mann can draw together. The episode may be melodramatic, but it is hardly tragic, for tragedy presupposes some substantial truth.

Thomas Mann's repeated claims of intimacy and praise now reveal themselves to be of crucial significance for an ultimate interpretation of Doctor Faustus. Mann's agony of creation shows us that he was not engaged in an ordinary way in this work, but that the whole undertaking was a supercharged release of guilt with music representing a camouflaged but extended and unrelieved orgy. It was an experience that nearly shattered the author in the same manner as the goatish dream of Aschenbach and the lustful piano fantasies of Hanno broke their brittle relationship to life. In the life of Adrian Leverkühn music is capable of reinforcing the Oedipal fantasies to such an extent that the impact they have on him is a total one, allowing him to revel even in the ecstasy of murder. One must remember that in his darkened room he is constantly experiencing secret thrills and immense transports of sexual release in his musical activities. The high state of ecstasy he achieves exhilarates him, and though pain and hostility are a part of his pleasure, they are being libidinally oriented, felt as piquantly attracting. In the same way that Dostoevsky was willing to give ten years of his life for the fraction of a minute bliss of voluptuousness, so too does Adrian find the delicious feeling of rapture in a moment of orgasm in music to be worth a whole life of love.

Adrian Leverkühn does in Doctor Faustus what Thomas Mann was unable to bring himself to in actual life: to surrender himself completely to the chaotic world of music, to the chthonian maternal forces. These same forces of the "mother-darkness" Mann saw triumphant in Germany under Hitler. According to Mann in Germany and the Germans, Germany paid a high price for inwardness, depth of culture, and musicality of soul "in the political, the sphere of human social life."[54] Such words come as a surprise in 1947, for we expect to find them back among the writings of the First World War, but we discover instead Mann busily warming up the old chestnuts of the Observations of a Non-Political Man. Although a generation has passed and the author is twenty-nine years older, nothing has changed radically from his war book of 1918. Germany is still the "maternal" land of music and cultural superiority as opposed to France or England with their concepts of political progress and enlightenment. Mann emphasizes Germany's lack of political acumen and contrasts the French tradition of social upheaval with Germany's inability to complete a successful revolution during her long history. He finds Germany to be the product of romanticism with its emphasis on irrational and demonic powers, and for that very reason she appears to him to be closer to the wellsprings of life. Germany's pessimistic outlook represents an honest position highly critical of all rhetorical virtues and idealistic euphemisms: "The Germans are a people of the romantic counterrevolution against the philosophical intellectualism and rationalism of the Enlightenment, a people with a rebellion of music against literature, with mysticism against clarity."[55]

Thus, as in the past, Mann's conception of history is polarized around his notion of the "musicality of the German soul," and the only difference between the Observations of a Non-Political Man and his remarks in Germany and the Germans is his apparent criticism of Hitler's role in events of the present. But while he inveighs against the National Socialists, his secret longing is still to be one with Germany, whose political backwardness, according to Mann in Germany and the Germans, began with Martin Luther. With poetic license Mann paints his own portrait in the Luther of the separatistic, anti-Roman, anti-European mentality. As an extremely musical and an anti-political devotee, Luther becomes a gigantic incarnation of the German soul, and to the author he is closer to the devil than to God. In Mann's sketch the theologian comes forth as a truly exemplary emanation of German musical inwardness; he is an intolerant leader whose anti-political dedication contributed as much as anything else to the German's political immaturity and who, like Thomas Mann himself, understood nothing and did not want to understand anything of political freedom. As Mann describes the Reformer in all his choler, coarseness, raging and vomiting hate, superstition, unchristian and even heathen tendencies, he could be portraying the dictator of Nazi Germany.* Mann grimly and categorically professes his

---

*Thomas Mann leaves us with no doubt about the kinship between Luther and Hitler: "Hitler's similarity to Luther is very actively felt, although there appear to be Lutherans who do not wish to know anything about that." (Sufferings for Germany [1946] Works, XII, 731.)

total antipathy to this "monstrous" theologian, as he did his repugnance for Hitler, but as we know from his past pronouncements couched in doctrinaire terms, indignation often conceals, ambivalently, an inner attraction.[56]

And thus we come once again to Thomas Mann's "Brother Hitler" theme. Hatfield is closer to the truth than he perhaps realizes: "It would be simplistic to call Mann's hero a symbol of National Socialism. He has too much distinction, intellectual, social and personal, for that. Yet he does share through his coldness, his ruthlessness, his hubris, in the guilt of modern Germany. The parallel is by no means exact, but it exists."[57] The author's unthinkable kinship with the dictator reaches more to the depths of his own soul than he is openly willing to admit. When Mann can say that there is too much Hitler, the paper hanger and adventurer, and too much latent Nazism in the works of Wagner whom he indirectly calls a barber and a charlatan, then he is not demonstrating an actual antipathy to the musician but rather a closer identification through him with Hitler.[58] Richard Wagner was the one man who continuously wove an hypnotic spell over Thomas Mann and to the end Thomas Mann never relinquished the dichotomies of Western civilization and German musical depth of soul. Perhaps the final word on the "Brother Hitler" motif is to be found in his comment on Hermann Goering's statement at the Nuremberg trials that he, had he been empowered, would have tried to induce Thomas Mann to stay in Germany. Mann's reaction: "What was that? He would of course have offered us a castle, a million, and each of us a diamond ring, if we had been willing to join the Third Reich. Go to your doom, fat and jovial murderer! You at least enjoyed your life, while your lord and master lived nowhere but in hell."[59] Thomas Mann apparently draws a curious distinction between the spellbinding dictator and his Nazi followers as he did between the authoritarian Moses and the coterie of brutal toughs surrounding him in The Tables of the Law. It should be left up to the reader to determine whether Hitler in Mann's appraisal is in a decisive measure to be divorced or absolved from culpability in the crimes of the National Socialists and that as the artist's brother he was of a different mental composition from the guttersnipe sadists who followed him blindly. Moses, we recall, did not go about and himself commit the outrages; instead, his destroying angel Joshua instigated and carried out those deeds that resulted in the deaths of

many, the implication being that Moses was not responsible for the frightful excesses of his adherents. And
in Doctor Faustus the doomed and inhuman Adrian Leverkühn, like Hitler, but unlike Hitler's subordinates,
was subjected to a mental hell of his own making, the
very same hell all Mannian artist figures incur by reason of their distance from and hatred of life.

Not only is Hitler the artist's brother in his
mental make-up, by his special position of loneliness
and grandeur, and by his inclination to explosive outbursts, but he is also the successful outcast exalted
to the highest post over the middle class which he
controls at his pleasure. Hitler's rise to power
represented to Mann the imposition of the dark underworld of the mother over the bourgeois father-world.
Mann's words about Wagner's music in his letter to Emil
Praetorius are especially apt in this context: "Believe it seriously--but you cannot really take it seriously!--that this triumphal procession over the bourgeois world, owes everything to yearning, 'to submerge
again in the reuniting abyss and divine night.'
. . . "60 And what is true for Hitler is equally true
for Adrian Leverkühn. His punishment granted him in
advance, Adrian becomes the unrepentant apostate to
the bourgeois father-world of politics as he gives himself up fully to the dark and destructive powers of
music. Through the sphere of music this protagonist,
whom the author loved more than all of his self-projec-
tions, is associated in spirit with the neo-romantic
Nazis, the very same Nazis who, with sadistic glee,
sought to crush the traditional middle class world.
Mann's Germany, where the apotheosis of the supreme
artist occurs, is akin to the house of the Buddenbrooks
in which the forces of dissolution and decay went hand
in hand with an increase in Hanno's musical (artistic)
activities. This artist hero's parricidal fantasies
did their share in destroying the Buddenbrook family
and bringing about, in Mannian terms, the collapse of
the old middle class. Now once again the end of an
era, the humanistic bourgeois era, takes place in the
unleashing of maternal forces under the leadership of
the omnipotent artist Brother Hitler. And it is significant that Adrian shows no real feelings of comradeship for Serenus Zeitblom, who, as his name indicates,
represents the optimistic and cheerful side of humanity. Adrian's relentless coldness remains completely
unaffected by the one-sided friendship this pedantic
humanist proffers. To Zeitblom's counterpart, Settembrini of The Magic Mountain, music was politically

347

suspect and it still is to Zeitblom; but to Adrian
music is never anything but a distinct pleasure and a
covert gratification. The impression left by the humanist Zeitblom is that his mentality is totally alien to
the profound spirit of musical Germany. Juxtaposing
Zeitblom and Leverkühn by implication in Germany and
the Germans, Mann reveals how undivided he felt about
his "maternal" Germany. "There are not two Germanies,
an evil and a good Germany, but on the contrary only
one, for whom the best it had to offer sprouted, by
means of the devil's cunning, into evil."[61]

To a great extent Doctor Faustus tells us where
Thomas Mann stood with regard to the revolutionary upheaval in Germany. During the immense carnage of the
great war, Mann's feelings rose to fever pitch as they
did in the first world holocaust. Indeed, the fact
that Mann decided to become a "musician" in World War
II is the best proof that he was mentally in the same
position as he was during the First World War. With
music Mann became a secret sharer of the ideology of
Hitler. The dictator struck a vibrant chord in the
author that equalled the electricity of emotion similar
to that of the Observations of a Non-Political Man.
Thomas Mann's two periods of leave-taking from his seat
on Olympus coincided therefore with the two instances
of the inner self of the artist being caught up in the
external world, his two great outbursts of emotion coming, as they did, during the World Wars when the savage
in man was unleashed.

During his stay in the United States, from the late
thirties to after the end of the war, Thomas Mann walked
a thin tightrope between what he conceived of as the
spirit of Western political civilization in the service
of humanity and that of the defiant and inward world
of mother-darkness on a rampage. Even though he became
a United States citizen, there must have been a measure
of unpleasantness in his living in America, for he had
to bear a double onus: his dispossession from the maternal homeland and his enforced captivity in the home of
the paternal West.

The forces of repression held the upper hand
throughout Thomas Mann's life which externally, at
least, may serve the world as a model of propriety and
correct bearing. These forces, so painfully formulated
and controlled in Doctor Faustus, were severely chal-
lenged throughout the Second World War, for the threat
of a breakthrough, in the sense of an Aschenbach's

giving way, was never more imminent in the author himself than at that time. This might also explain Mann's
immense polemical involvement on behalf of the British
Broadcasting Company. The vigor with which the apolitical author hurled himself into the fray against the
Nazis can be said to stand in direct proportion to the
strength of the bond he felt for the unbridled mother-
country. As a tyro writer Mann found an outlet for his
urges in the outbursts of his earliest heroes, and as
the gaunt monk of the First World War he brought his
artistic convictions in alignment with the maternal
fortunes of Germany, although now, paradoxically, the
apolitical author found in Western politics a counterbalance to the dangerous and misguided ebullience of
his desires. Thus, the ultimate paradox for Thomas
Mann was in being forced to take, superficially at
least, a political stand against the powers of romantic
inwardness and the musicality of the German soul.

One cannot, then, call Thomas Mann Olympian in
his treatment of Germany and her demise. His great insight is that he is fully aware of the Hitler in all
of us. But in this instance he is not dealing with a
case of recognition that could serve the intellect in
abjuring or exorcizing the devil. Instead he presents
us with a Hitler substitute in heroic garb and in arro-
gantly stoic proportion. His stress of the artist endowment in Hitler at the expense of the dictator's
other, more important traits represents a distortion
of history as well as a caricature of his own civilized
convictions. Objectivity is totally vanquished by such
a gross projection of the diabolical artistic nature.

Adrian Leverkühn's Humanity

The rigid life which Adrian Leverkühn leads coincides very closely to that of Gustav von Aschenbach in
Death in Venice. Both men are alone in the world, with
art sufficient unto themselves. Their daily regimen
consists of nerve-taxing and painstaking labor at the
expense of their instinctual life and both possess a
fear of trying to break out of the chrysalis of severe
repression which they have carefully imposed upon their
lives. In the Munich cemetery Aschenbach catches sight
of a hallucinatory figure which finds its parallel in
Doctor Faustus as Adrian Leverkühn's apparition of the
devil. Aschenbach's diabolus in his many forms reminds
Hirschbach of Leverkühn's devil who keeps changing his
shape but retains his reddish beard and bloodshot
eyes.[62] These figures represent the bite of the hero's

conscience in its diverse forms, for the more unbearable the hero's urges become under his burden of repression (that is, the closer to the breaking point
they are), the more threatening and imminent the visual-
ization of and the need for punishment becomes. The
visions would be tantamount to proportionately rising
doubts and anxieties, until finally a moment must arrive when release can no longer be postponed; the end
result is then a psychic explosion, an external collapse, a destructive excess. Leverkühn's last work,
The Lamentation of Dr. Faustus, reflects his imminent
insanity; it is an accomplishment of passion that
borders on a death-rattle, a musical composition that
resounds like a shriek of horror. The final note is
struck, his mad speech is over, and Adrian Leverkühn
collapses at the piano. The proof of his sin and suffering is now visible to all. His end, so similar to
Aschenbach's, constitutes a break with cold passivity
and a release from the iron grip of repression that
molded and held fast the cauldron of his emotions. The
result is complete disintegration of the entity. Yet,
despite the immediate gloom and stark despair which
pervade and conclude Doctor Faustus, several critics
have seen in the ending a certain positive note and
even overtones of humanity.[63] Perhaps the main reason
for this can be traced to Mann's footnote on the meaning of the abysmally sorrowful Lamentation of Dr.
Faustus:

> No, this dark tone-poem permits up to the
> very end no consolation, appeasement,
> transfiguration. But take our artist
> paradox: grant that expressiveness--
> expression as lament--is the issue of the
> whole construction: then may we not
> parallel with it another, a religious one,
> and say too (though only in the lowest
> whisper) that out of the sheerly irre-
> mediable, hope might germinate. It would
> be but a hope beyond hopelessness, the
> transcendence of despair--not betrayal
> to her, but the miracle that passes belief.
> For listen to the end, listen with me: one
> group of instruments after another retires,
> and what remains, as the work fades on the
> air, is the high G of a cello, the last
> word, the last fainting sound, slowly
> dying in a pianissimo-fermata. Then
> nothing more: silence, and night. But
> that tone which vibrates in the silence,

which is no longer there, to which only
the spirit hearkens, and which was the
voice of mourning, is so no more.   It
changes its meaning; it abides as a light
in the night.   (VI, 651)

After reading almost the entire paean to hopelessness and despair which Doctor Faustus represents, the
reader must wonder at the justification for this utterance which, in terms of what has passed, seems entirely
unmotivated. Mann's tack-on claim of humanity, this
"miracle that passes belief," likewise passes beyond
the credence of the reader. To Holthusen these final
words also remain unconvincing: "It is questionable
if this is really the place where modern Nihilism con-
quers itself, if this 'flight' of meaning can be believed."[64] Considering the tone and quality of the
novel, it is difficult to avoid the suspicion that the
"Light in the Night" is simply there for the sake of
appearances, a concession of questionable sincerity
appended to the main body of the novel. Thomas Mann
is asking us to believe that his hero of darkness is
now ready to embrace "light." The manner in which
Adrian Leverkühn strikes a bargain with his conscience
rules out completely any "friendliness to life" and
consequently any conception of humanity. His conflict
is too great for him to transcend. His is too much an
intense inner problem to be affirmative; he is too
abundantly concerned with self-punishment and atonement,
too much the seeker of death as penance to care at all
about the world. If he in his behavior represents a
step towards humanity, then it is a kind of humanity
which denies every modicum of comfort to his fellow men.
All his efforts are spent in resolving the two opposing
aims of feeling and repression, and the only way out
of the dilemma is to experience human emotions; but such
an undertaking is for him a vicious circle which would
only increase his sense of guilt. The fixed course of
his life lies in repetitiously acting out the guilt
within, a continual pursuit to palliate the secret
voice of doom.

FULL CIRCLE: THOMAS MANN'S LAST WORKS

As one moves ever closer towards the end of Mann's
works, the conviction persists that Mann's literary
creations may have frequently changed garb and substituted masks but they have never deviated from the worn
path established in his earliest works. Mann's heroes
find no new truths but seek only confirmation of the
old.

There is a tendency for Mann in these later works,
The Holy Sinner, The Black Swan, and Felix Krull, to
relax the stringent check-reining of his feelings and
desires that would be more important to a younger
author. However, one is not compelled to attribute
the tendency to age alone. After the stark and unrelieved intensity of Doctor Faustus which, in its
grimness and desperation, represented a catharsis or at
least a settling of accounts, Mann felt freer of the
rigidity which had continually forced itself upon him
and his works. Having paid for the creation of Doctor
Faustus with torturous doubts and physical illness, he
acquired an inner degree of freedom that in turn permitted a momentary open play of emotions and a lighter
tone in his next work, The Holy Sinner. But even if
this work, along with the whole final productive period, is characterized by a greater liberty of emotion,
one should not immediately attribute it to a newly
transformed and clarified state of mind, for, in truth,
the pendulum effect of oscillation between emotional
extremes is still completely in force in the aged
author. The easy and playful touch that marks The Holy
Sinner gives way immediately in The Black Swan to the
familiar restricted control of emotion, the cold attitude of reserve, and the heavy play of morbidity.
Again, as in the past, the dark drama is relieved in
turn by a more exuberant work, in this case, the last
jewel in the crown, Felix Krull. But even here, it
will be seen, the basic tenor is only slightly modified
from what preceded it, for its inviolable purpose is
again to recapitulate, confirm, and relive the repressed
past in the illusory present.

The Holy Sinner

The source of The Holy Sinner, Hartmann von Aue's
medieval verse epic, Gregorius, is sometimes called the
German Oedipus Rex. As the incestuous issue of the
twins, Sibylla and Wiligis, the infant protagonist

Gregorius is, in keeping with the traditional pattern of the mythic birth of the hero, cast adrift on the water. Found and raised by humble fisherfolk, he grows up to become the hero of his people, is instrumental in freeing the kingdom of his parents from an oppressor, and marries, eventually and unwittingly, his own mother. Upon learning of his incestuous union, Gregorius voluntarily seeks atonement by chaining himself to a rock in the middle of a lake where, reduced to a small animal-like creature, he exists for seventeen years until he is discovered, hailed for his act of penance, and made Pope of all christendom.

From this brief outline the reader's thoughts will, doubtlessly, first turn to the early novella, The Blood of the Walsungs, in which another set of twins, Siegmund and Sieglinde, the spoiled and pampered darlings of a high patrician household (equivalent to royal lineage), are also overtly guilty of the sin of incest. Weigand has made a close inspection of the two works: "We cannot fail to notice that Sibylla and Wiligis are, as it were, a reincarnation of the pair in The Blood of the Walsungs. As regards their figures, their manners, their poise, their obsession with a sense of their own exclusiveness, their preoccupation with the concept of Ebenbürtigkeit, the similarity is so striking as to preclude any element of chance. Thomas Mann was obviously at pains to make the Jewish twins of The Blood of the Walsungs live again in the fairy tale setting of The Holy Sinner."[1]

From here the focus shifts to Joseph in Egypt, in which there is also an incestuous liaison between brother and sister, the parents of Potiphar. And the parallel goes even further when we take the affair between Joseph and Mut, an obvious mother figure, into consideration. Joseph's rise, fall, and resurrection to the greatest heights is identical to the career of Gregorius. Despite the immediate difference in mood between Doctor Faustus and The Holy Sinner the tale of Gregorius can still be considered as an extension of the former in its exaggerated emphasis on the protagonist's withdrawal from the world and the absolute isolation of his nature. In Gregorius' penance on the rock there is reached a reductio ad absurdum of the Mannian hero's narcissistic yearning for a return to the womb inasmuch as the protagonist is actually successful in achieving his goal. He is literally dehumanized as he is transformed on the rock into a hedgehog-like creature; there he exceeds the musician

hero in the self-chastisement which stems from the
ecstatic guilt of a sexual transgression.

The figure of Clemens the Irishman, who, like
Serenus Zeitblom, tells the story for the author, contributes an even more obvious parallel between the two
novels. Again the author installs a narrator as a veil
between himself and his story, for by means of such a
mask, Thomas Mann, as Weigand notes, may project his
personality in a stylized and teasing way without assuming full responsibility for the narrator's slant.[2]
Both Clemens and Zeitblom possess a pedantic bent, hint
of humanistic interests, and are digressive. Both let
themselves get ahead of the story; both are guilty of
personal asides to the reader and tend to analyze subjectively while telling the story. The main difference
between the two is that Zeitblom, as a foil to Adrian
Leverkühn's gloomy pessimism and negative outlook, is
himself devoid of these nihilistic tendencies, whereas
Clemens reveals himself to be of the same ilk as the
previous protagonist. Clemens, it can be said, has in
him the same basic tendency to destruction, which, as
Karl Stackmann notes, has been held against the author
himself.[3] Further, as a medieval monk, skeptical of
the miracles which he relates, he is not always credible, destroying, as he does, the mood of belief when
the bells of Rome miraculously ring by themselves:
"To Clemens the entire affair is more or less an engaging exercise pursued with detachment, with polite
curiosity, courteous sympathy, feigned dismay, and
rhetorical indignation at daring details thoroughly
relished."[4] And one critic virtually accuses the author
of sacrilege in the telling of the medieval narrative:
"Self-awareness is Mann's signature, and however finely
drawn it may be, it is apparent everywhere, makes for
irony, derision, cynicism, sophistication, self-reflec-
tion, and an ill-hidden superiority complex. . . .
Mann's polite detachment is one of ethical indifference,
sardonic sophistication, amorality, blasphemy and religious frivolity, sexual display and eroticism of
death."[5]

Significantly, Mann immediately took a defensive
position in regard to this novel: "But if the old and
the pious are parodistically smiled upon, then this smile
is melancholy rather than frivolous, and this played-out
novel of style, the final form of the legend, preserves
in pure seriousness its religious nucleus, its Christianity, the idea of sin and grace, in complete earnest-
ness."[6] Once again Mann is not his own best critic.

What for Hartmann von Aue was originally a sparse and straightforward tale with a basic moral (the purifying power of penance to obtain the immeasurably great mercy of God),[7] is essentially for Mann a vehicle for parody. As before, Thomas Mann is motivated by the ambivalent desire to depict a "daring" set of emotions while concealing it at the same time in a veil of words. What is more consistent in Mann's creations than the process of sin and atonement? The concept of the saint, not to mention the many characters with ascetic tendencies, has long been predominant: from the figure of Savonarola in Fiorenza, Adrian ("Hadrian") Leverkühn, and the saintly virtues of the heroes of some essays, e.g., Dostoevsky and Nietzsche, to the Pope of this work.

We submit, therefore, that Clemens' function in the novel is conclusively no different from that of his counterpart in Doctor Faustus. Like Zeitblom he is the Apollonian figure behind the narrative who attenuates the stark outbreak of affect to create, as one critic notes, "a gaiety which stands in shart contrast to the mental and physical suffering described."[8] Mann's need for distance again results in special treatment of the subject matter, for the very nature of the material concerning the sin of all sins demands the utmost forbearance, and the author achieves his distance not only by creating an atmosphere of duplicity which hovers about the whole story but also by other means. In this fairy-tale novel (an epithet which Weigand continually applies), the element of time is purposely vague. History is suspended and Mann makes no effort to re-create the Middle Ages in his work. The end effect is to make relative the human situation confronting the protagonist.[9]

In some measure the puppet play, one of Adrian Leverkühn's compositions, is carried over into The Holy Sinner as a continuation of the composer's irony and parody. In nearly every situation the characters, wooden and doll-like, simulate and utilize emotions which they no longer feel sincerely, and consequently they fail for the most part to become true representatives of human anguish. And, too, a note of exaggeration accompanies their passions.

A partial exception to human coldness is the depiction of vivid intimacy on the "wedding night" of Wiligis and Sibylla. Weigand comments on this in detail: "While Hartmann narrates the scene of cohabitation with the utmost courtly discretion, Thomas Mann turns the spotlight on a riot of elemental passion, both exciting and repulsive in its stark moody cruelty, heightened by the proximity of the dead father's body lying in state (the son is getting even with his jealous sire), and deriving a peculiar piquancy from the symbolic Adam and Eve dialogue and the sister's artful poise and unabashed curiosity throughout the act of her violation. Here naturalistic detail is enveloped in an aura of surrealism that is without parallel in Thomas Mann's work, as regards the treatment of sex."[10] If Weigand's view is correct, we are witnessing the first real love-scene since Thomas Mann's initial work, Fallen, to carry itself along with its own power and excitement.

Only in high old age, it can now be speculated, is the author able to relent a bit in the severe restraint he has consistently placed on his characters' feelings. But even so, one can still detect a measure of abstention; at the height of their passion, the twins turn to Old French to express their most personal thoughts, an act reminiscent of Hans Castorp's babblings in French when he confesses his love to Clawdia Chauchat. But finally, and in the usual vein of ambivalent confusion, the intermingling of cruelty and death with tenderness--when Wiligis murders his pet dog Hanegriff --places the Mannian crest indelibly on this scene. This bloody deed recapitulates the sadistic fury of the hero of Tobias Mindernickel whose affection for his pet concealed equal amounts of cruelty. At this point Clemens breaks into the story to comment on Wiligis' outburst of parricidal hostility: "Oh God, the beautiful good dog! In my opinion that was the worst thing that happened on this night, and I find it easier to forgive the other incident, as illicit as it was."[11] The symbolic connection--of a pet dog with the ever vigilant father--which Mann has forged in previous works, serves as the requisite ingredient for the actual culmination of Wiligis' passion-filled sadism.

Mann's language in this work consists of a mixture of modern and archaic German, Middle High German, French forms, and even something of Pennsylvania Dutch.[12] Besides the use of archaic sentence constructions he forces American words into German orthography and transposes American expressions into his native tongue: smoothlich, Water, Hoax, Quarrel und Skramble, Suckling, tellen, Gentlevolk, fiddel-faddel, lackadesi, twelf Kiddens upbringen, bosten und swaggern, Kauert (coward), _Puhr Pipels Stoff, lamenten, lad, Pepp, Sparring, einen Fistiköff, ausfigurieren, zur Fallzeit, Grundwerk tun, an der anderen Hand gerechnet._[13]

Weigand wonders why Mann felt compelled to "cast his novel in so odd a linguistic mold." The answers he suggests are contradictory: that the author was consciously seeking new modes of expression and novel linguistic effects in the manner of James Joyce[14] and that he, whose mastery of the German tongue was becoming deficient by years of exile, deliberately fostered an "anti-aesthetic" style:

> These cases, and many others like them, show that Thomas Mann's "Sprachgefühl" is slipping. It should not be objected that some of these Anglicisms are deliberately planted: they may all be conscious and deliberate, for that matter. The fact is rather that they reveal a lack of concern for the inviolability of German idiom, a casual disregard of those safeguards with which every cultural language surrounds itself. I would even go so far as to say that Thomas Mann, as conscious a craftsman in the medium of language as the world has ever seen, here takes a rather malicious delight in nibbling away at the defenses which guarantee the integrity of his native language. . . . The mood of an all-forgiving divine grace that pardons the blackest iniquity of the repentant sinner should not blind us to the fact that an ineradicable _ressentiment_ against the spiritual core of that native heritage which repudiated the author is furtively woven into the tissue of this angelic story.[15]

Yet, one must wonder if there is not perhaps a better way to explain the fact that the respected _Sprachmeister_ purposely neglected the aesthetic to the detriment of his art. Weigand's charge is, it seems, somewhat drastic. A more consistent explanation is to be found in the author's need to disengage himself facetiously from his material; Mann is subject to an inner compulsion to play with language in order to lighten the dark mood when incest is so overtly depicted. The stamp of levity on the thoughts of his characters certainly serves to reduce the underlying tone of ser-

iousness in the more earnest situations. The humorous
touch is lower in quality than that of the Joseph tetralogy, but the reason for its presence in this work
is identical.

The total personality of Gregorius does not vary
substantially from that of Joseph's either. Like
Joseph, Gregorius, with his head inclined to one side,
pale countenance and bluish shaded eyes, is clean and
neat as a youth, finely dressed and elegant, and at
all times a paragon of urbanity. But he is stoical;
he does not cry aloud like the other boys when he
hurts himself, and he is able to concentrate all his
efforts and strength on a single aim. And one must
not overlook the fact that he is literally an outcast
among the villagers. Like Joseph he distinguishes himself in his aristocratic and lonely removal from the
crowd. The gulf between Gregorius and his foster-
siblings likewise appears to be more a matter of "innate merits," as in Goethe of The Beloved Returns, than
a result of his upbringing. He is even a stranger to
his fellow pupils of the cloister. And like Adrian
Leverkühn, he seems to learn without effort as he, imbued with arrogance, evinces an antipathy towards his
studies. He is known as "the mourner," one who is
overwhelmed by a sense of melancholy and who is possessed, like Hanno Buddenbrook, of a singular inability
to participate freely in life's pleasures. Like Hanno,
Friedemann and others, his fantasy is capable of profoundly affecting his life and of filling him with a
sense of evil and sinfulness, while his impact on
others is that of the creative artist. The feeling of
perpetual doubt which plagues every Mannian hero af-
flicts him as well; and so with beating heart Gregorius
listens to public commentary and gossip about himself.
To him any mention of his person seems like slander,
but internally he cannot help but feel that each word
hits the mark and that something is therefore wrong
with him. He is the target of hatred by the common
people, and in his fist fight with his foster brother
Flann--where the duel between Jappe and Do Escobar is
replayed--he meets face to face the crude embodiment
of life. The same could be said for the opponent in
his second encounter, Prince Roger,* the ruthless

---

*Prince Roger, who is vanquished by the hero in a
knightly duel before the city walls, is the rival suitor
of Gregorius for the hand of Queen Sibylla.

seducer of women.

It must appear to the modern reader that Gregorius'
guilt is hardly justified since his transgression was
committed in all ignorance, even though in the Middle
Ages of the poet Hartmann it was deemed correct to assign a sense of sin to him. In either case, guilty or
innocent, the punishment does not fit the crime. If
he is innocent, his sentence is incredibly severe:
extreme isolation and the loss of seventeen years.
But as a guilty man who committed the crime of mankind
he undergoes, ironically, a penance which, as we shall
see, has all the signs of paradise. The source of his
guilt, Oedipal hostility and desire, must replay itself in every new context if it is to find expressive
relief, if only for the moment. Mann's heroes obses-
sively seek punishment for their "original sins," but
nowhere has one of the author's protagonists found
such blissful punishment as here in The Holy Sinner.

Once again we are compelled to include a Mannian
protagonist among the long procession of artist heroes
who are marked men and sinners of the first order. We
know that unconscious guilt is ultimately the persistent product of a child's mind, and in the hero's narcissism we see the link, reinforced by omnipotence of
thoughts, between the actual transgression of Wiligis
and the fantasied sin of Gregorius. The guilt of the
latter is wholly symbolic and thus completely unamenable
to rational analysis, but it is no less real to him
than the deed itself, for the guilt achieved in fantasy
still cuts a wider swath on its possessor's fate than
thoughts acted out in reality. As a burdened penitent,
Gregorius is another reproduction of the artist figure
whose guilt is a figment of imagination, the end result
of a state of pure narcissism. The source of the forbidden fantasy is reflected in Gregorius' words to his
mother: "A young man who leaves home to look for his
mother and win a wife for himself, who, no matter how
beautiful, could be his mother, must reckon with the
fact that it is his mother whom he marries" (VII, 255).
Ironically, Gregorius' reasoning contains by projection
more than a grain of truth that almost embarrassingly
fits the mental pattern of all Mannian heroes whose
guilt consists primarily in thinking about, rather than
committing, a guilty act.

As drastic and severe as the hero's self-imposed
chastisement appears to be, it is a moot and almost
pleasantly humorous point whether the aims of this

penance are, in a traditional sense, satisfied in any degree at all. There is a real element of pleasure in Gregorius' prison on the rock, despite the author's dogmatic assertion that "Extreme guilt, extreme atonement, this sequence alone creates holiness."[16] Fürstenheim has drawn particular attention to the meaning of the rock, which, surrounded by water, represents a symbol of rebirth: "Constant references to 'Mother Earth' serve to stress the same associations of rebirth. A single paragraph contains the words Mutter, magna parens, Mutterleib, Muttergrund, uteri, mütterlich. Gregorius has become a child again, has shrunk in size, slobbers, sleeps most of the time and in the position of an embryo ('in sich selbst zusammengezogen, die Knie am Mund')."[17]

Indeed, the image of Gregorius obtaining nourishment from the rock that is supposed to be torturing him is undeniably that of a feeding infant. Far from being exposed to the miseries of Tantalus, he returns, rather, to a paradisical state. His stay on the "penitent" rock actually represents total regression to a stage which all the artist figures of Mann long for, and his expiation of guilt is carried out by a symbolic death, in which, however, nothing is lost or forsaken. What to Hartmann's Gregorius was originally a genuine ordeal of atonement, is to Mann's a return to the mother and, as such, a reverting to the pleasurably forbidden, to the desired incestuous. The Mannian hero, therefore, has his cake once again and eats it too. His trial is less a punishment, less a bitter mortification than the fulfillment of a wish. The emphasis in this story is on the pleasurable aspect of masochism, in keeping with the novel's light tone of parody and in striking contrast to the desperation and agony of Adrian Leverkühn in Doctor Faustus.

Mann himself informs us directly that there is a question mark as to the hero's penance: "I let the penitent be reduced to a creature of nature, to a hibernating animal, finally to merely a moss-covered thing of nature, insensitive to wind and weather. I had to consider that that simultaneously signified a reduction in the severity of his penance."[18] So in The Holy Sinner we are confronted with the ultimate irony concerning Christian atonement and salvation. Indeed, it is questionable whether the author makes any attempt at all to plumb the problem of sin and redemption. With only pleasure and no real punishment at stake it remains fully open as to whether or not there exists,

as several critics have asserted, a case that this
novel is another appeal to the idea of humanity.[19]

In the original story of Gregorius, Hartmann von
Aue had his hero suffer genuinely; and the end result
was grace in the form of excessive clemency by Gregorius as Pope. However, the sinner of Thomas Mann enjoys his stay on the rock, avoiding all responsibility
and concern for time and indulging in regression pure
and simple. Thus his reputation of mildness and mercy
does not logically follow from his penance. He has
made no real sacrifices, but has actually by-passed
them on the way to the throne of God. There is, therefore, no hard-earned right for him to stand above his
fellow men and pass judgment on them. The conception
of the chosen one, sufficient unto himself and akin to
the artist who is responsible to no one and who manipulates his puppets without fear of consequences, is not
a transformation, but rather a continuation, under more
adult circumstances, of the same prior process of narcissism. In fact, upon his release from the rock his
behavior is not that of a penitent, as Fürstenheim
shows, but that of play-acting, the very opposite in
spirit from Hartmann's truly contrite sinner:

> His first reaction in shrinking away from
> them is only natural in the circumstances.
> However, when he violently protests his
> own unworthiness and warns his visitors
> not to be polluted by his sinful presence,
> there can be little doubt that he is once
> more acting a part; Gregor demeans himself
> exactly as he feels a man in his situation
> ought to behave. Incidentally, he is thus
> able to hide his deeper emotions. Acting
> as he does, he draws attention to himself--
> he need only keep silent and no one would
> even suspect him of being human. He does
> not mean what he says when he urges these
> men to depart, for as soon as one of them
> shows any sign of taking him at his word
> Gregor changes his tune and points out
> firmly that he is the man they have come to
> find. When offered the triple crown he
> accepts at once, showing perfect composure
> and not the least surprise.[20]

Like Felix Krull, the hero to come, Gregorius is
an excellent actor, one whose emotions are totally on
the surface and whose deepest motives are hidden as

far as God and the world are concerned. This proclivity
to dissemble extends, interestingly enough, to Gregorius' mother, whose admission that she knew the Pope as
her son all along also gives serious doubt to the intensity and depth of her own penance, and indicates a
covert commission on her part to participate in the
strange fate and dubious ordeal of her son.

And as with most of Mann's heroes little or nothing
changes between being the highest or the lowest. Gregorius as Pope is still the outcast; only the external
surroundings have been altered. Raised to the position
as head of the state, like Goethe and Joseph, he is
nevertheless removed in spirit from the masses and from
any responsible contact with people on a personal and
equal level. The epithet "Son of God," which was applied to Joseph and also had its equivalent in The
Beloved Returns and in the Goethe essays, suits this
chaste leader of all Christianity even more. His special position above the common herd, bordering on arrogance and snobbery, has become the fixed stock in
trade of the Mannian hero. Szondi is even of the opinion that Gregorius' sin basically rests on pride and
arrogance and that the humanity of the novel consists
in purifying himself of these defects: "Incest in
The Holy Sinner has its origin not in itself but is
rather the ultimate consequence of pride."[21] But
Gregorius never really overcomes his arrogant manner.
In the end he is as narcissistically inclined as ever,
because it is just this narcissism for which there is
no cure. The Mannian hero cannot love another human
being unreservedly without endangering the precarious
balance in his own life and, as a result, he is forced
back on himself. To this extent Gregorius is faith-
fully consistent with the succession of Mann's past
heroes.

The Black Swan

Thomas Mann, as we have seen, has not always
proved himself a reliable critic of his own creations,
a dubious honor certainly, but one that is further supported in his assertation that The Black Swan* is by

---

*The German title is Die Betrogene which means the
deceived one. The English translation refers, curiously,
to an extremely brief scene near the end of the novel

no means connected to Death in Venice: "There have
been some asinine comparisons made: this [work] has
nothing to do with Death in Venice, neither in its
gravity nor in its theme. The only thing it has in
common with it is that it is my creation and to be
sure unmistakably mine."[22] Joseph Mileck's detailed
comparison, however, reveals that there are enough
striking similarities between the two works to clearly
label The Black Swan a companion piece to the earlier
creation.[23] Surveying Mileck's analysis, we find that
Rosalie von Tümmler, the widowed heroine of the novel,
succumbs pathetically, like Gustav Aschenbach, to a
wayward passion for a much younger person. In each
instance the accompanying moral and physical dissolution is emphasized and in each case moderate desire
turns into destructive passion in a relatively short
time. Both protagonists are overwhelmed by the physical qualities of the beloved; they stammer out a
feverish confession of love while alone, and they seek
rejuvenation in massages and cosmetics while attempting to still the hunger within, sacrificing all propriety and self-respect in the process. The mood of
The Black Swan just as that of Death in Venice is reflected in signs or symbols of death that accompany
an atmosphere of life in ferment: the black swans,
putrifying matter, and the castle in decay are set off
against the heavy and overpowering scent of spring and
the unbridled luxuriousness of the castle--the destina-
tion of the "exotic" excursion.[24] In Death in Venice
the jungle of life was contrasted with the Stygian
world of Venice.

     The story itself, as is the case of nearly all of
Mann's works, is uncomplicated in the extreme. Rosalie
von Tümmler has just passed through the change of life
when she becomes involved with a young American expatriate Ken Keaton. As soon as their affair approaches
the intimate stage, Rosalie's menses miraculously return, and soon after she confesses her love to Ken
Keaton and arranges for the consummation of her passion.
But what Rosalie ascribes to a miracle of rejuvenation
turns out to be merely a symptom of cancer on a rampage
which, speedily running its course, terminates her life
in a matter of days.

_____

where the heroine, on the way to her tryst, stops to
feed the black swans.

Rosalie, who has an overwhelming passion for nature, invests and animates it with her own sexually conditioned feelings. She was born in the spring as a child of May, and becomes ecstatic about nature's phenomena and fascinated by their forms: "She discoursed happily on wind pollination--or, rather, on Zephyrus' loving service to the children of Flora, his obliging conveyance of pollen to the chastely awaiting female stigma--a method of fertilization which she considered particularly charming."[25] Roses remind her of Cupid and Psyche, the sweet scents of nature stupefy her awareness, and the hot June days transport her into raptures. By contrast her daughter Anna epitomizes a rejection of emotional life by force of repression. She denounces nature and is physically discomfitted by its odors and vapors, contrary to her mother who accuses her of being opposed to natural phenomena and possessed by the idea of transposing her sense perceptions into frigidity. Rosalie finds in nature a projected preoccupation with sex, and she even associates an old oak tree with her early ebbing sexual life and its later rejuvenation. Subjectively and socially her words and thoughts cling to a nucleus of sexuality. She envies men because their sex life is less restricted and less subject to repression than hers, and originally her interest in Ken Keaton was captured in part by rumors of his success with women. The emphasis on sex places Rosalie in one mold with Aschenbach, whose very destruction arose from the fact that he could not disregard the ebullient urges within, urges, one must add, that are inexorably paired off with disaster.

Death in both novels comes in the form of a merciless and consuming disease that represents the final price paid for transgressing the command of conscience; and here as in the case of Gustav Aschenbach, death follows soon after the heroine has allowed her feelings to run freely. Rosalie von Tümmler's conscience demands that she atone through death as the final retribution for her permissiveness of feeling. What was once a symbolic punishment to Hanno Buddenbrook, and a deliberate self-sacrifice for Gustav Aschenbach, is an automatic physical penalty for Rosalie. As confirmation we learn from her physician Muthesius that her emotional license was directly responsible for her fatal cancer: "Mind you, I don't deny that the uterus itself is producing the voracious brood. Yet I advise you to adopt my opinion, which is that the whole story started from the ovary--that is, from immature ovarian cells which often remain there from birth and which, after the menopause, through heaven knows what process of stimulation, begin to develop malignantly" (VIII, 949).

The association of doom with the sexual is directly pointed up by the mouldy air and licentious statue of the castle's secret passageway which is the rendezvous of Rosalie and Ken Keaton. The same connection is also made in the scene in which Rosalie, on a walk with her daughter, encounters a pile of putrifying excrement: "[its] evil effluvium, which drew the blowflies by hundreds, was, in its ambivalence, no longer to be called a stench but must undoubtedly be pronounced the odor of musk" (VIII, 887). The scent of musk, a secretion of the sex glands of certain animals and consequently linked to procreation, is identified in this revealing passage with the last stages of decomposition, a commentary which would have little significance in the book if not used as a symbol of Rosalie's mental state.*

Although she calls it love, Rosalie's passion for Ken Keaton is, like that of Aschenbach, based on a need to find an outlet, a flight from inhibitions. Rosalie is exceedingly jealous of Ken Keaton's other affairs and her thoughts dwell constantly on his physical charms in a way that seems to challenge the basic composition of her nature. The primacy of the instinctual reveals that her whole person is being consumed in an inexorable quest for gratification, enhancing the fact that a drive to experience has been slumbering in her for a long time. The need to alter the unbearable and deadening effect of repression becomes irresistible and gnaws away at the demands of propriety: "Oh Anna, my loyal child, I harbor lust, shame and grievous lust in my blood, in my desires, and I can't free myself from it . . ." (VIII, 918). Indeed, Rosalie seems compelled to provoke fate and the ensuing punishment: she purposely plans an excursion to the castle to force a showdown and steals the bread from the mouths of the black swans, symbols of death, in almost open defiance.

The object of Rosalie's passion, Ken Keaton, is depicted as mediocre and commonplace. It is probably no accident, as W. H. Rey notes, that this blond-haired,

---

*Musk is used in the manufacture of perfume, a sexual lure.

broad-shouldered and narrow-hipped representative of
"life" possesses an alliterative name as did Hans
Hansen.[26] As an American expatriate who has rejected
his own society and leads an irregular existence, he
appears to deviate at first glance from Mann's conception of the middle class; but yet in his enthusiasm
for Europe and his knowledge of its history and traditions, he is, in a very real sense, less American than
a true German burgher with his aura of assurance and
sprinkling of knowledge.

But it is Rosalie, even more than Ken Keaton, who
seems to fall out of character as a typical Mannian
protagonist in spite of her inner plights and passions.
Simple and cheerful, she is sociable by nature and her
attitude towards art is naive. Rey finds her to be
enough of a bourgeois type to make The Black Swan
unique among Mann's works.[27] Yet on the other side of
the ledger she is invested with certain features and
traits which (besides those mentioned earlier by
Mileck) are consistent with other heroines. There are
bluish shadows around her brown eyes and a yellow pallor to her complexion. In addition to her moral degeneration and shamelessness, she possesses a measure
of exhibitionistic passion below a surface of propriety,
as we note, when Ken Keaton attempts to hurry their
affair.

Rosalie's love of water rivals that of Tonio
Kröger; during the boat trip on the Rhine she sings in
a surge of feeling: "Oh water-wind, I love you. Do
you love me too, Oh water-wind?" (VIII, 939)--words
of joy and release which recall Tonio's song to the
sea: "Oh you wild friend of my youth; once again we
are united. . . ." Rosalie's season is spring, that
time of the year when the Mannian hero's will is put
to the fullest test, and she is also a true stoic as
her ability to bear pain reveals.

Rosalie's position as the Mannian chief figure is
weakened, however, by the role of her daughter Anna,
who possesses the characteristics as well as the temperament of the artist. Crippled, and therefore "marked"
by a clubfoot, Anna is alienated from dancing, sports,
and other activities of people her own age. Endowed
with unusual intelligence, she even rejects the challenges of school as prosaic and ceases to pursue any
academic goals. Instead she turns to the creative and
becomes a kind of intellectual painter who operates
"in the firmly conceptual, the abstractly symbolical,

and often in the cubistic mathematical . . ." (VIII,
879). Like Adrian Leverkühn with his sense of parody,
and Tonio Kröger with his "frigid art," she purges
every element of feeling from her works. And just as
she rejects love in her life and emotionality in her
works, she also resents Ken Keaton's "primitive guile-
lessness."

However, this inconsistency in characterization
can be explained away rather easily if we only make the
assumption that mother and daughter complement each
other, that we are dealing here with a montage, and
that the two poles of the author's personality, the desire for sexual indulgence and the inner necessity for
repressive propriety, are each personified in two separate characters.

The montage device also serves to explain why
Rosalie is entrusted with more than the usual amount of
dangerous emotions and why she is permitted (as opposed
to the passive Aschenbach) to be actively involved in
a love affair. She embraces Ken Keaton in the secret
passageway at the castle and pours out a confession of
love that, in its excess of feeling and sensuality, is
rare or even absent among the creations of Thomas Mann.

In her final hour Rosalie confronts death with
these words:

> Anna, never say that Nature deceived
> me, that she is sardonic and cruel. Do
> not rail at her, as I do not. I hate to
> go away--from you all, from life with its
> spring. But how could there be spring
> without death? Indeed, death is a great
> instrument of life, and if for me it bor-
> rowed the guise of resurrection, of the joy
> of love, that was not a lie but goodness
> and mercy. . . .
> Nature--I have always loved her, and
> she--has been loving to her child. (VIII,
> 950)

An even fifty years after Tonio Kröger's pronounce-
ment, "I love life," another Mannian protagonist comes
to the same conclusion. Rosalie's view that death is
the great instrument of life also recapitulates the
remark by Hans Castorp more than a quarter of a century
before, and, consequently, nothing new is revealed in
the denouement of The Black Swan. What emerges from

368

behind the facade of Rosalie's words is a defensive reaction and contradiction, an inner misgiving concerning
the value of life. In Rosalie's yearning for the aristocratic black swans, which Rey calls the most striking
death symbol in the story,[28] we discern the most convincing confirmation of the recurrent death wish: "I
have suddenly now a deep longing for the black swans
. . ." (VIII, 937). This utterance, her subsequent defiance of the birds by eating their bread, her destructive passions, and her love-song to the sea (which can,
in accordance with other works, be interpreted as a
death-wish) run strangely, if not hypocritically, counter to someone who asserts and reasserts deep love of
life. Joseph Mileck is of the opinion that Rosalie's
final insight is less than adequately prepared for
beforehand and that she arbitrarily attains almost
overnight an understanding which took Hans Castorp two
years to gain.[29]

The heroine's spontaneity contrasts strangely to
her repeated avowals of love for nature. Justifying
her claim of love becomes in fact a central leitmotif
in the work. Perhaps this is why several critics have
found the language to be "false" and "stilted."[30]
Rosalie and Anna (who takes the opposite view from her
mother) literally endow nature with human qualities.

Thomas Mann tells The Black Swan with more pathos
than irony, perhaps more than he had intended; for in
"playing his trick" on his heroine, he is so successful
in undermining a feeling of love for life that Rosalie's
insistent claims come forth as hollow and unconvincing.
There is no real doubt where Mann actually stands in
this tale; the morbid feel of the work readily overrides
his attempts to achieve Apollonian distance. And in
the end it is Anna's viewpoint which prevails as she
asserts that "Heart is sentimental nonsense" (VIII, 910).
Her deeply ingrained distrust and suspicion of the world
and of love, the morbid common denominator of all Mannian heroes, is thus confirmed by the final, pitiless
mood. The ending of The Black Swan reechoes the beginning of Doctor Faustus where the hero's father, Jonathan
Leverkühn, demonstrates by means of his biological ex-
periments the belief that life is a fraud: weird phenomena of nature in which animate and inanimate forms
can scarcely be distinguished, e.g., insects and snails
which survive by trickery and deceit or which are death-
dealing in their beauty. By extending these analogies,
one concludes that the guilt-ridden Adrian Leverkühn,
unable to find a hold in the world through love, is

affected deeply by the illusions that blend life and
death in nature--hence the special delight of his morbid laughter. So, too, we find in The Black Swan that
the ambivalence in Nature and its phenomena of life,
love and beauty, are presented incongruously in protean
images of death. Thus the free exchange of allusions,
each with a morsel of death, serve to devaluate man's
natural sense impressions and vital reactions: the
crocus and the colchicum, the stench and the scent of
musk, and, of course, Rosalie's rejuvenation and its
basis of decay.

Confessions of Felix Krull, Confidence Man

In the hero of his final novel, Felix Krull, Thomas
Mann created the most adventurous and active protagonist
of his career, a character more daring and free in his
behavior than any previous leading figure. A picaresque
hero in search of adventure, Felix Krull guides us
through a series of escapades from which he always
emerges supremely victorious. After the death of his
father and the collapse of his family and its fortune,
Felix Krull takes up with the prostitute Rosza who initiates him into the mysteries of sex; some time later
he successfully feigns epilepsy before the induction
authorities and thus spares himself an enlistment in
the army; on his way to Paris he steals a box of jewelry
and builds a moderate fortune on its sale; in the French
capital he becomes an instant success, rising from an
elevator boy to headwaiter and pursued by wealthy women
and titled nobility; as a favor to his acquaintance,
the Marquis de Venosta, he assumes the latter's identity
and embarks on a tour of the world; but his first stop,
Lisbon, becomes the concluding scene of the work and
serves as a superbly fitting climax to the author's
quest for the maternal figure. Discovered in his attempts to seduce Zouzou, the bourgeois daughter of Professor Kuckuck, Felix Krull is shown embracing Mrs.
Kuckuck, the darkly exotic, Portuguese-speaking mother,
in her majestic fashion the epitome of Mann's conception
of the eternally feminine.

Although this protagonist is endowed with exceptional license, it is impressively astonishing how carefully he is cut from the same cloth as all of Mann's
heroes. Again, and for the last time, he is from a
well-to-do household in which there are gala banquets,
recurrent festivities and even the dubious honor ac-
cruing from the presence of an infantry lieutenant. A

difference is obvious, however, in that his father's
house and business are dissolute and irregular and a
carnival atmosphere prevails. The hero's father does
not resemble Thomas Buddenbrook closely, for he lacks
an overburdened conscience and a sense of propriety;
but yet his death, which is intimately connected with
bankruptcy, is as degrading as his business manipula-
tions are shady, qualities which echo the mood of
Buddenbrooks. After the father's death, the slovenly
and sensuous mother moves, like Consuelo Kröger, to
another city further down on the map. And Felix Krull
himself, like the hero of The Clown, gives full expression to his imagination by acting out theatrical
games in solitude. He is a lover of music, especially
opera. and hates school with a vengeance. People are
generally suspicious of young Felix as they were of
Gregorius in The Holy Sinner, and cast dark, contemptuous glances at him.*

However, Felix Krull is atypical in an important
way. As an active participant in the delights of love,
he stands in unique contrast to all the passive suf-
ferers who rarely did more than look on at life from
a safe distance. Felix's frenzied frolic in Madame
Diane Philibert Houpflé's boudoir and his eager enjoy-

---

*The resort Bad Langenschwallbach is to him what
Travemünde is to Hanno Buddenbrook. Felix Krull resembles Adrian Leverkühn of Doctor Faustus in his rejection of and distaste for anything which smacks of
the coarse and the off-color. His change of name, to
Armand Kroull, is comparable to the actions of Joseph
in Joseph and His Brothers and Gregorius in The Holy
Sinner, and like Joseph, he becomes a servant in a
great house (Hotel Saint James and Albany) in which an
obvious mother-figure, Madame Diane Philibert Houpflé,
ensnares him in a frenzy of passion. This woman, artistic and wealthy and whose husband is by implication impotent, reminds us of Mann's earliest stories. But
there are other refrains as well. The hero's ability
to feign sickness can be assumed to represent an extension of the typical, for it reveals him to be more
than usually interested in illness. His playing at
sickness when he simulates epilepsy before the military
suggests Joseph's trancelike behavior in the moonlight
before the well; his audience with the King of Portugal
recalls Axel Martini's conversation with Klaus Heinrich
in Royal Highness; and the impression he makes on roy-
alty is very much like Joseph's on the pharaoh.

ment with the prostitute Rosza have no parallel in all
of Mann's works for pure sexual excitement, free of
morbidity and perversion. One must go back to the
author's earliest literary effort, Fallen, to find a
descriptive account of sexuality between man and woman.
It is a striking fact that only on the pages of his
first work in 1894 and his last, sixty years later,
did Mann depict a consummation of heterosexual passion.
This fact may then contribute to the explanation of
why he delayed his composition of Felix Krull. He
broke off work on this novel in 1911 to turn to Death
in Venice and again in 1952 to begin The Black Swan.

In order to motivate his hero's behavior convincingly and to portray accurately a criminal roué capable
of evoking sympathy from the reader, Mann needed to
characterize him less rigidly than he did the repressed
heroes who preceded; moreover, his own conscience and
values had to be brought into line with artistic considerations. Only if perfunctorily concerned about the
dangers of his instincts and only if partially endowed
with a mordant conscience, could this hero take chances
in the real world and yet steer a middle course between
icy intellect and fatal eruption in sin. In the Rosza
and Houpflé episodes, for example, the hero has to ac-
quit himself in a virile manner without the usual destructive aspects and associations with death being
present. We draw support for this view from Wolff:
"Observed in itself the Diane-Philibert-episode is only
a comic satirical insertion, but it is significant when
seen from the biographical perspective because out of
it developed the narrative Death in Venice in the early
period and the theme of The Black Swan in the late period."[31] It was only at the age of seventy-nine that
Thomas Mann completed this work that was begun so long
ago and strangely enough, it was only at this advanced
age that he dared show such great relish for the details
of the sexual act.

When we spoke of the mellowing effect of old age
in conjunction with The Black Swan and The Holy Sinner,
we forwarded the assumption that Mann's repressive
forces were waning and that he was therefore able to
soften his position on the direct expression of his
emotions. Yet in Felix Krull as in the past, Mann is
not totally delivered from his conscience. Despite his
hero's fabulous success with women, the author reveals
that Felix Krull still harbors a modicum of reservation
about sex:

I have often indulged in excesses, for the
flesh is weak and I found the world all too
ready to satisfy my amorous requirements.
But in the end and on the whole I was of
too manly and serious a temper not to return
from sensual relaxation to a necessary and
healthful austerity. . . . For my part I
know many kinds of satisfactions finer and
more subtle than this crude act which is
after all but a limited and illusory satisfaction of an appetite; and I am convinced
that he has but a coarse notion of enjoyment whose activities are directed point-
blank to that goal alone.[32]

At the end of the novel, however, we discern the
familiar link between death and the sexual: during the
gory slaughter of the bullfight, Felix Krull's fiery
passion for Madame Kuckuck and her surging bosom is
kindled--a reminder that Mann cannot let his hero live
without his thoughts darkened by reflection, for the
author still, as Idris Parry notes, distrusts his instincts as the path to license.[33] But Felix Krull is
not even really free enough to be considered a Bohemian,
despite his apparent lack of conscience. He makes very
few friends, builds a protective wall of urbanity around
himself, and cultivates contact only with people of
distinction. Possessed by a drive for cleanliness,
inclined to sartorial perfection and distressed by overstimulation through coffee, he presents to the world the
very opposite of the undisciplined and ill-kempt dissolute. He is a natural gentleman in every sense of
the word. Despite the book's title, he scarcely resembles a criminal, but possesses on the contrary more
than his share of virtue: he obtains extreme satisfaction in giving money to the poor and has a kind word for
his fellow passenger or the man on the street. He does
not try to succeed at all costs, refusing to take advantage of the immature Miss Twentyman and disapproving
of the behavior of Lord Kilmarnock despite the possibilities of glory which the latter was prepared to bestow
on him.

To Elizabeth M. Wilkinson, Felix Krull is the story
of an artist without a medium: "Unable to give vent to
his artistic impulses in creation, he lets them run amok
into destruction and crime."[34] Yet, when we take a close
look at Felix Krull, we find that his criminal tendencies
are at most only a slight extension of a bad conscience.

Felix Krull does not really set store by swindling.
As a confidence man there is a singular lack of greed
in him. Though he steals the jewelry box from Madame
Houpflé, his theft was more a matter of momentary temptation than calculated robbery for he is even willing
to face ruin when he makes amends by confessing to his
deed. He is scrupulously fair in dealing with his shady
companion Stanko, considering the latter's attempt to
take advantage of him. Felix certainly possesses honor
above and beyond the code of most thieves when he vol-
unteers to place his fortune as security for assuming
the role of the Marquis de Venosta from whom he obtains
no material advantage from his impersonation. His
crimes are in fact of minor significance and are in
some measure directed only against some impersonal,
petty authority. The forgery of his father's signature
in order to play truant from school, the stealing of
candy as a boy, and his hoodwinking of the recruiting
officers are hardly enough to stamp him as a man with
criminal tendencies. At worst he is a boudoir thief,
but ultimately he is less a fraud than an astounding
personality who, almost God-like, lives in a somewhat
narcissistic self-made world of make-believe. Paul
Altenberg states that Felix Krull became a swindler as
a matter of conviction and stands outside the moral
law,[35] but he overlooks the fact that the hero's father,
who attempts to defraud the public with bad champagne,
is really more culpable in a criminal sense than Felix.

Though the hero writes his memoirs from jail, one
must wonder what put him there, and at the end we are
still not convinced of Felix Krull's improbity. His conscience and sense of propriety are still too much in
force to permit him to be less than kind to people de-
serving of consideration. His criminality, then, if
anything, would therefore appear to be more the fruit
of his imagination than a heinous violation of a physical law. He certainly had no feeling of guilt or remorse from the misdeeds he literally describes, which
he is in every instance able to rationalize away with
ease. The sins which Krull commits simply do not support his claims of having lived a vicious life. In
the relationship of Krull the narrator to Krull the
protagonist there exists a special incongruity in self-
reproaches which are not borne out by the burlesque
and essentially harmless tone of the total work. And
when Krull states at the outset that his frankness in
presenting this story is determined less by vanity than
by a desire to enhance its moral value, he is in reality
confessing to a sense of worthlessness and doubt of

his self and his life--both, one must add, the by-pro-
ducts of a guilty conscience.

Far from being a malefactor, Felix Krull closely
resembles Tonio Kröger, the model of correct manners
and aristocratic aloofness. Even his affairs with
Madame Houpflé and the prostitute Rosza are not out of
keeping with this resemblance. They are paralleled by
Tonio's adventures of the flesh. During his stay in
the South, Tonio descends into the depths of lust and
searing sin and later oscillates between two crass
extremes: icy intellect and scorching excess. The
difference is that in Felix Krull the hero's sexual
escapades assume central importance for the work. And
no less than Felix Krull, Tonio Kröger feels himself
to be a criminal. In fact, branded by an indelible
mark on his brow he acts as if he has a greater burden
to bear than Felix. But in both Tonio and Felix moral
turpitude is hardly an offense against the general public. Each leads an essentially moral life and wins
the acclaim and honor of society. The King of Portugal
is so impressed by Felix Krull that he decorates him
with the Order of the Red Lion, Second Class. In short,
Felix's scruples are especially remarkable considering
his early dissolute environment, for he, like Tonio
Kröger before him, follows a path that leads to an
honorable and socially acceptable vocation. Thus, their
only crime seems to be that they disdain the regular,
middle-class mode of life.

Though Felix Krull is Thomas Mann's most active
and adventurous protagonist, he is hardly an archcrimin-
al. We do not believe his self-accusations and mea
culpa, for his conscience is too strong for him to become truly unprincipled. His desire to hide behind a
role in life as an actor does on stage becomes his modus
vivendi, but, for the most part, his honesty is no more
questionable than that of the majority of his fellow
citizens. In this respect he is the culmination of a
long line of Mannian protagonists with bad consciences
who feel themselves to be heartless evildoers but behave essentially in a most correct manner.

In an interview entitled Return Thomas Mann states
that the final version of Felix Krull went in experience
and fullness beyond its original conception to become
a Bildungsroman.[36] This designation, however, must be
qualified. Felix Krull undergoes less of an inward
change after he goes to Paris than before--in that part

of the novel which was written first. He does grow
somewhat with his boyhood experiences, but what he
learns as an adult does not in the least transform a
basic attitude of narcissism that only becomes more
fully entrenched and almost autistic.

Afterwards, all emphasis is on the make-believe;
and Krull succeeds in making the world into a fairy
story so successful that the element of personal danger
is removed and he can emerge superior in every situation. There is little that he cannot do. He learns
a foreign language in a flash, draws like a finished
artist the first time he holds a brush, instinctively
charms a king, chooses the right wine, and even plays
a commendable game of tennis in his first encounter
with the sport. Krull is playing an imaginary role
which has somehow, by magic wish, turned into reality.
Somehow the gods favor him and allow him to become
more simply a person with a golden touch for he is
mechanically perfect and lacks even those flaws which
usually characterize one as human. Relying totally
on omnipotence of thought, he projects the wishes of
an infantile psyche into a world of his own making.
Consequently, all goes as he wants it: his education
is complete almost as soon as it begins, and he may
continue to adhere to a prescribed ethical code which
was his at the outset.

Considering Krull's conspicuous abundance of mental
reservations in dealing with others, we must question
Paul Altenberg's decision to classify this work on the
basis of "Humanity,"[37] and indeed, the question may
justifiably be asked if this term can be in any way
applied to the case of Felix Krull. The god-like protagonist of this novel is not liable for his actions,
which even in themselves are usually evaluated only in
terms of appearance. In addition he changes his name
in order to further obscure his identity and facilitate
his withdrawal from the ties of responsibility and to
cut himself off from his bourgeois past. His potent
narcissism provides him with a safe world, where he can
maintain his distance from others and yet continue to
play a role in a world of appearances.

Felix Krull is certainly a darling of the gods and,
as Mann himself points out, a man of innate merits, who
feels himself superior and distinguished from birth and
who makes every effort to correct his humble social
position by bringing it into harmony with his aristocratic soul.[38] The hero's drive to be an aristocrat

is essentially the prime mover of the novel in which the hero's inborn superiority becomes the most consistent leitmotif.

But, as we discussed the problem before, Mann's scheme recognizes the aristocratic principle as a commitment to death, which, in turn, opposes the democratic principle of life. Like the aristocratic bearing of Goethe in The Beloved Returns and Rosalie's longing for the aristocratic black swans, the hero of Felix Krull reveals in his striving for the aristocratic a disguised death-wish, an attitude which, as the product of a guilty mind, seriously detracts from any claim of humanity in his values or genuine nobility of his thoughts. Of course, one might counter, the hero comes to the defense of love when he contradicts Zouzou's hyperprudish commentary:

> However fair and smooth the skin,
> Stench and corruption lie within.
> (VII, 633)

But Felix Krull's answer to these morbid lines is less an inspired sermon on the beauties of life and the joy of living than an exercise in eloquence.

Long before the novel ends with Krull's final tryst with Zouzou, where her mother arrives to take, subsequently, the daughter's place in the love affair, we saw that the mother was in fact the hidden fixation and ultimate goal of his passion. We recall that even before his eloquent defense of love, he saw less appeal in Zouzou alone than he did in the combination of mother and daughter and that it was the mother who held the greater attraction for him at the blood ritual of the bullfight. Again the coexistence of symbolic slaughter with a forbidden attraction places a decisive onus on the hero. A taboo sexual relationship has its excitement, but for the Mannian hero its prohibitions and threats of retribution far outweigh any tender emotions that should evolve in a natural love relationship. Felix Krull, as other Mannian protagonists before him, ends his story by making a choice which can only succeed in compounding and intensifying his guilt. The real object of his desires is, as in previous stories, the forbidden wife of another rather than an unattached woman of his own age with whom one could normally devel-

op a genuine and meaningful relationship.* Again there
is no lasting affection nor full investment of the personality. Again, too, the hero has little recourse but
to confuse gratification with love.

Mann considered <u>Felix Krull</u> to be one of the best
things he ever wrote, and the general opinion is that
the author succeeded very well indeed with this novel.
Sections of it certainly have real force. Wolff, for
example, calls the military induction scene the best
farce ever written by Mann. It is certainly not in-
accurate to state that the strength of this work can
be explained by its vivid expression of the senses.
After a lifetime of reticence and reserve Mann breaks
out of his shell in <u>Felix Krull</u> and largely allows his
feelings to run their course unencumbered by verbiage.
This last book is in many respects still similar to
his first work, <u>Fallen</u>, for both possess a "felt" quality, something not found in other works that lacked
either the enthusiasm of youth or the mellowness of
high old age.

Because of the abrupt end of <u>Felix Krull</u>, the novel
gives the appearance of being a fragment. But actually
this work represents the full circle of completeness.
For such a scrupulously honest and correct swindler and
moralist as Felix Krull, it became only a matter of a
short time before Thomas Mann had fully plumbed the
depths of his hero's so-called criminality. To have
continued to describe his protagonist's escapades on a
tour of the world, would only have resulted in a pointless repetition and a piling up of dubious adventures.
And so in reality the novel had to terminate in the way
it did. With <u>Felix Krull</u> Mann does indeed make a full
circle, one befitting the author's last creative effort. He has his hero descend from his aristocratic

---

*In the sensuous and exotic "mother" of Latin
extraction, Madame Houpflé, we recognize a number of
familiar refrains. Her name, Diane Philibert, which
she as an authoress uses as a <u>nom de plume</u>, is associated in French history with aristocratic licentiousness
(Diane) and political reaction (Philibert) and contrasts
with the prosaic name of the impotent businessman she
has married, the toilet manufacturer Houplfé.

sphere into the middle-class world of Professor Kuckuck whose name is etymologically connected with cuckoo (a bird that lays its eggs in the nests of other birds) and, by extension, with cuckold--the fate in store for the Professor. From the outset Kuckuck appears to be more than a casual acquaintance on the train to Lisbon; a feeling of paternal acceptance emanates from the Professor who already knows a great deal about the personal life and family history of the Marquis de Venosta (the name assumed by Felix Krull). He finds it natural that he should bring Felix home with him, as if he were indeed a member of his family. Thus, it is certainly not by accident that Felix Krull seeks out and finds the imposing maternal figure, Madame Kuckuck of Lisbon. And it now takes no real imagination on the part of the reader to bridge the gap in geography from Portugal to Brazil, the home of the author's mother. The very last lines of Thomas Mann's very last work show the hero passionately clinging to the enormous bosom of the Portuguese-speaking mother, thus realizing a wish that was manifested in Mann's earliest works and one which, in no uncertain terms, threw its long shadow over all his writings.

CONCLUSION

Thomas Mann's works can be viewed as a remarkable personal confession, a kind of vast autobiography which chronicles his artistic genius at the same time it exposes his fascination with the Oedipal theme. Consequently, Mann's writing reflects a fixed preoccupation with incest, parricide, and subsequent feelings of guilt. Protagonists whose psyche is essentially inelastic, whose locus in society is stationary, and whose basic attitudes remain undeveloped, are neatly pinned and held fast by an inescapable pattern of guilt, and are compelled always to act and react in accordance with the terms of a rigorous conscience.

Guilt, more than any other single factor, constitutes the central unity of the works of Thomas Mann. And since guilt is a constant burden, the behavior of its possessor is characterized by a perpetual need to find some reprieve from the heavy imposition of conscience, even if that release must be obtained at the cost of life itself. There is scarcely a protagonist in Mann's works who does not long for death or at least for punishment that mortifies the flesh for the sake of psychic gratification. Punishment and defeat are therefore the real goals for the Mannian hero because they dull the edge of the unconscious pain generated in the conflict between severe repression and emotional release. The surface result is compulsive control or "frigid art" which functions as a firm container to hold craving and desire in check, to prevent open exposure to people and life, and to define a restricted area for the self-inflicted torture of exhausting work.

Because Mann's stock in trade is the eternal triangle, the range in his themes is consequently extremely narrow. He dispenses with elaborate plots, pressing social problems, and consistent development of character to concentrate on the tormented psyche of his hero. Gustav von Aschenbach, for example, merely takes a trip to Venice where he then passively gazes at the people around him. Very little really happens to his vegetative heroes unless it is a sudden paroxysm of futility and rage. In fact, Mann focuses essentially on the artist who needs to seek out and eliminate his Oedipal non-artistic rival-enemy while yearning for a woman who is unattainable, or, perhaps, not a "real" woman in any sense of the word: "There is no woman who holds the interest because of positive, spiritual greatness, none who inspires through self-sacrifice, renunciation, or the triumph of a pioneering, independent spirit."[1] The Mannian hero's love affair is morganatic, one which resembles a rigged game, vouchsafed by rules of distance and reserve. There is no give-and-take involvement between lovers, no sense of wonderment at the multihued spectrum of love and life. Women hold no immediate attraction for him at all unless they form an integral part of the incest-parricide relationship. As a result, his claims of affection are flimsy and superficial and his needs immediate and compelling, for the protagonist is motivated by fear as well as by libido, by power and domination more than by tender concern.

One who cannot love without calling forth destructive urges must in spite of all protestations and subterfuges be possessed in all things by inner doubts and a sense of worthlessness. In the words of Sigmund Freud: "A man who doubts his own love may, or rather must, doubt every lesser thing."[2] The Mannian hero's doubt of himself leads him to question the whole world; he is compelled to see the world on the verge of dissolution. Thus, when Thomas Mann remarked that Buddenbrooks represented the end of a bourgeois era, he was in effect telling us the theme of every one of his works. Since the existing social system or age represents the world constructed by the father, Mann's theme of bourgeois decay is in reality his triumph over the father. The projected decline of the paternal family or the age it stands for, the imposed end of vitality and robustness become in essence the weakling hero's revenge on the healthy law-givers of life, those who do not doubt life but enjoy it. The "end of an era" is therefore rooted to the death-wish and gives the lie to the often cited statement of Hans Castorp, for example, that whoever is interested in death is particularly interested in life.

As we look back at Mann's works, we see that they unfold in a receding line. His first and most emotional work, Fallen, the stories which immediately follow, and his first novel, Buddenbrooks, are all characterized by a youthful intensity. But with the passage of time, Mann refrains from letting his protagonist express feelings directly or protects him from emotionally laden situations. Using irony and diverse stylistic devices, Mann succeeds in making a virtue out of retreat from genuine passion. The culmination of this tendency is crystallized in the novel Doctor Faustus. Here Mann inserts an intermediary to tell his story in order to reduce the immediate vitality in a work that has already been reduced emotionally to zero grade by the dehumanized hero himself. Only at the end of his career does Mann make a gesture to recover some of the spontaneity of the early works but without much success.

Though the subject matter remains the same, a change of focus does take place in Tonio Kröger. Tonio Kröger is Mann's first mature hero, a famous, successful, and stoically dedicated artist who stands in marked contrast to the earlier restless, misfit heroes. With only minor exceptions he becomes the model for all subsequent protagonists. Henceforth the ironical hero achieves distance from threatening situations by assuming a superior role, by majestically beckoning the world to him instead of investing himself in it. Though the pose and posture are different, the needs remain the same.

Tonio Kröger also stands at the beginning of the hero's development into the role of "king" in the classic pattern of the mythical folk hero. As Mann progresses, his hero turns into a respected man of letters and then into a ruler of the people (Frederick the Great), and finally he becomes practically a god in Joseph and in The Holy Sinner. But here in this last work, too, we learn from the author the underlying reason for the near deification of the hero: "He [Clemens] too probably had an inkling that incest was a privileged taboo, permitted gods and kings and forbidden only to the common herd. . . ."[3]

In Tonio Kröger one finds also the first of a series of claims of love for life which are, however, repeatedly disproved by the actions of the heroes. But the more the author reiterates the love of life claim, the more suspect the avowal becomes. There would be no need for repeated confessions of love if the antipathy towards life were really overcome. The fact remains that the instinctually conditioned doubt recurs again and again and with it the compulsion to nullify it, if only by solemn pronouncements, which in turn become the refrain of loving life. Thomas Mann's big smokescreen is precisely this affection for life, but considering the heroes' morbid predilections and omnipresent death-wish, we are forced to conclude that the author's hatred towards life is more convincing than his professed love for it. Mann's antagonism is only slightly modified--if at all--in his later works, and so the claim that they represent a new found feeling

for humanity is also exposed as hollow and untenable.
This is strikingly demonstrated by the Mannian hero's
overwhelming relationship to music which excludes for
the author the possibility of an open acceptance of
humanity. The "musicality of the German soul" which
permeates all of Mann's heroes in one form or another
from the very first turns the protagonist inward and
away from the life experience, whereas the democratic
approach to life is, according to Mann, not musical
and rules out the artist hero's education in terms of
human relationships and personal maturation. Because
democracy is based on the premise of equality and fraternity of people, two concepts that Mann's superior
heroes could never subscribe to, the author's so-called
conversion to democracy therefore never took place.
Nowhere do we find an unqualified love for life, commitment to humanity, or engagement in democracy on
the part of either Mann or his protagonists. And since
the so-called conversions did not take place in Mann's
development as an artist, then one must conclude that
he sustained an original mental set throughout his
works, that all his works are variations on the same
theme, and that there can be, in other words, no place
for the concept of the Bildungsroman in the whole scope
of his writings. With the creation of Hanno Buddenbrook
and the earliest heroes the author had already cast
the mold and model for all subsequent protagonists:
"As early as 1900 his [Thomas Mann's] last works, Doctor
Faustus and Felix Krull were already there in his head
practically finished. For him the only question was
when would he get round to writing them down. He did
not use all his plans, but whatever plans he did use
in his work came from his youth, and one thing led on
to the next."[4]

    Imperative for an understanding of the last half
of Mann's creative life is the Observations of a Non-
Political Man. The author was already middle-aged
when he wrote this diatribe; it was therefore no quixotic and haphazard outburst, but rather a sustained
expression of his most interior convictions. We have
traced his attitude through World War II and have seen
that Mann was unable to give up many of the precious
and passionate ideas he held back in 1914-1918; the
fury of the Observations compels us to cast further
doubt on a metamorphosis in his approach and beliefs.
Despite the critics' views, Mann did not become a
liberal in politics. He never changed his outlook,
and any modification he claimed or implied actually
conformed to the past in a remarkable way.

Mann stood for the "good German" during the dark period of National Socialism when the word German became such an anathema to the West. Because he was forced to take a stand on the side of the West, he became the most important cultural name that the West could salvage from the Germany of the thirties. Eventually a cult developed around Thomas Mann which hindered later critics from looking at him and his works with a more discriminating eye, for when criticism turns in large part to reverence and praise, it tends to overlook basic truths and obvious weaknesses. Religious and Marxian interpretations especially have led to literary sociology where the grand and sweeping statement replaces a sober and precise look at the work and glosses over its textual content.

Many critics, unable to appreciate or apprehend the punishment refrain in Mann's early short tales, have neglected them or have made short shrift of them in their interpretations. Yet, in many respects these shorter works are more impressive than the long fictional creations. They, more than the thick novels, reflect the genius of an author who is at bottom a psychological writer. The characterizations of the heroes of these early tales are sure and true, and the protagonists there do not exist as abstractions or as bearers of the ironic temperament but come alive in all their frustrations and agony. They illustrate in a remarkable way the most modern views on depth psychology and show a precise correlation between the hero's passions and his crippling inhibitions. Thomas Mann instinctively possessed a deep understanding of his heroes' problems, their need to come to terms with their basic drives, their inability to master their inner problem, their compulsion to serve blindly and pitilessly the caprice of their conscience, and the accurate and subtle rationalizations by which they protected themselves. One could go so far as to say that Thomas Mann, intuitively closer to the theories of Sigmund Freud in his early tales than later in his career, demonstrated there as profound an understanding of psychology as any writer of his time.

Our study began on the close resemblance between the values and attitudes of the author with those of his heroes, and our progressive analysis of the hero's guilty actions confirms that there is an even deeper and more intense personal connection between the author and his creations than one might at first suspect.

Writing was for Thomas Mann more than a creative process in the service of the aesthetic, but something
closer to redemption through atonement. It represented
an agonizing self-appraisal as well as the most intimate
expression of the self. To say that his works are
strongly autobiographical is insufficient, for what
really characterizes them is an emotional outpouring
of the self similar to a patient's most personal revela-
tions to his psychiatrist. The recurrent autobiographical features, Mann's critical statements regarding his
own works, and his later repudiation of some of them,
make it clear that he felt he exposed perhaps too much
of himself in his leading figures; but at the same time,
Mann's virtuosity in divulging, unconsciously for the
most part, the mechanism of guilt and repression in an
artistic format and elevated style communicates to the
reader a great deal about the creative process--the
bent of mind that can so facilely split off, multiply,
and play off images in a dramatic fashion. In tracing
along the circular but fascinating paths which Mann
laid out in his literary outpouring of fantasy, the
reader may also cherish this remarkable personal confession which accurately records his deepest attitudes
towards the processes of life and death.

NOTES

Chapter I: THE PATTERN OF GUILT

[1] Erika and Klaus Mann, "Portrait of Our Father," The Stature of Thomas Mann, ed. Charles Neider (New York: New Directions, 1947), p. 69. Hereafter cited as STM.

[2] Bilse and I (1906), Thomas Mann, Collected Works in Twelve Volumes (Oldenburg: S. Fischer, 1960), X, 22. Nearly all citations from Mann's writings, unless otherwise stated, are to this collection as Works plus the date and volume number.

[3] On "Royal Highness" (1910), Works, XI, 571.

[4] Chamisso (1911), Works, IX, 54.

[5] Thomas Mann: Sein Leben und sein Werk (Berlin: S. Fischer, 1925), p. 12.

[6] Arthur Burkhard, "Thomas Mann's Appraisal of the Poet," PMLA, 46 (1931), 883-89.

[7] Brother Hitler (1939), Works, XII, 848.

[8] See Burkhard, PMLA, 46, 880-881; William Valentine Glebe, "The Relationship Between Art and Disease in the Works of Thomas Mann," diss. University of Washington 1959, p. 8; Ferdinand Lion, Thomas Mann: Leben und Werk (Zurich: Oprecht, 1947), p. 39; Charles Neider, "The Artist as Bourgeois," STM, pp. 352-55.

[9] Peter Heller, "Thomas Mann's Conception of the Creative Writer," PMLA, 69, 774.

[10] ibid., 780.

[11] Lion, p. 39.

[12] See Henry Hatfield, Thomas Mann (Norfolk, Conn.: New Directions, 1951), p. 33. See also Hermann Kesten, "Works and Deeds," STM, p. 24; Ludwig Lewisohn, "Death in Venice," STM, p. 125.

[13] Burkhard, PMLA, 46, 880.

[14] Willy Tappolet, "Das Problem des Künstlers bei Thomas Mann," Schweizerische Pädagogische Zeitschrift, 31 (1921), 146.

[15] Thomas Mann: Der Dichter und der Schriftsteller (Berlin: Wiegandt and Grieben, 1927), p. 22. See also Jean Fougère, Thomas Mann oder die Magie des Todes (Baden-Baden: Hans Bühler Jr., 1948), pp. 7 and 37.

[16] Gerhart Piers and Milton B. Singer, Shame and Guilt (Springfield, Ill.: Thomas, 1953), pp. 5-6.

[17] ibid., p. 5.

[18] The Complete Psychological Works of Sigmund Freud, Standard ed. (London: Hogarth, 1961), 19, 166. Hereafter cited by volume number.

[19] Ives Hendrick, Facts and Theories of Psychoanalysis, 3rd ed. (New York: A. Knopf, 1958), p. 77.

[20] Freud, Three Essays on the Theory of Sexuality, 7, 158.

[21] ibid., p. 159.

[22] Cf. Freud, Totem and Taboo, 13, 29.

[23] See ibid., 13, 159-60.

[24] ibid., p. 87.

[25] Hendrick, p. 26.

[26] The Infant Prodigy (1903), Works, VIII, 346.

[27] An Elementary Textbook of Psychoanalysis (New York: International Universities Press, 1955), p. 121.

[28] Schopenhauer (1938), Works, IX, 574.

[29] Monika Mann, "Papa," STM, p. 80.

[30] Bruno Walter, "Recollections of Thomas Mann," STM, p. 105.

[31] ibid., pp. 104-05.

[32] Monika Mann, STM, p. 80.

[33] See The Book Closest to My Heart (1954), Works, XI, 686-87.

[34] "Die Kunst Thomas Manns," Zeitschrift für deutsche Bildung (Frankfort on the Main), 1 (1925), 108-09.

[35] Communication to the Bonn Literary Society (1906), Works, XI, 716-17.

[36] The Last Year of Thomas Mann (New York: Farrar, Straus and Cudahy, 1958), p. 10.

[37] ibid., p. 33.

Chapter II: BUDDENBROOKS

[1] Hans Eichner, Thomas Mann (Berne: Francke, 1953), p. 12.

[2] Frank Donald Hirschbach, The Arrow and the Lyre (The Hague: M. Nijhoff, 1955), p. 41.

[3] Buddenbrooks (1901), Works, I, 747-50.

[4] R. Hinton Thomas, Thomas Mann (Oxford: Clarendon Press, 1956), p. 43.

[5] Works, XI, 394.

[6] Works, XI, 111. In 1918 Mann also makes this claim in his Observations of a Non-Political Man (Works, XII, 72), and as late as 1954 he includes Thomas Buddenbrook, while omitting Hanno, from a list of his heroes: Gustav von Aschenbach, Hans Castorp, Joseph, Goethe, and Adrian Leverkühn; see The Book Closest to My Heart (Works, XI, 686).

[7] Works, IX, 559.

[8] Hatfield, p. 32.

[9] See Thomas Mann: A Study (London: Secker, 1933), pp. 23-24. The name Bilse refers to the pseudonym of an obscure writer of the time who indiscreetly and transparently portrayed prominent persons and acquaintances in his novel.

[10] Works, XI, 380-81.

[11] Preface to a Recording of "Buddenbrooks" (1940), Works, XI, 550.

[12] Works, XI, 113.

[13] Lübeck as an Intellectual Way of Life, Works, XI, 380.

[14] Paul Scherrer, "Bruchstücke der Buddenbrooks-Urhandschrift und Zeugnisse zu ihrer Entstehung, 1897-1901," NRs, 69 (1958), 273.

[15] See ibid., pp. 276-277.

[16] Alfred Kantorowicz, Heinrich und Thomas Mann (Berlin: Aufbau, 1956), p. 66.

[17] See Kantorowicz, p. 65; see also Works, XI, 550.

[18] Kantorowicz, p. 76.

[19] Golo Mann, "Memories of My Father," Inter Nationes (Bonn, 1965), p. 4.

[20] See Eloesser, p. 22.

[21] Hatfield, pp. 32-33.

[22] Wir waren fünf: Bildnis der Familie Mann (Konstanz: Südverlag, 1949), pp. 20ff. Referred to in this study as There Were Five of Us.

[23] Portrait of My Mother (1930), Works, XI, 420.

[24] Erich Heller, The Ironic German (London: Secker and Warburg, 1958), p. 45.

[25] Eichner, p. 10.

26 loc. cit.

27 Hans M. Wolff, Thomas Mann: Werk und Bekenntnis (Berne: Francke, 1957), p. 19.

28 Hatfield, p. 48.

29 Wolff, pp. 22-23.

30 ibid., p. 20.

31 Max Lorenz, "Buddenbrooks," Preußische Jahrbücher, 110 (1902), 151.

Chapter III: THOMAS MANN'S PYRRHIC VICTORS

1 See James Cleugh, pp. 77-78; Hans Eichner, p. 18; Hans M. Wolff, p. 14. The only detailed discussion of these works, that of Martin Havenstein, dates from the nineteen-twenties, but often his remarks reflect no more than personal prejudices; e.g., in reference to the novella Little Lizzie he says: "I do not know at all what I am to make of this scandalous story, told with such admirable art" (p. 153).

2 Henry Hatfield finds fault with those critics who see only the problem of the outcast artist figure in these tales: "The basic contrast between the isolated individual and the normal majority is easy enough to grasp; and if one focuses on it, the tendency is to reduce all the narratives to a rather wearying monotony, to accuse Mann of repetitiousness or even of sterility. Clearly, the fault lies more in the interpreters than in the author" (p. 14).

3 See Hans Eichner and Hans M. Wolff; see also Roger Nicholls, "Nietzsche in the Early Works of Thomas Mann," UCPMP, 45 (1955).

4 Frederick J. Beharriell is an exception, but he has not analyzed them in detail or as literature per se, but has regarded them from the standpoint of their anticipation of Sigmund Freud's theories. "Psychology in the Early Works of Thomas Mann," PMLA, 77, (March, 1962), 149-55.

5 In essence, critics have failed to apply in a literal way Mann's own criticism of these stories. In his Observations of a Non-Political Man (1918) he says that in these works he was a "chronicler and commentator of decadence, a lover of the pathological and death, and an aesthete with inclinations towards the abyss" (XII, 153).

6 A Short Account of Psycho-Analysis, 19, 200. The work which dealt directly with an explanation of masochism, Three Essays on the Theory of Sexuality, was published in 1905, two years after Thomas Mann wrote Tristan and Tonio Kröger.

[7] Beharriell, pp. 150-55.

[8] Gladius Dei (1902), Works, VIII, 214.

[9] Fiorenza (1905), Works, VIII, 1067.

[10] Nicholls, p. 50; Hatfield, p. 23.

[11] Kantorowicz, p. 61.

[12] Cleugh, p. 105.

[13] Nicholls, pp. 10-11.

[14] Havenstein, p. 151.

[15] Revenged (1899), Works, VIII, 166-67.

[16] Nicholls, p. 10; Wolff, p. 13; Hirschbach, p. 26.

[17] The Will to Happiness (1896), Works, VIII, 47.

[18] Tobias Mindernickel (1898), Works, VIII, 141.

[19] Fallen (1894), Works, VIII, 40.

[20] See Erich Ebermayer, "Thomas Manns Jugendnovelle Gefallen," Die Literatur, 27 (1925), 459-61; Wolff, p. 12; Eloesser, pp. 51-53; Hatfield, p. 13; Hirschbach, pp. 4-5.

[21] loc. cit.

[22] Wolff, pp. 12-13; Nicholls, p. 13.

[23] loc. cit.

[24] Disillusionment (1896), Works, VIII, 66.

[25] Little Lizzie (1900), Works, VIII, 180.

[26] The Wardrobe (1899), Works, VIII, 160.

[27] PMLA, 77, 154.

[28] ibid., p. 153.

[29] Death (1897), Works, VIII, 74.

[30] The Clown (1897), Works, VIII, 138.

[31] Tristan (1903), Works, VIII, 244-47.

[32] Wolff, p. 32.

[33] Hatfield, p. 19.

[34] Cleugh, p. 105.

[35] Hirschbach, p. 11.

[36] Introduction to a text edition of Tonio Kröger (Oxford: Blackwell, 1944), p. xv.

[37] Introduction to a text edition of <u>Tristan</u> (Boston: Ginn and Company, 1960), p. x.

Chapter IV: THE REPRESSIVE OUTLOOK: FROM TONIO KRÖGER TO DEATH IN VENICE

[1] <u>The Hungry</u> (1903), <u>Works</u>, VIII, 266.

[2] Kantorowicz, pp. 63-64.

[3] Heller, p. 68.

[4] Wolff, p. 34.

[5] <u>Tonio Kröger</u> (1903), <u>Works</u>, VIII, 337.

[6] Cleugh, p. 98.

[7] Heller, p. 70.

[8] Hirschbach, p. 15.

[9] <u>The Infant Prodigy</u> (1903), <u>Works</u>, VIII, 341.

[10] <u>A Gleam</u> (1904), <u>Works</u>, VIII, 356.

[11] <u>At the Prophet's</u> (1904), <u>Works</u>, VIII, 362.

[12] Wolff, p. 41.

[13] <u>A Weary Hour</u> (1905), <u>Works</u>, VIII, 375-76.

[14] <u>The Blood of the Walsungs</u> (1906), <u>Works</u>, VIII, 388.

[15] Hirschbach, p. 10.

[16] Wolff, p. 42.

[17] See Curt Moreck, "Eine Novelle Thomas Manns und ihre Geschichte," <u>WuW</u>, 5 (June 1950), 236.

[18] <u>ibid</u>., p. 235.

[19] <u>A Sketch of My Life</u> (1930), <u>Works</u>, XI, 117.

[20] <u>The Railway Accident</u> (1909), <u>Works</u>, VIII, 419.

[21] Wolff, p. 43.

[22] <u>A Sketch of My Life</u>, <u>Works</u>, XI, 118.

[23] On "Royal Highness," <u>Works</u>, XI, 570.

[24] <u>loc. cit.</u>

[25] <u>Observations of a Non-Political Man</u>, <u>Works</u>, XII, 96-97.

[26] <u>Works</u>, XI, 570.

[27] <u>Observations of a Non-Political Man</u>, <u>Works</u>, XII, 96.

[28] Wolff, pp. 30-31.

[29] Royal Highness (1909), Works, II, 25.

[30] Paul Scherrer and Hans Wysling, Quellenkritische Studien zum Werk Thomas Manns (Berne: Francke, 1967), p. 35.

[31] Viktor Mann, pp. 195-200.

[32] The Fight Between Jappe and Do Escobar (1911), Works, VIII, 432.

[33] "Death in Venice," STM, p. 138.

[34] Hirschbach, pp. 17-18.

[35] See Hirschbach, p. 21; Wolff, pp. 46-50; Heller, pp. 98-99; Eichner, p. 44.

[36] Death in Venice (1912), Works, VIII, 452.

[37] Wolff, p. 50.

[38] "'Death in Venice' by Thomas Mann: A Story about the Disintegration of Artistic Sublimation," Psychoanalytic Quarterly, 26 (1957), 220-21.

[39] Thomas, pp. 65-68.

[40] Heller, p. 107.

Chapter V: THE ARISTOCRATIC BEARING

[1] Observations of a Non-Political Man, Works, XII, 66.

[2] Klaus Mann, The Turning Point (New York: L. B. Fischer, 1942), pp. 38-39.

[3] Heller, pp. 117-18.

[4] Hatfield, p. 65.

[5] Thoughts in War (1914) in Das Thomas Mann-Buch, ed. Michael Mann (Hamburg: Fischer Bücherei, 1965), p. 82. Hereafter cited as T.i.W. This article was not included in Thomas Mann's collected works.

[6] Letter to Count Hermann Keyserling (1920), Works, XII, 595.

[7] Klaus Mann, p. 8.

[8] See After-Dinner Speech in Amsterdam (1924), Works, XI, 354.

[9] T.i.W., pp. 83-84.

[10] ibid., p. 85.

[11] loc. cit.

[12] T.i.W., p. 89.

[13] ibid., p. 86.

[14] Frederick and the Grand Coalition (1915), Works, X, 113.

[15] Heller, p. 122.

[16] A Man and His Dog (1919), Works, VIII, 554.

[17] Disorder and Early Sorrow (1925), Works, VIII, 648.

Chapter VI: AN INTERNAL TRIANGLE: THE MAGIC MOUNTAIN

[1] See Hatfield, p. 68.

[2] Thomas Mann's Novel "Der Zauberberg" (New York: Appleton-Century, 1933), pp. 3-12.

[3] Heller, p. 191.

[4] A History of the German Novelle (Cambridge: Cambridge University Press, 1949), p. 245.

[5] The Magic Mountain (1924), Works, III, 890-92.

[6] Weigand, p. 20.

[7] Works, XII, 575.

[8] ibid., p. 580.

[9] Hirschbach, p. 70.

[10] Introduction to "The Magic Mountain" (1939), Works, XI, 602-03.

[11] Weigand, p. 75.

[12] Hirschbach, p. 69.

[13] ibid., pp. 58-59.

[14] Wolff, p. 57; Weigand, p. 97.

[15] Weigand, p. 13.

[16] Wolff, p. 73.

[17] Thomas, p. 98.

[18] Heller, p. 184.

[19] Introduction to "The Magic Mountain," Works, XI, 612.

[20] Works, II, 88.

[21] UCPMP, 45, 68.

[22] Weigand, p. 111.

[23] Heller, p. 207.

[24] "The Magic Mountain," *STM*, p. 145.

[25] Wolff, p. 73.

[26] Thomas, p. 98.

[27] See *The Story of a Novel* (1949), *Works*, XI, 278; see also *Letter to Gerhart Hauptmann* (1925), *Works*, XI, 597-99.

[28] "Gerhart Hauptmann and Mynheer Peeperkorn," *GLL* N.S., 5 (April, 1952), 164.

[29] *Works*, VIII, 419.

[30] Wolff, p. 73.

[31] Kantorowicz, p. 114.

[32] Weigand, p. 23.

[33] Hirschbach, p. 75.

[34] *ibid.*, pp. 72-73.

[35] Wolff, pp. 62-63.

[36] Hirschbach, p. 78.

[37] Hatfield, p. 85.

[38] "My Brother," *STM*, p. 87.

[39] "Death and Thomas Mann," *STM*, p. 286.

[40] *Introduction to the Magic Mountain*, *Works*, XI, 617; *My Time* (1950), *Works*, XI, 315.

[41] *On the Spirit of Medicine* (1925), *Works*, XI, 595.

[42] *Thomas Mann/Robert Faesi, Correspondence*, ed. Robert Faesi (Zurich: Atlantis, 1962), p. 15. See also *My Time*, *Works*, XI, 315.

[43] Hatfield, p. 70.

[44] Wolff, p. 57.

[45] *The German Novel* (Toronto: University of Toronto Press, 1956), p. 269.

[46] Weigand, p. 5.

[47] Introduction to a text edition of *Tonio Kröger*, p. xvi. See also Hermann Stresau, *Thomas Mann und sein Werk* (Frankfort on the Main: S. Fischer, 1963), p. 131.

[48] Thomas Mann oder die Magie des Todes, p. 42.

[49] Wolff, p. 72.

[50] Thomas Mann an Ernst Bertram (Pfullingen: Neske, 1960),
p. 109

[51] Wolff, p. 63.

[52] My Time, Works, XI, 313.

[53] Letter to Count Hermann Keyserling (1920), Works, XII,
602-03.

[54] Thomas Mann an Ernst Bertram, p. 112.

[55] Culture and Socialism (1928), Works, XII, 639.

[56] Introduction to the Magic Mountain, Works, XI, 610;
A Sketch of My Life, Works, XI, 134.

Chapter VII: JOSEPH AND HIS "FATHERS"

[1] Sixteen Years: Foreword to the American Edition of
"Joseph and His Brothers" in One Volume (1948), Works, XI, 672.

[2] ibid., p. 671.

[3] Cleugh, p. 202.

[4] "Thomas Mann's Mario und der Zauberer," GR, 21 (1946),
307.

[5] loc. cit.

[6] Mario and the Magician (1930), Works, VIII, 691.

[7] Hatfield, pp. 92-93.

[8] ibid., p. 93.

[9] "Tonio Kröger in Egyptian Dress," NY, July 22, 1944, p. 53.

[10] Joseph and His Brothers (1948), Works, IV, 78-79. The
publication dates of the individual volumes are as follows:
Joseph and His Brothers (1933), Young Joseph (1934), Joseph in
Egypt (1936), and Joseph the Provider (1943).

[11] Thomas Mann in der Epoche seiner Vollendung (Munich:
K. Desch, 1952), p. 74.

[12] Hirschbach, pp. 102-03.

[13] Thomas Manns Roman "Joseph und seine Brüder" (Stockholm:
Bermann-Fischer, 1945), pp. 41-42.

[14] Hatfield, pp. 110-11.

[15] Hamburger, p. 148.

[16] Heller, p. 253.

[17] A Word Beforehand: My "Joseph and His Brothers" (1928), Works, XI, 627; Works, XI, 659.

[18] Hirschbach, p. 91.

[19] Works, IX, 498-99.

[20] Thomas, p. 132.

[21] Hirschbach, p. 26; J. M. Lindsay, Thomas Mann (Oxford: Blackwell, 1954), p. 105; Hatfield, p. 102; Heller, p. 255; STM, p. 87; Arnold Bauer, Thomas Mann (Berlin: Colloquium, 1960), p. 60; Jürgen Scharfschwerdt, Thomas Mann und der deutsche Bildungsroman (Stuttgart: Kohlhammer, 1967), pp. 175-227.

[22] Hans Bürgin and Hans-Otto Mayer, Thomas Mann: Eine Chronik seines Lebens (Frankfort on the Main: S. Fischer, 1965), p. 70.

[23] Hatfield, p. 97.

[24] ibid., p. 98.

[25] loc. cit.

[26] See "Once Upon a Time," The Nation, 138 (1934), 678-79.

[27] "Thomas Mann Begins Trilogy," NYT Book Review, June 10, 1934, p. 1.

[28] Kenneth Burke, "Permanence and Change," The New Republic, 79 (1934), 186.

[29] Edith Hamilton, "Joseph in Egypt: A Heterodox View of Thomas Mann's Novel," SRL, 18 (1938), 11-13.

[30] "The Alexandrian Mode," The Commonweal, 28 (1938), 693.

[31] "Thomas Manns Joseph in Aegypten," Monatshefte, 29 (1937), 242-43.

[32] Joseph and His Brothers: A Lecture (1942), Works, XI, 657.

[33] ibid., pp. 666-67.

[34] "Joseph in the Land of the Dead," The Nation, 146 (1938), 303. [35] Works, XI, 657; Briefe an Karl Kerényi (1945), Works, XI, 651 and 653.

[36] About the Joseph Story (1928), Works, XI, 625.

[37] Bürgin and Mayer, p. 122.

[38] Edwin Berry Burgum, "The Sense of the Present in Thomas Mann," Antioch Review, 2 (1942), 404-06; Cleveland, op. cit., p. 694.

[39] Davis, _op. cit._

[40] _Op. cit._, pp. 253-54. See also Ignace Feuerlicht, _Thomas Mann_ (New York: Twayne Publishers, 1968), p. 46 and p. 58.

[41] _loc. cit._, p. 255.

[42] Hatfield, p. 110.

[43] Wolff, p. 95.

[44] Hamburger, p. 130 and p. 142.

[45] See Hatfield, p. 96; Lindsay, p. 110; Paul Altenberg, _Die Romane Thomas Manns_ (Bad Homburg: Gentner, 1961), p. 153. Thomas Mann, too, calls Joseph a "symbol of humanity." (_Works_, XI, 665).

[46] Hatfield, p. 111.

[47] Bürgin and Mayer, p. 153.

[48] _Works_, XI, 677-78.

[49] Wolff, pp. 107-08.

[50] Hatfield, p. 113.

[51] See _The Boy Henoch_ (1934), _Works_, VIII, 951-57. This fragment represents a chapter which was deleted from the final version of _Young Joseph_.

[52] _Psychoanalytic Quarterly_, 26, 222.

[53] See _Nietzsche's Philosophy in the Light of Contemporary Events_ (1947), _Works_, IX, 679.

[54] Wolff, p. 107; Harry Slochower, _Thomas Mann's Joseph Story_ (New York: A. Knopf, 1938), pp. 54-56; Hatfield, pp. 118-19; Malcolm Cowley, "The Golden Legend," _The New Republic_, 94 (1938), 170; see also Mann's concession: _Works_, XI, 663.

[55] Cowley, _op. cit._, p. 170.

[56] Slochower, _op. cit._, p. 56.

[57] _Brother Hitler_, _Works_, XII, 849.

Chapter VIII: SEQUELS AND INTERLUDE: THE BELOVED RETURNS, THE TRANSPOSED HEADS, AND THE TABLES OF THE LAW

[1] Hatfield, p. 122.

[2] _Works_, XI, 354.

[3] _Fantasy on Goethe_ (1948), _Works_, IX, 724.

[4] _ibid._, p. 735.

[5] _The Beloved Returns_ (1939), _Works_, II, 728.

[6] Thomas Mann und Goethe (Berne: Francke, 1949), pp. 101-02.

[7] Fantasy on Goethe, Works, IX, 754.

[8] Fantasy on Goethe, Works, IX, 734; To the Youth of Japan (1932), Works, IX, 290; Goethe and Democracy (1949), Works, IX, 759-62, 780, 782; Goethe's Career as a Man of Letters (1932), Works, IX, 360.

[9] Fantasy on Goethe, Works, IX, 738.

[10] Goethe as Representative of the Bourgeois Age, Works, IX, 318.

[11] Works, IX, 123.

[12] Works, IX, 302-03.

[13] Fantasy on Goethe, Works, IX, 742.

[14] Blume, p. 108.

[15] Fantasy on Goethe, Works, IX, 743.

[16] The Transposed Heads (1940), Works, VIII, 713.

[17] See Karl Kerényi, "Die goldene Parodie: Randbemerkungen zu den Vertauschten Köpfen," NRs, 67 (1956), 552-53.

[18] The Story of a Novel, Works, XI, 154.

[19] The Tables of the Law (1943), Works, VIII, 808.

[20] The Myth of the Birth of the Hero (New York: The Journal of Nervous and Mental Disease Publishing Company, 1914), p. 87.

[21] Wolff, p. 109.

[22] Bürgin and Mayer, p. 169.

[23] Dorothy Donnelly, "Pulling the Lion's Teeth," The Commonweal, 42 (1945), 503.

[24] Wolff, p. 109; Käte Hamburger, Thomas Manns Mose-Erzählung "Das Gesetz" auf dem Hintergrund der Überlieferung und der religionswissenschaftlichen Forschung (Frankfort on the Main: Ullstein, 1964), pp. 98-99.

[25] Neue Schweizer Rundschau, N.F., 12 (1945), 550.

[26] Armin L. Robinson, ed., The Ten Commandments (Preface by Hermann Rauschning) (New York: Simon and Schuster, 1944), p. x.

[27] Thomas Mann: Briefe 1889-1936, ed. Erika Mann (Frankfort on the Main: S. Fischer, 1961), p. 398.

Chapter IX: *CAVE MUSICAM*

[1] "Säkularisierung des Teufels," NRs, 59 (1948), 197.

[2] "Thomas Manns Doktor Faustus," OL, 13, Fasc. i-ii (1958), 87-88.

[3] See Wolff, p. 112.

[4] loc. cit.

[5] See "Thomas Mann's Doktor Faustus: The Enigma of Frau von Tolna," GR, 23, 249-53.

[6] Doctor Faustus (1947), Works, VI, 23.

[7] See Calvin S. Brown, "The Entomological Source of Mann's Poisonous Butterfly," GR, 37, 116-20.

[8] See Wolff, p. 113.

[9] See Hirschbach, p. 122.

[10] Works, IX, 575.

[11] Works, XI, 155.

[12] Hatfield, p. 131.

[13] Blume, p. 137.

[14] See Lesser, p. 375.

[15] Dostoevsky--Within Limits (1946), Works, IX, 661.

[16] ibid., pp. 660-61.

[17] Works, XI, 1131-32.

[18] "Die Welt ohne Transzendenz," Merkur, 3 (1949), 42.

[19] loc. cit.

[20] ibid., p. 1142.

[21] Proem to a Musical Nietzsche-Celebration (1924), Works, X, 182.

[22] Sufferings and Greatness of Richard Wagner (1933), Works, IX, 373.

[23] ibid., p. 405.

[24] ibid., p. 404.

[25] ibid., p. 402.

[26] ibid., p. 400.

[27] Works, XI, 421ff.

[28] Works, X, 217.

[29] See "The 'Break-Through'--Thomas Mann and the Deeper Meaning of Disease," Ciba Symposium, 9, No. 1, 36-43.

[30] Nietzsche's Philosophy in the Light of Contemporary Events, Works, IX, 678.

[31] Dostoevsky--Within Limits, Works, IX, 664.

[32] The Story of a Novel, Works, XI, 164.

[33] Schopenhauer, Works, IX, 546.

[34] P. M. Pickard, "Thomas Mann's Doctor Faustus: A Psychological Approach," GLL, N.S., 4 (1950), 91.

[35] See Heller, p. 260.

[36] Hatfield, p. 141; Basso, "A New Deal with Old Nick," NY, Oct. 30, 1948, p. 106.

[37] See "Bemerkungen über Thomas Manns Doktor Faustus," Neophil., 41 (1957), 195-96.

[38] Merkur, 3, 55.

[39] Heller, p. 283.

[40] NRs, 59, 198.

[41] Charles J. Rolo, "Mann and His Mephistopheles," Atlantic, 182, 94.

[42] ibid., p. 92.

[43] Lesser, p. 466.

[44] GLL, N.S., 4, 91.

[45] See Works, XI, 146.

[46] Hatfield, p. 130.

[47] Works, XI, 681-82.

[48] Peter de Mendelssohn, "Tagebuch des Zauberers," NRs, 66 (1955), 515.

[49] The Book Closest to My Heart (1954), Works, XI, 686.

[50] "Thomas Mann's Docktor Faustus: Prolegomena to an Interpretation," GR, 23 (1948), 206.

[51] GR, 23, 249.

[52] Works, XI, 291-96.

[53] ibid., p. 291.

[54] Works, XI, 1132.

[55] ibid., 1143.

[56] ibid., 1132-36; 1142.

[57] Hatfield, p. 129.

[58] Letters of Richard Wagner (1951), Works, X, 797.

[59] The Story of a Novel, Works, XI, 239.

[60] Wagner Without End (1949), Works, X, 926.

[61] Works, XI, 1146.

[62] Hirschbach, p. 20.

[63] William H. Rey, "Selbstopfer des Geistes," Monatshefte, 52 (1960), 153; Hatfield, pp. 134-35; Lindsay, p. 124.

[64] Merkur, 3, 169-70.

Chapter X: FULL CIRCLE: THOMAS MANN'S LAST WORKS

[1] Hermann J. Weigand, "Thomas Mann's Gregorius," GR, 27 (1952), 88.

[2] GR, 27, 83.

[3] See "Der Erwählte: Thomas Manns Mittelalter-Parodie," Euph, 53 (1959), 61.

[4] Thomas O. Brandt, "Narcissism in Thomas Mann's Der Erwählte," GLL, N.S., 7 (1954), 236.

[5] ibid., pp. 238-39.

[6] Remarks on the Novel "The Holy Sinner" (1951), Works, XI, 691.

[7] See Stackmann, Euph, 53, 62-63.

[8] E. G. Fürstenheim, "The Place of Der Erwählte in the Work of Thomas Mann," MLR, 51 (1956), 55.

[9] See Weigand, GR, 27, 30.

[10] ibid., p. 24.

[11] The Holy Sinner (1951), Works, VII, 36.

[12] Brandt, GLL, 7, 236.

[13] See Fürstenheim, MLR, 51, 55; Weigand, GR, 27, 91.

[14] ibid., p. 89.

[15] ibid., p. 92.

[16] The Story of a Novel, Works, XI, 242.

[17] MLR, 51, 65.

[18] Remarks on the Novel "The Holy Sinner," Works, XI, 690.

[19] See Stackmann, Euph, 53, 74; William H. McClain, "Irony and Belief in Thomas Mann's Der Erwählte," Monatshefte, 43 (1951), 323. This implication is also present in Fürstenheim's article, MLR, 51, 62.

[20] loc. cit.

[21] Peter Szondi, "Versuch über Thomas Mann," NRs, 67 (1956), 562. See also Fürstenheim, MLR, 51, 58.

[22] Return (1954), Works, XI, 529.

[23] "A Comparative Study of Die Betrogene and Der Tod in Venedig," MLF, 42 (1957), 124.

[24] See Mileck, MLF, 42, 124-27.

[25] The Black Swan (1953), Works, VIII, 884.

[26] "Rechtfertigung der Liebe in Thomas Manns Erzählung Die Betrogene," DVLG, 60 (1960), 434-35.

[27] ibid., p. 440.

[28] ibid., p. 442.

[29] Mileck, MLF, 42, 128.

[30] See Brendan Gill, "Lean Years," NY, July 10, 1954, p. 70; Gilbert Highet, "Life and Health, Disease and Death," Harpers, 209 (July 1954), 93; Richard Plant, "The Late Sorrow," NYTBR, June 6, 1954, p. 6; Charles J. Rolo, "Of Love and Death," Atlantic, 194 (July 1954), 83. Mann in Return admitted that the dialogues between mother and daughter were unreal. (Works, XI, 530).

[31] Wolff, pp. 135-36.

[32] Confessions of Felix Krull, Confidence Man (1954), Works, VII, 315.

[33] "Thomas Mann's Latest Phase," GLL, N.S., 8 (1954-55), 250.

[34] Introduction to a text edition of Tonio Kröger, p. xiv.

[35] "Thomas Manns letztes Werk," SchM, 36 (1957), 792.

[36] Works, XI, 531.

[37] SchM, 36, 796.

[38] Introduction to a Chapter of "The Confessions of Felix Krull, Confidence Man" (1953), Works, XI, 704.

CONCLUSION

[1] Erna H. Schenk, "Women in the Works of Thomas Mann," Monatshefte, 32 (April, 1940), 164.

[2] Notes upon a Case of Obsessional Neurosis, 10, 241.

[3] William McClain, "Ein unveröffentlichter Thomas Mann Brief über den Erwählten," Monatshefte, 54 (Jan., 1962), 9.

[4] Golo Mann, "Memories of My Father," Inter Nationes (Bonn, 1965), p. 3.

WORKS BY THOMAS MANN

COMPLETE EDITIONS

Collected Works [in individual editions]. Berlin: S. Fischer, 1922-1935, Vienna: Bermann-Fischer, 1936-1937.

Collected Works in Ten Volumes. Berlin: S. Fischer, 1925.

Stockholm Edition of Thomas Mann's Complete Works. Stockholm: Bermann-Fischer, 1938, Amsterdam: 1948, Vienna: 1949, Frankfort on the Main: S. Fischer, 1950 --.

Collected Works in Twelve Volumes. Berlin: Aufbau, 1955-1956.

Collected Works in Twelve Volumes. Oldenburg: S. Fischer, 1960.

COLLECTIONS IN GERMAN

Der kleine Herr Friedemann (Short Stories) 1898.

Tristan (Six Tales) 1903.

Der kleine Herr Friedemann und andere Novellen (Short Stories) 1909.

Rede und Antwort (Discussions and Articles) 1922.

Novellen (Short Stories) 1922.

Ausgewählte Prosa (Selected Prose) 1924.

Bemühungen (Discussions and Articles) 1925.

Die Forderung des Tages (Speeches and Articles) 1930.

Leiden und Große der Meister (Essays) 1935.

Achtung, Europa! (Political Articles) 1938.

Die schönsten Erzählungen (Best Tales) 1939.

Adel des Geistes (Essays on the Problem of Humanity) 1945.

Ausgewählte Erzählungen (Selected Tales) 1945.

Meistererzählungen (Selected Tales) 1947.

Neue Studien (Essays) 1948.

Tonio Kröger und andere Erzählungen (Tales) 1953.

Altes und Neues (Prose of Five Decades) 1953.

Der Tod in Venedig und andere Erzählungen (Short Stories) 1954.

Erzählungen (Tales) 1955.

Zeit und Werk (Diaries, Speeches and Writings) 1955.

Nachlese (Prose) 1956.

Sorge um Deutschland (Six Essays) 1957.

Erzählungen (Tales) 1958.

INDIVIDUAL WORKS

SHORT STORIES

Fallen (Gefallen) 1894.

The Will to Happiness (Der Wille zum Glück) 1896.

Disillusionment (Enttäuschung) 1896.

Death (Der Tod) 1897.

Little Herr Friedemann (Der kleine Herr Friedemann) 1897.

The Clown (Der Bajazzo) 1897.

Tobias Mindernickel (Tobias Mindernickel) 1898.

The Wardrobe (Der Kleiderschrank) 1899.

Revenged (Gerächt) 1899.

Little Lizzie (Luischen) 1900.

The Way to the Cemetery (Der Weg zum Friedhof) 1900.

Gladius Dei (Gladius Dei) 1902.

Tristan (Tristan) 1903.

The Hungry (Die Hungernden) 1903.

Tonio Kröger (Tonio Kröger) 1903.

The Infant Prodigy (Das Wunderkind) 1903.

A Gleam (Ein Glück) 1904.

At the Prophet's (Beim Propheten) 1904.

A Weary Hour (Schwere Stunde) 1905.

The Blood of the Walsungs (Wälsungenblut) 1906.

Anecdote (Anekdote) 1908.

The Railway Accident (Das Eisenbahnunglück) 1909.

The Fight Between Jappe and Do Escobar (Wie Jappe und Do Escobar sich prügelten) 1911.

Death in Venice (Der Tod in Venedig) 1912.

A Man and His Dog (Herr und Hund) 1919. (Also translated as
    Bashan and I.)

Disorder and Early Sorrow (Unordnung und frühes Leid) 1930.

Mario and the Magician (Mario und der Zauberer) 1930.

The Transposed Heads (Die vertauschten Köpfe) 1940.

The Tables of the Law (Das Gesetz) 1943.

The Black Swan (Die Betrogene) 1953.

DRAMA

Fiorenza (Fiorenza) 1905.

NOVELS

Buddenbrooks (Buddenbrooks) 1901.

Royal Highness (Königliche Hoheit) 1909.

The Magic Mountain (Der Zauberberg) 1924.

Joseph and His Brothers (Die Geschichten Jaakobs) 1933. (Also
    translated as The Tales of Jacob; the title of the entire
    tetralogy has been translated as Joseph and His Brethren.)

Young Joseph (Der junge Joseph) 1934.

Joseph in Egypt (Joseph in Ägypten) 1936.

The Beloved Returns (Lotte in Weimar) 1939.

Joseph the Provider (Joseph der Ernährer) 1943.

Doctor Faustus (Doktor Faustus) 1947.

The Holy Sinner (Der Erwählte) 1951.

Confessions of Felix Krull, Confidence Man (Bekenntnisse des
    Hochstaplers Felix Krull) 1954.

CONFESSION

Observations of a Non-Political Man (Betrachtungen eines
    Unpolitischen) 1918.

ESSAYS

The Old Fontane (Der alte Fontane) 1910.

Chamisso (Chamisso) 1911.

Thoughts in War (Gedanken im Kriege) 1914.

Frederick and the Grand Coalition (Friedrich und die große Koalition) 1915.

Goethe and Tolstoy (Goethe und Tolstoi) 1921.

Goethe's "Elective Affinities" (Zu Goethes "Wahlverwandtschaften") 1925.

Kleist's "Amphitryon" (Kleists "Amphitryon") 1927.

Lessing (Rede über Lessing) 1929.

Theodor Storm (Theodor Storm) 1930.

Platen (August von Platen) 1930.

To the Youth of Japan (An die japanische Jugend) 1932.

Goethe as Representative of the Bourgeois Age (Goethe als Repräsentant des bürgerlichen Zeitalters) 1932.

Goethe's Career as a Man of Letters (Goethes Laufbahn als Schriftsteller) 1932.

Sufferings and Greatness of Richard Wagner (Leiden und Größe Richard Wagners) 1933.

Voyage with "Don Quixote" (Meerfahrt mit "Don Quixote") 1934.

Freud and the Future (Freud und die Zukunft) 1936.

Richard Wagner and the Ring (Richard Wagner und der Ring des Nibelungen) 1937.

Schopenhauer (Schopenhauer) 1938.

Goethe's "Faust" (Über Goethes "Faust") 1939.

"Anna Karenina" ("Anna Karenina") 1940.

Goethe's Werther (Goethes Werther) 1941.

Dostoevsky -- Within Limits (Dostojewski -- mit Maßen) 1946.

Nietzsche's Philosophy in the Light of Contemporary Events (Nietzsches Philosophie im Lichte unserer Erfahrung) 1947.

Fantasy on Goethe (Phantasie über Goethe) 1948.

Goethe and Democracy (Goethe und die Demokratie) 1949.

The Erotic of Michelangelo (Die Erotik Michelangelos) 1950.

Bernard Shaw (Bernard Shaw) 1951.

Gerhart Hauptmann (Gerhart Hauptmann) 1952.

Old Fontane Once Again (Noch einmal der alte Fontane) 1954.

Heinrich von Kleist and His Tales (Heinrich von Kleist und seine Erzählungen) 1954.

On Chekhov (Versuch über Tschechow) 1954.

On Schiller (Versuch über Schiller) 1955.

AUTOBIOGRAPHICAL WORKS

Sleep, Sweet Sleep (Süßer Schlaf) 1909.

After-Dinner Speech in Amsterdam (Tischrede in Amsterdam) 1924.

Underway (Unterwegs) 1925.

Paris Reckoning (Pariser Rechenschaft) 1926.

Lübeck as an Intellectual Way of Life (Lübeck als geistige
Lebensform) 1926.

A Sketch of My Life (Lebensabriß) 1930.

Portrait of My Mother (Das Bild der Mutter) 1930.

Curriculum Vitae (Lebenslauf 1930) 1930.

Intellect in Society (Der Geist in der Gesellschaft) 1932.

Curriculum Vitae (Lebenslauf 1936) 1936.

The Story of a Novel (Die Entstehung des Doktor Faustus) 1949.

My Time (Meine Zeit) 1950.

Return (Rückkehr) 1954.

LETTERS

Thomas Mann: Briefe 1889-1936, ed. Erika Mann, Frankfort on the
Main: S. Fischer, 1961.

Thomas Mann: Briefe 1937-1947, ed. Erika Mann, Frankfort on the
Main: S. Fischer, 1963.

Thomas Mann: Briefe 1948-1955, ed. Erika Mann, Frankfort on the
Main: S. Fischer, 1965.

Thomas Mann Briefe an Paul Amann 1915-1952, ed. Herbert Wegener,
Lübeck: Schmidt-Römhild, 1959.

Thomas Mann an Ernst Bertram, Briefe aus den Jahren 1910-1955,
ed. Inge Jens, Pfullingen: Neske, 1960.

Thomas Mann -- Karl Kerényi. Gesprach in Briefen, ed. Karl
Kerényi, Zurich: Rhein,1960.

Thomas Mann -- Robert Faesi. Briefwechsel, ed. Robert Faesi,
Zurich: Atlantis, 1962.

Heinrich und Thomas Mann, ed. Alfred Kantorowicz, Berlin:
Aufbau, 1956.

THOMAS MANN'S MOST SIGNIFICANT CRITICAL
AND MISCELLANEOUS WORKS

Bilse and I (Bilse und ich) 1906.

Communication to the Bonn Literary Society (Mitteilung an die Literaturhistorische Gesellschaft in Bonn) 1906.

On "Royal Highness" (Über "Königliche Hoheit") 1910.

Thoughts in War (Gedanken im Kriege) 1914.

Letter to Count Hermann Keyserling (Brief an Hermann Grafen Keyserling) 1920.

The German Republic (Von deutscher Republik) 1923.

An Experience in the Occult (Okkulte Erlebnisse) 1924.

After-Dinner Speech in Amsterdam (Tischrede in Amsterdam) 1924.

Proem to a Musical Nietzsche-Celebration (Vorspruch zu einer musikalischen Nietzsche-Feier) 1924.

Letter to Gerhart Hauptmann (Brief an Gerhart Hauptmann) 1925.

On the Spirit of Medicine (Vom Geist der Medizin) 1925.

For the Reception of Gerhart Hauptmann in Munich (Zur Begrüßung Gerhart Hauptmanns in München) 1926.

Culture and Socialism (Kultur und Sozialismus) 1928.

A Word Beforehand: My "Joseph and His Brothers" (Ein Wort zuvor: Mein "Joseph und seine Brüder") 1928.

About the Joseph Story (Über den Joseph-Roman) 1928.

Freud's Position in the History of Modern Thought (Die Stellung Freuds in der modernen Geistesgeschichte) 1929.

Appeal to Reason (Ein Appell an die Vernunft) 1930.

An Exchange of Letters (Ein Briefwechsel) 1937.

The Coming Victory of Democracy (Vom zukünftigen Sieg der Demokratie) 1938.

This Peace (Dieser Friede) 1938.

Europe, Beware! (Achtung, Europa!) 1938.

Culture and Politics (Kultur und Politik) 1939.

Brother Hitler (Bruder Hitler) 1939. (English Translation was A Brother.)

Introduction to "The Magic Mountain" (Einführung in den "Zauberberg") 1939.

410

The Problem of Freedom (Das Problem der Freiheit) 1939.

This War (Dieser Krieg) 1940.

Preface to a Recording of "Buddenbrooks" (Vorwort zu einer
  Schallplattenausgabe der "Buddenbrooks") 1940.

Joseph and His Brothers: A Lecture (Joseph und seine Brüder:
  Ein Vortrag) 1942.

Listen Germany! (Deutsche Hörer!) 1942.

Germany and the Germans (Deutschland und die Deutschen) 1945.

On "Doctor Faustus" (Über den "Faustus") 1947.

Sixteen Years: Foreword to the American Edition of "Joseph and
  His Brothers" in One Volume (Sechzehn Jahre: Zur
  amerikanischen Ausgabe von "Joseph und seine Brüder"
  in einem Bande) 1948.

Wagner Without End (Wagner und kein Ende) 1949.

Letters of Richard Wagner (Briefe Richard Wagners) 1951.

Remarks on the Novel "The Holy Sinner" (Bemerkungen zu dem
  Roman "der Erwählte") 1951.

Praise of Transitoriness (Lob der Vergänglichkeit) 1952.

The Artist and Society (Der Künstler und die Gesellschaft) 1952.

Introduction to a Chapter of "The Confessions of Felix Krull,
  Confidence Man" (Einführung in ein Kapitel der "Bekenntnisse
  des Hochstaplers Felix Krull") 1954.

The Book Closest to My Heart (Das mir nächste meiner Bücher) 1954.

BIBLIOGRAPHIES

Bürgin, Hans. Das Werk Thomas Manns. Eine Bibliographie unter
  Mitarbeit von Walter A. Reichart and Erich Neumann. Frankfort
  on the Main: S. Fischer, 1959.

Jonas, Klaus W. Fifty Years of Thomas Mann Studies. A Biblio-
  graphy of Criticism. Minneapolis: University of Minnesota
  Press, 1955.

---------- and Ilsedore, B. Thomas Mann Studies Vol. II.
  Philadelphia: University of Pennsylvania Press, 1967.

SECONDARY SOURCES

Altenberg, Paul. "Thomas Manns letztes Werk," Schweizer
  Monatshefte, 36 (Jan. 1957), 790-97.

----------. Die Romane Thomas Manns. Bad Homburg: Gentner, 1961.

Baer, Lydia. "Death and Thomas Mann," The Stature of Thomas Mann, ed. Charles Neider. New York: New Directions, 1947, pp. 281-86.

Basso, Hamilton. "A New Deal with Old Nick," New Yorker, Oct. 30, 1948, pp. 95-96 (Vol. 24).

----------. "Tonio Kröger in Egyptian Dress: Joseph the Provider," New Yorker, July 22, 1944, pp. 53-57 (Vol. 20).

Bauer, Arnold. Thomas Mann. Berlin: Colloquium, 1960.

Beach, Joseph Warren. "The Magic Mountain," The Stature of Thomas Mann, ed. Charles Neider. New York: New Directions, 1947, pp. 103-17.

Beharriell, Frederick J. "Psychology in the Early Works of Thomas Mann," Publications of the Modern Language Association of America, 77 (March 1962), 149-55.

Belitt, Ben. "Art as Discipline," The Nation, 112 (June 1936), 814-15.

Bennett, E. K. A History of the German Novelle. Cambridge: Cambridge University Press, 1949.

Blume, Bernhard. Thomas Mann und Goethe. Berne: Francke, 1949.

Boehlich, Walter. "Thomas Manns Doktor Faustus," Merkur, 2 (1949), 588-603.

Brandenburg, Hans. "Aus Thomas Manns Münchener Zeit Erinnerungen von Hans Brandenburg," Neue literarische Welt (Darmstadt), 3 (March 1952), 3-4.

Brandt, Thomas O. "Narcissism in Thomas Mann's Der Erwählte," German Life and Letters, N.S., 7 (July 1954), 233-41.

Brenner, Charles. An Elementary Textbook of Psychoanalysis. New York: International Universities Press, 1955.

Brown, Calvin S. "The Entomological Source of Mann's Poisonous Butterfly," Germanic Review, 37 (March 1962), 116-20.

Buisonjé, J. C. de. "Bemerkungen über Thomas Manns Doktor Faustus," Neophilologus, 41 (July 1957), 185-99.

Bürgin, Hans, and Mayer, Hans-Otto. Thomas Mann: Eine Chronik seines Lebens. Frankfort on the Main: S. Fischer, 1965.

Burgum, Edwin Berry. "The Sense of the Present in Thomas Mann," Antioch Review, 2 (1942), 387-406.

Burke, Kenneth. "Permanence and Change," The New Republic, 79 (June 1934), 186-87.

Burkhard, Arthur. "Thomas Mann's Appraisal of the Poet," Publications of the Modern Language Association of America, 46 (Sept. 1931), 880-916.

Cleugh, James. Thomas Mann: A Study. London: Secker, 1933.

Cleveland, C. O. "The Alexandrian Mode," The Commonweal, 28 (April 1938), 693-94.

Cowley, Malcolm. "The Golden Legend," The New Republic, 94 (March 1938), 170-71.

Davis, Elmer. "Thomas Mann Begins Trilogy," NYT Book Review, June 10, 1934, p. 1.

Donnelly, Dorothy. "Pulling the Lion's Teeth," The Commonweal, 42 (1945), 503-04.

Ebermayer, Erich. "Thomas Manns Jugendnovelle Gefallen," Die Literatur, 27 (May 1925), 459-61.

Eichner, Hans. Thomas Mann. Berne: Francke, 1953.

Eloesser, Arthur. Thomas Mann: Sein Leben und sein Werk. Berlin: S. Fischer, 1925.

Feuerlicht, Ignace. Thomas Mann. New York: Twayne Publishers, 1968.

Fougère, Jean. Thomas Mann oder die Magie des Todes. Baden-Baden: Hans Bühler, Jr., 1948.

Freud, Sigmund. The Complete Psychological Works of Sigmund Freud, ed. and trans. James Strachey and Anna Freud. Standard ed. Vols. 2-21. London: Hogarth, 1953--.

Fürstenheim, E. G. "The Place of Der Erwählte in the Work of Thomas Mann," Modern Language Review, 51 (Jan. 1956), 55-70.

Gill, Brendan. "Lean Years," New Yorker, July 10, 1954, 70-71 (Vol. 30).

Glebe, William Valentine. "The Relationship Between Art and Disease in the Works of Thomas Mann," diss. (University of Washington, 1959).

Gronicka, André von. "Thomas Mann's Doktor Faustus: Prolegomena to an Interpretation," Germanic Review, 23 (Oct. 1948), 206-18.

Hamburger, Käte. Thomas Manns Roman "Joseph und seine Brüder." Stockholm: Bermann-Fischer, 1945.

----------. Thomas Manns Mose-Erzählung "Das Gesetz" auf dem Hintergrund der Überlieferung und der religionswissenshaft-lichen Forschung. Frankfort on the Main: Ullstein, 1964.

Hamilton, Edith. "Joseph in Egypt: A Heterodox View of Thomas Mann's Novel," Saturday Review of Literature, 18 (1938), 11-13.

Hatfield, Henry. Thomas Mann. Norfolk, Conn.: New Directions, 1951.

----------. "Thomas Mann's Mario und der Zauberer," Germanic Review, 21 (Dec. 1946), 306-12.

Havenstein, Martin. Thomas Mann: Der Dichter und der Schriftsteller. Berlin: Wiegandt and Grieben, 1927.

Heller, Erich. The Ironic German. London: Secker and Warburg, 1958.

Heller, Peter. "Thomas Mann's Conception of the Creative Writer," Publications of the Modern Language Association of America, 69 (Sept. 1954), 763-96.

Hendrick, Ives. Facts and Theories of Psychoanalysis, 3rd ed. New York: A. Knopf, 1958.

Highet, Gilbert. "Life and Health, Disease and Death," Harpers, 209 (July 1954), 93.

Hirschbach, Frank Donald. The Arrow and the Lyre. The Hague: M. Nijhoff, 1955.

----------. "Götterlieblinge und Hochstapler," German Quarterly, 32 (Jan. 1959), 22-33.

Holthusen, Hans Egon. "Die Welt ohne Transzendenz," Merkur, 3 (1949), 38-58, 161-80.

Kahler, Erich. "Säkularisierung des Teufels," Neue Rundschau, 59 (1949), 185-202.

Kantorowicz, Alfred. Heinrich und Thomas Mann. Berlin: Aufbau, 1956.

Kerényi, Karl. "Die goldene Parodie: Randbemerkungen zu den Vertauschten Köpfen," Neue Rundschau, 67 (1956), 549-56.

Kesten, Hermann. "Works and Deeds," The Stature of Thomas Mann, ed. Charles Neider. New York: New Directions, 1947, pp. 22-30.

Kohut, Heinz. "'Death in Venice' by Thomas Mann: A Story About the Disintegration of Artistic Sublimation," Psychoanalytic Quarterly, 26 (1957), 206-28.

Krutch, Joseph Wood. "Once Upon a Time," The Nation, 138 (June 1934), 678-79.

Kümmel, W. G. "Das Mosesbuch Thomas Manns und die Bibel," Neue Schweizer Rundschau, N.F., 12 (Jan. 1945), 544-50.

Lesser, Jonas. _Thomas Mann in der Epoche seiner Vollendung._
Munich: K. Desch, 1952.

Lewisohn, Ludwig. "Death in Venice," _The Stature of Thomas Mann,_
ed. Charles Neider. New York: New Directions, 1947, pp.
124-28.

Lindsay, J. M. _Thomas Mann._ Oxford: Blackwell, 1954.

Lion, Ferdinand. _Thomas Mann: Leben und Werk._ Zurich: Oprecht,
1947.

Mann, Erika. _The Last Year of Thomas Mann._ New York: Farrar,
Straus and Cudahy, 1958.

----------. ed. _Thomas Mann: Briefe 1889-1936 and 1937-1947._
Frankfort on the Main: S. Fischer, 1962 and 1963.

---------- and Mann, Klaus. "Portrait of Our Father," _The
Stature of Thomas Mann,_ ed. Charles Neider. New York:
New Directions, 1947 pp. 59-76.

Mann, Golo. "Memories of My Father," _Inter Nationes_ (Bonn, 1965),
1-15.

Mann, Heinrich. "My Brother," _The Stature of Thomas Mann,_
ed. Charles Neider. New York: New Directions, 1947,
pp. 83-90.

Mann, Klaus. _The Turning Point._ New York: L. B. Fischer, 1942.

Mann, Michael, ed. _Das Thomas Mann-Buch,_ Hamburg: S. Fischer,
1965.

Mann, Monika. "Papa," _The Stature of Thomas Mann,_ ed. Charles
Neider. New York: New Directions, 1947, pp. 77-82.

Mann, Viktor. _Wir waren fünf: Bildnis der Familie Mann._
Konstanz: Südverlag, 1949.

McClain, William H. "Irony and Belief in Thomas Mann's _Der
Erwählte,_" _Monatshefte,_ 43 (Nov. 1951), 319-25.

----------. "Ein unveröffentlichter Thomas Mann Brief über den
Erwählten," _Monatshefte,_ 54 (Jan. 1962), 9-10.

Mendelssohn, Peter de. "Tagebuch des Zauberers," _Neue Rundschau,_
66 (1955), 511-17.

Mileck, Joseph. "A Comparative Study of _Die Betrogene_ and _Der
Tod in Venedig,_" _Modern Language Forum,_ 42 (Dec. 1957),
124-29.

Moreck, Curt. "Eine Novelle Thomas Manns und ihre Geschichte,"
Welt und Wort, 5 (June 1950), 234-36.

Neider, Charles. "The Artist as Bourgeois," The Stature of Thomas Mann, ed. Charles Neider. New York: New Directions, 1947, pp. 330-57.

Nicholls, Roger A. "Nietzsche in the Early Works of Thomas Mann," University of California Publications in Modern Philology, 45 (1955), 1-119.

Oswald, Victor A. "Thomas Mann's Doktor Faustus: The Enigma of Frau von Tolna," Germanic Review,23 (Dec. 1948), 245-53.

Parry, Idris. "Thomas Mann's Latest Phase," German Life and Letters, N.S., 8 (July 1955), 241-51.

Pascal, Roy. The German Novel. Toronto: University of Toronto Press, 1956.

Pickard, P. M. "Thomas Mann's Doktor Faustus," German Life and Letters, N.S., 4 (Jan. 1951), 90-100.

Piers, Gerhart, and Milton B. Singer. Shame and Guilt. Springfield, Ill.: Thomas, 1953.

Plant, Richard. "The Late Sorrow," NYT Book Review, June 6, 1954, p. 6.

Politzer, Heinz. "The 'Break-Through'--Thomas Mann and the Deeper Meaning of Disease," Ciba Symposium, 9, No. 1, 36-43.

Rank, Otto. The Myth of the Birth of the Hero. New York: The Journal of Nervous and Mental Disease Publishing Company, 1914.

Rey, William H. "Rechtfertigung der Liebe in Thomas Manns Erzählung Die Betrogene," Deutsche Vierteljahrsschrift für Literaturwissenschaft und Geistesgeschichte, 60 (Nov. 1960), 428-48.

----------. "Selbstopfer des Geistes," Monatshefte, 52 (April-May 1960), 145-57.

Rice, Philip Blair. "Joseph in the Land of the Dead," The Nation, 146 (March 1938), 303-04.

Robinson, Armin L., ed. The Ten Commandments (Preface by Hermann Rauschning). New York: Simon and Schuster, 1944.

Rolo, Charles J. "Mann and His Mephistopheles," Atlantic, 182 (Nov. 1948), 92-94.

----------. "Of Love and Death," Atlantic, 194 (July 1954), 83.

Scharfschwerdt, Jürgen. Thomas Mann und der deutsche Bildungsroman, Stuttgart: Kohlhammer, 1967.

Schenck, Erna H. "Women in the Works of Thomas Mann," Monatshefte, 32 (April 1940), 145-64.

Scherrer, Paul. "Bruchstücke der Buddenbrooks-Urhandschrift und Zeugnisse zu ihrer Entstehung, 1897-1901," Neue Rundschau, 69 (Aug. 1958), 258-91.

---------- and Wysling, Hans. Quellenkritische Studien zum Werk Thomas Manns. Berne: Francke, 1967.

Schochow, Maximilian. "Die Kunst Thomas Manns," Zeitschrift für deutsche Bildung (Frankfort on the Main), 1 (1925), 106-12.

Slochower, Harry. Thomas Mann's Joseph Story. New York: A. Knopf, 1938.

Sorensen, Bengt Algot. "Thomas Manns Doktor Faustus. Mythos und Lebensbeichte," Orbis litterarum, 13, Fasc. i-ii (1958), 81-97.

Stackmann, Karl. "Der Erwählte: Thomas Manns Mittelalter-Parodie," Euphorion, 53 (1959), 61-74.

Stirk, S. D. "Gerhart Hauptmann and Mynheer Peeperkorn," German Life and Letters, N.S., 5 (April 1952), 162-75.

Stresau, Hermann. Thomas Mann und sein Werk. Frankfort on the Main: S. Fischer, 1963.

Szondi, Peter. "Versuch über Thomas Mann," Neue Rundschau, 67 (1956), 557-63.

Tappolet, Willy. "Das Problem des Künstlers bei Thomas Mann," Schweizerische Pädagogische Zeitschrift (Zurich), 31 (June 1921), 139-48, 174-82.

Thomas, R. Hinton. Thomas Mann. Oxford: Clarendon Press, 1956.

Walter, Bruno. "Recollection of Thomas Mann," The Stature of Thomas Mann, ed. Charles Neider, New York: New Directions, 1947, pp. 103-07.

Weigand, Hermann J. "Thomas Manns Joseph in Aegypten," Monatshefte, 29 (Oct. 1937), 241-56.

----------. "Thomas Mann's Gregorius," Germanic Review, 27 (Feb., April 1952), 10-30, 83-95.

----------. "Thomas Mann's Novel Der Zauberberg." New York: Appleton-Century, 1933.

Weimar, Karl S. Introduction to a text edition of Tristan. Boston: Ginn and Company, 1960.

Wilkinson, Elizabeth M. Introduction to a text edition of Tonio Kröger. Oxford: Blackwell, 1944.

Wolff, Hans M. Thomas Mann: Werk und Bekenntnis. Berne: Francke, 1957.

Books of Related Interest

Cromwell's Press Agent: A Critical Biography of Marchamont Nedham, 1620-1678
  Joseph Frank, University of Massachusetts, Amherst

A Due Sense of Differences: An Evaluative Approach to Canadian Literature
  Wilfred Cude, Concordia University at Montreal

The Flight from Women in the Fiction of Saul Bellow
  Joseph F. McCadden, Burlington County College

Jane Austen and Samuel Johnson
  Peter L. DeRose, Lamar University

A Middle English Treatise on the Playing of Miracles
  Clifford Davidson, Western Michigan University

Passing the Love of Women: A Study of Gide's **Saul** *and its Biblical Roots*
  Anne Lapidus Lerner, Jewish Theological Seminary

Realism in Shakespeare's Romantic Comedies: "O Heavenly Mingle"
  Marvin Felheim, University of Michigan; Philip Traci, Wayne State University

The Search For An Eternal Norm: As Represented by Three Classics
  Louis J. Halle, Graduate Institute of International Studies, Geneva

Stephen Crane at Brede: An Anglo-American Literary Circle of the 1890's
  Gordon Milne, Lake Forest College

Theology As Comedy—Critical and Theoretical Implications
  George Aichele, Jr., Adrian College

0-8191-2858-9